# LITERARY CRITICISM AND CULTURAL THEORY

*edited by*
William E. Cain
Wellesley College

*A ROUTLEDGE SERIES*

# OTHER BOOKS IN THIS SERIES:

A COINCIDENCE OF WANTS
*The Novel and Neoclassical Economics*
Charles Lewis

MODERN PRIMITIVES
*Race and Language in Gertrude Stein,
Ernest Hemingway, and Zora Neale
Hurston*
Susanna Pavloska

PLAIN AND UGLY JANES
*The Rise of the Ugly Woman in
Contemporary American Fiction*
Charlotte M. Wright

DISSENTING FICTIONS
*Identity and Resistance in the
Contemporary American Novel*
Cathy Moses

PERFORMING LA MESTIZA
*Textual References of Lesbians of Color
and the Negotiation of Identities*
Ellen M. Gil-Gomez

FROM GOOD MA TO WELFARE QUEEN
*A Genealogy of the Poor Woman in
American Literature, Photography and
Culture*
Vivyan C. Adair

ARTFUL ITINERARIES
*European Art and American Careers in
High Culture, 1865–1920*
Paul Fisher

POSTMODERN TALES OF SLAVERY
IN THE AMERICAS
*From Alejo Carpenter to Charles Johnson*
Timothy J. Cox

EMBODYING BEAUTY
*Twentieth-Century American Women
Writers' Aesthetics*
Malin Pereira

MAKING HOMES IN THE WEST/INDIES
*Constructions of Subjectivity in the
Writings of Michelle Cliff and Jamaica
Kincaid*
Antonia Macdonald-Smythe

POSTCOLONIAL MASQUERADES
*Culture and Politics in Literature, Film,
Video, and Photography*
Niki Sampat Patel

DIALECTIC OF SELF AND STORY
*Reading and Storytelling in Contemporary
American Fiction*
Robert Durante

ALLEGORIES OF VIOLENCE
*Tracing the Writings of War in Late
Twentieth-Century Fiction*
Lidia Yuknavitch

VOICE OF THE OPPRESSED IN THE LANGUAGE
OF THE OPPRESSOR
*A Discussion of Selected Postcolonial
Literature from Ireland, Africa and
America*
Patsy J. Daniels

EUGENIC FANTASIES
*Racial Ideology in the Literature and
Popular Culture of the 1920's*
Betsy L. Nies

THE LIFE WRITING OF OTHERNESS
*Woolf, Baldwin, Kingston, and Winterson*
Lauren Rusk

FROM WITHIN THE FRAME
*Storytelling in African-American Fiction*
Bertram D. Ashe

THE SELF WIRED
*Technology and Subjectivity in
Contemporary Narrative*
Lisa Yaszek

THE SPACE AND PLACE OF MODERNISM
*The Little Magazine in New York*
Adam McKible

# THE FIGURE OF CONSCIOUSNESS

## William James, Henry James, and Edith Wharton

Jill M. Kress

ROUTLEDGE
NEW YORK & LONDON

Published in 2002 by
Routledge
29 West 35th Street
New York, NY 10001
www.Routledge-NY.com

Published in Great Britain by
Routledge
11 New Fetter Lane
London EC4P 4EE

Routledge is an imprint of the Taylor and Francis Group.

10  9  8  7  6  5  4  3  2  1

*Library of Congress Cataloging-in-Publication Data*

Kress, Jill M., 1968–
    The figure of consciousness : William James, Henry James, and Edith Wharton / by Jill M. Kress.
        p. cm. — (Literary criticism and cultural theory)
    Includes bibliographical references and index.
    ISBN 0-415-93979-8 (acid-free paper)
    1. Wharton, Edith, 1862–1937—Knowledge—Psychology. 2. Consciousness in literature. 3. American fiction—20th century—History and criticism. 4. James, Henry, 1843–1916—Knowledge—Psychology. 5. James, Henry, 1843–1916. Portrait of a lady. 6. Wharton, Edith, 1862–1937. Age of innocence. 7. Wharton, Edith, 1862–1937. House of mirth. 8. James, Henry, 1843–1916. Golden bowl. 9. James, William, 1842–1910—Influence. I. Title. II. Series.

PS3545.H16 Z6885 2002
813'.409353—dc21

                                                            2002021319

Printed on acid-free, 250 year-life paper
Manufactured in the United States of America

*For my parents*
*and for Keith*

# Contents

Acknowledgments ix

Preface xi

Chapter One
Studies in Nature and Interiors:
The Discourse of Consciousness in Nineteenth-Century Science 1

Chapter Two
Contesting Metaphors and the Discourse of
Consciousness in William James 27

Chapter Three
The Structure of Consciousness:
Henry James's *Portrait of a Lady* and the Drama
of Social Relations 61

Chapter Four
Relations, Receptacles and Worlds of Experience:
Gendered Metaphors and *The Golden Bowl* 87

Chapter Five
Designing Our Interiors:
Self-Consciousness and Social Awareness in Edith
Wharton's *The House of Mirth* 131

Chapter Six
The Price of a Conscious Self in Edith Wharton's
*The Age of Innocence* 161

Notes 187

Bibliography 237

Index 261

# Acknowledgments

It is with pleasure that I acknowledge the people who have helped to shape this project from beginning to end. I am indebted, first and foremost, to James Longenbach for his valuable advice during this book's development. His meticulous and tireless readings have given insightful direction to my project throughout its many stages. For his generosity and continued graciousness to me, I am deeply grateful. I also thank John Michael, Anita Levy and Kenneth Gross for their assistance and encouragement on these chapters. I am fortunate to have had the support of many dear friends as I was writing. In particular, I would like to thank Emily J. Orlando for her expertise, and for giving lavishly of her time and friendship. Special thanks go to Kara Molway Russell, who read the entire manuscript, offering me intelligent and heartening responses along the way. I am tremendously blessed to count her among my friends.

The editors at *The Journal of the History of Ideas* granted me permission to use portions of "Contesting Metaphors and the Discourse of Consciousness in William James." At Routledge, Damian Treffs has been kind and attentive to all of my concerns. Sharon Cameron, one of my many wonderful teachers, first introduced me to Henry James years ago. I remember those initial readings with fondness and think of her with admiration. I extend a warm thank you to my family, especially my parents, who have always given me abundant love. Finally, my greatest debt, which I delightedly record, is to my husband, Keith, who is also my greatest gift.

# Preface

In her essay on the novels of Dorothy Richardson, published in the *Little Review*, April 1918, May Sinclair includes what is probably the first use of the term "stream of consciousness" in relation to a literary work.[1] Sinclair conceives of the dilemma of the modern novelist in terms of her contact with "reality," a realm "too fluid," too "thick and deep," for us to carve out any individual portion for study. As a response to these teeming surroundings, Sinclair maintains that novelists must simply "plunge in," that the best of novels, in fact, are more or less "sustained immersion" in the waters of life. Sinclair's production of a fluid universe extends beyond the current of the outside world to express the "inside" of a character's mind, an inside equally formless and changeable. Though the figure of the stream comes from William James's *The Principles of Psychology* (1890), Sinclair's essay reveals the ways in which this metaphor directs her study, the ways in which it constructs an argument and engenders a reality of its own. Moreover, her review, answering as it does both Richardson's *Pilgrimage* and James's textbook of psychology, elucidates the problem of creating form in a formless world, of embracing identity when experience remains fluent.

Certainly, William James often forms the focal point for the philosophical and psychological study of consciousness in America, but my reading of turn-of-the-century scientific and literary writings together helps to reevaluate the cultural narrative of consciousness and to reveal the crucial ways in which metaphor constructs each of its manifestations. In the works of both the social scientists, Charles Darwin, George Henry Lewes, Herbert Spencer, Alfred Russel Wallace, and William James, and the fiction writers, Henry James and Edith Wharton, metaphors for consciousness emerge in a variety of ways. What these works share, however, is the repeated attempt to understand questions about the mind through figurative representation, as well as a deep ambivalence regarding the multiplying tendency of words.

The metaphorical aspect of the discourse of consciousness proves significant precisely because figurative language becomes a means to establish identity, to render accessible a self. At the same time, an anxiety over language, so prevalent in texts that develop theories of consciousness, reminds us that though these authors invest in the power of words, they also betray extreme distrust of any symbolic system. Since the culture at large shapes their figures, writers are not always in control of their own designs. Thus the discourse of consciousness in both science and fiction produces an equivocal version of the self. Identity shifts relentlessly, changing with every new linguistic configuration.

Many studies of consciousness address Henry James's fiction, yet readers often consider consciousness as a thematic expression in his texts, rather than analyzing its formal properties. Even those studies that link William and Henry James rarely provide a look at the syntactical complexities of language and metaphor. Reading *The Principles of Psychology*, I demonstrate the profound ways in which metaphor directs William James's arguments; for though James constructs a series of metaphors out of which consciousness materializes, the structures come undone. James's writings display a repeated effort to portray consciousness even while he questions its existence. His equivocation over consciousness underscores a characteristic trait of texts in the whole of this study: that is, authors remain uncertain about whether they are naming an entity or explicitly creating it. James's metaphors, at once, direct us inward to a stable, individualized self and propel us outward to find consciousness materializing in the fluxional cycle of the natural world. He struggles over appropriate "names" and "terms" for consciousness, a gesture that presupposes some clearly delineated concept around which we might wrap a verbal expression, yet James also seems painfully aware that every new metaphor launches an entirely new theory. Even when James dismantles earlier images of consciousness, his reluctance to abandon certain figurative constructions arises less out of scientific conviction than from aesthetic commitment to what he has created in language. James, in fact, possesses a heightened awareness of what he crafts with words; he also, perhaps more penetratingly, acknowledges the inadequacy of any linguistic system to realize ideas thoroughly.

Psychological scientists such as Lewes and Spencer, following upon the heels of Darwin, anticipate William James's elaborately conflicting metaphors as well as his indecision over how and where to place consciousness. Despite their grounding in the natural sciences, these writers often generate a spiritual essence for the human mind when they cannot locate mental experience in the natural world. Making consciousness metaphysical preserves its elusiveness and, in some sense, suspends scientific investigation. Alfred Russel Wallace's belief in a metaphysical force that, combined with evolution, directed the development of human consciousness, demonstrates how the extravagance of metaphors carries scientific theory beyond the strict circumference of natural causes. My analysis of a variety of works by these evolutionary writers highlights the figurative language in their texts in order to discuss the methods by which science brings consciousness into being. Generating competing theories about the human mind, these studies confirm that a shared figurative discourse exists between scientific lexicons and imaginative writing. The language of Darwinian science, with its rhetoric of "survival," imparts a sense of urgency to the powers of selective attention that consciousness presumably sustains; affirming consciousness, therefore, amounts to an act of self-preservation. But the more these authors admit that the problem of consciousness is a problem of language, the more their carefully constructed designs begin to fall apart.

Nevertheless, consciousness must be something (these writers insist), for if consciousness does not exist, then it remains the greatest illusion human beings have ever invented. Forfeiting the claim of consciousness would mean abandoning all notions of a coherent self, one that thinks, feels, wills, and reflects on its actions; but the notions of selfhood do indeed unfasten in these texts, indicating the ways in which social realities give rise to mental realities. As a result, we become aware of the tension between those enticing and disquieting movements towards transcendence and the ways in which discursive symbols are inevitably bound by social and cultural contexts. Whether they are expressed abstractly in philosophical discourse or with respect to certain characters in the course of a novel, figures for the human mind rely upon social systems. Though scientific and philosophical theories appear devoid of references to their specific cultural arena, the erupting metaphors often make concrete imprints of gender and social class. The language of the novels of this study, specifically, is outfitted with metaphors that occasion a split between "natural" and socially constructed versions of the self. The division is realized both through explicitly interiorized images that point us to a character's "insides" as the locus of identity, and opposing networks edging outward.

Henry James, especially, reveals the anxiety about exchanges between two worlds, brought into being by his contradictory figures: the exclusive territory of the mind and the maze of social relations. Though the interior world may be symbolized by items from the social world— rooms, curtains, clothing, money, houses—James scrupulously crafts separate spaces as representative of an inner life. In *The Portrait of a*

*Lady* the tension between a desire for self-transcendence and the exigency of personal definition manifests itself through metaphors of openness and closure. James fashions intellectual frameworks for Isabel's self-defense against the limitlessness of an unruly social world. Eventually, though, the membrane around the self exposes its permeability and enclosures for consciousness become crowded with the stuff of what was once clearly the "outside" world. Isabel learns that one's identity issues from the social envelope, the world in which we live.

James realizes consciousness through the drama of social relations in both *Portrait* and *The Golden Bowl*, but always by way of controlled experiment, always inside meticulously defined containers. James's later novel, which I read in conjunction with an essay by William James, "A World of Pure Experience," fashions consciousness out of social exchanges, thus exposing the social and cultural inflections of the metaphors used to produce it. *The Golden Bowl*, in particular, highlights a tension between the rewards and the cost of consciousness for female characters, revealing the ways in which Henry James's work complicates gender as a vehicle for personal identity. Though irrevocably bound to the idea of the individual, the concept of a private interior as consciousness falls apart in these texts, revealing the jumble of rhetorical arrangements, contrived relations and social configurations, that constitute what we call the self.

James's formulation of the conscious minds of characters inevitably produces ambivalent ground for the self's position in a complex world. Similarly, Edith Wharton's fiction exposes the ambiguities of human subjectivity, multiplying the anxiety over the status of selves, namely because those selves get characterized by gender and social class. The contending forces of social awareness and self-consciousness in Wharton's fiction demonstrate how rigid codes for society manufacture selves. *The House of Mirth*, as I argue in my fifth chapter, dramatizes the conflict between a natural self, or what Wharton calls the "real" self, and the notion of a self fluent with the world around it. While Lily Bart becomes the centerpiece for speculation and social intrigue, we are also paradoxically asked to conceive of her sensibility as the essence of personal identity. Metaphors for consciousness in Wharton's prose generate competing accounts of subjectivity, sometimes fabricating a self identical to social texture, sometimes preserving a version of consciousness that indicates some separate, intrinsically private, room inside the mind.

*The Age of Innocence* dismantles any notion of privacy as a means of establishing identity, and, as my final chapter demonstrates, reveals the hazards of self-consciousness for characters defined by a profoundly open social system. The permeability of consciousness in Wharton's late novel rubs up against the intense desire of its main character, Newland Archer, for a fulfilling inner life. Archer aches for sanctuary, a respite from the social machine that rules him. Compared to his literary ancestors Maggie Verver and Isabel Archer, whose meditative vigils provide refuge and power, Newland finds no existence outside of society. Wharton shows this world to be a perpetual stage, with no place for retreat, no voice or personal agency to separate or individuate a self. Archer's dream of a life that transcends social boundaries remains unattainable in this novel, which is, perhaps, its enticement. Yet Wharton's repeated references to a "real" life and "real" selves—a gesture she repeats both in *The House of Mirth* and *The Age of Innocence*—reveals her reluctance to abandon the notion of an authentic, personal interior. Accordingly, Wharton's impulse to suspend the imaginative life of a character, to leave the wondering and deliberating we might attribute to a conscious mind unspoken, remains rigorously balanced against her understanding of the self as a product of its social and historical sphere.

Edith Wharton's texts reveal the tension between a singular conception of the self and the idea of a self that is continually shifting. Indeed, the anxiety over language that all of these authors manifest originates in their belief in the power of verbal expression, a stance that requires that they balance delicately the disruptive with the fertile tendencies of words. Consciousness undergoes a series of rhetorical shifts in these works of philosophy, science and fiction at the turn of the century, occasioning just as many revisions in concepts of the self and mind. What emerges in this study is a fuller understanding of the striking path that metaphor creates for the course of any narrative as well as the significance of figurative language in a variety of discourses. Reading the figure of consciousness as it materializes through metaphors of nature and place, social categories and spiritual essences, we come to discover that if the fluctuations of language expose us to the precariousness of identity, they also open up possibilities for its continual transformation.

# THE FIGURE OF
# CONSCIOUSNESS

## CHAPTER ONE

# Studies in Nature and Interiors:
## The Discourse of Consciousness in Nineteenth-Century Science

> "Nature, in passing through the medium of the imagination, is necessarily transposed and in a manner conventionalized; and it is this transposition, this deliberate selection of certain characteristics to the exclusion of others, that distinguishes the work of art from a cast or a photograph."

> Edith Wharton, *The Decoration of Houses*

In the introduction to her first book, *The Decoration of Houses* (1897), Edith Wharton stipulates two distinct ways to decorate a home: "by a superficial application of ornament" independent of the structure of the building, or "by means of those architectural features which are part of the organism of every house, inside as well as out."[1] Accentuating the technical significance of her study, Wharton cites the "unscientific methods" of the lay person's designs that "sever" the "natural connection between the outside of the modern home and its interior."[2] Her aim, throughout detailed discussions of cornices and vestibules and mouldings, is to repair this rift. In addition to its directions on how to decorate each room of a house, Wharton's textbook in interior design provides us with a metaphorical figure for the self that might be understood both through its psychological "interior" and its biological "structure." Her language, furthermore, exposes the relationship between the architectural metaphors that give shape to notions of private life and questions, prevalent at the turn of the century, about the role of "nature" in the creation of human subjectivity.

Meditations on the conventionalization of nature seem oddly placed inside a book about interior design; yet Wharton's figurative construction of the imagination as a place nature visits provides a helpful introduction to the connections I would like to draw between scientific language and what is usually considered "literary" language, in nineteenth and early twentieth-century texts. Throughout their varied writings, scientists and novelists alike use metaphors as a means to express their understanding of the workings of the human mind. What we find happening, however, is that while authors might consider metaphors productive for the explanation of a particular theory, they often underestimate just how productive figurative language can be. Metaphors move beyond the simple function of defining concepts to generate vast perceptual networks of their own. Writers consequently lose control over their scrupulously composed texts.

Nineteenth-century scientific texts often rely upon evolutionary theory to inquire into the origin of human life and to answer questions about mental activity; in addition, psychological scientists employ figurative language in order to compose theories about the human mind, to materialize those experiences that we have come to consider intensely personal or "inward," and to substantialize the self's place in a fluid, changing universe. Among the work of Charles Darwin, Alfred Russel Wallace, George Henry Lewes and Herbert Spencer metaphors for consciousness proliferate; these texts, in turn, share some of the same figures that we see in the Jameses and Wharton. It is precisely the metaphoricity of all of these texts that demonstrates, as the designs for Wharton's interiors remind us, that no discourse is set apart from nor immune to the intricacies of figurative language. Science does not borrow from the literary lexicon, nor does a scientific text merely supply the imaginative writer with his or her vocabulary; rather, as the following discussion will demonstrate, the prominence of metaphors in all of these textual explorations of human subjectivity indicates a shared discourse. As consciousness materializes through metaphor across genres we begin to recognize a common concern over language; indeed, writers repeatedly betray their anxiety over the creative and disruptive power of words. Specifically, the convolutions and involutions of metaphor in both psychology and fiction suggest that the universe around us can also enter inside us; thus the quest for a stable language system with which to conceive of consciousness becomes a crucial component of our understanding of the world and the integration of self-identity.

With the advent of Charles Darwin's theory of evolution, the exploration of the notion of consciousness became a portion of scientific study rather than the exclusive realm of philosophers pondering the mind-body problem. Because Darwin's first book, *On the Origin of Species* (1859), shifts attention to origins, the terms of his inquiry into consciousness likewise reflect an interest in finding a "natural" origin for the mind or the origin of consciousness in evolution.[3] Though the *Origin* deals minimally with consciousness, this work proves important since it helps us to contextualize the conflict between natural and supernatural explanations for human mental events. As a naturalist, Darwin's challenge was to try to imagine a way that consciousness—that experience we feel as private and subjective, that seemingly unique inwardness—could have been derived from mere matter. Darwin argues, however, that consciousness is not in matter *per se*; it is, more accurately, the fundamental property of all living things. He further insists that mental structures, though they vary according to species, are subject to the same evolutionary nudges as corporeal structures. Nonetheless, Darwin's lengthy chapter title (in an essay that anticipates *Origin*) signals "the difficulties of this subject," just as his language betrays discomfort with theorizing in order to discover *the* point from which all species evolved.

> I have as yet only alluded to the mental qualities which differ greatly in different species. Let me here premise that . . . there is no evidence and consequently no attempt to show that all existing organisms have descended from any one common parent-stock, but that only those have so descended which, in the language of naturalists, are clearly related to each other. Hence the facts and reasoning advanced in this chapter do not apply to the first origin of the senses, or of the chief mental attributes, such as of memory, attention, reasoning, &c., &c., by which most or all of the great related groups are characterised, any more than they apply to the first origin of life, or growth, or the power of reproduction. The application of such facts as I have collected is merely to the differences of the primary mental qualities and of the instincts in the species of the several great groups.[4]

Conducting his reader through fascinating mutations of the mental peculiarities of certain species, Darwin circumvents questions about how or *when* a distinctly human consciousness and mind evolved. The "language of naturalists" is the language of relations. And indefatigable naturalist that he is, Darwin steers his analysis of mental instincts via this "language," indicating a network of transfers rather than a solitary occasion of creation. Gillian Beer has pointed out that "Darwinian theory requires that we accept forgetfulness and the vanishing of matter" as preconditions of its method of explanation. Because the notion of "origin" is antecedent to language and consciousness, no origin—whether it is the origin of species, of mental qualities, or of individual experience—can ever fully be regained or rediscovered.[5] Darwin's language directs us towards certain ideas and away from others, though his metaphors sometimes undermine the careful course he has set. *Origin* eludes the question of origins repeatedly, still its persistent pull comes not simply from the promise of the book's title, but also through metaphors that frequently confound Darwin's suspension of a primal source.[6]

While Darwin makes clear that he will explain the "variation" of mental characteristics, he assures his readers that there is no "evidence" that reveals "one common parent-stock": he will not address the "first origin of senses" any more than the "first origin of life." Focusing on diversity, on shifts and deviations rather than some vestige that might remain, a thread that might reach back to "one" original essence, Darwin creates a text that multiplies, a linguistic project enhanced by his famous figure of the Tree of Life.[7] Strikingly, Darwin's lush metaphor refers again and again to extensions— "thin straggling branches," "great branches," "budding twigs," even "fallen branches"—but never to the hidden root, or a once presumably existent, if barely visible seed.[8] His caution against finding any "root" appears again in *Origin* even more bluntly; it is a repetition of his testimony from the 1844 essay: "I may here premise that I have nothing to do with the origin of mental powers, any more than I have with that of life itself. We are concerned only with the diversity of instinct and other mental faculties in animals of the same class."[9] In his early essay, as in *Origin*, Darwin piles example after example of domestic animals and their "dispositions," "temper," "habits," "manners," "expressions," and "tendencies"—all "facts" that "must lead to the conviction, justly wonderful as it is, that almost infinitely numerous shades of disposition, of tastes, of peculiar movements, and even of individual actions, can be modified or acquired by one individual and transmitted to its offspring."[10] Just as these traits undergo metamorphoses from one generation to the next, so too they suggest an uninterrupted link among separate organisms; pushing this to its extreme realization, Darwin will argue that human consciousness or mental capacity is continuous with other species.

Certainly Darwin's work pretends to be neither philosophy nor psychology. He admits that his "conjectures" about mental capacity and the inheritance of certain cognitive traits are sometimes "vague and unphilosophical," yet he lures his readers towards the gradual acceptance of each step along the evolutionary trail, guiding them towards a place of abundant "possibility":

> Once grant that dispositions, tastes, actions and habits can
> be slightly modified, either by slight congenital differences
> (we must suppose in the brain) or by the force of external
> circumstances, and that such slight modifications can be
> rendered inheritable,—a proposition which no one can
> reject,—and it will be difficult to put any limit to the com-
> plexity and wonder of the tastes and habits which may pos-
> sibly be thus acquired.[11]

The repeated reference to "slight" modifications (the word appears
three times in this paragraph) underscores the logical tone of this passage, as well as the sense that the author asks little from his readers.
Even his vague pronouncements, Darwin urges, should serve to
"delay" one's first impulse "utterly" "to reject" a theory. Darwin
takes the reader through each consecutive phase of his hypotheses
until our concessions feel as "gradual" as the acquirement of differing characteristics in a species might. With limitless possibility as the
destination, the point of departure might seem immaterial; and
Darwin's language is often provocative, if not conflicted, precisely in
the ways he invites a thought only to follow it with ambiguous and
open conclusions.

Conceptually and theoretically, Darwin's text remains muddled
and yet the implications of his materialist theory resonate, a phenomenon that indicates increasing belief in scientific method as *the*
technique for examining human experience. Darwin repeatedly
rewrites the *Origin*; aware of complications, he still pursues methods
of empirical observation, which make his discoveries sound quite
matter-of-fact. Always, his tone reveals a keen awareness of his audience. This text, which reads like a humble enquiry by a cultivated
man to a cultivated group of readers, nonetheless, contains astonish-
ing facts. Thus it is fitting that the conclusion to the *Origin*, with its
famous reference to the "tangled bank," should display a caution that
verges on contradiction and indecision. Providing, first, an elegant
display of lofty Victorian rhetoric, Darwin speaks of species "enno-
bled" by their link to the first few beings of the world, and the security of a future where natural selection leads us to "perfection."
Finally, Darwin's vision of "open fields," referring, certainly, to scientific research yet to come, culminates in the image of the "tangled
bank," a captivating figure that nonetheless obstructs the view of the
"fields":

> It is interesting to contemplate a tangled bank, clothed with
> many plants of many kinds, with birds singing on the bush-

es, with various insects flitting about, and with worms
crawling through the damp earth, and to reflect that these
elaborately constructed forms, so different from each other,
and dependent upon each other in so complex a manner,
have all been produced by laws acting around us.[12]

This passage purposely enmeshes plants and animals in a "tangle"—
the numerous plants arched and bending; the animal life alternately
"singing," "flitting," "crawling"—and makes them simultaneously
"different" and "dependent" as if to suggest that the union of such
"complex" life forms would always create a chaotic and tumultuous
association. Though Darwin explains that the plants, worms, birds
are united under the same "laws" that ultimately produce "the higher animals," he remains cagey about the place of human beings in this
evolutionary portrait. Except, of course, for the silent observer who
"contemplates" this scene with interest. And here Darwin's metaphor
seems to proliferate and split beyond his control. The implicit human
presence stands as a conscious investigator, definitively removed from
the tangle, yet curiously examining the spectacle. Embodied in the
contemplative spectator, consciousness—a presumably modern product of evolution—seems here to have existed from the beginning.
Darwin, at least, must grant the conscious mind a place in this picture
in order to examine his evolutionary construction. Consider, also, the
subsequent gesture, as the naturalist includes another overseer who,
while still peripheral to the scene, sustains life on the embankment.
Darwin's prose gets convoluted as he closes, switching to the passive
tense, expressing a "view of life, with its several powers, having been
originally breathed by the Creator into a few forms or into one." A
profoundly ambivalent gesture, Darwin not only vacillates on the
question of singular or multiple origins for life, but he also hints at a
version of the Genesis story where a divine Creator "breathes" life
into human beings.

When Darwin attempts to tackle the question of human origins
head on, in his second most important book, *The Descent of Man,* he
immediately states his reluctance to publish such a work; in fact, he
explains that he collected notes with "no intention of publishing on
the subject, but rather with the determination not to publish."
Concerned that he might add to the prejudices against his views,
Darwin also states that he considered the *Origin* "sufficient" because
his first edition of that text stated that "'light would be thrown on the
origin of man and his history' and this implies that humans must be
included with other organic beings in any general conclusion respect-
ing his manner of appearance on this earth."[13] At the core of this text

stands Darwin's continuity hypothesis: "The sole object of this work is to consider, firstly, whether man, like every other species, is descended from some pre-existing form"; and in his chapter on the Mental Powers of Man he expresses this aim with respect to mental life: "My object in this chapter is to show that there is no fundamental difference between man and the higher mammals in their mental faculties." Even though Darwin's title suggests more attention to the human species, the naturalist is always more comfortable with plants, insects and animals. He will speak of "man" only to the extent that human experience resembles or parallels animal experience. Such a restriction forces Darwin to make incredibly naive equations: "As man possesses the same senses as the lower animals, his fundamental intuitions must be the same." Darwin demonstrates this correspondence by showing the maternal affection of baboons, the reasoning power of an elephant, the curiosity and jealousy of monkeys, the attentive watchfulness of a wild cat, a dog's dreaming; each example that Darwin employs raises the respective animal to the level of a subject, an informing subject, from whom the human (reader) is meant to understand his or her experience of emotions and mental events.[14]

In one memorable instance, relegated to a footnote, Darwin himself imitates the action of a baboon, thus defying a critic's attempt to "discredit" his work. In order to prove that maternal affection is a continuous emotion from female human to female animal, Darwin cites the case of a mother baboon who "had so capacious a heart" that she adopted young monkeys of other species, young dogs and even a kitten. When the kitten scratches her, however, this baboon examines the kitten's feet and promptly bites its claws off. Both startlingly funny and oddly disturbing, Darwin's footnote requires that we see ourselves in the baboon at the same time it indicates how forcefully he sees a baboon in himself: "A critic, without any grounds . . . disputes the possibility of this act as described by Brehm, for the sake of discrediting my work. Therefore I tried, and found that I could readily seize with my own teeth the sharp little claws of a kitten nearly five weeks old."[15] In order to authenticate his work, to restore his credibility and confirm his data, Darwin makes viable the baboon's act; he preserves the accomplished scientist's reputation by replicating a strikingly bestial gesture. Oddly enough, Darwin seems more invested in proving that the act—the "seizure"—is possible than insisting upon the interfacing of mental and emotional states among humans and animals. But his identification with the mother baboon serves as an allegory for *The Descent of Man*. And though allegory emphasizes symbolic affiliation between two otherwise differing things, Darwin consistently attempts to integrate man and animal, to make their actions, mental capacities, attitudes synonymous; Darwin then argues that human self-integration involves our complete integration with all animal species.

*The Descent of Man* includes a chapter devoted to the Moral Sense which, for Darwin, emerges out of social instinct. Establishing an affiliation between moral sense or conscience, social instinct and sympathy—"an essential part of the social instinct . . . indeed its foundation stone"—Darwin gets caught between a desire to preserve the unique position of human conscience and his thesis regarding the continuity between all species. From the start, Darwin suggests that human sensibility remains distinct: "It may be well first to premise that I do not wish to maintain that any strictly social animal, if its intellectual faculties were to become as active and as highly developed as in man, would acquire exactly the same moral sense as ours." Moreover, the text bows repeatedly to what appears to be inescapably *human* about the capacity to retain impressions from former states of being. Darwin refers to this power as an "inward sense" or "inward monitor" that allows past impressions to be compared "during their incessant passage through the mind." He stresses repeatedly that "man cannot avoid reflection; past impressions and images are incessantly and clearly passing through his mind"; "alone ranked as moral," human beings constantly contemplate their actions and approve or disapprove them. Consciousness, in this assessment, operates as an obsessive agent of self-inspection.[16]

Natural selection requires that each species fit flawlessly into a taxonomy while simultaneously expanding beyond that system of classification. Each species, as Darwin resolutely reminds us, moves toward "perfection." But moral sense or conscience, that highest human faculty, emerges out of a quagmire of unpredictable instincts; how, therefore, might we record its progress or ensure its perfected state? Consciousness, presumably an outgrowth of moral sensibility, becomes exceedingly capricious in this account. In a later work, Darwin admits that the terms "will," "consciousness" and "intention" present him with difficulty because they suppress the progression of habit and inheritance. Although actions—which were first voluntary, soon became habitual and finally, hereditary and automatic—often reveal the state of the mind, this result was not, according to Darwinian logic, intended or expected. Furthermore, Darwin claims that most of our expressive actions are innate or instinctive, derived for some specific use rather than indicative of a particular mental state. Crying, screaming, drawing down the corners of the mouth, bearing the teeth were all performed for a definite object—to escape some danger, relieve some distress, gratify some desire.[17] Darwin effectively empties out consciousness through the evolutionary process until it is difficult to locate any function at all for this self-reflective capacity. By relegating emotional expression to the realm of innate or instinctive actions, Darwin removes reflection or intentionality from human development, though he does leave open the question of whether or not "we have any instinctive power of recognizing" emotions by their respective expressions. Darwin says elsewhere, somewhat bewilderedly: "We are indeed all conscious that we do possess such sympathetic feelings, but our consciousness does not tell us whether they are instinctive, having originated long ago in the same manner as with the lower animals, or whether they have been acquired by each of us during our early years."[18] Without the ability to monitor its own evolutionary process, consciousness proves uninteresting and unproductive to Darwin, a baffling commodity for nature to have "selected" and preserved.

Though Alfred Russel Wallace presented his theory of evolution in conjunction with Charles Darwin (1858), this less famous, codiscoverer of natural selection differed with Darwin on the question of consciousness and the development of the human mind. Darwin's insistence on continuity in evolution may make his notions of consciousness seem narrow, yet Wallace's explanation of consciousness, because it relied on spiritualism, threatened to expunge him from the scientific community altogether. A theory of consciousness dependent upon metaphysical imposition went against the scientific establishment as well as the rules of natural causes. Wallace, however, found the theory of natural selection inadequate when applied to humans and, to the disturbance of Darwin and other fellow scientists, he spent the latter part of his career endeavoring to understand the chasm between the materialist theory he supported and the metaphysical implications he could not deny. For Wallace, there had to be more to the evolution of the human mind than mere matter, struggle and survival. His initial recognition of the role of the human brain as a totally new factor in the history of life received admiring endorsement from Darwin. Wallace concurred with Darwin on all aspects of natural selection for corporeal structures; yet he conceived of the human body as having reached a point where the skeleton remained stationary, while the cranial cavity changed and the brain, in turn, developed radically superior capabilities.[19]

Wallace devotes an entire volume to *Darwinism*, mapping the intersections between his own views and those of his friend and fellow scientist, Charles Darwin; with respect to questions about consciousness, the most interesting segment comes at the close of his book. "Although, perhaps, nowhere distinctly formulated," Wallace submits that Darwin's argument "tends to the conclusion that man's entire nature and all his faculties, whether moral, intellectual, or spiritual, have been derived from their rudiments in the lower animals," a "conclusion" that rests upon Darwin's countless demonstrations of such "rudiments" as he detects them in animals. Wallace wants to suggest that proving continuity between animals and humans is not the same as proving that mental and moral faculties have been developed by natural selection. Walking a tight line, Wallace proposes that "certain definite portions" of the human mind, "of man's intellectual and moral nature," could not have been developed by variation and natural selection alone; that "some other influence, law or agency is required to account for them."[20] This conviction that certain portions of the mind are parceled out for consciousness pervades nineteenth-century scientific and philosophical texts; often, writers include subtle undercurrents of this belief rather than exploring its consequences. Wallace traces his hypothesis outside science into mysticism and modern spiritualism.[21]

Entrenched in metaphysics, Wallace often loses his grounding; at these troubled moments, he repeatedly explodes into raptures about the moral history of humanity and the endless possibilities, therefore, for moderns:

> Thus alone we can understand the constancy of the martyr, the unselfishness of the philanthropist, the devotion of the patriot, the enthusiasm of the artist, and the resolute and persevering search of the scientific worker after nature's secrets. Thus we may perceive that the love of truth, the delight in beauty, the passion for justice, and the thrill of exultation with which we hear of any act of courageous self-sacrifice, are the workings within us of a higher nature which has not been developed by means of the struggle for material existence.[22]

Never mind that Darwin spends the entire text of *Origin* matching these "human" faculties to a series of like expressions in animals; Wallace relegates these elevated emotions to humans alone, to the workings of a "higher nature." Such noble qualities are neither "material," nor the product of "struggle." Nature, for Wallace, is more than the world around us. Though nature transcends the outdoors, it also gets enfolded within. Wallace internalizes the "workings" of nature as if there were a protected inner space for each human, unaffected by environmental pressures. Appropriately, Wallace mystifies the work of the scientist, making nature's "secrets" the object of his inquiry. And though he uses the language of the natural scientist, figuring certain levels of "nature" allows Wallace to fashion a distinctly human variety, and to re-locate it "within us."

While Wallace might be remembered most for his departures from legitimate scientific study, he did not abandon his initial findings entirely; his theories that coincided with Darwinian science provided a basis, though Wallace would continually work to make that foundation more elusive. In *Darwinism*, however, he reminds his readers that he debates "solely" with the capability of Darwin's theory to "account for the origin of the *mind*, as well as it accounts for the origin of the *body*." He feels compelled to recognize some origin for special faculties of consciousness that is distinct from what explains the "animal" characteristics of humans. In addition to the moral nature of human beings, Wallace addresses the mathematical faculty, musical and artistic faculties, as well as what he calls "the metaphysical faculty," which enables us to form abstract conceptions, and the faculty of wit or humor. Wallace argues that these "special faculties" clearly point to "the existence in man" of something that has not been derived from animal progenitors. Best referred to as "a spiritual essence or nature," this something more that Wallace constructs becomes superadded to the "animal nature" of humans. In moments such as these, the generative power of metaphors is welcome; authors of consciousness might, to this extent, embrace figurative discourse precisely because they need its tendency to multiply. When Wallace locates the mystical asset *in* the human being, however, he effectively contains it as well as emphasizes its exclusivity. Only when we admit to some distinct and differentiating inwardness are we able to understand what is "otherwise mysterious or unintelligible" with respect to human life, especially the "enormous influence of ideas, principles, and beliefs" over everyday life and actions.[23]

Wallace creates a term for this "new power"—"vitality"—because "it gives to certain forms of matter all those characters and properties which constitute Life." This first stage, where the force of "vitality" turns inorganic matter into organic is followed by a stage "more marvellous," and "still more completely beyond all possibility of explanations by matter, its laws and forces": the introduction of consciousness. Through its resistance to explanation, its transcendence of natural "laws," Wallace invents consciousness as an extra-material force, one that affects him with wonder. He refutes the possibility that the evolution of complications in structures produces something as profoundly unique as consciousness; it is "preposterous," he claims, to assume that mere stages of complexity might result in this sensibility. That "an *ego* should start into existence, a thing that *feels*, that is

*conscious* of its own existence"—these developments must be the
result of "something new." More important, perhaps, than these
statements that indicate Wallace's resistance to the idea of continuity,
and his desire to make consciousness a singular, unparalleled pocket
of the human mind, are his remarks that consciousness cannot be elu-
cidated with words. Consciousness remains irresistibly obscure: "No
verbal explanation or attempt at explanation . . . can afford any mental satisfaction, or help us in any way to a solution of the mystery."
We have no adequate words, no access to a vocabulary that would fit
the "mystery" of consciousness because this special human faculty,
more than any other, points to the unknown world of spirit, "an
unseen universe." Wallace implies that consciousness entered human
beings by means of some "spiritual influx," a process that stands little chance of scientific analysis; though oddly enough, he classifies
this agent along with the "marvellously complex forces which we
know as gravitation, cohesion, chemical force, radiant force, and
electricity." Thus Wallace simultaneously inserts consciousness into
the world of the physical sciences, conscientiously listing those
"forces" that hold up the material universe, at the same time he constructs consciousness as a metaphysical quandary, the ultimate enigma
of spiritualism. Symptomatic of a characteristic dilemma in countless
texts on consciousness, Wallace's equivocal claim discloses the desire
for scientists to locate consciousness within a scientific paradigm and
the simultaneous wish to preserve its mystical properties. Accentuate
its elusiveness, establish its impenetrability, and one might guarantee
human beings—specifically, the human mind—a select standing in
natural history.[24]

Yet once Wallace crossed the line from permissible scientific inquis-
itiveness into a blatant conviction of supernatural phenomena, his
work lost credibility. Theories about the mystical properties of consciousness, in fact, occasioned an increasingly materialist view from
evolutionary scientists. Post-Darwinian philosophical and scientific
texts embodying this response, consequently, often assume consciousness does nothing at all, appears as a helpless spectator, making
human beings "conscious automata." Consciousness was either *the*
vital force in human development or it was completely written out of
the narrative. The writings of G.H. Lewes seem to provide careful
criticism of the problems of philosophy rather than an innovative system of his own, yet his work represents a compromise between a radically materialist view of consciousness and the dubious traces of
mysticism.[25] Along with many philosophers and psychologists of his
era, Lewes finds deplorable the "extreme laxity with which the term
Consciousness is employed"; his solution is to avoid the word alto-

gether. Just as William James will experiment with different words to exchange for consciousness, Lewes considers using "Feeling" instead, but doubts that feeling is the proper term for the "whole activity of the sentient organism, inasmuch as there is, on the one hand, the activity which is unfelt, being unconscious; on the other, there is the activity of Thought."[26]

Lewes decides upon "Sentience" as a less ambiguous term than consciousness and he will create another term for what he considers to be the "plexus of sensibilities," the "Sensorium." The Sensorium, Lewes painstakingly points out, does not refer to a single organ or "portion" of the central mass of the organism: it is the ideal conception of a "movable centre"; the "blending" of impressions and sensations; a "chamber of images"; a "storehouse of experience." Lewes repeatedly reminds the reader that Mind is a system, a function of the organism, not an internal principle. Notice almost immediately, though, how his metaphors contradict this claim, consistently establishing nuclear images and figures of enclosure—centres, chambers, houses. Furthermore, though Lewes eschews the term consciousness, he retains the expression "inner life" and claims the activities of the Sensorium to be synonymous with this concept. Certainly, Lewes presses the reader to rethink metaphysical notions of inwardness as he groups "nutritive activity" in all organic tissue, "neural processes still in action" along with the more nebulous category of "experience" and its "residual effects"; but bringing these together under the title of The Inner Life seems an odd reversal of Lewes's otherwise careful avoidance of metaphysical notions of interiority.[27]

Lewes's language intensifies as he discusses the network of sensations and feelings that reach the "Sensorium"; indeed, he creates a drama in which the entire organism modifies and becomes modified as a result of each encounter—encounters at once neurological, biological and linguistic. At the close of his chapter on The Inner Life, he reaches this almost poetic crescendo: "If we understand that not a sunbeam falls upon a garden wall but the wall is altered by that beam; much more is it comprehensible that not a thrill passes through the body but our Sensorium is altered by it." An odd comparison. Still, the "thrill" that alters the Sensorium presents a charge unlike the sunbeam gracing the garden wall; the sunbeam merely "falls upon" the wall while the obscure "thrill" physically inserts itself inside the Sensorium as it "passes through the body" with an almost sexual titillation. Here Lewes appears to sever mental functions and biological/bodily functions: the body receives the thrill, the Sensorium reacts in turn. Moreover, these modifications leave "traces" on the Sensorium, the sum of which, Lewes states, *is* the Inner life.[28]

Strikingly, Lewes makes consciousness a thrilling sensation, a seemingly physical energy though its changing force remains tenuous. Consciousness nevertheless materializes into "traces," as if leaving behind, and leaving *inside* us, some language we must decode. Comprehensive and evaluative, Lewes's text tends to rehearse the myriad definitions of consciousness, often alerting the reader to convolutions of the word. Lewes composes "consciousness" out of his audience's readings—and misreadings—of the term, making elaborate deciphering always necessary. Understanding consciousness thus becomes a process of "disengaging" one meaning from another, of "extricating our science" from the errors of other theories.[29] Lewes anticipates, certainly, William James, and a host of turn-of-the-century philosophers and psychologists in identifying the problem of consciousness as a problem with language. Whether these "scientists" admit it or not, their frustration often registers as a lack of control over terms, definitions, naming. Lewes addresses "general usage" of the term consciousness at the same time he hopes to detach, if not the term then at least his belief in the concept, from the imprecise discourse surrounding it. Though his text constructs intricate remappings of the functions of consciousness, though he replaces names and transforms interpretations, *Problems of Life and Mind* (1880) reverts to the term "consciousness" again and again with a relentlessness that appears beyond Lewes's control. Despite his explicit desire to forfeit the name, Lewes returns to "consciousness" as a sort of catchall. Placing unconscious sentient process next to subconscious and conscious processes among the data of psychology, Lewes concludes that

> Consciousness is the abstract term for all states, whether discriminated or not. In the first case, to have a sensation and to be conscious of having it, are two different states; in the second case, they are one in the same state. Whatever ambiguity there may be in this must be submitted to as inevitable. Language was not formed by philosophers. They must employ the terms at hand.[30]

Surrounded by "inevitable" ambiguity, it is no surprise that consciousness here accommodates two, polarized meanings at once. Lewes explains, however, that this ambiguity is not philosophical, but linguistic. Throughout *Problems of Life and Mind*, Lewes does everything to avoid using "the terms at hand" because he deems them inaccurate; but here he seems to submit to the inexorable pull of "consciousness," a word that invariably leaves its signature on his text. Lewes rescues some clarity by relegating the term to the abstract—consciousness speaks for "all states"; but if consciousness is everything, it may as well be nothing. What Lewes cannot evade, finally, are the figures that accompany the term. His language is more powerful than his attempts to maneuver it: consciousness is simultaneously interiorized and ubiquitous; a core of each human being that still shifts uncannily.

Discussing "personality," Lewes illuminates an irksome problem for nineteenth-century philosophers and scientists seeking to explore ideas without the entanglement of language; that is, the contradictions inherent in Lewes's prose reveal the impossibility of "studying" consciousness without entering a verbal contest. That these writers characteristically call attention to their discourse, regretting the inadequacies of language, imagining a way to relate their findings without the bother of metaphorical expression, actually serves to secure the existence of consciousness until it appears as an unshakable conviction, troubled only by our limited vocabulary. G.H. Lewes's work characteristically betrays the desire his fellow philosophers had to banish figurative language from "science," to unmask concepts from their obscuring descriptions. At the same time, of course, the text shows how these authors must build their theories with linguistic, often explicitly literary, tools. To explain "personality," Lewes formulates a "center" inside each human being; he claims that feelings, sometimes obscure enough to appear instinctive, may not enter "the daylight of consciousness" in certain minds. Nevertheless: "They form the moral core of our Personality: as generalised conceptions form the intellectual core, and generalised sensations form the sensible core. Every sensible impression, every proposition, every social action, is *apperceived* by this personal centre. Our individuality, or idiosyncrasy, is its expression."[31] With this elaborate distribution of "cores" whose respective functions and substances Lewes details, it is difficult to tell whether we have one "personal centre" or many centers. Like his concept of the "movable centre," these shifting cores build a network, a complex infrastructure through which a multitude of experiences find their way. Given Lewes's reference to "individuality" it seems we are meant to imagine a singular center for each person. But where do we locate this center; and with a language so slippery, how might we stabilize something like "personality" or individual identity?

Lewes's chapter on "Consciousness and Unconsciousness" in *The Physical Basis of Mind* (1893) begins: "Science demands precision of terms"; with these words Lewes issues an immediate warning about language as a portion of scientific inquiry. Unlike physicists and chemists who have only to "settle the significance of the facts observed," Lewes argues that biologists and social theorists must "settle the significance of the terms they employ in expressing the facts observed. Hence more than half their disputes are at bottom verbal." Most of his chapter, in fact, overtly engages the question of consciousness as one irrevocably influenced by the verbal—the "ambiguity of current terms," unsatisfactory "definitions," the use of "popular language," and "special meanings" versus "general meanings" of words. Specifically, Lewes finds that consciousness, at once, resists definition and needs no definition: "In one sense, no definition of Consciousness can be satisfactory, since it designates an ultimate fact, which cannot therefore be made more intelligible than it is already. In another sense no definition is needed, since every one knows what is meant by saying, 'I am conscious of such a change, or such a movement.' It is here the equivalent of Feeling." Ironically, what "everyone knows" consciousness to be comprises a great majority of Lewes's critique of the term. The title of Lewes's book, moreover, designates his project as one that attempts to merge the barriers between the physical and the mental; "feeling" equates to consciousness only insofar as we understand its physiological basis as well as its psychological sway. Consciousness is, above all else, a function of the organism. This definition leaves room for Lewes's discussion of conscious, subconscious, and unconscious (or "latent") states that differ solely in the degree of complication in the neural processes. Lewes expresses the distinctions consciousness makes with a simple, yet striking, statement of the human mind's limitations: "We can only discriminate one thrill at a time."[32]

To elucidate the concept of the unconscious, Lewes formulates an image in his text and then asks the reader to picture one for him or herself. Experiences, when they enter the unconscious, enter a latent state; they get "stored up in Memory, remaining in the Soul's picture-gallery, visible directly [when] the shutters are opened." Though most of his text emphasizes the importance of accuracy in scientific language, Lewes here inserts a metaphysical entity, the Soul, into his discussion of unconsciousness as if distracted by the beauty of the gallery he has figuratively entered. He is quick to follow up his point with a criticism of such linguistic extravagances, however: "As a metaphorical expression of the familiar facts of Memory this may pass; but it has been converted from a metaphor into an hypothesis." And here, succinctly stated, is the problem with metaphor: though we need it to elucidate theories, it surreptitiously engenders "hypotheses" of its own. Of course, we might ask which of Lewes's "hypotheses" are *not* dependent upon metaphor. Indeed, though he implicates metaphor in the confusion over the term "consciousness," Lewes ends this chapter with another elaborate figure, accompanied by an imperative that the reader "picture" the theory he has proposed, place it, that is, in the soul's own private museum. The picture gallery inclines toward a restrictive view of high culture and aesthetic awareness; to unfasten the "shutters" further, as it were, Lewes makes the final metaphor in this chapter open out onto the natural world:

> Picture to yourself this sentient organism incessantly stim-
> ulated from without and from within, and adjusting itself
> in response to such stimulations. . . . Besides the stream of
> direct stimulations, there is a wider stream of indirect or
> reproduced stimulations. . . . The term Soul is the personi-
> fication of this complex of present and revived feelings, and
> is the substratum of Consciousness (in the general sense),
> all the particular feelings being its states. . . . [W]e may
> compare Consciousness to a mass of stationary waves. If
> the surface of a lake be set in motion each wave diffuses
> itself over the whole surface, and finally reaches the shores,
> when it is reflected back towards the centre of the lake.
> This reflected wave is met by fresh incoming waves, there is
> a blending of the waves, and their product is a pattern on
> the surface.[33]

Identity, Lewes subtly suggests, is a product of environmental response, constructed and reconstructed through each "adjustment" the organism makes. Furthermore, Lewes draws on a well-established tradition of using natural metaphors to explain mental phenomena— flowing streams, substratums (of the earth?), disturbances on the surface of a lake. The "picture" of this "sentient organism" becomes increasingly involved as Lewes winds up his metaphor. Lewes asks us to picture not one, but two, parallel "streams." Complicating the relatively simple image of the stream, however—the same image that William James adopts—Lewes compares consciousness to "a mass of stationary waves," as if to add another layer to this figural representation. Though the waves enter a rather unnatural, "stationary" condition, they simultaneously get set in motion, "blending" with other waves until we ascertain a surface pattern. This does not, however, belie their finding a "centre." Lewes focuses on the "surface," but he attaches a foundation, a bottom tier, to this multivalent image. The "substratum" suggests a geological comparison, though he identifies this portion of his figure with the unearthly "term" Soul. More accurately, Lewes proposes that the Soul provides this "substratum," an under layer, for the entire figurative landscape. But what is the language of the "Soul"? Does it fit into a scientific discourse—whether that be biological, psychological, or geological—a purely metaphysical discourse, a religious or a literary discourse? Lewes's metaphors seem to be at cross-purposes here, indicating an uncertain "fit." Though the streams are in constant flux, the Soul furnishes a bedrock; the surface of the lake may ripple with movement, but the waves appear fixed. Through this wedding of contradictory images, Lewes's text exemplifies the prevalent notion that consciousness cannot be "captured," neither inside the laboratory nor inside a stable linguistic system. He also complicates the concept of identity: is it fixed or fluid? And if consciousness emerges out of this union of conflicting metaphors and incongruous verbal entities, then it will always remain elusive even, or especially, at the moment of its most complex articulation.

George Henry Lewes questions the autonomy of consciousness, making Mind the sum total of all sensations of an organism; he refutes the possibility of a singular, authoritative core that governs human thoughts and feelings, though his metaphors often appear to crystallize toward such a center or fix themselves compulsively to build a foundation for the self. The clashing metaphors in Lewes's psychology reflect his theoretical stance regarding consciousness; in Lewes's system, a series of conflicting sensations, rather than a unified source, governs mental life. Though Lewes sometimes seems aware of his diametrical figures of speech, as if employing linguistic paradoxes were the only way to demonstrate the mind's multivalent permutations, an underlying discomfort with the fluctuating tendencies of language chafes against his theories. In challenging the autonomy of consciousness, Lewes, of course, threatens the autonomy of the self and presses us to ask how we are to read ourselves within these conflicting models and discourses. Whether biology, philosophy or Lewes's brand of physiological psychology offers the objections, the loss of a distinctly human, appropriately sacrosanct notion of consciousness signals a reconsideration of all assumptions we hold about a coherent, singular self.

While Lewes's studies communicate vexed uncertainties about the place of consciousness in science and in scientific expressions of human life, the work of Herbert Spencer exposes the foreboding suspicion that consciousness is a mere causal event in evolution, an outgrowth of increasing complexities in animal nervous systems, which, finally, emerges as a useless entity in human existence. Strangely, however, the relinquishment of consciousness to its post as futile observer, does not preclude lengthy discussions of the term. Indeed, Spencer's writings bring forth beautiful metaphors uniting physiological clarifications with suggestive hypotheses about the "substance" and "composition" of what he deems most inexplicable—the human mind. Herbert Spencer's studies are often read in conjunction with the writings of G.H. Lewes; the work of these scientists, in fact, concurs on almost every point except for the question of continuity in consciousness. Thus, these writers expose a crucial split in the theories of consciousness during the nineteenth century: a cursory rendition of this disparity shows consciousness as either an organic, cohesive procession of experience that varies according to social and environmental influences, or a specialized portion of the self that remains a distilled, inviolable essence of identity. While G.H. Lewes attempts to pull apart any impression of constancy for consciousness—exposing, instead, its disparate strands—Spencer creates a concept of consciousness as an endless thread, a unified linear progression following the laws of evolution. Neither writer, however, plots to make consciousness an essential component of selfhood; on the contrary, both Lewes and Spencer acknowledge "consciousness" only insofar as they must address the misuse of the term, or in order to resituate it properly in the narrative of mental history. Immeasurable, however, are the consequences of their metaphors. As we have seen, Lewes uses metaphor to build a framework for identity by suggesting the notion of a center; though Lewes maneuvers this "center" regularly, he paradoxically establishes its rootedness in the self through references to a core, gestures toward inwardness, and the assemblage of figurative chambers and houses for our interiors. Spencer pays more attention to relations; rather than a framework, he invests his theory with images of networks. According to Spencerian psychology, the more the mind evolved, the closer it came to complete integration.

Spencer spends a great deal of time accounting for the structure of nervous systems, from the minutest organisms to the highest forms; hence something called a "nervous shock is the ultimate unit of consciousness."[34] Significantly, he conceives of nerve systems through a series of metaphors: "threads," "clusters," "bundles," and "fibres" being his most common figures.[35] As if meticulously knitting together the strands of his argument through these figurative remnants, Spencer subsequently creates a magnificent image of the "fabric of Mind":

> And now, having roughly sketched the composition of Mind—having, to preserve clearness of outline, omitted details and passed over minor qualifications; let me go on to indicate the essential truth which it is a chief purpose of this chapter to bring into view—the truth that the method of composition remains the same throughout the entire fab-

ric of Mind, from the formation of its simplest feelings up
to the formation of those immense and complex aggregates
of feeling which characterize its highest developments.[36]

In addition to highlighting the way that Mind materializes, that is, becomes a "fabric" that we might presume to use, (possibly to wear?), Spencer's metaphor suggests a maker, a workshop, perhaps even, a tailor. Yet he also uses metaphors of writing: "sketches" and "outlines" suggest multiple drafts, revised versions of what he deems the "truth." For despite the hastiness that he acknowledges drives this chapter, the gaps that it might contain, Spencer writes in order to reveal an "essential truth." Drawing attention to the "sketchiness" of his presentation, Spencer admits that he has kept his "outline" incomplete in order to preserve clarity; one wonders if it is also to preserve beauty. Nevertheless, Spencer's metaphor of the craftsman working with his "fabric" makes way for the place of the writer, always behind the scenes in scientific studies. As Peter Dear points out, scientific *literary* practice is worth investigating as a crucial feature of scientific practice as a whole since the account of an experiment is an essential part of its performance. Because it is in texts that knowledge is made, the literary constitution and function of experience in scientific argument proves fertile ground for analysis.[37] Spencer's "experiments" are mental excursions, not laboratory investigations, though they are always extremely provocative in their verbal or "literary" realization. The "method of composition" for the mind in Spencer's *Principles of Psychology* sounds remarkably like a writer's method, building gradually, sentence per sentence, paragraph per paragraph. This, Spencer seems to indicate, is also how the mind gets composed.

Spencer's images, both of the "fabric" and the "composition" of the mind, lend themselves to extensions and various addendum. When discussing the internal or unconscious processes of the mind, Spencer maintains his assumptions about continuity, much like Darwin does; in fact, additions to his theories merely strengthen the figures he fashions. Spencer acknowledges the existence of the unconscious: "Out of a great number of psychological actions going on in the organism, only a part are woven into the thread of consciousness." Yet he asserts that the disparate strands of mental life do not remain separate, where they might evoke psychological conflict or threaten the cohesion of individual identity; rather, they move progressively toward organic wholeness: "Gradually, as the nervous system becomes more and more integrated, the twisting of these various strands of changes into one thread of changes becomes more complete."[38] Though he maintains plurality in the "changes," the final image is solitary: "one thread." An integrated nervous system, like strands intertwined, serves as the ideal figure for the nervous system's ultimate phase in Spencerian psychology. In "The Composition of Mind," Spencer assembles "harmony," "unity" and "correspondences," terms that appear throughout what he calls, appropriately, his "synthetic philosophy."[39] So many of Spencer's metaphors give rise to some sort of synthesis; combinations and re-combinations of the elements of consciousness or "units of feeling," as he calls them, point us to the closest thing to a definition of Mind that he offers: "Mind, as known to the possessor of it, is a circumscribed aggregate of activities; and the cohesion of these activities, one with another, throughout the aggregate, compels the postulation of a something of which they are the activities."[40] The possessor of each Mind knows its periphery, measures its confines: individual vision is limited to a certain "circumscribed" collection of activities that we imagine exist together. And because they "cohere," we induce a "something" of which "Mind" becomes the symbol. Spencer here seems to discount words as mere "symbols" whose inadequacy keeps the mind permanently "unknowable." Just as Motion and Matter are "unknowable forms of existence,"

> Mind is also unknowable . . . the simplest form under which we can think of its substance is but a symbol of something that can never be rendered into thought; we see that the whole question is at last nothing more than the question whether these symbols should be expressed in terms of those or those in terms of these—a question scarcely worth deciding; since either answer leaves us completely outside of the reality as we were at first.[41]

Spencer's irritation about questions of language—"terms" and "symbols"—emerges clearly from this passage; not only are symbols hopelessly insufficient, but the symbolic appears to alienate us from the "real" question. Symbols always exist "outside of" "reality"; language cannot penetrate the dominion of Mind. Indeed, Spencer's Mind remains inexpressible, untouched by language, as if it were *the* absolute quantity in psychology.

With a subtle rhetorical shift, Spencer makes consciousness and mind equivalent, identifying each through the pivotal property of cohesion: "Every element of that aggregate of activities constituting a consciousness, is known as belonging to consciousness only by its cohesion with the rest." In this passage, Spencer approaches a tautological discourse: that which constitutes consciousness is known to belong because it coheres, because it forms an aggregate—in short, because it *belongs*. Rather than delineating the functions and activities of consciousness, a list that authors of consciousness inevitably deliver, he literally defines its boundaries, drawing a circle around the concept with his repetitive logic. Of course, his gestures in defining consciousness presuppose that such an entity exists, thus what "belongs" to consciousness, what "coheres" to this aggregate, comes to distinguish it from other things and allows Spencer to outline it. Appropriately, Spencer follows this description with a discussion of what exists beyond the bounds of consciousness. Consequently, that which is "beyond the limits" of consciousness, "disconnected" from consciousness, "cut off," "made foreign," un-"incorporated," not "linked," materializes as the unconscious.[42]

Spencer must rely upon inside/outside dichotomies to devise the character of human consciousness; this correspondence might explain why his language circles back on itself when he attempts to realize consciousness separately. What "distinguishes Psychology from the sciences upon which it rests," Spencer relates, is that "each of its propositions takes account both of the connected internal phenomena and of the connected external phenomena to which they refer." "Connections" both within and among the terms seem to engender thought. According to Spencer, we cannot "frame any psychological conception" without looking at what he calls internal and external "co-existences and sequences." Reflecting on the example of the representation of a concept to one's self, Spencer demonstrates the impossibility of remaining inside one or the other frameworks. Take the "involved sentiment" of justice: one "cannot represent to himself this sentiment, or give any meaning to its name, without calling to mind actions and relations supposed to exist in the environment: neither this nor any other emotion can be aroused in consciousness even vaguely, without positing something beyond consciousness to which it refers." Consciousness sustains itself through a constant interchange between its own discrete boundaries and the "environment" around it. To put it more boldly, Spencer may construct a carefully delineated border around consciousness, but he makes it impossible for his configuration to exist on its own. Indeed, while consciousness houses emotion, it remains a mere crucible requiring outside energy to stir its contents. The functions of consciousness—one of which is "arousing" emotions—always depend upon something outside of itself.[43]

Despite this interrelatedness, Spencer still maintains that "the thoughts and feelings which constitute a consciousness . . . are absolutely inaccessible to any but the possessor of that consciousness"; to this extent he closes off what appeared to be a permeable border. Or does he awaken our latent access to it by suggesting that each "possessor" of consciousness makes their own truth? Such questions prove arbitrary and elusive in *The Principles of Psychology*. The text unfolds, that is, as mysterious and deliberately estranging. Spencer continually assures the reader that discoveries, which elucidate the peculiarities of the nervous system and even suggest how it incorporates Mind and consciousness, do not provide an answer to what Mind or what consciousness *is*.[44] Whenever we come close to answers, Spencer halts the progression of his text to reiterate the impossibility of entire revelation: "though accumulated observations and experiments have led us by a very indirect series of inferences to the belief that mind and nervous action are the subjective and objective faces of the same thing, we remain utterly incapable of seeing, and even of imagining, how the two are related. Mind still continues to us a something without any kinship to other things." Elaborate proof of the relatedness of "inside" and "outside," mental and social life, disappears each time Spencer comes face to face with Mind. Always capitalized, set apart linguistically through near personification, Mind is "a something without any kinship"; we cannot see how its illustrious relations work.[45]

Spencer's texts demonstrate the simultaneous rigor and resistance in the study of mind and consciousness, a polarization that, as we have seen, often gets formulated through conflicting metaphors. It is as if evolutionary scientists approach questions about the nature of consciousness reluctant to discover any answers; perhaps were we to uncover the "mysteries" of consciousness, we would be a lot less interesting to ourselves. But the compulsive investigations, the concern over proper names and symbols for consciousness, the paradoxical character of the metaphors indicate that the ambivalence runs deeper than a desire to retain enigmas surrounding human mental life. Though evolutionary scientists would deny the doctrine of divine creation, their work exemplifies a profound discomfort with the loss of creative power in mental life. Once consciousness is named, delineated, its secret functions divulged, it is necessarily limited as is the mind that is imagined to contain it. Thus, scientists in the hub of the evolutionary period seem to want paradoxical things: to place consciousness inside the elaborate classification systems that frame their findings and yet to maintain some elusive property of conscious life in its creative relation to experience.

Darwin, Wallace, Lewes and Spencer, among other evolutionary scientists, wrestled with questions about the natural origin of the mind; they attempted to unhinge consciousness in the same way they composed it—with the unwieldy tool of language. About a decade later, when William James began publishing his new psychology, he integrated their notions of the natural origin of organic forms, the continuity of physical and mental processes, as well as the evolutionary scientist's equivocation with language and metaphor.[46] As we will see, the ultimate principle of Jamesian consciousness is its creative capacity. The human mind, according to James, is constantly "shaped" and reshaped by experience, by the imaginative energy "inside" it and by its connection to the fluid world outside of it:

> Only those items which I notice shape my mind—without selective interest, experience is an utter chaos. Interest alone gives accent and emphasis, light and shade, background and foreground—intelligible perspective, in a word. It varies in every creature, but without it the consciousness of every creature would be a gray chaotic indiscriminateness, impossible for us even to conceive.

This passage, taken from James's *Principles of Psychology*, indicates the significance of the creative element of the human mind, here rendered explicitly artistic. James also formulates a distinct contrast between the imagined outside and inside, a division that inflects most studies of consciousness in the nineteenth and early twentieth century. "Items," James asserts, "shape" the mind, make sense of the chaos, even compose a picture out of it, with traditional artistic components such as "light," "shade," "perspective," "foreground." Thus it might seem, at first, that it is the outside world that forms the mind out of what is otherwise confusing darkness. Looking more closely at the development of James's figure, however, we see that the subject "I" (whose job it is to "notice") actually molds the mind, this time more like a sculptor. Further, the "intelligible perspective" that "selective interest" brings not only generates a mind, the possessor of this selective attention seems, ultimately, to "conceive" of consciousness.[47]

William James's figure of consciousness here brings us back to Edith Wharton and to the connections between artistic and scientific discourse with which we began. Just as Wharton positions nature inside the imagination in order to create art, James repeatedly conflates interiors with exterior spaces, sometimes making consciousness the streams and birds of the natural world, and sometimes establishing it as a fortress that offers neither entry, nor access to the outside. These fluctuations in metaphors amount to a continual shift in the meaning of consciousness. Thus, the experiments with language that scientists, philosophers and novelists perform repeatedly reinvent consciousness, as if to suggest that keeping human subjectivity autonomous, coherent and credible amounts to building, dismantling and recreating, compulsively, those figures that bring it into being.

## CHAPTER TWO

# Contesting Metaphors and the Discourse of Consciousness in William James

> "When I say *every 'thought' is part of a personal conscious-ness*, 'personal consciousness' is one of the terms in question. Its meaning we know so long as no one asks us to define it, but to give an accurate account of it is the most difficult of philosophic tasks."

> William James, *The Principles of Psychology*

William James's lifelong attention to questions about human mental experience elucidates the development of the concept of consciousness through its realization in fields as disparate as natural science, radical empiricism and religious mysticism. Over the course of a career that both establishes and traverses disciplinary boundaries, James's work embodies tensions between scientific explanation for mental phenomena and the inescapability of metaphysical arguments.[1] Most readers of James puzzle over the theoretical contradictions within his work, debating central philosophical dilemmas concerning the status of the conscious self. Perhaps the most paradoxical aspect of James's theories, his response to dualism, emerges as he attempts to negotiate ethereal explanations for consciousness with bodily processes.[2] The mind-body problem disrupts James's more delicately balanced theories, a disruption registered explicitly through the metaphors in his texts.

Reading *The Principles of Psychology* (1890) alongside "Does 'Consciousness' Exist" (1904), this chapter demonstrates how figurative language directs the study of consciousness for William James. I argue that metaphor does more than describe consciousness; metaphor constructs James's arguments, governs his conflicting theories of mind through a series of rhetorical configurations, and provokes the continual reconstruction of his ideas of human subjectivity. Furthermore, while it is impossible for James to explain and to study consciousness without metaphor, he experiences great anxiety about using language—figurative or otherwise—to represent his object of study. The language becomes more powerful than his intentions or designs and, indeed, raises implications that James cannot control. James possesses a heightened awareness of what he crafts with words; he also, perhaps more penetratingly, acknowledges the inadequacy of any linguistic system to realize concepts thoroughly.[3] Struggling over appropriate "names" and "terms" for consciousness, James presupposes some clearly delineated concept around which we might wrap a verbal expression, yet he also seems painfully aware that every new metaphor launches an entirely new theory. Fluid and unpredictable, consciousness becomes like language itself—it yields its power precisely because it can be so many things at once. The ultimate principle of Jamesian consciousness seems to be its creative capacity; still, once James admits that the problem of consciousness is a problem of language, his carefully constructed designs begin to unravel. Though consciousness will be translated into James's notion of "pure experience" by the time he writes the radical empiricism essays, James remains simultaneously committed to his figures (especially of the *stream of consciousness*") and ambivalent about the account of consciousness that they provide. James helps create the modern self with its enhanced individuality, though his metaphors at once direct us inward to a centered, private self and propel us outward to find consciousness materializing in the fluxional cycle of the natural world.

In presenting his initial theory of the stream of our thoughts, James argues for its coherence. His most famous metaphor of the "stream" of consciousness appears to saturate the varied material of the mind; its water washing over and through any distinctions or separations that the mind might present:

> Consciousness, then, does not appear to itself chopped up in bits. Such words as 'chain' or 'train' do not describe it fitly as it presents itself in the first instance. It is nothing jointed; it flows. A 'river' or a 'stream' are the metaphors by which it is most naturally described. *In talking of it hereafter, let us call it the stream of thought, of consciousness, or of subjective life.*[4]

We notice that James's first impulse in this chapter on "The Stream of Thought" is to dispute words like "chain" or "train" when applied to consciousness. Though James often refers to a "section" of consciousness, he places this dubious word in quotation marks.[5] Thus undermining the word, he emphasizes the unity of this indivisible flow as well as the sense that language feels inadequate for the task of producing consciousness.

It is not surprising that James should refrain from words that implicate a machinery behind consciousness as "chain" and "train" do; he suggests, instead, that consciousness is organic, natural, uncontrived. Water, then, is what "naturally" describes consciousness. James intuitively harkens back to literary Romanticism by locating the picture of the mind in nature. It is difficult to tell if James, in reiterating the tropes of Romanticism, wishes to place consciousness in an historical narrative or whether he is arguing that such a "natural" phenomenon is, in fact, ahistorical. He does not try to define consciousness so much as he tries to locate it in its "natural" realm. Like William Wordsworth, James might wish to strip away the contrivances of society and return to a purer version of the human mind, a version that he can imagine existed before him and will continue to exist after him.[6] James rejects words that allude to the mind or body as a machine. His version of consciousness seems fluid, unpredictable, diverging and converging: a stream, for instance, meanders, a "chain" and a "train" do not. Moreover, such mechanical words are not "fit" because they imply a connected series of links rather than an uninterrupted issue. For James, consciousness allows no such gaps. James's desire to find words that are more "natural" is as much an aesthetic motion as it is an attempt at correcting false theories.[7] While James initially and explicitly designates these words as "metaphors," he effectively reclaims them in order to give a name *and* an image to consciousness. Metaphors that merely "describe" consciousness, suddenly become means of creating it. James effects this transformation partly because he must give imaginative substance to the insubstantial region of thought, mind, and feeling in order to make clear what he is studying.

As Peter Marcus Ford points out in *William James's Philosophy*, the metaphors "matter" metaphysically.[8] A "stream" and a "chain" have different characteristics and, therefore, produce differing accounts of consciousness. James reminds us that "Metaphysics means nothing but an unusually obstinate effort to think clearly" *(PP*, 1.148). In discerning the proper metaphor with respect to consciousness, James's choice of words helps him to create a particular theory of knowledge—a gesture, incidentally, which is exactly the province of metaphysics. However, if con-

sciousness "appears to itself" as a "stream" and it cannot be
"chopped up in bits," James's dilemma is still how to study these
sensibly continuous, always changing "sections" called thoughts
that seem logically to comprise consciousness. Thinking about this
dilemma in a later, abridged edition of *Principles*, James testifies to
the difficulties of inspecting consciousness:

> We first assumed conscious "states" as the units with
> which psychology deals, and we said later that they were
> in constant change. Yet any state must have a certain
> duration to be effective at all. . . . Consciousness, as a
> process in time, offers the paradoxes which have been
> found in all continuous change. There are no "states" in
> such a thing, any more than there are factors in a circle,
> or places where an arrow "is" when it flies. . . . Where
> everything is change and process, how can we talk of
> "state"? Yet how can we do without "states," in
> describing what the vehicles of our knowledge seem to
> be?[9]

Like the flying arrow that cannot be fixed, consciousness, "as a
process in time," offers no beginning or end to commence a study
of it. However, James is invested in questions about how we think
and how we receive knowledge; consciousness is one "vehicle" for
our knowledge and so he endeavors to explore it, systematically, as
a scientist. Interestingly enough, though James here equivocates
over the view of consciousness he originally formulated in *The
Principles of Psychology*, he adheres to his metaphor of the
"stream" throughout his career. James's reluctance to abandon the
figure seems to arise less out of scientific conviction and more from
aesthetic commitment to what he has created in language. As a
philosopher and a scientist, he rigorously questions his formulation; yet he cannot abandon the picture he designed as an artist.
James was committed to finding the stream in the mental landscape
he had fashioned.[10]
     In his chapter, "The Stream of Thought," James ventures to
prove that thought is in constant change within each personal consciousness. Variation is one of the properties of the stream. He
speaks of fluctuating "experience," successive "brain-states,"
"pulses" of change: "Experience is remoulding us every moment
. . . our brain changes like the aurora borealis, its whole internal
equilibrium shifts with every pulse of change . . . like the gyrations
of a kaleidoscope" *(PP,* 1.228–9). James's version of experience is

colorful and fluid; no one thought is identical with another. Furthermore, *we* are fluid, plastic beings, constantly "remoulded" by the sculpting hands of experience. James's sense that the mind is a living being and that we are created and re-created by its flux seems to have an almost dizzying effect here.[11] Our internal equilibrium forever "shifts"; the streaming, swirling motion signified by the aurora borealis and the gyrating kaleidoscope make the brain chaotic. Consciousness ostensibly steps in to create order, to sift and to "select."[12]

According to James, consciousness "from our natal day is of a teeming multiplicity of objects and relations" *(PP,* 1.219). Our brain confronts this abundant variety of thoughts: thoughts that are always in transition and impressions that blend and merge. Given the concentration of Jamesian metaphors that make blurry outlines in the world of impressions, it is not surprising that James expresses the importance of relations in understanding thoughts and feelings. Furthermore, James uses the transitional qualities of language in order to emphasize the relational aspect of consciousness. As Daniel Bjork notes, "Declensions, conjunctions, and prepositions were linguistic signs that consciousness was relational and inherently dynamic rather [than] substantive and static."[13] Relations, in fact, become the means by which one follows the stream; impressions must be seen in a continuum so that consciousness suffers no breach. James depicts this quite suggestively: "an impression feels very different according to what has preceded it; as one color succeeding another is modified by the contrast, silence sounds delicious after a noise. . . ." *(PP,* 1.228). At another point, he states: "Into the awareness of the thunder itself the awareness of the previous silence creeps and continues; for what we hear when the thunder crashes is not thunder *pure*, but thunder-breaking-upon-silence-and-contrasting-with-it" *(PP,* 1.234). The silence and the thunder rely on each other for impact; "thunder *pure*" cannot exist because our sense of it comes in the "contrast" it makes to silence. James strings together the image of "thunder-breaking-upon-silence-and-contrasting-with-it" because he must create a "single" word for the impression comprised not simply of thunder, but the edges of silence surrounding it.[14] Elsewhere, James laments the inadequacies of language to express the fullness of a thought or feeling. It is almost impossible, he persuades us, to imagine a feeling so limited that it has no inkling of anything that went before. We are woefully imprecise, therefore, in naming our thoughts: "Here, again, language works against our perception of the truth. We name our thoughts simply . . . as if each knew its own thing and nothing else. What each really knows is clearly the thing it is named for, with dimly perhaps a thousand other things" *(PP,* 1.234). The "dim" perception of the "thousand other things" of which our thoughts consist is often represented, in *Principles,* by recurring words that seem to indicate that there is an inescapable fuzziness in the language of consciousness. Some of James's favorites are: "echo," "halo," "fringe," "penumbra," "shadow," "suffusion." Significantly, all of these words share a lingering quality, as if, when attached to consciousness, they had the ability to spread or cling or float or leave a trail. James's sense that there is more to a thought or feeling than its traditional label can express, drives him to keep words in suspense.

Because much of James's work in *The Principles of Psychology* involves correcting mistaken assumptions as well as erroneous definitions, he is especially disturbed by scientific and philosophical inaccuracy in naming:

> We ought to have some general term by which we desig
> nate all states of consciousness merely as such, and apart
> from their particular quality or cognitive function.
> Unfortunately, most of the terms in use have grave
> objections. 'Mental state,' 'state of consciousness,' 'con
> scious modification,' are cumbrous and have no kindred
> verbs. The same is true of 'subjective condition.'
> 'Feeling' has the verb 'to feel,' both active and neuter,
> and such derivatives as 'feelingly,' 'felt,' 'feltness,' etc.,
> which make it extremely convenient. But on the other
> hand it has specific meanings as well as its generic one,
> sometimes standing for pleasure and pain, and being
> sometimes a synonym of 'sensation' as opposed to
> thoughts; whereas we wish a term to cover sensation
> and thought indifferently. *(PP,* 1.185)

I quote James at length here to show that his thoroughness with respect to the question of naming (a thoroughness that is sometimes exhausting) reveals the extent to which the issue vexes him. James continues to try out other possible words and phrases to illustrate what he calls here "all states of consciousness." He entertains: *psychosis,* but this has no verb or grammatical form allied to it; 'affections of the soul,' 'modification of the ego,' 'states of consciousness,' all of which he dismisses as "clumsy"; idea, Locke's word, but it has not "domesticated itself within the language"; thought, but it doesn't cover sensation. He says we may be forced to adopt some *"pair* of terms" like Humes's 'impression and idea' or Hamilton's 'presentation and representation' or "the ordinary" 'feeling and thought' *(PP,* 1.186). This "quandary" which James settles indecisively by choosing "sometimes one, sometimes another of the synonyms I have mentioned" produces a kind of explosion of terms, none of which satisfy James's probing mind.

Trying to build a vocabulary for consciousness, James stumbles through a series of possible "names" until he settles his question by remaining unsettled. The choice to vacillate between names, and especially the pairing of terms, allows James to create a space without a name. James is cagey about definitive labels and images; he prefers to enhance what he sees as a more supple string of relations. However, James does conclude this passage in *Principles* with the statement that his own partiality is for "either FEELING or THOUGHT. I shall probably use both words in a wider sense than usual, and alternately startle two classes of readers by their unusual sound" *(PP,* 1.186). James is able to remain ambivalent, swinging between two alternate points (*either* feeling or thought); he is not fixed because he establishes a bridge between the terms, even if that bridge is the "unusual sound" of the words together. The delicacy with which James approaches this question of naming becomes fascinating in itself. If a word is "cumbrous" or not "domesticated" within the language, he rejects it, which seems to suggest that James wants to avoid attributing an unwieldy or alien quality to consciousness. Naming this entity, then, appears to be partly a process of finding a language with which to tame it. And James is simultaneously curious and cautious about such a task.

At the beginning of this passage in *Principles,* James alludes to the importance of naming; he begins, in fact, with an imperative: "We ought to have some general term by which we designate all states of consciousness merely as such, and apart from their particular quality or cognitive function." James wants a term to cover all, a "general term" for consciousness that can exist "apart from" its functions.[15] While we might guess that this is the job of the word "stream," we sense an underlying discomfort for James with his own terms of choice—perhaps because he protests so systematically to every word or pair of words that he considers. He protests too much; that is, he pursues the question relentlessly, approaching term after term, discarding each one until he reaches a resting place. Only here, as we have seen, he chooses to rest within a transition; he rests "in between," in the fluctuating waters of a vagrant stream.[16]

A series of particularly acute images for consciousness occurs as James explains the rate of change of the subjective states of our mental content, the "successive psychoses which shade gradually into each other" *(PP,* 1.236). James's language mirrors the image of consciousness he creates: like the bird flying, it is always getting away from us; yet perched and static, it gives us the illusion that we can examine it. In the same fashion, James shows that words slip and flutter, but they also provide arresting imagery.

> As we take, in fact, a general view of the wonderful stream of our consciousness, what strikes us first is this different pace of its parts. Like a bird's life, it seems to be made of an alternation of flights and perchings. The rhythm of language expresses this, where every thought is expressed in a sentence closed by a period. The resting-places are usually occupied by sensorial imaginations of some sort . . . the places of flight are filled with thoughts of relations, static or dynamic. . . . *Let us call the resting-places the 'substantive parts,' and the places of flight the 'transitive parts,' of the stream of thought.* (PP, 1.236)

The gesture toward naming ("let us call") at the end of this passage is significant; James attempts to fix a definition by creating an image that is utterly unfixable—the bird's "flights and perchings." We are reminded again of James's focus on natural imagery to describe consciousness: the metaphors of water and birds occupy the landscape for consciousness. Indeed, James states that we have a privileged "view," a panoramic scope for consciousness that shows us the stream and the flying bird as well as the bird at rest. James becomes a landscape artist, "painting" a scene out of nature; he explicitly avoids mind-as-machine language or any systematic, mechanical language. Acutely aware that his image must remain true to the flow of what he calls here, the "wonderful *stream* of our consciousness," James uses words like "passage," "transition," "rhythm," and "pace" to ensure that the stream is still progressing. In this sense, the scene is like a moving picture. Though James speaks of "parts," thus indicating a division of the stream, his metaphors and analogies serve to compose a dynamic consciousness, not to pick it apart. James examines by constructing and comparing. If we can imagine the soaring and the suspenseful stillness of a bird's life, if we feel the rhythm of a sentence as we read— as it commences, then closes with a period—we have some sense of the pulse of consciousness.

James uses a new metaphor in order to explain how different parts of the stream of consciousness have differing paces, like a bird both flying and perching. This new metaphorical construction is yet another visual invention, possibly distracting the reader from the sense that analyzing consciousness could amount to division. Nevertheless, James maintains that the illusion of "parts" or "sections" in what he defends as a steady stream, is the psychologist's error; and yet it proves to be a necessity for his study of the phenomenon. James rebukes the "traditional psychology" that

> talks like one who should say a river consists of nothing but pailsful, spoonsful, quartsful, barrelsful, and other moulded forms of water. Even were the pails and the pots all actually standing in the stream, still between them the free water would continue to flow. It is just this free water of consciousness that psychologists resolutely overlook. (*PP*, 1.246)

Despite James's superior awareness of the water that flows in addition to the "moulded forms" of water, he too must fill the pails, spoons, quarts, and barrels in order to inspect the "free water of consciousness." The metaphor here is easier to understand because it is in keeping with the "stream" of consciousness; and though James does not mistake the spoonful for the whole river, he does examine its contents. Thus he figuratively "contains" consciousness even while he insists on its steady rush.

The Jamesian stream metaphor is a practical method for the conceptualization of the mind thinking. We may trace the metaphorical resonance of the mind's "stream" in the arrangement of a sentence and the cadence of spoken language. James refers to the "rhythm of language" in a sentence *(PP,* 1.236) to express something like the passage of consciousness. More specifically, James locates consciousness in what he calls the "shading" of relations between words and thoughts:

> There is not a conjunction or a preposition, and hardly an adverbial phrase, syntactic form, or inflection of voice in human speech, that does not express some shading or other of relation which we at some moment actually feel to exist between the larger objects of our thought . . . it is the stream of consciousness that matches each of them by an inward coloring of its own. In either case the relations are numberless, and no existing

> language is capable of doing justice to all their shades.
> We ought to say a feeling of *and*, a feeling of *if*, a feel-
> ing of *but*, and a feeling of *by*, quite as readily as we say
> a feeling of *blue* or a feeling of *cold*. Yet we do not. . . .
> (PP, 1.238)

We use certain words metaphorically when we describe thoughts or
feelings, such as feeling blue; other words have some basis in the
physical world like a feeling of cold. Somehow the "inward coloring" of our consciousness also finds a "match" for the feeling of
*and, it, but, by*, which do not reveal their metaphorical "shades"
so clearly. We are reminded here of James's sense that consciousness "steeps and dyes" (PP, 1.246) the images it washes over; that
no words are exempt from the stream, even words we would not
consider necessarily "descriptive," further emphasizes James's
notion that his stream is ubiquitous. Though language cannot
always do justice to these words and their figurative colors, James
asserts that we "feel" this relation to exist nonetheless. If James is
to study the minute particulars of consciousness, he must also
study the minute particulars of the words he uses to construct consciousness—most explicitly, the "feelings" attached to them. Here,
James wants to see beyond language, to expand the possibilities of
words and to imagine what they "ought to say" when we use them.
Even to imagine the "inward coloring" they might assume for our
individual consciousnesses. The meaning of words might be easily
lost in what James later calls this "mob of abstract entities, principles, and forces" (PP, 1.238); but the stream of consciousness
keeps thought and word coherent.
     Examining consciousness is, at once, imagining and inspecting.
If the object of James's psychology is a product of his imagination,
he can maintain the illusion that he has control over what he will
subject to scientific scrutiny. For James, then, inspecting is intro-
specting. James seems loath to define introspection; his impatience
in explaining its meaning implies that a definition is unnecessary:
"The word introspection need hardly be defined—it means, of
course, the looking into our own minds and reporting what we
there discover" (PP, 1.185). Such "discoveries" are certainly no
matter of course, however. While James's mind might produce picturesque accounts of thought and its movement, it is hardly a given
that others have the ability, not to mention the imaginative vocabulary, to realize what James "reports," when looking into his own
mind. Despite a confident definition of the process, James does
readily admit that the introspective method is fallible and diffi-

cult.[17] Though its definition may be obvious, its results are not. In continuing his discussion of the transience of thought within each personal consciousness, James concedes:

> Now it is very difficult, introspectively, to see the transitive parts for what they really are . . . stopping them . . . is really annihilating them. . . . Let anyone try to cut a thought across in the middle and get a look at its section, and he will see how difficult the introspective observation of the transitive tracts is. The rush of the thought is so headlong that it almost always brings us up at the conclusion before we can arrest it. Or if our purpose is nimble enough and we do arrest it, it ceases forthwith to be itself. As a snowflake caught in the warm hand is no longer a flake but a drop, so, instead of catching the feeling of relation moving to its term, we find that we have caught some substantive thing with . . . its function, tendency and particular meaning in the sentence quite evaporated. (*PP*, 1.236–7)

James uses different angles to "get a look at" this thought; he imagines cutting the thought across the middle to consider a cross-section, but the "rush of the thought" is so fast that we reach the conclusion before we can investigate it in process. Speed is important, but ultimately irrelevant because "stopping" the thought is equivalent to "annihilating" it. James's language occasions his conviction that he cannot capture "relation moving"; what he catches is "some substantive thing," while the rush or "tendency" of the thought suffers the same fate as the snowflake—it "evaporates." James creates images that express the impossibility of "catching the feeling of relation" without altering it: "The attempt at introspective analysis in these cases is in fact like seizing a spinning top to catch its motion, or trying to turn up the gas quickly enough to see how the darkness looks" (*PP*, 1.237). The spinning top, like the snowflake, "ceases" to be itself once it is caught. The notion that one might be able to "see how the darkness looks" by turning up the gas is as ridiculous as it is compelling. With intricate analogies such as these, James makes consciousness appear to be an elusive entity—an entity that only *his* configurations can tease out.

The tip-of-your-fingers feeling that consciousness sometimes acquires in the Jamesian narrative proves particularly haunting when James discusses memory and namelessness.

Suppose we try to recall a forgotten name. The state of
our consciousness is peculiar. There is a gap therein; but
no mere gap. It is a gap that is intensely active. A sort of
wraith of the name is in it, beckoning us in a given direction, making us at moments tingle with the sense of our
closeness, and then letting us sink back without the
longed-for term. If wrong names are proposed to us this
singularly definite gap acts immediately so as to negate
them. They do not fit into its mould. And the gap of one
word does not feel like the gap of another, all empty of
content as both might seem necessarily to be when
described as gaps. (*PP*, 1.243)

A name is more than just a lexical tag; it is a description that brings
to bear an experience—makes it available to thought, available as
an object of thought, and therefore, an object of experiment under
the Jamesian introspective system. We feel, at once, the "gap" that
awaits the proper label, but also the "wraith" of the name, like an
alluring apparition. That name, so close it makes us "tingle," calls
to us to find it. We have a consciousness of emptiness that is
intensely active, "beckoning us in a given direction." It is evident
from this passage that while words engender Jamesian consciousness, they must also fit into a distinct "mould." However, words
or, specifically, names are sometimes ghostlike; they summon us
and tease us with their illusory power. If, as James insists, namelessness is compatible with existence, then:

The rhythm of a lost word may be there without a sound
to clothe it; or the evanescent sense of something which
is the initial vowel or consonant may mock us fitfully,
without growing more distinct. Everyone must know the
tantalizing effect of the blank rhythm of some forgotten
verse, restlessly dancing in one's mind, striving to be
filled out with words. (*PP*, 1.243–4)

Words have what we might call a mental residue. Their vanishing
pattern lingers and "mocks" us without sound. Here, the words do
more than tease; they defy the mind to capture them. James's image
of the "forgotten verse, restlessly dancing in one's mind, striving to
be filled out with words" is an appropriate analogue for consciousness. James's repeated metaphors, his sumptuous prose, are
an attempt to "fill out" consciousness with words, to locate it, to

"clothe" it, as it dances its tantalizing dance in the mind. Giving attention to the "evanescent," James attributes rhythm, color, and even flavor to this "sense of something," waiting to be captured.

The further we follow the stream in James's classic chapter on consciousness, the more we realize it is suffused with experiences of all of the senses: "A tune, an odor, a flavor sometimes carry this inarticulate feeling of their familiarity so deep into our consciousness that we are fairly shaken by its mysterious emotional power" *(PP,* 1.244). This Proustian impression on our consciousness, of tune, odor and flavor, reaches deep. Significant for our understanding of this passage is the connection between emotion and consciousness for James; emotions are not ghostly or bodiless like the words that we might search for to describe them. A feeling or a sensation enters so deeply into our consciousness that we are "shaken"; the emotion may be elicited without words and the familiarity felt without clear articulation.

James describes ambiguity with exquisite precision; and rather than obscuring his thoughts, these gestures toward the ambiguous lend themselves to beautiful, vivid imagery. Claiming that the "definite images" of psychology form only the smallest part of our actual minds, James strives to account for the tenuous, streaming remainder:

> Every definite image in the mind is steeped and dyed in the free water that flows round it. With it goes the sense of its relations, near and remote, the dying echo of whence it came to us, the dawning sense of whither it is to lead. The significance, the value of the image is all in this halo or penumbra that surrounds and escorts it,— or rather that is fused into one with it and has become bone of its bone and flesh of its flesh; leaving it, it is true, an image of the same thing it was before, but making it an image of that thing newly taken and freshly understood. *(PP,* 1.246)

"Definite" images are not set apart from their surrounding atmosphere; that is, the images James develops are "steeped in," and imbued with, the touch of the water flowing around them, the sound of the echo trailing after them, the sight of the halo accompanying them. By formulating consciousness as water, James suggests that as each image is immersed in this "free water," it is also somehow changed by it. The Jamesian stream contains no ordinary water—saturation and some sort of tainting are the effects of a dip in its currents. Consciousness possesses transforming power as it "dyes" those images that it encounters. A potent, all-pervasive force, Jamesian consciousness flows "round" each image in the mind so that it seems we are meant to notice the water perhaps more than the definitive "image." James speaks of a fusion between the "relations" round this image—the "dying echo" of its imagined origin, the "dawning sense" of its direction—and the image itself. The "value" of the image exists in its seemingly untraceable relations, and yet, that which "escorts" the image becomes one with the image. For James, it is impossible to ignore the "free water" of consciousness that flows round the containers—the "definite images" and "moulded forms of water"—that hold the details of our conscious life.[18] Moreover, in this "bone of its bone and flesh of its flesh" marriage of image and shadow, fusion amounts to re-creation.

At one point in the *Principles*, James tells a story about four men taking a trip to Europe. He depicts their different ways of seeing in order to show how the mind "chooses to suit itself, and decides what particular sensation shall be held more real and valid than all the rest" *(PP,* 1.275). Empirical thought, James tells us, depends upon experience while perception is an "exquisite example" of selective industry. Much of what we see and experience depends upon our habits of attention. Something may be present to us countless times and we will fail to notice, or a thing met only once in a lifetime may leave an impression which makes it an "indelible experience."

> Let four men make a tour in Europe. One will bring home only picturesque impressions—costumes and colors, parks and views and works of architecture, pictures and statues. To another all this will be non-existent; and distances and prices, populations and drainage-arrangements, door- and window-fastenings, and other useful statistics will take their place. A third will give a rich account of the theatres, restaurants, and public balls, and naught beside; whilst the fourth will perhaps have been so wrapped in his own subjective broodings as to tell little more than a few names of places through which he passed. Each has selected, out of the same mass of presented objects, those which suited his private interest and has made his experience thereby. *(PP,* 1.275-6)[19]

Each man in this hypothetical account of the trip to Europe has "selected" what "suits" him and has thereby "*made* his experience." These words seem especially significant both because James's own attention to consciousness allows him, in a sense, to "make" it and also because consciousness itself is a "selective" agent. Moreover, this notion of "experience–made" indicates that the episode is frozen, not fluid; it becomes an image (or a series of images, afforded to different sensibilities) whose pieces can be examined, whose individual strands can, in some sense, be taken apart. The account of consciousness James thus gives is layered with meaning; he tells the story of four men who tell a story of their consciousnesses, their perception of the visual, their subjective modes of experience. One man seems almost purely aesthetic, bringing home the "picturesque" that exists as much in his mind as in the "colors," "costumes" and "statues" he physically sees; another man finds only the abstract world of "prices" and "populations"; still another provides a voluptuous account of a more active experience—the world of "theatres, restaurants and public balls." For the fourth man, "Europe," per se, seems to be non-existent. What he "sees" and perceives is only the world in his mind. He is "wrapped" in his "subjective broodings" and merely "passes" through, contained in this cocoon of his thoughts with only a bare memory of names and places.

That consciousness is imagined to contain all of these portraits—from the aesthetic to the abstract, from the public to the intensely private—allows for a fuller examination of the stream of human thought. Consciousness not only brings together different languages, but it also operates as a threshold for differing modes of thinking, studying, imagining, dreaming, perceiving, experiencing. As James states, "we see that the mind is at every stage a theatre of simultaneous possibilities. Consciousness consists in the comparison of these with each other, the selection of some, and the suppression of the rest by the reinforcing and inhibiting agency of attention" *(PP,* 1.277). The mind as a "theatre of possibilities" becomes a wonderful model for Jamesian consciousness. James states explicitly that consciousness "consists in the comparison of these [possibilities] with each other"; consciousness that is full and multifaceted, yet also selective. James must, in some sense, draw a circle around the "simultaneous possibilities" that consciousness offers in order to provide his sketch; interestingly, he suggests that it is one of the properties of consciousness to do just that.

Consciousness creates its own world through this gesture of selection; without it, James suggests, we would be lost in the "chaos of sensation":

The mind, in short, works on the data it receives very much as a sculptor works on his block of stone. In a sense the statue stood there from eternity. But there were a thousand different ones beside it, and the sculptor alone is to thank for having extricated this one from the rest. Just so the world of each of us, howsoever our several views of it may be, all lay embedded in the primordial chaos of sensation, which gave the mere matter to the thought of all of us indifferently. We may, if we like, by our reasonings unwind things back to that black and jointless continuity of space and moving clouds of swarming atoms which science calls the only real world. But all the while the world we feel and live in will be that which our ancestors and we, by slowly cumulative strokes of choice, have extricated out of this, like sculptors, by simply rejecting certain portions of the given stuff. (*PP*, 1.277)

Reminiscent of Emerson's call— "build, therefore, your own world"[20]—James's words depict the mind as creator, sculpting a world from the "primordial chaos" of what science calls "real." James implicitly states that science is wrong in claiming that the "black and jointless continuity of space and moving clouds of swarming atoms" is "the *only* real world." Moreover, his description of the world suddenly resembles terms he used for consciousness— "swarming," "moving," and "jointless"—while consciousness itself solidifies into stone. Figuring the creator as an artist, a "sculptor" who "extricates" out of this the world we *feel*, not simply the world we study, James redefines the "real" by locating it in experience. Just as his example with the four men in Europe illustrates, we *choose* what is "more real and valid" (*PP*, 1.275) because we consciously experience it as such. Not scientists alone, but also "each of us" with our several views have access to the "world-stuff" (*PP*, 1.277) and possess the ability to create and recreate it. We join our ancestors in constructing this world, by the "slow cumulative strokes of choice." The worlds of our consciousnesses, therefore, are of our own making. What's more, we know they exist because we "feel" that they exist; we live and experience their reality.

One consequence of the mind's ability to fashion its own world is that consciousness acquires a sacred status. The stream as a whole is associated with the self, yet there is something more, an inner core or what James will call "a self of selves." James submits that "If the stream as a whole is identified with the Self far more than any outward thing, a *certain portion of the stream abstracted from the rest* is so identified in an altogether peculiar degree, and is felt by all men as a sort of innermost centre within the circle, of sanctuary within the citadel, constituted by the subjective life as a whole" *(PP,* 1.284–5). James begins with the image of his stream, yet here this stream seems to have a vortex, drawing its waters about a center. As such, a certain "portion" of the water is "abstracted from the rest." The abrupt shift in figures apprises us of James's problem: in trying to account for this specialized "portion" of consciousness, he has broken his fluid stream. When looking at the stream of consciousness, we are suddenly asked to recognize that certain "portions" run deeper or run into what James imagines as a "centre" within the "circle."[21] James places metaphor upon metaphor such that we lose the sense of how the stream and the circle fit together into one image. The figures of the "innermost centre" of the circle and the "sanctuary within the citadel" all imply a place set apart, an interior space, a stronghold—contained, holy, and separate. However, as we have seen, the stream also appears more random, exploring, even vagrant. This tension in the account of Jamesian consciousness, between consciousness as nucleus and consciousness as outpouring stream, occurs repeatedly in *Principles.* In setting apart this holy of holies for the self, James impresses a spiritual essence onto his notion of consciousness. Attention to that which is "within" emphasizes the peculiar uniqueness of each individual consciousness as opposed to the permeating quality James often attributes to it. Here, he seems to argue for something deep within the subjective self that constitutes consciousness. He asks: *"what is this self of all other selves?"* and answers:

> Probably all men would describe it in much the same way up to a certain point. They would call it the active element in all consciousness; saying that whatever qualities a man's feelings may possess, or whatever content his thought may include, there is a spiritual something in him which seems to go out to meet these qualities and contents, whilst they seem to come in to be received by it. It is what welcomes and rejects. It presides over the perception of sensations . . . it is the home of interest,— not the pleasant or the painful, not even pleasure or pain, as such, but that within us to which pleasure and pain, the pleasant and the painful speak. . . . Being more incessantly there than any other single element of the

mental life, the other elements end by seeming to accrete
round it and to belong to it. (*PP*, 1.285)

The center of consciousness is vividly portrayed as James describes
the "spiritual something" in us around which all other things
"accrete" and "belong." All other elements seem to move toward
it, as if this "active element" possessed some centrifugal force. And
yet it also acts as a forceful presence, it "goes out" and "presides"
over our perceptions as both judge and host, welcoming and rejecting, meeting and receiving. James conceives of it as if it were
explicitly locatable; it is where we find the spiritual, it is a "home,"
it is more incessantly "there" than any other single element of mental life.

At this point in *Principles*, James has just begun his chapter on
"The Consciousness of Self"; he moves from his "general sketch"
to "finer work"; where he will "trace the psychology of this fact of
self-consciousness" *(PP*, 1.278). "Tracing" this "finer work"
appears to involve minute analysis, a more delicate, intricate
"sketch" that leads James to what he calls the "central nucleus of
the Self." But once James gets there, his language remains elusive,
even baffling. Because he strings his referents along, continuing to
refer to "it" instead of naming his object of study, his language
begins to undermine itself. He states: "One may, I think . . . believe
that all men must single out from the rest of what they call themselves some central principle of which each would recognize the
foregoing to be a fair general description,—accurate enough, at
any rate, to denote what is meant, and keep it unconfused with
other things" *(PP*, 1.285). Getting beyond the confusion of this
statement is difficult; even given the context it is hard to trace
James's figure here. James's use of the conditional tense ("would
recognize"), his "at any rate," the "general description" leave us in
a vague tangle of qualifiers. Immediately following the assessment
of how "all men" would "probably describe" what he deems the
"self of selves," this quintessentially vague statement becomes
couched in the "specifics" of James's list. Presenting an inventory
of qualities to describe this peculiar component of consciousness,
James tells us: "*it* presides"; "*it* is what welcomes or rejects"; "*it* is
the home of interest"; "*it* is the source of effort"; "*it* connects with
how ideas are reflected"; "*it* plays a part analogous to the psychic
life." And yet James also expresses that we can find this "central
principle," that we "*must* single [*it*] out." But we want to ask, after
reading his list: what exactly is *it*? Consciousness, the stream, the
Self, the language to describe these things, something beyond or
underneath consciousness that he has yet to imagine?

In fact, James partly addresses these questions even as he attempts further analysis of his version of the Self:

> Some would say that it is a simple active substance, the soul, of which they are conscious; others, that it is nothing but a fiction, the imaginary being denoted by the pronoun I. . . . *Now*, let us try to settle for ourselves as definitely as we can, just how this central nucleus of the self may *feel*, no matter whether it be a spiritual substance or only a delusive word. (*PP*, 1.286)

James imagines this "it," this incontrovertible part of ourselves of which we are conscious, as either the soul or an imaginary being called "I," a "spiritual substance" or "only a delusive word." The split between substance and word, where substance is "active" and word is "imaginary" and "delusive," hinges, finally, on a feeling. For James, it does not matter whether this part of the self is "spiritual substance" (a description which is itself paradoxical) or only a word—fictional, delusive, imaginary. What matters is that we "feel" this central nucleus of the self; and it is with the confidence of that feeling which James proceeds. This passage helps to illustrate the shift from a presumably objective to a consciously subjective mode of scientific observation that scholars of this period articulate as *the* major change in theories of knowledge. In *Consciousness and Society*, Stuart Hughes identifies this shift as the central concern for writers of philosophy, sociology, psychology, and literature during the period between 1890–1930.[22] Hughes reminds us that scientists were beginning to recognize the disparity between an external reality and their own inner appreciation of that reality. With this change in perception comes a change in scientific analysis.

Immediately before one of the salient moments in James's *Principles*—where he introduces the metaphor of the stream—James speaks of consciousness as "sensibly continuous." James makes clear that his discovery of this characteristic is the result of a feeling: "Such consciousness as this, whatever it be for the onlooking psychologist, is for itself unbroken." And how does he know this? Because, as James continues: "It *feels* unbroken. . . ." *(PP*, 1.231). James rests a great deal of his theory of consciousness and his development of the notion of Self on "feeling" and on introspection, and yet his findings, for the most part, were considered legitimate, scientific study resulting in professional recognition. During James's time, psychology was still a branch of philosophy and James's fluid movements between these two disciplines—manifested in his academic career and within the body of his writings—reflect psychology's concern with central philosophical problems such as the mind-body relation, and origins of knowledge.[23] Though we can see retrospectively the overriding influence of experience as a "touchstone" for knowledge,[24] at the time these writers were producing their accounts of consciousness, there was skepticism about labeling such conjectures "science." Studies that appealed to experience and did not purport to be objective could potentially make philosophy and psychology seem no different from imaginative literature.

The narrative of consciousness makes its historical mark because James "produces" consciousness in an institutional context. Nevertheless, the language that gives rise to consciousness—the metaphors, analogies, and figures that form its narrative—often suggests that consciousness is an all-pervading, universal, but still evasive entity that writers across centuries have spent pages of prose trying to capture. This juncture between the historical position of consciousness and its presumable powers of transcendence makes the linguistic aspect of consciousness especially important to an analysis of the culture of the mind in modern American literature. In *Principles*, James's metaphorical language allows him to design the object he purports to be discovering; his later work radically challenges the existence of consciousness while still doing the linguistic work to produce it. The figural language remains a part of his analysis, though James vacillates between the notion of consciousness as a wandering stream and consciousness as the ultimate center or core of our being. At moments in *Principles*, the concept of consciousness seems to contain everything; in James's *Essays in Radical Empiricism*, he will reduce it to almost nothing.

In his 1904 essay, "Does 'Consciousness' Exist?", James appears to reverse his findings in *Principles*, arguing for the "non-existence" of consciousness. James speaks as if he could strip away all metaphors and point beyond the text, beyond words, toward another reality: "For twenty years past I have mistrusted 'consciousness' as an entity; for seven or eight years past I have suggested its non-existence to my students, and tried to give them its pragmatic equivalent in realities of experience. It seems to me that the hour is ripe for it to be openly and universally discarded."[25] The irony of James's bold statements in this piece, however, exists in his simultaneous insistence on the non-existence of consciousness along with his still frequent use of metaphors to draw out this "non-entity." Stressing the "cognitive *function*" of consciousness rather than any particular label, James seems happy to do away with the name because it has become an obstacle. Yet James's obsession with naming continues in this later essay, and gives us some insight into the linguistic aspect of his overall project:

> 'Thoughts' and 'things' are names for two sorts of objects, which common sense will always find contrast- ed and will always practically oppose to each other. Philosophy, reflecting on the contrast, has varied in the past in her explanations of it, and may be expected to vary in the future. At first, 'spirit and matter,' 'soul and body,' stood for a pair of equipollent substances quite on par in weight and interest. But one day Kant under- mined the soul and brought in the transcendental ego, and ever since then the bipolar relation has been very much off its balance. The transcendental ego seems nowadays in rationalist quarters to stand for everything, in empiricist quarters for almost nothing. (*ERE*, 1)

James uses names to make a "common sense" distinction: "thoughts" and "things" are separate entities, differing "sorts of objects" because they have different names. The disquieting motion comes, however, when this fine contrast is set "off bal- ance." Kant is the culprit here and James sets up the shift in our understanding of the "bipolar relation" between such concepts as "spirit and matter," "body and soul," as if he were telling a story.[26] Once the world of terms was equally balanced, all was well; then "one day," Kant came in and set the philosophical world off balance. And now we cannot tell whether this term ("transcendental ego") means "everything" or "nothing." We are plunged into uncertainty—meaning is arbitrary or vanishing—as this formerly balanced world begins to tip. Having given "Philosophy" a chance to explain herself, James continues his essay by offering his own "explanation" of consciousness and naming:

> I believe that 'consciousness,' when once it has evapo- rated to this estate of pure diaphaneity, is on the point of disappearing all together. It is the name of a nonenti- ty, and has no right to a place among first principles. Those who still cling to it are clinging to a mere echo, the faint rumor left behind by the disappearing 'soul' upon the air of philosophy. (*ERE*, 2)

Placing "consciousness" in quotation marks (in his title as well as throughout the essay) is the first indication that James has become suspicious of it; more significant, however, is what happens to the figure of consciousness that only fourteen years before, was James's illustrious stream. The once freely flowing water is "on the point of disappearing all together"; once deep enough to "steep" the images it encountered, the water has now "evaporated."

James will maintain in this later collection of essays that there is no "stuff" of consciousness, though he seems to produce relentless puns on his own language from *The Principles of Psychology*, a text that essentially created the stuff of consciousness. Readers familiar with the earlier James will undoubtedly recognize the reappearance of the metaphor of water; but James also brings back the figure of the echo. Though James originally encouraged his readers to attend to this "echo"—a vestige of what he called the "definite images" of the mind *(PP,* 1.246)—he now chides those who persist in chasing it. Consciousness transforms into "the faint rumor," left behind "upon the air of philosophy." Brought to the status of a "rumor," consciousness becomes mere idle talk, something waiting to be confirmed, tentative and unreliable hearsay. Immediately before this passage, James states that "the spiritual principle," which is often associated with consciousness, "attenuates itself to a thoroughly ghostly condition." Consciousness, in fact, gets so thin that it is "pure diaphaneity," or transparency. James's boldest assertion also contains one of the subtler ironies of this passage; he states that once consciousness becomes vaporized, something we can see through, or something that we secretly whisper to the winds, it has "no right to a place among first principles." James seems to be playing with the title of his first book which coined the famous metaphor for consciousness—a metaphor that, in turn, became a theory of consciousness. If consciousness no longer has a place among "first principles," James may in fact be trying to deny or to rewrite its place in *Principles.*

In his initial formulation, James would emphasize the spiritual or ethereal quality of consciousness with words like "echo," "halo" and descriptors that call it "wraith-like," "evanescent," and "fused." What was once a fascination with and even an anxiety about naming becomes a dismissal of names and of existence. In *The Principles of Psychology*, James searched for words that would convey the slippery edges of the pool of consciousness. He seemed, in fact, to revel in words that played with the paradoxes of a substance that was also spirit—a tenuous thread that was vanishing even as we placed it. Fourteen years later, under the influence of his radical empiricism, his language appears to vaporize that pool, pushing consciousness to the point where he questions, does it exist? But as my own language in this paragraph illustrates (along with the language of practically every study of William James), it is impossible to speak of consciousness without metaphors. James invites us to indulge in such figures even as he criticizes them; he makes it difficult not to notice his language though he simultaneously persists in negating its significance:

> To deny plumbly that 'consciousness' exists seems so absurd on the face of it —for undeniably 'thoughts' do exist—that I fear some readers will follow me no farther. Let me then immediately explain that I mean only to deny that the word stands for an entity, but to insist most emphatically that it does stand for a function. . . . 'Consciousness' is supposed necessary to explain the fact that things not only are, but get reported, are known. Whoever blots out the notion of consciousness from his list of first principles must still provide in some way for that function's being carried on. (*ERE*, 4)

Calling our attention to "the word" consciousness, by repeatedly placing quotation marks around it, James purposely subverts the status of consciousness as "entity." The literalness of the word is clear— "writing" consciousness is equated to creating it, just as "blotting it out" can effectively eliminate it. James seems somewhat haphazard in aligning consciousness with "thoughts" and "knowing"—as if he had forgotten his own elaborate ponderings in *Principles* for appropriate words for these very concepts. James bows to his readers when he says that denying consciousness would be "absurd" for undeniably "thoughts" do exist and the function they perform is "knowing." However, his tone here seems dismissive; he sounds as if he has lost patience with words and instead, wishes to give a bare-bones account of this portion of experience.

But if James intends to "blot out" the notion of consciousness, he must also "provide in some way" (provide an account, a narrative, a new figure?) for the task of reporting that consciousness performs. Revising and rewriting his theories becomes a tricky business for James at this point; for the question of existence is intimately tied to questions of consciousness—being, and making note of that being; tracing the origins of the self, of knowledge, of thought; not just feeling and thinking, but being *aware* that we are feeling and thinking. Questions about such processes involve a radical readjustment of our notions of the way the mind works. James's empiricism is "radical" in the same way because it goes back to the root, in an attempt to locate the origin of these concepts of experience, consciousness, knowing. James states that those who abandon the notion of consciousness and substitute "absolute experience" for it are "not quite radical enough"—that is, they do not go far enough. But James will take us to the extreme. The uncanny twist in the narrative of consciousness, however, comes when James gets to that extreme; indeed, he finds that the tools with which he created his "citadel" are also necessary to disarm it.

James spends much of the essay stating what consciousness is *not,* before he determines what it is, whether it exists, and what we find its existence to be. He dismisses those psychologists and philosophers who continue to read consciousness (and thereby experience) as something that can stand out, like "a kind of impalpable inner flowing," *(ERE,* 6) or be "brought out by analysis" as if it were "one element, moment, factor . . . of an experience of essentially dualistic inner constitution from which, if you abstract the content, the consciousness will remain revealed to its own eye" *(ERE,* 8). James explicitly objects to this model:

> *Experience, I believe, has no such inner duplicity; and the separation of it into consciousness and content comes, not by way of subtraction, but by way of addition . . .* paint will also serve here as an illustration. In a pot in a paint-shop, along with other paints, it serves in its entirety as so much saleable matter. Spread it on a canvas, with other paints around it, it represents, on the contrary, a feature in a picture and performs a spiritual function. (*ERE,* 9)

As we found in *Principles,* consciousness has a transforming power—like the waters that "dye" those images that enter the stream—here it is explicitly linked with the spiritual that, for James, summons the world of art. He begins with the figure of paint in a pot in a paint-shop. There is nothing particularly significant about this paint, indeed, it seems to have commercial value only—it is "saleable matter." When this paint is "spread on a canvas," however, it begins to "represent" something more; or is it merely something different? It is difficult to tell whether James attaches more "value" to the "spiritual function" than any other;

though when this paint becomes a "picture," it certainly becomes something other than the liquid color with which we started. It acquires a different value not only as it touches the canvas, but also, arguably, as it is "touched" (perhaps even "tainted"?) by the consciousness of both artist *and* observer. James glosses his own analogy by stating that the issue is one of context: "a given undivided portion of experience, taken in one context of associates, play[s] the part of a knower, of a state of mind, of 'consciousness'; while in a different context the same undivided bit of experience plays the part of the thing known, of an objective 'content'*(ERE,* 9–10). James does not want to divide these "parts" or to separate the paint into menstruum (oil) and pigment *(ERE,* 8), rather, he imagines the paint simply "playing a part" or "performing" different functions. And the part that it plays (either knower/state of mind/consciousness *or* "the thing known") determines the resulting product—merchandise or art, "saleable matter" or "spiritual function."

Consciousness or content, subjective or objective, "thought" or "thing"—these are all terms that James contrasts throughout this essay. He offers a reading of them, within the context of philosophy, reminding us that the affair of consciousness is always an "affair of relations":

> The dualism connoted by such double-barrelled terms as 'experience,' 'phenomenon,' 'datum,' 'Vorfindung'— terms which in philosophy at any rate, tend more and more to replace the single-barrelled terms of 'thought' and 'thing'—that dualism, I say, is still preserved in this account, but reinterpreted, so that, instead of being mysterious and elusive, it becomes verifiable and concrete. It is an affair of relations, it falls outside, not inside, the single experience considered, and can always be particularized and defined. (*ERE,* 10)

Unwilling to separate experience into "consciousness and content," James is nevertheless comfortable with "preserving" the dualism of those "double-barrelled" words such as "experience" and "phenomenon." As long as it is one word, serving a double purpose, "dualism" is appropriate. Yet we cannot ignore the connotations of the word in the discipline of philosophy, for dualism implies that there are two basic, irreducible principles—mind and body. Consequently, James's double-barrelled word is doubly loaded. It is precisely this mind-body split that he wants to avoid.

"Reinterpreting" dualism allows James to make "verifiable and concrete" what could instead be "mysterious and elusive." No longer cultivating the mystery and elusiveness of consciousness, James seems, in fact, to "reinterpret" his own figures, erasing what once seemed hopelessly evasive—translating mystery into matter. The ever-elusive "consciousness" needs to be deleted. And yet challenging consciousness necessitates reiteration. Quotation marks are one way to disable the word; reinterpretation is another.

In some sense, consciousness is reinterpreted or we might even say re*named* as "experience." James explains that the separation of experience into two parts comes about because we confuse "other sets of experiences" with the experience at hand—we add something "other" to the "given concrete piece of it" *(ERE,* 9). But experience is not split; the illusion that it comes in two parts, therefore, must be the "other" of experience that "falls outside" and that James confidently states, "can always be particularized and defined." The certainty of definition is made emphatic by James's separation of what falls "outside" and what remains "inside" the *single* experience considered. We read "defining" as the attempt to trace a line around the experience and set its boundaries. Yet metaphors do not obey boundaries, they are extravagant figures that wander out of bounds.[27]

"Pure experience" remains a "numerically single thing," though James admits that "experience is a member of diverse processes that can be followed away from it along entirely different lines" *(ERE,* 12). "Following" these "different lines" is tantamount to a certain kind of vagrancy.[28] James wanders through these experiences, which he imagines as "rooms"—the room in which his reader "really" sits and the room in/of the mind:

> If the reader will take his own experiences, he will see what I mean. Let him begin with a perceptual experience, the 'presentation,' so called, of a physical object, his actual field of vision, the room he sits in, with the book he is reading at its centre. . . . The physical and the mental operations form curiously incompatible groups. As a room, the experience has occupied that spot and had that environment for thirty years. As your field of consciousness it may never have existed until now. . . . As a room, it will take an earthquake, or a gang of men, and in any case a certain amount of time, to destroy it. As your subjective state, the closing of your eyes, or any instantaneous play of your fancy will suffice. In the real world, fire will consume it. In your mind, you can let

> fire play over it without effect. As an outer object, you
> must pay so much a month to inhabit it. As an inner
> content, you may occupy it for any length of time rent-
> free. (*ERE*, 11;14).

Ironically, James constructs a metaphor that enhances our sense
that consciousness is "inner," "subjective," closed off from the rest
of the world—the mind with a house inside. The "room" as "inner
content" becomes our field of consciousness, thus its existence
depends upon things like "the closing of our eyes." In the "real
world" this room takes up time and space; it can be destroyed by
earthquake, fire, or a gang of men. James must build these rooms
in order to use them for his illustration of experience; so in effect,
both of these "rooms" are figurative. And yet one is figured as
physical and one mental; one is "in the real world" and the other
is "subjective," "inner content" that can disappear "instanta-
neously," according to the whims of our mind.

James's "last word" in this essay on radical empiricism constitutes a final attempt to rein in his metaphors and, once and for all,
to redefine "consciousness." Metaphors continually test and
redraw the boundaries, offering new and improved versions of
consciousness. However, each metaphorical construction remakes
consciousness until James's epistemology gets entangled in the
elaborate language he uses to articulate it. It is not clear, finally,
where we end up in this essay. James will argue for his own "intuition" against what he assumes is his readers'. James began, "Does
'Consciousness' Exist?" with a nod to the "principles" of his "larger Psychology"; he will end with another such motion. To answer,
in part, the thought/thing dichotomy, James addresses the dilemma
of dualism straight on; for the difference between thought and
thing, if there be any, is reminiscent of the mind/body split. James
imagines his audience repeatedly objecting to his claims:

> 'All very pretty as a piece of ingenuity,' they will say,
> 'but our consciousness itself intuitively contradicts you.
> We, for our part, *know* that we are conscious. We *feel*
> our thought, flowing as a life within us, in absolute con-
> trast with the objects which it so unremittingly escorts.
> We can not be faithless to this immediate intuition. The
> dualism is a fundamental *datum*: Let no man join what
> God has put asunder.' (*ERE*, 36)

James pokes fun at his audience as he gives voice to their objections. The audience who says we *know*, we *feel* our thoughts, relies upon "intuition"; they could also rely upon the pronouncements of an earlier Jamesian text. James hears the remonstrances to his argument in exactly the same language that he first used to render consciousness in *Principles*. For if James's readers speak of "thought, flowing as a life within us," it is because he himself coined those terms as a way to imagine consciousness. The reference to his work as a "pretty piece of ingenuity" is suggestive of James's uneasiness about his manipulation of dualism, as if he wondered whether his "ingenious" theory could be no more than a carefully contrived sham.

By playfully inverting the language of the marriage ceremony, James speaks for an audience who finds the mind/body split "fundamental." "Let no man," they cry, "join what God has put asunder." James, of course, will be the man to attempt the reversal of this "fundamental *datum*." For James must, he tells us, "obey" *his* intuitions, even when the stakes are this high. Hence, under the new regime of experience, the "stream" of thought becomes "only a careless name": "Let the case be what it may in others, I am as confident as I am of anything that, in myself, the stream of thinking (which I recognize emphatically as a phenomenon) is only a careless name for what, when scrutinized, reveals itself to consist chiefly of the stream of my breathing" *(ERE, 36–7)*. Immediately upon establishing this notion, however, James shifts his figure from consciousness as breathing to consciousness as "breath." James states that "breath, moving outwards, between the glottis and the nostrils, is, I am persuaded, the essence out of which philosophers have constructed the entity known to them as consciousness." That *"entity,"* James continues, *"is fictitious, while thoughts in the concrete are fully real" (ERE, 37)*. Consciousness has been fictitiously "constructed" out of what is, in essence, "breath"; but thoughts are somehow "fully real" when they are "in the concrete" because "thoughts in the concrete are made of the same stuff as things are" *(ERE, 37)*. It is difficult to keep track of what is "real" or "fictitious," "constructed" or "concrete" in this passage. James's reasoning is convoluted; the conclusion to his essay seems to spin out of control here, opening up the possibilities for more words, rather than providing the proverbial "last word."

James rebuilds his theory of consciousness, sliding from one figure to another. Because the word "essence" implies a spiritual or immaterial entity, what James "grieves" might "sound materialistic" turns on itself as he formulates yet another trope for consciousness: consciousness as spirit. We move from thinking to breathing to breath to spirit. Finally, what appears to be a radical statement equating the flow of our thoughts with the passage of air through our lungs, actually brings us back to the latent spiritualism of the account of consciousness in *Principles*. "Breath" seems to have more to do with the ethereal qualities of consciousness than the corporeal because breath, "ever the original of 'spirit'" *(ERE,* 37), disappears as it comes into being. But how can thinking be like breath if thoughts are only "real" when they are "in the concrete"? How are thoughts "concrete"? And what does it mean to imagine that thoughts are "made of the same stuff" as things? James ends his essay with a series of cryptic suggestions that generate more questions than answers. His language is deliberately figurative (naming thoughts "concrete," for example) and though there seems to be little danger that a reader would expect thoughts to be made of solid matter any more than they would mistake thinking for an actual stream of liquid water, such literalization is not completely outrageous. After all, the *Essays in Radical Empiricism* ask us to replace "consciousness" with the movements of our body's respiratory system.

The problem, of course, is that respiration is not the only way James imagines consciousness in the course of this essay. Moreover, as breathing turns into breath, we seem to lose biology in exchange for metaphysics. James uses metaphor against itself; language twists in and out of its literal and figurative meanings until the reader is forced to conclude that consciousness may, in fact, be impossible to define in one particular way, with one specific image—perhaps even impossible to place with words. Consequently, we do not rest at the end of "Does 'Consciousness' Exist?" There seem to be countless, contradictory answers to that question; and James hints at the potential for his argument to unravel as he concludes with a "wish": "I wish I might believe to have made that plausible in this article" *(ERE,* 38). It is not clear what exactly the "that" is which James wants "made plausible"—typical of his work, James remains vague, especially under the pressure to conclude. Significantly, he does not merely wish for plausibility; rather, he wishes that he might *believe* he has *made* something plausible—a statement that emphasizes the role of subjectivity in his argument as well as the sense that consciousness (hence, experience) is what we believe it and make it to be.

"Does 'Consciousness' Exist?" leaves us uncertain whether Jamesian consciousness is spirit or matter, fluid function or concrete entity. Rather, "pure experience" becomes a container for everything—mental, physical, and metaphysical—a substitute for consciousness because it includes consciousness, because it is the origin of consciousness.[29] The essays, however, are not the first place where James begins to question whether our physical acts (such as the movement of our eyelids, the adjustments of our muscles) may in fact explain our inward lives. Folded within the text of *The Principles of Psychology,* in a portion of James's chapter on "The Consciousness of Self," we find the same suspicion. Namely, that everything introspected in the stream of consciousness can be explained physiologically:

> This palpitating inward life is, in me, that central nucleus which I just tried to describe in terms that all men might use. . . . But when I forsake such general descriptions and grapple with particulars, coming to the closest possible quarters with the facts, *it is difficult for me to detect in the activity any purely spiritual element at all. Whenever my introspective glance succeeds in turning round quickly enough to catch one of these manifestations of spontaneity in the act, all it can ever feel distinctly is some bodily process, for the most part taking place within the head.* (PP, 1.287)

Disenchanted with his own "general descriptions," aiming for "the closest possible quarters with the facts," James is forced to divulge his secret: consciousness is really just in our heads. That is, it is literally *in there* as a "bodily process," not the paradoxical spirit-substance that cannot be explained. At this point, we are forced to ask: what exactly is inwardness or, as James calls it, "this palpitating inward life"? How is the self conscious of itself (if indeed it is at all)? What happens when consciousness (the inner core) is conflated with the body (the physical/exterior self)? For the next few pages of this chapter, James entertains the possibility that his enchanting model of the self as sanctuary is actually just a collection of physical activities— "a fluctuating play of pressures, convergences, divergences, and accommodations in my eyeballs," "the opening and closing of the glottis," "the movements of the muscles of the brow and eyelids" *(PP,* 1.287–8). If James's "introspective glance" is quick enough, he can, presumably, "catch" one of these palpitations; under such scrutiny, consciousness becomes mere anatomical adjustment.

    Tentative at first, James issues one of a series of qualifiers: "I do not for a moment say that this is all it [the 'Self of selves'] consists of, for I fully realize how desperately hard is introspection in this field" *(PP,* 1.288). And though James speaks less boldly here than he will in the radical empiricism essay, he does replace what he calls "spiritual activity" with bodily activities. Yet as we see with his stipulation about introspection, James leaves room for the possibility that there is more to the inner self than physical sensations. Moreover, he sets up his theory as a "hypothesis" that acts as a theoretical "what if": "Now, without pledging ourselves in any way to adopt this hypothesis, let us dally with it for a while to see to what consequences it might lead if it were true" *(PP,* 1.288). James remains cagey, playing with the possibilities, thinking hypothetically rather than stating his case indefinitely. One of the consequences of our "dallying" is a readjustment of our notions of objectivity and subjectivity. The conclusion: if everything inner is physiological, then all that is experienced is objective:

> If they really were the innermost sanctuary, the *ultimate* one of all the selves whose being we can ever directly experience, it would follow that *all* that is experienced is, strictly considered, *objective.* . . . Instead, then, of the stream of thought being one of *con*-sciousness . . . it might be better called a stream of *Scious*ness pure and simple, thinking objects of some of which it makes what it calls a 'Me,' and only aware of its 'pure' Self in an abstract, hypothetic or conceptual way. *(PP,* 1.290)

Self-awareness, like subjectivity, gets eased out of this account of consciousness; the "innermost sanctuary" takes on a different meaning here because the self is an abstract concept—a section of the stream like any other thought—not that which contains or causes the stream. James's desire to dissect consciousness is literalized in this passage; though James has relentlessly denied the possibility of division, here he severs the word to transform the concept. Consciousness becomes "Sciousness" so that James can speculate on the nature of the self.

These conjectures from *Principles,* in "The Consciousness of Self," contradict much of what James emphatically asserted in the previous chapter on "The Stream of Thought." As if anticipating such a critique, James recovers from his digression and issues an open-ended conclusion:

> Speculations like this traverse common-sense; and not only do they traverse common-sense (which in philoso-

> phy is no insuperable objection) but they contradict the
> fundamental assumption of every philosophic school. . . .
> I will therefore treat the last few pages as a parentheti-
> cal digression, and from now to the end of the volume
> revert to the path of common-sense again. I mean by this
> that I will continue to assume (as I have assumed all
> along, especially in the last chapter) a direct awareness
> of the process of our thinking as such, simply insisting
> on the fact that it is an even more inward and subtle
> phenomenon than most of us suppose. (*PP*, 1.291)

James sounds as if he is chastising himself for this "parenthetical
digression," vowing to stay on course— "the path of common-
sense"—for the rest of the volume. Though philosophy, apparently, does not object to "traversing" common sense, James will not.
He explains what walking down the "path" with *him* will mean.
We can continue to assume that we have a direct awareness of the
"process of our thinking"; yet James inserts a modification of his
doctrine as "subtle" as the phenomenon itself. That inwardness
which is most vividly felt "turns out" to consist of physical movements that James locates mostly in the head; but "over and above
these there is an obscurer feeling of something more," a phenomenon which, James states, "must at present remain an open question"
*(PP*, 1.292). What is most striking about this rather inconclusive
"conclusion" is how quickly James abandons it. For the rest of the
chapter, he stays true to his promise, virtually ignoring his discovery (his "parenthetical digression") that grounds consciousness in
physiology. James seems more interested in the "obscurer feeling,"
the unnamable "something more."

The path that James will follow for the remainder of *The
Principles of Psychology*—the path that leads him, finally, to radical empiricism, a path, as he deems it, "of common sense"—may
be crooked, but it inevitably directs us inward to the self. An
intensely individualized self. As the metaphorical language of
*Principles* takes us "even more inward," Jamesian consciousness
gets established as intrinsic, natural, a fundamental "something"
inside us. "Does 'Consciousness' Exist?" will confirm this direction, though the essay ends with ambivalence—its metaphors
changing with every challenge to the theory James can imagine.
The discourse of consciousness in the Jamesian text produces an
equivocal version of the self—sacred, central, inward core, *and*
wandering, tenuous flow of experience. In the Jamesian account of
consciousness, words keep us suspended, questions are left unan-

swered, and theories remain open-ended. If James is writing a narrative of consciousness—perhaps even an allegory that begs us to read into and under and beyond its figures—he is also continually gesturing toward what exists outside of his narrative. James's elaborate attempts to form something elusive that cannot be apprehended may, in fact, be disclosing an anxious suspicion that nothing exists beyond what he has created. Hence his frenetic revisions, deletions, and rehearsals of metaphors for consciousness. It is inconceivable for us to imagine "mind," as we understand that concept in the twenty-first century, without the notion of consciousness (one might even say without a Jamesian notion of consciousness). James creates a series of metaphors out of which consciousness materializes, yet he systematically deconstructs his own creation throughout the course of his career. Metaphor, however, seems to regenerate itself. Liquid metaphors, nuclear metaphors, ethereal metaphors, corporeal metaphors—consciousness measures inwardness with figures such as these. What we inherit from James are both the tools to construct the self and the subsequent claim continually to remake it.

## CHAPTER THREE

# The Structure of Consciousness:
## Henry James's *Portrait of a Lady* and the Drama of Social Relations

"In other words consciousness is an illimitable power, and though at times it may seem to be all consciousness of misery, yet in the way it propagates itself from wave to wave, so that we never cease to feel, and though at moments, we appear to, try to, pray to, there is something that holds one in one's place, makes it a standpoint in the universe which it is probably good not to forsake."

Henry James

In a letter to Grace Norton, written in response to her expression of intense isolation and sorrow, Henry James speaks "with the voice of stoicism" about how she must face suffering.[1] His letter swells with metaphors that make the world a fluid universe, and we, floundering individuals, sometimes blinded by darkness, sometimes close to drowning. James writes imploringly that one must not "melt too much into the universe" but be as "solid and dense and fixed" as one can. If James begins by saying "I don't know *why* we live" he ends by giving some sense of *how* we can live; that is, he imagines how one can endure pain, prevail over that enticement to "melt" away and, ultimately, keep one's place despite the shifting currents of life. Personal survival, as James sees it, comes through the power of consciousness. Thus, the figures for consciousness in James's letter to Grace Norton elucidate the problem of creating form in a formless world, of embracing identity when experience comes with the rush of waves. And though James's language here is explicitly naturalistic, his emphasis on the contrast between inner and outer spheres corresponds to the question of private versus public identities as a means to understand subjectivity.

The language in James's letter suggests that consciousness, which presumably exists inside us, takes on the qualities of the outside world. More precisely, in his novels, consciousness becomes *the* site for a contest between the personal and the social world. While William James forges a study of consciousness by examining a generic notion of mind, Henry James formulates consciousness through the experience of particular characters in his fiction. Together, Henry and William James provide a moment of intersection between philosophy and literature through their investigations, both theoretical and aesthetic, of the concept of consciousness. Each author creates a world for the self that guarantees stability but is open to possibility. Consciousness is that fund of self-knowledge, protected like a treasure. It is also an ever-changing current, a growing awareness. Despite these contradictory images, perhaps because of its flexible metaphors, consciousness becomes something that we both believe in and consider representative of an interior reality.

Most studies of the James brothers give little sense of the way that linguistic configurations get reworked in both philosophy and fiction, nor is it clear what significance we should place on words that overlap in these genres. I want to consider how both philosopher *and* fiction writer comprehend, and ultimately, create the concept of consciousness through a shared language of metaphors. Building a model for subjectivity out of figurative language, both brothers make consciousness the key to an understanding of the self. I begin this chapter with a series of letters from William to Henry James, mostly in reference to Henry's work. In using these letters, it is not my intention to offer a critique of the relationship between the brothers; but rather, the relationship between the language that both writers use to articulate consciousness as a process of thought. I then consider Henry James's first important novel, *The Portrait of a Lady*, in order to read metaphors of consciousness as they invent the inner life of a character. Both letters and novel reveal the struggle to find a language adequate to what each author envisions consciousness to be. The friction between enclosure and openness highlights the letters as well as the drama of *Portrait*. Yet for James's main character, Isabel Archer, we see most explicitly that the conflict is between a consciousness that is private and a consciousness that must be shared; a self that develops inwardly, and a self that becomes socialized.

Critics have afforded ample attention to the link between the James brothers, often attending to the commentary that the James brothers make on each other's work.[2] William's appraisals of Henry's style are often read as some of the earliest critiques of the developing Jamesian method of narration. Henry's sense that he has "unconsciously pragmatised" becomes a hinge for the philosophical interpretation of his novels.[3] Psychoanalytical readings of Henry's fictional characters as well as psychological speculations on the Jameses themselves have emerged through analysis of their letters, some of which, for instance, reflect William's impatience with Henry's late manner.[4] All of these critical gestures rely upon the reconstruction of some Jamesian persona, making personality the basis for a study of this family's place in literature, autobiography, psychology, and philosophy. Readers of the Jameses thus fall prey to and often perpetuate certain family myths, especially when it comes to the two elder brothers: William is a philosopher (and a man) of action; he dismisses purely intellectual speculation in favor of the more practical world of "science." Henry is the aesthete, absorbed in the world of words, obsessed with the nuances of a complex social system; an exquisite observer, he does not experience, he examines.[5] However, as we focus on the metaphorical language exhibited in Henry's novels and William's philosophy, we find that what look like extremes in their methods (and, as some critics would have it, their "artistic temperaments") often fuse in strange and interesting ways.

Despite his own cultivation of an elusive consciousness, when William responds to Henry's work, he will ask that Henry conform to a more definitive course. As he tells him in an early letter (1870) "In my opinion what you should cultivate is directness of style. Delicacy, subtlety and ingenuity will take care of themselves."[6] Explicit in this letter (and implicit in his own work) is William's insistence that "style" matters. Indeed, representations of thought begin to compose the characteristics of thought; in other words, the language used to describe a self that is conscious ends up creating the concept of consciousness. Still a certain tension exists within this language; metaphors offer various renditions of consciousness, many of which contradict each other. Early in Henry's career, for example, his brother sends him this encouraging response to *The Tragic Muse* (1890): "The whole thing hangs together most intimately and well; and it is truly a spectacle for rejoicing to see that by the sort of practice a man gives himself he attains the plenitude and richness which you have at last got. Your sentences are straighter and simpler than before, and your felicities of observation are on every page." Here the praise William gives seems directly related to what is "straight" and "simple" about Henry's prose. A mere sentence later, however, William contends that "the whole thing is an exquisite mirage which remains afloat in the air of one's mind."[7] William's image of the mirage hints at some uncertainty about what exactly Henry's language has created; floating in the "air" of one's mind, the mirage deceives us into thinking it is real. Arguably, this "exquisite" form of deception is exactly the aim of fiction. Yet the contradictions in William's letter indicate a more fundamental quandary over language, one that deeply influences each writer's imagination of consciousness.

William's response to *The Golden Bowl* (1904) gives a more extensive critical analysis of Henry's method and highlights this polarity in the account of consciousness.[8]

> It put me, as most of your recenter long stories have put me, in a very puzzled state of mind. . . . [T]he method of narration by interminable elaboration of suggestive reference (I don't know what to call it, but you know what I mean) goes agin the grain of all my impulses in writing; and yet in spite of it all, there is a brilliancy and cleanness of effect, and in this book especially a high-toned social atmosphere that are unique and extraordinary. Your methods and my ideas seem the reverse, the one of the other—and yet I have to admit your extreme success in this book. But why don't you, just to please Brother, sit down and write a new book, with no twilight or mustiness in the plot, with great vigor and decisiveness in the action, no fencing in the dialogue, no psychological commentaries, and absolute straightness in the style? Publish it in my name, I will acknowledge it, and give you half the proceeds. Seriously, I wish you *would*, for you *can*; and I should think it would tempt you, to embark on a 'fourth manner.' You of course know these feelings of mine without my writing them down, but I'm 'nothing if not' outspoken.[9]

William worries about how Henry presents his own consciousness as well as the consciousnesses of his characters. His critique points to an explicit discomfort with circumlocution—Henry fills his writing with "suggestive reference" rather than overt statement, "psychological commentary" as opposed to action. William claims he was put in "a puzzled state of mind" upon reading the novel, especially because it "goes agin the grain of all [his] impulses in writing." The exquisite irony of William's declaration is made more emphatic by his own vacillations in this passage—rhetorical swings that leave *us* a bit "puzzled." Contrasting images seem to exist simultaneously in William's imagination of the novel. The philosopher, for instance, finds in it both "twilight" *and* "brilliancy"; "mustiness" *and* "cleanness." William asks Henry, finally, to aim for "absolute straightness in style." He phrases it as if he knew it were an unpleasant task that required restraint: "But why don't you, just to please Brother, sit down and write a new book . . . with great vigor and decisiveness in the action . . . and absolute straightness in style?" *Sit down and write a new book.* This remark sounds as much like a challenge as it does a commission. Though, as William goes on to say, he knows Henry "can" write this way, he also implies that such a work would not really be Henry's. It would have to be published, instead, in *his* name.

William asks for "decisiveness" but cannot write decisively about what his brother appears to be doing; Henry, so William argues, produces a "unique and extraordinary" atmosphere, which seems both potently clear in its "brilliance" and hopelessly dark because it is sinuous rather than "straight." William reluctantly acknowledges the "success" of Henry's later works in their subsequent correspondence, but he cannot justify his brother's wayward manner. "I have to admit that in *The Golden Bowl* and *The Wings of the Dove*, you have succeeded *in getting there* after a fashion, in spite of the perversity of the method and its *longness*, which I am not the only one to deplore."[10] William concedes Henry's "getting there," though he is preoccupied with the novelist's deplorable "fashion" in doing so. Moreover, it is not exactly clear where it is that Henry has arrived. Again in a later letter, this time in reference to *The American Scene* (1907), William's commentary reproduces the discourse he feels compelled to critique. Moreover, the language with which William describes Henry's attempts to capture "a thing," echoes the language that William used in *Principles* to establish the built-in evasiveness of his own version of consciousness.

> You know how opposed your whole 'third manner' of execution is to the literary ideals which animate my crude and Orson-like breast, mine being to say a thing in one sentence as straight and explicit as it can be made, and then to drop it forever; yours being to avoid naming it straight, but by dint of breathing and sighing all round and round it, to arouse in the reader who may have had a similar perception already (Heaven help him if he hasn't!) the illusion of a solid object, made (like the 'ghost' at the Polytechnic) wholly out of impalpable materials, air, and the prismatic interferences of light, ingeniously focused by mirrors upon empty space. But you *do* it, that's the queerness! And the complication of innuendo and associative reference on the enormous scale to which you give way to it does so *build out* the matter for the reader that the result is to solidify, by the mere bulk of the process, the like perception from which *he* has to start. As air, by dint of its volume, will weigh like a corporeal body; so his own poor little initial

perception, swathed in this gigantic envelopment of suggestive atmosphere, grows like a germ into something vastly
bigger and more substantial. But it's the rummiest method
for one to employ systematically as you do nowadays; and
you employ it at your peril.[11]

What is perhaps most striking about William's protestations, as readers of Jamesian philosophy and psychology will be aware, is that in
his own work, confusions abound between the "impalpable" and the
"corporeal," "ghostly" objects and "solid" objects, "envelope" and
"substance." As a philosopher attempting to delineate consciousness,
William finds that "language works against our perception of the
truth. We name our thoughts simply . . . as if each knew its own
things and nothing else. What each really knows is clearly the thing it
is named for, with dimly perhaps a thousand other things."[12] And he
spends much of *Principles* trying to put words around these "dim perceptions" that a name alone cannot secure. William James experiences anxiety over the issue of "naming thoughts" because language
fails to be more accurately attuned to relations and, therefore, misses
the "thousand other things" which accompany the thought itself.
William suggests that Henry avoids naming altogether, though he
does produce "perceptions" for the reader that somehow get solidi-
fied into "objects" once they are "swathed" in the atmosphere of
innuendo and suggestion.

William contrasts his own method with Henry's in this letter:
"mine being to say a thing in one sentence as straight and explicit as
it can be made, and then to drop it forever; yours being to avoid naming it straight." William indicates that Henry's avoidance of
"straight" naming springs out of a desire to arouse his reader to join
him in the work of perceiving. The "breathing and sighing all round
and round" the object to be named seems to generate the filmy,
abstract envelope to which William protests. If Henry wants the reader to believe that there is something to discover, however, his intima-
tions, his "breathing and sighing," seem to be exactly the strategy to
induce this belief. William concedes that Henry's fiction "builds out
the matter" for his readers, that he "solidifies" these disembodied
words through "ingenious" techniques that, with "mirrors" and
"prismatic interferences of light," sound a lot like magic. Expressing
his frustration *and* fascination with Henry's attempts to express the
intangible, William seems to delight in the fact that Henry can pull it
off: "But you *do* it, that's the queerness!" Even though William celebrates Henry's accomplishment, he also maintains that his brother's
method is dangerous. Illusions, innuendoes, and suggestions rely

upon readers to bring them to completion and understanding; the "peril" exists in giving over the work of hermeneutics to an unskilled audience. William's own anxiety about audience is reflected in his appraisal of Henry's work. As the letter continues, William imagines Henry's readers protesting to his "perverse" method; he couches his own voice in the "cries" of an audience who demand a "directer manner":

> The method seems perverse: 'Say it *out*, for God's sake,' they cry, 'and have done with it.' And so I say now, give us *one* thing in your older directer manner, just to show that, in spite of your paradoxical success in this unheard-of method, you *can* still write according to accepted cannons. Give us that interlude; and then continue like the 'curiosity of literature' which you have become. For gleams and innu-endoes and felicitous verbal insinuations you are unap-proachable, but the core of literature is solid. Give it to us *once* again! The bare perfume of things will not support existence, and the effect of solidity you reach is but per-fume and simulacrum.[13]

William shows a desire to see through the words, to find a stable source, a solid "core," that might substantialize what is otherwise insinuation. His worries about Henry's method derive from the questions pressing on his own work: what can language produce and how does its object become real or "solid"? Is all that we establish simply "perfume and simulacrum," a faint scent or an illusory substance? William alerts us to the significance of these questions as he warns Henry that the "bare perfume of things will not support existence." It is not clear exactly what he means here: "existence" could refer to the reality or truth of the things presented—whether or not they have actual being. It might also refer to life. Thus, the bare perfume, the perceptions themselves, will not support life. What *does* support life, presumably, is the solid core. But where do we find that core? And is it any more stable than the "envelopment" of suggestions? William urges Henry to "Give it to us once again!" He believes Henry is capable of finding the solid core through a "directer manner"; in effect, he encourages his novelist brother to find the core by *creating* the core. We might ask, then, what is the difference between the language that creates "gleams" or "perfumes," and the language that creates a "core"?

At the beginning of this letter, William acknowledges his own "literary ideals" as "crude"; yet his approach to Henry's work is not so much literary as linguistic. He criticizes Henry's use of language as he determines what a text can create. Words such as "illusion," "'ghost,'" "impalpable," "empty," "innuendo," "perfume," and "simulacrum," become a string of mysterious referents. Similar words flood the (William) Jamesian lexicon and are reflected in his projected probings of consciousness.[14] Choosing between the elusive paradigm and the central core is expressed as a disparity between "suggestive reference" (which is also "avoidance") or "absolute straightness." In other words, it is a question of the circuitous path versus the straight one. Perversity or directness. William covets straightness, direct language, the solid core. Significantly, he is unable to realize it himself, though he encourages Henry to stick to this path in his fiction. Henry's language, however, is perhaps even more equivocal than William suggests. In his fiction and his own commentaries on his novels, Henry expresses ambivalence about the proper way to present his "story," especially when that story gives an account of a character's process of thought. Indeed, his equivocation is most apparent in the metaphorical language he uses to dramatize consciousness. Metaphors of expansion in James's texts explain a rise in a character's self-consciousness, the growth of their powers of perception, an increase in knowledge. However, metaphors of enclosure impart a sacredness to consciousness, portioning it off as a protected "core," giving us the sense that it is the most "inward" of characteristics, and therefore, the most inviolable.

Though readers might deem *The Portrait of a Lady* to be exactly the straightforward realist style to which William wanted his novelist brother to return, the text is filled with contradictory metaphors for consciousness that reveal its ambiguity about "method" and "idea." The ambiguity intensifies precisely around James's imagination of a conscious life. In the Preface, in an attempt to sort out his own compositional course, James produces metaphors that seem, at once, to contain and to spread. James builds a series of structures that become analogues for narrative, for consciousness and for the mind. His well-known "house of fiction" is one illustration; it is erected with all the discrimination of an architectural blueprint, but also with a roundabout method and a gathering sense of the potential for his subject to "burst" out of its frame. Garden metaphors occur throughout *Portrait* and enhance the sense that consciousness as awareness, or one's relation to oneself (as James will call it), is itself a growing thing. In a famous passage from the Preface, James speaks of the "moral" sense of a work of art as it is connected to life; almost immediately, his metaphors signal a conflict in what gets "projected" from the mind:

> There is, I think, no more nutritive or suggestive truth in
> this connexion than that of the perfect dependence of the
> 'moral' sense of a work of art on the amount of felt life
> concerned in producing it. The question comes back thus,
> obviously, to the kind and the degree of the artist's prime
> sensibility, which is the soil out of which his subject
> springs. The quality and capacity of that soil, its ability to
> 'grow' with due freshness and straightness any vision of
> life, represents, strongly or weakly, the projected morality.[15]

Words such as "sense," "sensibility," "felt life," "vision" sound like
synonyms for consciousness; through metaphor, James's substantial-
izes these abstract terms, casting them in a physical landscape. The
image of the "soil" becomes an important foundation for the growth
that James speaks of in this passage as well as the "growth" that will
occur as metaphors regenerate themselves throughout the Preface.
James tells us that the "soil" is the artist's "sensibility." Out of this
soil "springs" the artist's "subject"; furthermore, the soil supports the
artist's blossoming "vision of life," and, presumably, the "moral"
sense of a work of art. James traces backward from the moral to the
"amount of felt life," to the sensations of the artist. Significantly, he
imagines that the question rests upon the artist's ability to "grow" a
moral that, in turn, relies upon his or her ability to experience life.
"The quality and capacity of that soil, its ability to 'grow' with due
freshness and straightness any vision of life, represents, strongly or
weakly, the projected morality." James's predicament is how to cultivate the soil of the mind while still maintaining control over its yield;
as he imagines that the soil can grow a vision with "due freshness and
straightness" we are reminded of William's injunction that he aim for
"straightness." But a garden or, more specifically, growth itself is not
usually easy to control—whether it be the growth of a plant or the
growth of the mind. Plants, in fact, do not grow "straight," though
they can be manicured to appear to do so.[16] As James implies, if the
soil is to produce a moral—if life is to produce art—the garden must
be carefully cultivated.

The contrast (in both the Preface and the novel) between
metaphors that contain and metaphors that expand is exemplified in
the name of one of the houses in *The Portrait of a Lady*—
Gardencourt.[17] This name unites the two worlds in *Portrait*, both of
which become figures for the conscious self: the garden, where knowledge and self-awareness grow, and the court, where one is identified
and often restrained by one's particular role in society. In her reading

of the novel, Sandra Fischer argues that houses, rooms, corners, curtains, walls, doors, keys all contribute to our understanding of human inter-relationships, manifestations of personality, and individual self-images in the *Portrait*. She states that Henry James "experiments with metaphors of enclosed space" primarily to "enforce his literary concern with psychological reality."[18] James experiments with other metaphors for psychological reality as well, combining models for the self through conflicting figures. If the self is what gets hidden behind closed doors, it is also what exceeds physical boundaries. Composed for the New York Edition in 1908, the Preface to *Portrait* reveals the same sort of friction in language as William's letters (written close to this time), namely the necessity to establish a secure vocabulary with which to define the self while simultaneously exploring its potential for development. Specifically in this Preface, James's metaphors express both the growth of an individual represented in his fiction (the "subject" that is Isabel) and his own growth as an artist. Here, "one's imagination" is quite explicitly a garden in which the "seed" of an idea grows "as tall as possible" and, presumably, with great force as it "pushes into the light and air" to "thickly flower there."

> These are the fascinations of the fabulist's art, these lurking forces of expansion, these necessities of upspringing in the seed, these beautiful determinations, on the part of the idea entertained, to grow as tall as possible, to push into the light and the air and thickly flower there; and, quite as much, these fine possibilities of recovering, from some good standpoint of the ground gained, the intimate history of the business—of retracing and reconstructing its steps and stages. (vii)

The Prefaces allow James the opportunity to study not only the imaginations he has drafted for his characters, but also his sense of his own imagination, both of which originate in metaphor. Though there are hints that the garden could be a wild and uncivilized place, mostly, it appears to reflect a careful system. James is confident in his attempts at "retracing and reconstructing" what he names a history; he is able to conduct the thickly flowering branches of his story into the discrete units he calls "steps and stages."[19] He admits that his model is a "*projection* of memory upon the whole matter of the growth." Thus, James's comparison sounds like a mixed metaphor, as if he had to build his structure around a plant that could grow out of control. This strange metaphor indicates James's predicament over the representation of his own (artist's) mind, and consequently, the minds of his characters; the language he uses to appreciate "the growth of imagination" must be generative, yet finely wrought—a combination of natural imagery and artificial contrivance.

James reiterates the theme of expansion in this passage; it is the "fabulist," the storyteller, whose "lurking forces of expansion" seem something like the mirrors and catches of light with which William fancies his brother makes his magic. Indeed, "forces of expansion" lurk around every corner in the Preface and appear equally threatening throughout *The Portrait of a Lady*. The prefatory remarks become an attempt to contain these forces, through an account of the method of storytelling, and through the careful reconstruction of the phases of an author's imagination. In this sense, Henry James creates an exchange with his brother's work that also endeavors to draw figures for the imagination, human consciousness and the mind. As we have seen, William expresses anxiety over Henry's roundabout methods—his avoidance—but what Henry may be avoiding is the permanent confinement of the "forces of expansion" that, he muses, drive his imaginative productions. Nevertheless, almost every time Henry James presents a metaphorical construction that expresses an image of expansion, he turns on his figure and produces a metaphor to contain it.[20] James's metaphors figure largely in the novel as representations of both character and narrative; houses in the novel translate into the house-*as*-novel and the mind-as-house. An interesting corollary to the house metaphor can also be found in William's essay, "Does 'Consciousness' Exist?" (1904), that comes four years before James's Preface (1908). In it, William creates an elaborate metaphor for the "field of consciousness." He compares the field of consciousness to "the room in which you sit," constantly shifting from the physical room to a room inside the mind: "As a room, the experience has occupied that spot and had that environment for thirty years. As your field of consciousness it may never have existed until now. . . . As a room, it will take an earthquake . . . to destroy it. As your subjective state, the closing of your eyes, or any instantaneous play of your fancy will suffice."[21] It is not always clear what these rooms or houses contain, who dwells in them, or what occurs within their walls. These are questions of experience—questions that Henry James indirectly raises, but also leaves ambiguously answered.

Specifically, in the Preface, James assembles a house (the "house of fiction") that seems to enclose all of his other structures. In detailing the "house of fiction," oddly, James makes note of the windows as much as those who look through them, as if the frame around their vision determines what they will see:

These apertures, of dissimilar size and shape, hang so, all
together, over the human scene that we might have expected of them a greater sameness of report than we find . . . .
But they have this mark of their own that at each of them
stands a figure with a pair of eyes, or at least with a field-
glass, which forms, again and again, for observation, a
unique instrument, insuring the person making use of it an
impression distinct from every other. He and his neighbors
are watching the same show, but one seeing more where the
other sees less, one seeing black where the other sees white,
one seeing big where the other sees small, one seeing coarse
where the other sees fine. And so on, and so on; there is for-
tunately no saying on what, for the particular pair of eyes,
the window may *not* open. . . . (x–xi)

Though the windows hang together, the lookers do not share a common vision. Gazing upon the same scene, these "pairs of eyes" still
seem to form an infinite number of "impressions." In other words,
their (individual) vision is complicit in the construction of the scene.
This group of observers brings to mind William James's account of
four travelers in his *Principles of Psychology*. Just as Henry's imagined neighbors that stand "watching the same show . . . one seeing
black while the other sees white, one seeing big where the other sees
small," so William's travelers see the same Europe, but create individual accounts of experience.[22] William James will state it more
emphatically, insisting that beyond simply "bringing home" the experience they obtained in Europe, each traveler has, in fact, *made* his
experience. William writes: "Each has selected, out of the same mass
of presented objects, those which suited his private interest and has
made his experience thereby."[23] While William's analogy shows how
the observers "make" experience, Henry's indicates how they "make"
art. And yet, for Henry, experience is readily transformed into art; all
that is needed is the proper visual frame. Indeed, Henry James's theory of art rests on his image of the house, one which reminds us that
metaphors for (creating) fiction are comparable to metaphors for consciousness.

As other readers have also suggested, James draws from his literary
predecessors, Hawthorne and Emerson, in order to craft his theory of
narrative and his image of the mind—both in terms of architectural
form.[24] Emerson explicitly combines organic metaphors with structural metaphors in his essay, "The Poet" (1844): "For it is not
meters, but a meter-making argument that makes a poem,—a
thought so passionate and alive that like the spirit of a plant or an
animal it has an architecture of its own, and adorns nature with a new
thing."[25] Thoughts as well as plants have an "architecture"—nothing

seems to escape form—and yet the form does not seem static. Emerson calls attention, instead, to a process: it is not meter, but "meter-making," in the progressive tense. This is the "argument" or "spirit" of the work; it becomes part of nature, a living thing—the implication being that the spiritual aspect transcends the boundaries of poetic form. Thus Emerson prefigures James, erecting structures and surreptitiously inserting them in "nature"; designing forms while simultaneously defying their ability to contain. He ends his essay, accordingly, by naming a world where the poet can find Beauty "wherever are forms with transparent boundaries."[26]

As James reconsiders *The Portrait* years later, he seems to illuminate these paradoxes between structure and nature, between the way words keep us bound and still invite infinite perspectives. James imagines his novel with a form or "mould" that, nonetheless, it "strains."[27] Despite frequent mention of the mind's fecundity, human beings seem restricted to mere "vessels" that bear the story, or the "treasure" of human affections. And James's now famous "house of fiction"—which has "not one window, but a million"—must be "pierced" in order to permit the observers inside to look out upon the "spreading field, the human scene" (xi). These particular figures show the ambivalence of James's gesture toward containment; he speaks of the "growth of imagination" while simultaneously delighting in "locked up" treasures, precious objects, vessels, cornerstones, houses, and framed portraits—such as the "picture" hung in the light of the international scene, the final image in the Preface that encapsulates his desire for closure by enclosure (xii; xxi).[28] But perhaps "containment" or "enclosure" is simply another way to refer to definition. Language, in this sense, is restrictive by its very nature; words define by closing off other possibilities for meaning.

Henry James, however, will maintain the dubious balance between boundlessness and boundaries as he states: "Tell me what the artist is, and I will tell you of what he has *been* conscious. Thereby I shall express to you at once his boundless freedom and his moral reference" (xi). Coming at the end of James's elaborate metaphor of the "house of fiction," this statement about consciousness shows that it is intimately tied to the vision of the observer; more emphatically, James contends that the human scene is "nothing without . . . the watcher," nothing, that is, without consciousness. It is as if the "watcher" who is separate from everyday life validates the human scene precisely because he is not in it, precisely because his consciousness reflects, rather than embodies, it. James renders consciousness suspended somewhere between expansive vision and individual perspective, the whole of life that we might imagine walking "straight upon," and the perched window that holds us aloft. He also, simultaneously places consciousness within the artist/observer. Thus, "boundless" and inevitably bound, consciousness becomes a moral register, representing both the artist's "freedom" and his or her point of "reference."

Within both Preface and novel, author and character, Jamesian consciousness remains extraordinarily flexible; frames and walls "house" it, but do not appear to confine it. In her study entitled *Literary Architecture*, Ellen Frank discusses the relationship between architecture and literature or what she calls "the architecture of literature as external configuration, as form and embodiment, of consciousness." She names the larger subject of her book as "the nature of experience" which she takes to mean "our way of noticing or perceiving, our activity of being in the world."[29] Specifically, Frank argues that James's Prefaces become a sort of "paradoxical frame that seems to enclose and enter the picture at once." James complicates matters, she notes, by "tucking outdoor scenes inside."[30] Outside and inside are repeatedly confused in the *Portrait* which itself refers to a framed object. The subject of James's portrait, Isabel's consciousness, materializes through metaphors of nature, landscape, and lush gardens, as well as confined spaces, bolted doors, and formidable structures that seem particularly difficult to escape. Narrating his initial conception of Isabel in the Preface, James will imagine her as a structure he will erect, a piece of a house yet to be built:

> The point is . . . that this single small corner-stone, the conception of a certain young woman affronting her destiny, had begun with being all my outfit for the large building of 'The Portrait of a Lady.' It came to be a square and spacious house . . . it had to be put up round my young woman while she stood there in perfect isolation. (xii)

If the concept of Isabel's encounter with her destiny is the "cornerstone," then the house gets built around her (or on top of her); the same house—a "neat and careful and proportioned pile of bricks"— which James has named "a literary monument" (xvi). Critics have pointed out that Isabel gets "framed" in this story, in all senses of the word, trapped by the artist's controlling vision and contained within the frame of observing male consciousness.[31] In this passage from the Preface, a house is built round her; thus she herself becomes a container within a container, a "fair vessel," but nonetheless a self-enclosed monument inside a "spacious house."[32] This sense of an Isabel Archer who exists "in perfect isolation" is part of the fantasy that James maintains in the novel; this Isabel, presumably, springs out of the soil of the artist's mind, free from any other "impressions": "Thus I had my vivid individual—vivid, so strangely, in spite of being still at large, not confined by the conditions, not engaged in the tangle, to which we look for much of the impress that constitutes an identity" (xi). James implies that when he first created Isabel, it was without reference to her social environment; he keeps that mess of "conditions" and "tangles" away from his creation. James is most concerned with Isabel's "relation to herself" (xv). First and foremost an individual, Isabel becomes what James "preserves, protects, enjoys" (xii).[33] As James presents it, what constitutes Isabel's identity is Isabel herself.[34]

Reading representations of the mind in *The Portrait of a Lady* means understanding the intersection between consciousness and knowledge. The split between metaphors of enclosure and expansion, inside and outside, reveals something about this connection; for Isabel's journey toward self-discovery is often imagined in terms of these opposing metaphors. She begins on a wandering search (through continents, countries, and a variety of houses) for the coveted prize of "knowledge" and ends up with a quieter, yet more direct insight that James expressly depicts as a result of looking inward. Thus knowledge, a sum that is represented outside of the self, transforms into consciousness, an inner bounty that James creates inside the character of Isabel Archer. The formation and transformation of Isabel Archer's consciousness is largely dependent upon both her desire and capacity for knowledge. Knowledge that Isabel pays for with exacting, moral deliberation. Appointed a "precious vessel," Isabel functions as a carrier of knowledge; yet she must contract her expansive vision into a properly contained, scrupulously socialized self. Among the many contradictions in Isabel's character is her famed "love of knowledge"—investigative and exploring, this passion is, nevertheless, accompanied by fear.[35] What's more, it clashes with her penchant for romanticizing and thereby re-creating the world around her. James reveals the struggle between the ways we seek knowledge and our methods for creating it as he represents metaphors that enhance the transcending self alongside metaphors that inevitably compress it.

James represents the conflict between an externalized body of knowledge, symbolized by books, and the knowledge that originates in Isabel: "[T]his young lady had been seated alone with a book. To say that she was so occupied is to say that her solitude did not press upon her; for her love of knowledge had a fertilising quality and her imagination was strong" (1.27). Isabel's mind is represented as fecund and productive, her love of knowledge, "fertilising." Loving knowledge amounts to growing knowledge—a growth that resists the oppressiveness of solitude. Yet even though Isabel seems free to wander, with "uncontrolled use" of the library of books (1.29), she reads in a mysterious chamber with a bolted door. Growth occurs despite the "pressing" weight of solitude; freedom is found within a locked chamber rather than outdoors. Isabel embodies these conflicting metaphors; indeed, James repeatedly imagines them occupying space within her body, mind, and soul. Isabel's mind, for example, is "a good deal of a vagabond," but she trains it "to a military step . . . to halt, to retreat, to perform . . . complicated maneuvers" (1.31).[36] At the start of the novel, Isabel is "too wide-eyed," she "see[s] too many things at once. Her imagination was by habit ridiculously active; when the door was not open it jumped out the window. She was not accustomed indeed to keep it behind bolts" (1.42). Structures outside the self suggest various models for structures *of* the self: the bolted chamber in the Albany house where Isabel reads now becomes the bolted chamber of her imagination. Like many of the critics who read her, however, Isabel seems to recognize that her mind is prone to imaginative wandering, and consequently, that she is sometimes a poor "reader."[37] Thus, she makes efforts to contain herself, closing her eyes, in this early instance, so as not to "see" so much.

The rhythm between poles—the exploring mind, the restricted vision; the growing self, the pressure of confinement—is maintained by a constant exchange of metaphors. Isabel wants knowledge that comes from life, not the printed page. Thus she is "constantly staring and wondering," looking, presumably, outside of herself. Yet James also expresses that she "carried within herself a great fund of life and her deepest enjoyment was to feel the continuity between the movements of her own soul and the agitations of the world" (1.45). It is not clear whether the "life" outside, at which Isabel stares in wonder, is the same as the life she "carries within herself." In this passage, James places this flux and activity in her "soul"; in the Preface, he will target her "consciousness."[38] James repeatedly represents the something-inside Isabel as if it were a "fund," a bank account that she is reluctant to spend. "Giving one's self," therefore, is automatically connected to spending money; and the ultimate gift of one's self—presumably, in marriage—merely becomes a depletion of one's funds:

> Few of the men she saw seemed worth a ruinous expenditure. . . . Deep in her soul—it was the deepest thing there—lay a belief that if a certain light should dawn she could give herself completely; but this image, on the whole, was

too formidable to be attractive. Isabel's thoughts hovered
about it, but they seldom rested on it long; after a little it
ended in alarms. (1.71–2)

This "thing" deep in Isabel's soul—the "deepest thing there"—seems
separate from her hovering "thoughts." James calls it a "belief," and
he places it within this separate space in Isabel, making the "depths"
of his heroine a privileged chamber. In this same passage, however, we
are taken into the "recesses" of Isabel's "spirit" and, rather than a
private sanctum, we find an open garden:

> Her nature had, in her conceit, a certain garden-like quali-
> ty, a suggestion of perfume and murmuring boughs, of
> shady bowers and lengthening vistas, which made her feel
> that introspection was, after all, an exercise in the open air,
> and that a visit to the recesses of one's spirit was harmless
> when one returned from it with a lapful of roses. But she
> was often reminded that there were other gardens in the
> world than those of her remarkable soul, and that there
> were moreover a great many places which were not gardens
> at all—only dusky pestiferous tracts, planted thick with
> ugliness and misery. (1.72)

James represents the picture of the garden-like spot as coming from
Isabel's mind; it is her "conceit," her image. We are clearly "inside"
something in this description, which James alternately calls one's
"nature," "spirit," "soul"; yet it is an inside replete with the scent
and the shade of outdoors, and with long walking paths that provide
a view. Moreover, one "returns from it" with a bouquet of roses, as
if one could capture a material souvenir from a spiritual "visit." What
does it mean to imagine introspection (which means literally "looking
into") as a walk in the open air? And why the concern that it be
"harmless"? If one's inner world is merely a reflection of the outside
world, then any sense of a hidden, secret self disappears. Still, Isabel's
spiritual garden seems not only safe, but also particularly pleasant;
though the very mention of the "harmlessness" of these retreats
makes them suspect.

In fact, in *The Portrait of a Lady*, the self is often a dangerous, certainly painful, place to visit. We find it "planted thick with ugliness
and misery" alongside its roses. Moreover, just as the metaphor of the
garden of introspection suggests, inside and outside can be arbitrary
measures; boundaries between private and public selves are not
always clear. At the start of the novel, Isabel sees the self as a private,

privileged quarter that contains a treasure. "The gates of the girl's confidence were opened wider than they had ever been . . . it was as if she had given to a comparative stranger the key to her cabinet of jewels. These spiritual gems were the only ones of any magnitude that Isabel possessed, but there was all the greater reason for their being carefully guarded" (1.267). Just as "giving herself" is likened to a "ruinous expenditure," here, Isabel recognizes that she must carefully guard the "gates of her confidence," "the key to her cabinet" because she finds herself opening them more than ever before. The woman with whom Isabel shares her "spiritual jewels" is, of course, Madame Merle. Yet Madame Merle has no such sacred view of the self; if Isabel protects a coffer of gems, Serena Merle submits to limitlessness and inevitable flow:

> When you've lived as long as I you'll see that every human being has his shell and that you must take the shell into account. By the shell I mean the whole envelope of circumstances. There's no such thing as an isolated man or woman; we're each of us made up of some cluster of appurtenances. What shall we call our 'self'? Where does it begin? where does it end? It overflows into everything that belongs to us—and then it flows back again. I know a large part of myself is in the clothes I choose to wear. I've a great respect for *things*! One's self—for other people—is one's expression of one's self; and one's house, one's furniture, one's garments, the books one reads, the company one keeps—these things are all expressive. (1.287–8)

Madame Merle's theory explodes the privatized version of self, though the metaphor of the "shell" and the "envelope" hint that there is something inside that is being protected or contained.[39] Madame Merle belies confinement, though, when she questions what the boundaries of the self are. The self appears to have no beginning or ending; rather, in an echo of William James's language for the stream of consciousness, it "overflows" and "flows back again" from some place "inside" to all other "outside" things—clothes, houses, books, and friends—that express us. Most significantly, Madame Merle cannot deny the social implications of identity. For her, the self is composed through interactions and acquaintances with other things and other people in a world that is, first and foremost, open.

Isabel reads what Madame Merle calls "expressions" as limiting. They are also potentially threatening. If one's self is no different than one's clothes or one's house or one's books, then Isabel has no choice but to express herself. Such a self cannot be private; on the contrary, this version of self remains susceptible to public consumption—to be observed, inhabited or read. Unlike Madame Merle, Isabel insists upon a self that is separate from these externals. In fact, for Isabel, "the whole envelope of circumstances" obstructs a clear view of the self: "I don't know whether I succeed in expressing myself, but I know that nothing else expresses me. Nothing that belongs to me is any measure of me; everything's on the contrary a limit, a barrier, and a perfectly arbitrary one" (1.288). Madame Merle's "appurtenances" are arbitrary clutter—possessions and "belongings," mere restrictions. Echoing James's Preface (which sets up an isolated Isabel who "naturally" springs out of the soil of an artist's mind), Isabel denies any sense that social influences construct the self. Instead, she envisions a bare, pure self, sequestered from society, totally free of relations. Thus, Isabel not only keeps her own self in a sanctuary, but by refusing to read the "envelope of circumstances," she contributes to the enigma of other characters, especially Serena Merle. In fact, she sees herself "wander[ing], as by the wrong side of the wall of a private garden, round the enclosed talents, accomplishments, aptitudes of Madame Merle" (1.270). This metaphor of inaccessibility amplifies Isabel's wish to be like Madame Merle; the image of the "walled garden" also reiterates her imagination of the self as an enclosed but fertile place. The *Portrait*'s contrast between a socially encoded self (defined by accessories) and the sacrosanct self (identified by what is *inside* the "shell" or "envelope") reminds us of Isabel's relationship to knowledge and consciousness. Represented as outside the self, knowledge becomes the object of a quest, whereas consciousness turns inward to settle somewhere inside a character. The distinction is similar to one that Isabel notes in a conversation with Ralph. He fantasizes that she wants to "drain the cup of experience"; yet Isabel responds: "I only want to see for myself" (1.213). For her, experience is a "poisoned drink"—perhaps because the cup has been touched by other lips. In contrast is what Isabel "sees for herself," a vision that she believes is individual and unmediated.

The notion of "seeing for oneself" becomes tantamount to consciousness.[40] However, though James's metaphors intensify his construction of an inner world, consciousness becomes more than the question of personal introspection. In her discussion of *The Portrait of a Lady*, Millicent Bell brings together issues that she finds are too often held apart by other critics: "the role in the novel of transcendental individuality, with its belief in the limitless extension of personal being; the practical issues of personal self-definition in the social world, particularly as these presented themselves to nineteenth-century women; and the formal-aesthetic contest of openness and closure, which might be said to express both of these themes."[41] In posing

these questions all at once, Bell suggests that personal vision is directly related, even contingent upon, the tension between both transcendence of the self and definition of the self—a definition that occurs
through such "forms" as language and society. Furthermore, she
makes clear that the conflict between openness and closure is precisely that struggle between a consciousness that is "limitless" and one
that provides a "standpoint" (as Henry James own words remind us).
Bell suggests that the contest of openness and closure is formal, aesthetic; I would only qualify her statement to insist that it is explicitly
a contest of metaphors. As James ushers in consciousness to take over
what began as a narrative about knowledge, images of Isabel's social
relations enter into its encapsulated world. Eventually, the outline
around the self threatens to burst. James authors a self-involved consciousness that corresponds to terms like self-awareness, self-reflection, inward contemplation. Nonetheless, as the novel progresses,
Isabel's "self" gets crowded with representations from what was once
clearly the "outside" world. The dramatization of consciousness is no
longer a rehearsal of abstract notions of selfhood—freedom, choice,
beauty, knowledge. The drama becomes a drama of social relations.

Indeed, relations or relationships in the *Portrait* occasion both a
transformation in consciousness and the re-imagination of self.[42]
Relationships also cause a threat to the self because they demand a
change in one's habit of mind, one's point of view. Marriage to Lord
Warburton, for example, would necessitate habitation in a new
house, a space that impinges upon her very "existence." Isabel cannot
think of him as a companion for life, partly because she cannot see
herself in his home: "I cannot think of your home—your various
homes—as the settled seat of my existence." She continues with this
explanation: "we see our lives from our own point of view"
(1.166–7). Isabel also resists the confinement she imagines from a life
with Caspar Goodwood; refusing Goodwood is one of the first exercises of Isabel's "love of liberty" which, until that point, "was as yet
almost exclusively theoretic" (1.233). A confession of love from
Gilbert Osmond does not close in on Isabel so obviously as
Warburton's many houses or Goodwood's ability to "make people
work his will" (1.164); rather Osmond's effect on Isabel occasions
"dread" because his pull is ambiguous:

> The tears came into her eyes: this time, they obeyed the
> sharpness of a pang that suggested to her somehow the slip-
> ping of a fine bolt—backward, forward, she couldn't have
> said which. . . . What made her dread great was precisely
> the force which, as it would seem, ought to have banished

> all dread—the sense of something within herself, deep
> down, that she supposed to be inspired and trustful pas-
> sion. It was there like a large sum stored in a bank. If she
> touched it, it would all come out. (2.18)

Isabel cannot say which way this "bolt" moves—to shut her in or to release her; the ambivalent gesture of this insecure lock for the self connects to Isabel's sense that the something "deep down" within herself could be lost after the slightest "touch." Here the self appears vulnerable, an uncontrollable "sum" that cannot be portioned out, but must be spent all at once. Gestures toward containment offer protection for the self, though James represents them as confining as well—Warburton's houses, Goodwood's persistent hold on Isabel, Ralph's projected visions of her future, and Osmond's domineering mind all restrict Isabel's imagination of freedom. Inevitably, Isabel finds that an expansion of self, an increase in consciousness, comes with sacrifice; comes, that is, as a result of "spending" oneself. It is no surprise then, that Isabel would "give anything" for lessons from Madame Merle in the art of suppressing the self. "She had become aware more than before of the advantage of being like that—of having made one's self a firm surface, a sort of corselet of silver" (2.155). Though Isabel envisions a sanctuary that comes in the guise of armor for the self, she also discovers that such protection comes close to suffocation.

Isabel's famous night-long vigil makes clear her persistent struggle to press against the stifling structures that restrain her, even as she simultaneously yearns for masks, screens, draperies, costumes, corsets, silence, and shadows to screen her from the truth of her situation. Social "appurtenances," once a hindrance to the self, ironically hold the possibility for seclusion or self-protection. Indeed, the vigil scene provides Isabel a respite from social interaction, per se; and yet her entire meditation consists of sorting out the social intrigues carried on around her. Though Isabel sits silently and motionlessly by a dying fire, this long passage constitutes one of the most active, vivid portions of the novel precisely because its metaphors enact the expansion and contraction of consciousness. James calls the vigil a "picture"; and it is a picture encircled by his larger portrait. Yet even "reduced to its essence," James's "long statement" still multiplies image upon image, propagating metaphors for consciousness and expanding beyond its frame to "throw the action further forward than twenty 'incidents' might have done" (xx–xxi). James creates a consciousness that reels with images, each of which speaks to the relationships Isabel experiences. It is here that Isabel faces the reality that marriage is a social act, not an intimate personal exchange. The "ugly possibilities" for alliances—especially between Pansy and Lord Warburton, Lord Warburton and herself, herself and her husband— reveal this truth to her. Further, they constitute a "labyrinth" in which Isabel loses her way (2.188).

The labyrinth is one of a series of structures into which Isabel must enter, and out of which she must emerge. And the only way out is through: life is surrounded by dead walls (2.189); the mind becomes a darkened mansion (2.196); social systems are hung with heavy tapestries (2.199); and the world is a circle (2.203) that threatens to get smaller and smaller. As we have seen throughout *Portrait*, houses and gardens are looming representations of consciousness; during Isabel's searching vigil, however, they no longer represent increased perspective or openness. Instead, both house and garden suddenly embody the threat of enclosure:

> [S]he went with him freely, and his warning had contained nothing ominous. But when, as the months had elapsed, she had followed him further and he had led her into the mansion of his own habitation, *then*, then she had seen where she really was. She could live it over again, the incredulous terror with which she had taken the measure of her dwelling. . . . It was the house of darkness, the house of dumbness, the house of suffocation. Osmond's beautiful mind gave it neither light nor air. Osmond's beautiful mind indeed seemed to peep down from a small high window and mock at her. (2.196)

Reminiscent of James's "house of fiction," Osmond's "mansion" is equated to Osmond's "beautiful mind"; but rather than opening up possibilities for vision, its restricting "darkness," dumbness," and eventual "suffocation," encroach upon Isabel's mind, controlling her from a mocking stance at the window. Neither a sign of intimacy, nor a welcome retreat, social exchange (entering another's mind), involves a dangerous, terrifying passage. The image here reminds us of James's warning that Isabel had "a certain nobleness of imagination which rendered her a good many services and played her a great many tricks" (1.68). Isabel is lured into Osmond's lair and only then ascertains the extent of her trap, "the measure of her dwelling."[43] She is tricked by her own imaginative devices. If, as Isabel admits during her vigil, "she had effaced herself when he first knew her; she had made herself small, pretending there was less of her than there really was" and mistaken Osmond, in the same way, by seeing only "half of his nature" (2.191), then the conflict between Isabel and Osmond arises partly as a struggle over the amount of space allowed for the self to dwell. Isabel's "deception" reveals that the self can be erased or at least hidden; and when she chooses to reveal the whole there does not seem to be room for it in Osmond's mind. He imagined she would only be a reflection of him: "a polished, elegant surface" (2.79). Isabel, however, brings depths that Osmond cannot accommodate. Just as Isabel must shrink herself to fit into Osmond's mansion, her introspective garden must become part of a larger piece of property; its growth inhibited by the over-meticulous owner: "The real offence, as she ultimately perceived, was her having a mind of her own at all. Her mind was to be his—attached to his own like a small garden-plot to a deer-park. He would rake the soil gently and water the flowers; he would weed the beds and gather an occasional nosegay" (2.200). While James once portrayed Isabel entering the garden of her mind to gather roses, now she seems detached from this space: the garden is part of a larger plot; and someone else is gathering its flowers. Isabel is to remain passive, her mind, a decorative piece of Osmond's own.

Isabel's crime, however, is that her mind—far from passive—makes spirited, heroic leaps. More offensive still, she never imagines that her mind is *not* her own. Isabel can neither forfeit the possession of her mind to Osmond, nor can she efface her consciousness completely. Toward the close of the novel, James's metaphors reveal Isabel's desire to sink into an oblivion—an explicit escape from consciousness. Isabel returns to Gardencourt in the final chapter of the novel, hoping for such refuge; she is a passive traveler "with the sense of being carried," yet her mind's "fitful images" culminate in an architecture of their own:

> On the long journey from Rome her mind had been given up to vagueness; she was unable to question the future. She performed this journey with sightless eyes. . . . Her thoughts followed their course through other countries—strange-looking, dimly-lighted, pathless lands . . . the truth of things, their mutual relations, their meaning, and for the most part their horror rose before her with a kind of architectural vastness. (2.390–1)

Isabel appears to receive a respite from a consciousness that acts and directs; here her thoughts are "vague"; her normally keen eyes, "sightless." The course of her thought is indirect and "pathless." And though she does not see a clear path yet, James represents her seeing "truth," "meaning" and "horror" as a structure whose "architectural vastness" she cannot ignore. Isabel's bewilderment consists in finding that "horror" is as integral a part of the structure as "truth." Thus figured, consciousness becomes an unwelcome faculty whose only interruption is death: "She envied Ralph his dying, for if one were thinking of rest that was the most perfect of all. To cease utterly, to give it all up and not know anything more—this idea was as sweet as the vision of a cool bath in a marble tank, in a darkened chamber, in a hot land" (2.391). "Ceasing utterly" is, for Isabel, an evasion of both consciousness and of knowledge; to "not know anything more" is to take a secluded rest. The belabored "vision" of the "cool bath *in* a marble tank, *in* a darkened chamber, *in* a hot land," paradoxically offers what seems like limitless extension, but what is actually a series of images closing in on one another. James makes clear that a cessation of consciousness would mean a negation of the self; he also suggests that such a motion is impossible.

For no matter how vividly Isabel imagines an end to consciousness, James makes even the imagination of an end dependent upon the power of consciousness. Each image present to the reader makes up a portion of Isabel's inward life—the center of the subject of the novel—which is Isabel's consciousness. Thus its ending must leave us "*en l'air*" because, apart from death, a closure of Isabel's consciousness cannot occur. Instead, the portrayal of consciousness, even in the last pages of the novel, continues to be figured ambiguously and continues to veer from a personal to a social faculty. Ironically, when Caspar Goodwood presents himself to Isabel in the famous and final scene of the kiss, he tells her that she must "save what [she] can of her life" (2.434). Yet when Goodwood pushes Isabel to the edge, when his desperate words bring her beyond the imagination of death as a retreat from suffering, to imagine a *life* free from suffering, Isabel regains the full extent of her consciousness and "saves" herself. Isabel, that is, chooses to maintain the history and the self she knows—limited as her independence might be in Rome. She even chooses the freedom to suffer against the unreal life, the blank beginning, that Goodwood offers. First, Goodwood's words open up the world for her, but it is too vast; his "help" comes with an abundance that threatens to submerge her. She thinks: "The world, in truth, had never seemed so large; it seemed to open out, all round her, to take the form of a mighty sea, where she floated in fathomless waters. She had wanted help, and here was help; it had come in a rushing torrent" (2.435). Isabel begins to "sink and sink" rapturously in Goodwood's imagined embrace. During his actual embrace, however, this auspicious sinking turns to drowning: "His kiss was like white lightning, a flash that spread and spread again, and stayed. . . . So she had heard of those wrecked and under water following a train of images before they sink. But when darkness returned she was free" (2.436). The kiss brings bright flashes, "a train of images" that Isabel sees like a drowning person's last visions; the darkness brings freedom and sudden enlightenment:[44]

> She never looked about her; she only darted from the spot. There were lights in the windows of the house; they shone far across the lawn. In an extraordinarily short time—for the distance was considerable—she had moved through the darkness (for she saw nothing) and reached the door. Here only she paused. She looked all about her; she listened a little; then she put her hand on the latch. She had not known where to turn; but she knew now. There was a very straight path. (2.436).

After "floating," "sinking," and moving through darkness, Isabel turns to "a very straight path." James's language here is direct and active: she "darts" from the spot; "moves" swiftly across the lawn; she "reaches" the door; "pauses," and enters. The "straight path" is a literal one—most often read as the route that Isabel takes straight back to the Palazzo Roccanera in Rome. In a narrative that repeatedly comments on the fertile, romantic, tangled course of Isabel's mind, however, this final statement about her "direction" begs interpretation.[45] Consciousness shifts abruptly from the "confusion, the noise of waters" in Isabel's "swimming head" (2.436) to a more direct, composed course. Critics are caught in the question of why Isabel returns to Rome, but we might also read James's final gesture with respect to the metaphors themselves. What, for instance, does this "path" tell us about consciousness? And why must it be "straight"? We remember that it is James too who chooses the "very straight path" as the denouement—the final disentangling of his plot. Nevertheless, consciousness suggests *both* the drowning sensation *and* the straight path that we "know" to take. Fluid, interactive, enigmatic, and transforming, consciousness is also constructed as settled, solid, internal, and direct. By ending with straightness, James reminds us of his brother William's advice for his fiction, promoting "directness" or "straightness in style." James suggests, furthermore, that Isabel learns something about the power of consciousness, that she plumbs its depths even as he creates them for her to explore. If Isabel *began* on a straight path, she might have avoided suffering, but she would also have surrendered freedom. Consciousness, as Isabel comes to understand, cannot bolt the door against the public world; even the innermost sanctuary of personal thought expands to include social relations. As Kristin Boudreau reminds us, Isabel must learn that there is no reality beyond the confines of her community or her history within it.[46] James shows how experience in the world continually transforms his heroine, indicating that he prizes the self's ability to remake itself as much as he esteems the sacredness of individuality. Consciousness materializes out of suffering and comfort alike. Still, James suggests that consciousness might indeed establish a path, a position, a standpoint that, if we refuse to forsake it, will hold the self in place.

## CHAPTER FOUR

# Relations, Receptacles and Worlds of Experience:
## Gendered Metaphors and *The Golden Bowl*

"In general terms, then, whatever differing contents our minds may eventually fill a place with, the place itself is a numerically identical content of the two minds, a piece of common property in which, through which, and over which they join. The receptacle of certain of our experiences being thus common, the experiences themselves might some day become common also. If that day ever did come, our thoughts would terminate in a complete empirical identity, there would be an end, so far as those experiences went, to our discussions about truth. No points of difference appearing, they would have to count as the same."

William James, "A World of Pure Experience"

"Experience, as I see it, is our apprehension and our measure of what happens to us as social creatures—any intelligent report of which has to be based on that apprehension. The picture of the exposed and entangled state is what is required, and there are certainly always plenty of grounds for keeping down the complexities of a picture."

Henry James, *The Art of the Novel*

Whether we encounter them in the psychology and philosophy of William James or the novels of Henry James, metaphors for consciousness in turn-of-the-century American literature make manifest the tension between establishing notions of selfhood and considering possibilities for its transcendence. Specifically, as we have seen in Henry James's *The Portrait of a Lady*, consciousness exists in the pulse between contraction and expansion, inside and outside, nature and culture, the private self and the socialized self. Rather than becoming strained by this tension, moreover, consciousness appears to expand as does the character whose consciousness moves back and forth between these conflicting worlds. Isabel Archer learns that while she craves a consciousness that is inward and sacred, she lives in a social world; she discovers, in other words, that one cannot live one's life as she does her meditative vigil. Then again, the narrative allows her this respite from the tangle of social relations. The frame of the *Portrait* extends, as it were, to provide space for intense, personal self-reflection. Nevertheless, if there is one thing that emerges in the discourse of consciousness from this nineteenth century novel, it is the movement from the personal to the social, the rhetorical gesture away from a self-enclosed consciousness and toward a fluid, interrelational consciousness. More than an inward journey, consciousness becomes both a portrait of the interior life *and* a commentary on the self's place in society. Even though consciousness appears to be irrevocably bound by the idea of the individual (or perhaps we might say that the idea of the individual is bound by the idea of consciousness), making its way into the discussion of consciousness at the turn of the century is the question of social relations.

Looking closely at two texts, one an essay by William James, the other a novel by Henry James (both published in 1904) we can begin to see how metaphors for consciousness enact a social drama, making consciousness an affair of relations. Philosophy and fiction meet upon the ground of consciousness, and yet, it becomes clear that the language of interiority is not adequate for an understanding of the conscious mind and its functions, in either genre. As important as the question of how the mind interacts with itself is the question of how the mind interacts with other minds, how one mind might reach another, what means of communication each has for the thoughts that fill it, where its boundaries lie, which things remain within the mind and which can be shared. This shift, from a focus on the inner self to a preoccupation with relationships, is apparent in William James's essay "A World of Pure Experience" as well as in Henry James's last completed novel, *The Golden Bowl*. While William James's *Essays in Radical Empiricism* make the mind generic—an entity without explicit reference to its cultural context (class, race, gender, ethnicity)—James emphasizes the significance of the mind's status as a social entity in "A World of Pure Experience" because it depends upon its relationship with others. Radically challenging the boundaries of the self, James composes the tantalizing picture of a fusion of minds, a communion of selves, through his metaphorical discourse. It is important to note, however, that despite his attention to the relational aspect of both consciousness and experience, James's philosophy still preserves the sacredness of the individual, still secures a space where the self alone can abide.[1] Significantly, James will maintain the breach between one mind and another—a breach that he calls "absolute,"[2]—while continuing to attend to the ways in which this gap can be fused.

When the notion of self unfastens to include relationships with others, we become aware of the intricacies of these relations whether they are expressed abstractly in the philosophical discourse or with respect to certain characters in the course of a novel. In *The Golden Bowl*, more than in any of Henry James's novels, communication looks like a meeting of minds; relations and relationships, in fact, seem to determine the quality of a character's conscious life. Therefore, we need to open up our understanding of the journey toward self-awareness that guides so many critical readings of the Jamesian novel in order to consider that consciousness is more than an account of the interior life, the self interacting with itself. *The Golden Bowl*, most emphatically, reminds us that the self emerges out of certain social acts, that it is made up of so many experiences, and that consciousness is a product of the performances proceeding from each self.

Both William and Henry James inquire about the nature of identity, alluding to the post-evolutionary debates of their contemporaries over an intrinsic, organic notion of the self (one that science would introduce as definitive), and a variable notion of the self that relies upon certain social frameworks. In their attempts to understand human consciousness and mind, the relation between biology and sexual identity, connections between the body and individual sensibility, turn-of-the-century writers, across genres, ask questions that anticipate current debates over the social construction of identity. The logic that the Jameses and their contemporaries assume, and sometimes confound, carries over into our discussions of the politics of identity. In both cases, writers challenge our conventional understandings of the self and ask where to locate identity—through the body, inside the mind, or in light of social behavior. The dispute revolves around the question of whether or not there is a fundamental core, a true essence that defines a human being. Because consciousness is often designated as both spirit and body, it seems to be a part of a fluxional universe at the same time it furnishes a stronghold for the self.

Questions implicit in the exchanges between philosophy and fiction of the turn-of-the-century resonate conspicuously: Is consciousness intrinsic to the self or dependent upon something outside the self? Might we ground consciousness in biology or is it inevitably bound by the terms of the society in which we live? If we replace "consciousness" with "gender," we hear how the debates of the late nineteenth and early twentieth century repeat themselves. Judith Butler, for instance, argues that gender is an "act" which, like other ritual social dramas, requires a performance that is repeated.[3] What Butler calls the "performance" of gender, she also reminds us, looks dangerously like a natural, preexisting identity mostly because the repetition of the deed or the reenactment of gender reinforces a set of meanings that are already socially established. Emphasizing discourse, its directions and its limitations, helps focus discussions of consciousness and the question of gendered subjectivity. The discourse of gender, like the discourse of consciousness, issues from elaborate metaphors that make its subject appear natural—as well as elusive and mysterious—in order to conceal its reliance upon certain social configurations. The symbolism that pictures the human mind becomes that which constitutes identity; thus a study of the metaphors in both of the Jameses' texts exposes the tension between those enticing and disquieting movements toward transcendence and the ways in which discursive symbols are inevitably bound by social and cultural relations.

In "A World of Pure Experience," William James uses the term "relations" somewhat ambiguously, or at least abstractly, as he writes about human experience through the lens of radical empiricism.[4] Though empiricism may hold that all knowledge is derived from experience, James, the most fundamental of fundamentalists, brings his empiricism to the extreme:

> Empiricism is known as the opposite of rationalism. Rationalism tends to emphasize universals and to make wholes prior to parts in the order of logic as well as in that of being. Empiricism, on the contrary, lays the explanatory stress upon the part, the element, the individual, and treats the whole as a collection and the universal as an abstraction . . . to be radical, an empiricism must neither admit into its constructions any element that is not directly experienced, nor exclude from them any element that is directly experienced. For such a philosophy, *the relations that connect experiences must themselves be experienced relations, and any kind of relation experienced must be accounted as 'real' as anything else in the system.* (ERE, 42)

James first fractures experience: we are looking at the "part," the "element," the "individual" in order to understand the whole; only then can "relations" become the connecting links. While we cannot understand experience apart from relations, it is not so clear whether there is a distinct thing called *an* experience. James's convoluted prose doubles back on itself, calling attention to the attachment between the way relations do their connecting and the fact that such relations must also, always, be experienced in order to be counted as "real." James uses the term "relations" here, I presume, to refer to the way that events, observations, and encounters, are grouped in our minds. But because "relations" serves as the most integral expression in this essay, we can read James's convolutions as disclosing his vexed sense of social relationships—they enhance at the same time they might threaten the individual. James begins by considering the self and its network of associations; he will also address how that self interacts with other minds. James's use of the term, *individual*, resonates, summoning Emersonian rhetoric that establishes the sanctity of the individual. Here the term rubs against, and possibly rends asunder, the idea of relations and continuity that infuses "A World of Pure Experience." What James gives us is a world in which individuals are fundamentally divided from each other, at the same time, he relentlessly insists upon an elaborate system which interlaces these "individuals" together.

"Relations," James tells us, "have different degrees of intimacy. Merely to be 'with' another in a universe of discourse is the most external relation that terms can have." The most intimate, on the other hand, is "the relation experienced between terms that form states of mind, and are immediately conscious of continuing each other" *(ERE,* 44–5). The mind is not an aggregation of discrete units; rather, different "states of mind" overspread each other. James emphasizes this transfusion of mind states as he explains what makes up the self: "The organization of the Self as a system of memories, purposes, strivings, fulfillments, or disappointments, is incidental to this most intimate of all relations, the terms of which seem in many cases actually to compenetrate and suffuse each other's being" *(ERE,* 45). The organization of the individual remains fluid; thus the procession of mind states that *is* the self moves on, changing, shifting constantly. Water symbolism, which James often uses, conveys a sense of relatedness, a fluency among terms: rather than simply touching each other or being connected through their proximity to one another, James imagines the various mind states spreading over each other, steeped in "each other's being." James must create a word, in fact, to show how this process is enacted. The terms actually *"compenetrate,"* by which I suppose he means they jointly diffuse or, completely and mutually, enter through each other; though the word suggests a sexual union as well.

It seems that James is playing with the way that words come together (with their various prefixes and suffixes) as much as trying to understand how mind states do. Indeed, James uses the medium of language, specifically grammar, to make his point about relations: "Philosophy has always turned on grammatical particles. With, near, next, like, from, towards, against, because, for, through, my—these words designate types of conjunctive relations arranged in a roughly ascending order of intimacy and inclusiveness" *(ERE, 45)*. James establishes the order of "intimacy and inclusiveness" amongst prepositions, conjunctions and pronouns; as if these "particles" could themselves show how parts and particles of our minds are connected; as if the mind were specifically structured like language. All of these words forge some sort of relation—whether it be geographical or emotional, causal, comparative, or possessive—mirroring the intimacy of the mind's relations. Despite his desire to invent a system (or something like a grammar) for "relations," James, in fact, finds the universe "chaotic" because "no one single type of connection runs through all the experiences that compose it." Space-relations are inadequate because they do not connect minds into a "regular system," the self-relation is "extremely limited and does not link two different selves together" *(ERE, 46)*. However, James will find a way to "link" these different selves as he constructs a rather bizarre metaphor for the empiricist's universe:

> *Prima facie,* if you should liken the universe of absolute idealism to an aquarium, a crystal globe in which goldfish are swimming, you would have to compare the empiricist universe to something like one of those dried human heads with which the Dyaks of Borneo deck their lodges. The skull forms a solid nucleus; but innumerable feathers, leaves, strings, beads, and loose appendices of every description float and dangle from it, and, save that they terminate in it, seem to have nothing to do with one another. Even so my experiences and yours float and dangle, terminating, it is true, in a nucleus of common perception, but for the most part out of sight and irrelevant and unimaginable to one another. (*ERE,* 47)

The universe of absolute idealism is made of crystal (a clear, brilliant glass), and is shaped like a globe (perfectly round and symmetrical). We can see through to the inside where goldfish are swimming. Seeing the universe of absolute idealism as such, James tells us we would "have to" compare the empiricist's universe to "something like" a dried human skull hanging on the lodge of the Dyaks, a notorious tribe of headhunters. James borrows boldly from the discourse of anthropology, one of the new social sciences emerging in conjunction with the establishment of the science of psychology. Though it is hard to imagine what other image could be "like" this one, James tosses off his metaphor with a cavalier flourish; there is something disturbing, in fact, about the way he constructs this image as if symbols for the mind could be, simultaneously, easily accessible and wildly grotesque. Quite nonchalantly, moreover, James divorces the mind from the body by literally cutting it off at the head. One wonders whether these heads are men's or women's, especially since the figure punctuates James's argument with a sort of savage vehemence. The extravagant ornamentation of the heads might indicate feminine rituals of dress, but the question of sex gets violently obliterated since the bodies once attached to these heads no longer exist.

Certainly, a decapitated head is a strange model for what counts as perception in this elaborate figure. Unlike the crystal globe, the skull is dense, opaque, and impossible to penetrate. Moreover, James pays more attention to what adorns the head—the "innumerable feathers, leaves, strings, beads, and loose appendices of every description"—than he does to the skull itself. He seems to suggest that the mind cannot be contained; if these shrunken heads represent a nucleus of experience, we are somehow always exceeding our own containers. Biological sex does not matter, then, since neither the brain nor the body can sum up identity. The skull's various ornaments furnish "appendices of every description," as if the skull were the text and these dangling pieces, supplements to the main document. These decorative extravagances seem mere surfeit, however, since our experiences do not see each other, do not know each other; nevertheless, they "terminate" in the same place, ending in a "nucleus" that provides a common ground. Presumably, perception is the key to this commonality. But James takes away as much as he gives by indicating that such connections between experiences only allow for an "imperfect intimacy":

> This imperfect intimacy, this bare relation of *withness* between some parts of the sum total of experience and other parts, is the fact that ordinary empiricism over-emphasizes against rationalism, the latter always tending to ignore it unduly. Radical empiricism, on the contrary, is fair to both the unity and the disconnection. It finds no reason for treating either as illusory. (*ERE*, 47)

Though James took for granted the continuity that evolutionary biologists maintained, he would complicate it inexhaustibly; unity *and* disconnection must be maintained and only radical empiricism honors each, resists "treat[ing] either as illusory." Both the unity and the disconnection are real. But these experiences are "irrelevant" to each other except that they meet in a *dead* center. The metaphor of the shrunken heads, therefore, exotic and shocking as it is, does not answer the problem of how minds know each other or are conscious of each other's thoughts and experiences. The image of decapitation also obscures the question of how we perceive our own experience since a shriveled skull does not have the power to see inside itself any more than a crystal bowl can glimpse its own reflection.

Though James is fair to both the unity and the disconnection of "my experiences and your experiences," the essay claims that "forces at work" tend to make the unity greater—one of these elusive forces being "continuity." Underscoring the continuity of all experiences, James points toward the importance of taking relations at their "face value." To take the relation, in other words, "just as we feel it" *(ERE,* 48).[5] James says the most troublesome "conjunctive relation" for philosophy is the "co-conscious transition . . . by which one experience passes into another when both belong to the same self. About the facts there is no question. My experiences and your experiences are 'with' each other in various external ways, but mine pass into mine, and yours pass into yours in a way in which yours and mine never pass into one another" *(ERE,* 47–8). The continuity here is clearly *within* each person's experience; it is not a continuity that transcends the boundaries of the self. James makes clear that "within each of our personal histories, subject, object, interest and purpose are continuous or may be continuous. Personal histories are processes of change in time, and the change itself is one of the things immediately experienced" *(ERE,* 48). Here the "personal" stands in contradistinction to the social; personal identity exists within, remains an inward experience. There is no danger of confusing your experiences for mine. Though I may experience flux in my own experiences, they are always continuous; more importantly, I will never mistake them for your experiences. For James there is "no question" about this. Still, if these experiences are "'with' each other in various external ways," that is, if they are originally connected, we are compelled to ask how they know which way to "pass." Experiences might seem free flowing here, moving in and out of one another; but James makes us aware of boundaries. While he enacts a subtle push, throughout the essay, toward the unity of all experience, James is also adamant about taking the relations we experience for what they are. Ironically, he is concerned that logic and skillful argument—literally that "words"—could make them what they are not:

> [T]o be a radical empiricist means to hold fast to this conjunctive relation of all others [continuous transition or 'change'], for this is the strategic point, the position through which, if a hole be made, all the corruptions of dialectics and all the metaphysical fictions pour into our philosophy. The holding fast to this relation means taking it at its face value, neither less nor more; and to take it at its face value means first of all to take it just as we feel it, and not to confuse ourselves with abstract talk *about* it, involving words that drive us to invent secondary conceptions in order to neutralize their suggestions and to make our actual experience again seem rationally possible. (*ERE*, 48–9)

The crux of radical empiricism is, as we might have anticipated, a relation—a relation that we "feel" and that we must take at "face value," without too much questioning. The relation, apparently self-explanatory, is positioned at a "strategic point" which is a sort of Achilles heel for James's philosophy. If a hole be made, "the corruptions of dialectics"—argumentative words or perhaps too much logic—will pour in, disturbing the "purity" of this world of *pure* experience. Let us not, James consequently implores, confuse ourselves with "abstract talk *about* it" because "words" are no better than "inventions" that neutralize and rationalize "our actual experience." The "actual experience" seems to take on a mysterious quality here, as if words could not record but only counteract its effect. How exactly we should "take" our experience, then, is not clear. James suggests, though, that "feeling" the relation is the best way to experience it; we should take it without attributing words to it. Words only serve to confound us.

James tries to hold an untenable position, considering that his essay, of course, rests on his ability to use words convincingly and, thus, sway his audience toward his philosophy. For though he believes that minds are "turning in a direction" towards radical empiricism, he concedes at the end of this essay: "If they are carried farther by my words, and if then they add their stronger voices to my feebler one, the publication of this essay will have been worth while" (*ERE*, 91). The characteristic dismissal of the strength of his own voice does not diminish James's desire that *his* words will "carry" readers in the proper "direction." Certainly, it is not entirely surprising that James should be attempting to maintain this position—where words are both the necessary tools for one's argument *and* hopelessly inadequate to convey one's thoughts. He must, in some sense, insist upon it in order to maintain the paradox between some fundamental unity of all minds and the utter mystery one mind presents to another. In a similar vein, James will posit that while we have a "shared 'reality'" through which our experiences come together, they remain, at any rate, the experiences of individual minds:

> Round their several objective nuclei, partly shared and common and partly discrete, of the real physical world, innumerable thinkers, pursuing their several lines of physically true cogitation, trace paths that intersect one another only at discontinuous perceptual points, and the rest of the time are quite incongruent; and around all the nuclei of shared 'reality,' as around the Dyak's head of my late metaphor, floats the vast cloud of experiences that are wholly subjective . . . that find not even an ending for themselves in the perceptual world—the mere day-dreams and joys and suffering and wishes of the individual minds. These exist *with* one another, in deed, and with the objective nuclei, but out of them it is probable that to all eternity no interrelated system of any kind will ever be made. (*ERE*, 66)

Applying the language of physics, James presents several "nuclei" around which float our experiences like a "vast cloud." Similar to his Dyak's head, but differing in the sense that these experiences are not connected by their terminating points (as were the beads and feathers attached to the skull), our experiences, this time, are specifically named and can be placed within a social, rather than a purely abstract, context. They are the subjective collection of "mere day-dreams and joy and sufferings and wishes"; still, they float around like the imperceptible particles the physicist studies. Though they exist *with* one another—and with the objective nuclei they surround—their individuality seems to account for the impossibility that an "interrelated system" will ever be made to reveal how they can be understood. The picture that emerges is less sensational than the Dyak's head, yet more attentive to the chaotic nature of human social experience. We are the "innumerable thinkers" whose "several lines" of thinking "trace paths" that intersect with one another, but tend to be quite incongruous. Were we to try, it seems we could not find a pattern that these "paths" create.

The effect of this metaphor of the nuclei and cloud is to leave us a bit dazed. James states, immediately after this metaphor, that the next step in the development of his philosophy is the most critical. His goal is to "carry us safely through the pass" *(ERE, 66)*. The message that there is something dangerous in attempting to understand the phenomenon of "pure experience" seems implicit in James's metaphors. Tracing the paths our minds make is a dizzying task that, considering the "discontinuity" and "incongruities" along the way, might lead us to a deadly gap—an abyss that we must learn to pass or over which we must be "carried." Discussing what he calls "virtual knowledge," James states more explicitly the importance of moving forward (on whatever path), as if we knew we would be safe, and with complete faith in the reality of the relatedness of the terms of our experiences. To illustrate his point, James explains the difference between "knowing as verified and completed, and the same knowing as in transit and on its way" *(ERE, 67–8)*. We are "*virtual* knowers" before we are "certified" to be "actual knowers." The most potent example of our virtual knowledge is our knowledge of our own mortality: "Just so we are 'mortal' all the time, by reason of the virtuality of the inevitable event which will make us so when it shall have come" *(ERE, 68)*. Knowledge, thus, always appears to point forward, assuming a direction; its power is in its effect rather than its actuality.

> Now the immensely greater part of all our knowing never gets beyond this virtual stage. It never gets completed or nailed down. . . . *To continue thinking unchallenged is, ninety-nine times out of a hundred, our practical substitute for knowing in the completed sense.* As each experience runs by cognitive transition into the next one, and we nowhere feel a collision with what we elsewhere count as truth or fact, we commit ourselves to the current as if the port were sure. We live, as it were, upon the front edge of an advancing wave-crest, and our sense of a determinate direction in falling forward is all we cover of the future of our path. (*ERE*, 69).

James accentuates the sense of constant motion and transition by using the progressive tense: "knowing," "thinking," "advancing," "falling." Though the passage is filled with words that imply action, the overriding image is strikingly passive. We may live on the "front edge of an advancing wave-crest," dodging collisions, following the current, still our direction is determined simply by our "falling forward." But perhaps rather than considering this to be passive resignation, James imagines our sallying forward without "knowing" as the ultimate commitment. We must trust in what is at the end of our passage: "we commit ourselves to the current as if the port were sure." The way we live contrasts deeply with the notion that our "knowing" might ever go beyond the virtual stage to be "completed or nailed down." James's mixed metaphor (water cannot be nailed down) here emphasizes the disparity between the transitions we move through and the sense that anything can ever be concluded or arrested.

Water imagery is conducive to James's developing sense that we cannot locate discrete states of our experience; we can only count on their fluidity. James will return, however, to something like his Dyak's head in order to express the seemingly limitless "view" of our experience that we might miss if we were looking for its borders. "Our fields of experience have no more definitive boundaries than have our fields of view. Both are fringed forever by a *more* that continuously develops, and that continuously supersedes them as life proceeds" *(ERE,* 71). The fringe exceeds its boundaries and, like the "innumerable" accessories that hang from the Dyak's head, it suggests that there is something *more*—a something more which "continuously develops" and "continuously supersedes" both the nucleus and the expanse of field. Like the unnamable "something more" whose existence James preserves in his discussion of consciousness in *Principles of Psychology,*[6] these metaphors make experience a growing body, something that cannot quite be captured. Thus the mind is to be understood not as an entity that contains, but rather as an expanding, continuing sequence of experiences and transitions. James states this explicitly as he informs us: "On the principles which I am defending, a 'mind' or 'personal consciousness' is the name for a series of experiences run together by certain definite transitions, and an objective reality is a series of similar experiences knit by different transitions" *(ERE,* 80). Oddly enough, James allows for "definitiveness" in the transitions—as if to warn us, yet again, not to overlook them. Otherwise, edges are irrelevant because one experience "runs" over into another. "Knitted" together, experiences form a fabric or rather, as James calls it earlier in the essay, "the tissue of experience" *(ERE,* 57). This "tissue of experience," a metaphor which brings to mind an intricately woven cloth as well as human tissue, gets stretched in this essay as James imagines an ideal union that comes to be a kind of dwelling place for our minds:

> In general terms, then, whatever differing contents our minds may eventually fill a place with, the place itself is a numerically identical content of the two minds, a piece of common property in which, through which, and over

> which they join. The receptacle of certain of our experiences being thus common, the experiences themselves might some day become common also. If that day ever did come, our thoughts would terminate in a complete empirical identity, there would be an end, so far as *those* experiences went, to our discussions about truth. No points of difference appearing, they would have to count as the same. (*ERE*, 85–6)

James introduces this passage, which also serves as my epigraph, by referring to "your and my mental intercourse with each other." We use the term "intercourse" to express a variety of relations, verbal, social, sexual, which involve communication. Intercourse implies some sort of reciprocal action such that we change places with one another in order to understand what the other is thinking or feeling; thus, we figuratively enter into each other's minds. James, however, will take this prosaic metaphor and extend it; more than "changing places" with each other, in his vision, our minds seem to empty their contents into a common place. Further, James envisions that the "differing contents" of our minds actually "fill a place" outside of each of us, *created* by each of us; a place that becomes common property because it is the overlap of two minds.

James presses against the membrane of the individual as he elaborates on his image: the content of the two minds, which initially "differ[s]," becomes "identical" at this juncture. Identification seems to occur upon release into a "common" space— "in which, through which, and over which" the contents join—suggesting that as individual experience enters the basin, particulars somehow become mingled and mutual. This correspondence between different minds leads to James's musings about the possibility that they might be completely identical one day. Reading this moment, it is difficult to ignore the possibility that such "complete" identification would mean that *our* thoughts, as we understand ourselves to possess them, would not only "terminate in a complete empirical identity," they might simply terminate. Period. In radical empiricism, then, there would seem to be no individual thought. And James comes close to implying that this would be a positive transformation—"discussions about truth" would become unnecessary because "points of difference" would disappear; conflicts could be systematically erased because each mind's experience would "have to count as the same." But perhaps this is taking it further even than James would go. Something must continue to fill this receptacle, after all; that "something" being the contents of minds that continue to experience life. And they experience it, James

makes abundantly clear throughout the essay, with their own perspectives. He will simultaneously insist, however, that the series of
experiences that make up a mind run together, overspread, *compenetrate*, suffuse, continue from, and intersect with the procession of
experience that makes up another mind.

Furthermore, experience itself, James writes, "taken at large, can
grow by its edges. That one moment of it proliferates into the next by
transitions which, whether conjunctive or disjunctive, continue the
experiential tissue. . . . " *(ERE,* 87). Transitions, themselves experienced, bond experiences together. In turn, experience (that intercon-
nective tissue) "grows by its edges"; it is organic; one moment of it
"proliferates" into the next. James will amplify this statement in
order to stress the importance of locating life in these moments of
transition that link our experiences. "Life is in the transitions as
much as in the terms connected; often, indeed, it seems to be there
more emphatically, as if our spurts and sallies forward were the real
firing-line of the battle, were like the thin line of flame advancing
across the dry autumnal field which the farmer proceeds to burn"
*(ERE,* 87). This metaphor, eloquent as it sounds, seems oddly
destructive at first. Our "spurts and sallies forward" exemplify the
transitions in life, but as they are compared to the movements in a
battle—they are its "real" firing line—their motion seems particularly dangerous. This "firing-line" becomes another, equally hazardous,
line of fire as James imagines "the thin line of flame" advancing
across an arid field that a farmer proceeds to burn. It is in this "line"
that we live; its spurts and rushes go before us, literally, to blaze a
trail. And though the fire must burn its path for us, such devastation
is also necessary for the field's regrowth. Perhaps it is this growth to
which James alludes at the end of "A World of Pure Experience." He
imagines that as "trains of experience, once separate, run into one
another" the universe "continually grows in quantity by new experiences that graft themselves upon the older mass" *(ERE,* 90). The
world is renewed, then, and unified through a series of such trans-
plants, as pieces of "experiential tissue" are "grafted" on to one
another.

Envisioning "the world of pure experience" as a place where transitions between experiences become as important as the experiences
themselves, James suggests that we need to understand the self as a
continuous series of such experiences as well as to consider how the
self is continuous with other selves. James's work represents a characteristically modern deployment of personal experience as *the* model
for subjectivity; certainly, the advent of psychology as a life science
on par with evolutionary biology underscores the importance of the

study of the mind at this cultural and historical moment in America. Given the metaphor of the continuum that both sciences share, we might be tempted to trace some sort of evolution in James's own writing from a notion of "consciousness" that appears to be attached to the individual, to a broader view of "experience," to the final flowering into "*pure* experience," a term that opens up to include everything and that indicates a continuity among minds over and above their private consciousnesses. But James's writing always resists such systematic readings; his most thorough defense of any one of these positions contains deliberate gestures to overturn it. As such, this late essay does not elide the notion of a personal consciousness; indeed, James refers us to "the chapters on 'The Stream of Thought' and on 'The Consciousness of Self'" from his own *Principles of Psychology* as he explains the continuity we experience "within each of our personal histories" *(ERE,* 48n). What does happen, however, is that the emphasis on relations brings us to reconsider the self in conjunction with other selves, other minds; to place the self in its social milieu in order to understand the production of personal identity. James invites us to imagine a meeting of minds—he pushes the figurative expression to invite a picture of the literal fact. If our minds were to converge, somehow to establish a common ground or to fill a receptacle, how would such a union transform human relations? Communication, most certainly, would be transformed. We might, in fact, lose our need for language as we know it. After all, if "discussions about truth" cease because we achieve complete identification with another mind, might not all discussion cease? Might we find that we do not need words at all? There seems to be nothing disturbing in this possibility for William James; he continually represents his imagination of the mind as something that exceeds language, is even disabled by language. Thus the great receptacle is filled with our mind's "contents," but is somehow emptied of words. It is an image of complete unity, one might even say closure, for the human mind.

Of course, James represents this complete unity as a hypothesis: "some day" our experiences might become common, shared, and we would count them as "the same." Practically speaking, however, discontinuity is impossible to avoid. When we move from our experiences to someone else's we are moving from "a thing lived to a thing only conceived" *(ERE,* 49). Yet the notion of continuity persists for James if only, as he states, because it confirms the existence of other minds:

> To me the decisive reason in favor of our minds meeting in
> *some* common objects at least is that, unless I make that

> supposition, I have no motive for assuming that your mind
> exists at all. Why do I postulate your mind? Because I see
> your body acting in a certain way. Its gestures, facial move-
> ments, words and conduct generally, are 'expressive' so I
> deem it actuated as my own is, by an inner life like mine.
> (*ERE*, 77)

The back-and-forth motion of James's essay—from an emphasis on
continuity to discontinuity and back again—emerges out of an
attempt to understand the mind in relationship with other minds. The
assumption of a common meeting place is crucial if only because it
allows us to presuppose the reality of other minds besides our own.
We "postulate" another mind because we witness what comes from
another's body. James's justification is strikingly visual: the "outer
life" of the body reveals the "inner life" of the mind. Thus the mind,
in some sense, becomes tangible; and the physical self turns inside
out, or becomes transparent, in order to reveal its interior. We "see"
the mind, that is, through what is "expressive" about the body. A
strange departure from the sexless, genderless, disembodied mind
that floats through this essay, James's attention to the body here star-
tles us because it implies a material self, a subject connected to its
physical casing. But perhaps James wants to suggest that identity is
as fluid and adaptable as those "gestures" and "expressions" that we
daily perform. In that case, the body may be the site upon which
these signs get placed, but it does not seem to limit the possibilities
for self-transformation. Gestures, facial "movements," conduct and,
oddly enough, words (which James slips into this otherwise congru-
ent list) are somehow visible signs issuing from our bodies or
expressed *on* our bodies. The philosopher does not say, however, that
these physical signals the body sends are just as ambiguous a language as the spoken or written word.

James endeavors to control words carefully, though he likewise
cultivates the notion of language as unwieldy and mysterious, like the
various human phenomena he attempts to define. As we have seen,
James's work is preoccupied with the ways that consciousness manifests itself through the complex and abundant "relations" between
minds. Like the invisible particles of physics, however, Jamesian relations appear to consist of theoretical structures outside of a specific
social framework. James attempts, through his abstractions, to keep
the category of mind universal—heads and bodies may exist in this
essay, but they remain ambiguously encoded, functioning generically,
not engaging socially. Thus social categories, such as gender, may be
of importance in William James's philosophy and psychology pre-

cisely by virtue of their absence. Indeed, James's "relations" always remain disembodied; his notion of mind, ungendered. Universalizing experience, James makes the idea of a "shared reality" more plausible; in fact, James comes close to erasing all distinctions inside the "world of pure experience." In that great receptacle two minds become one, discussions cease, and we achieve complete, empirical identification with another. Constructions such as gender or class divisions would appear irrelevant, even invisible. Of course, James's philosophy is, he practically confesses from the outset, never that rigorously clear; even in its loveliest moments, James's language is convoluted and confused just, as he says, life is. Though James speaks theoretically about the mind, and apparently without reference to the social world, he relies upon his own status—his class, race and gender—to give authority to his words. Moreover, when we consider how metaphors for consciousness in philosophy overlap with certain figures in the fictional discourse of this time period, we see that propelling consciousness into the social realm brings with it a critical transformation in our understanding of the self.

In Henry James's *The Golden Bowl*, extraordinary unions take place between the minds of characters and, in some sense, the golden bowl itself will become a symbol for such mergers—something like the "receptacle" William James imagines. But Henry James's late novel is equally attentive to what is difficult and enigmatic about this marriage of minds, and to consequent impediments against complete communication. Henry James also constructs consciousness through social relations. Reading consciousness, accordingly, through the channel of relationships, we notice a conflation of images from William's essay and Henry's novel. The receptacle that William James envisions goes through a metamorphosis in the cramped world of this novel: it is a literal bowl intended as a gift, a metaphorical bowl into which characters spill their desire, an image for the body, and a figure for the mind. Moreover, the discourse of consciousness that philosophy and fiction share shows how, as William would have it, we might postulate another's mind. Indeed, characters in *The Golden Bowl* understand their own minds precisely by imagining the minds of others.[7]

In the Preface, James compares his main character, Maggie Verver, to other "intelligent" heroines, stating that "the Princess, in fine, in addition to feeling everything she has to, and to playing her part just in that proportion, duplicates, as it were, her value and becomes a compositional resource, and of the finest order, as well as a value intrinsic."[8] As the consummate reader of his cast of characters, James indicates that Maggie possesses the ability to interpret the surrounding social and cultural contexts; at the same time, James renders Maggie in such literary terms as to suggest that she becomes a figure for the novel itself. In making Maggie *the* compositional value of his text, James relies upon certain notions of femininity that show consciousness, when attached to a female character, as always "feminine," meaning always superior. A more refined registry, "femininity" in the Jamesian text finds ethereal connections; it correlates with intuition, highly-tuned sensibilities, heightened perceptual abilities.[9]

What becomes apparent in the novel, however, is that James is both relying upon these notions of gender identity and, simultaneously subverting them. For instance, James implies that Maggie, like a text, embodies multiple intricacies as well as fecundity: she is productive and reproductive.[10] Interestingly, while Isabel Archer's fertility is mostly metaphorical, restricted to the garden of her mind (she becomes pregnant, but her body houses a child only for it to die); Maggie Verver gives birth to the Principino, an heir. Moreover, the image of femininity that James composes in *The Golden Bowl* is complicated by the mind/body split. James is preoccupied both with what gestates in the woman's body and with what develops in her mind. As we have seen in *The Portrait of a Lady*, Isabel's garden is quite explicitly an imaginary or spiritual garden; so too, the garden that accommodates itself for the famous pagoda Maggie discovers is entirely fanciful, blossoming out from the inner regions of her mind. That James vacillates between images of enclosure (houses, corridors, locked rooms) and images of openness and growth (gardens) in both of these novels that feature female centers of consciousness, gives us some indication of his ambivalence toward the representation of the female mind. James complicates the familiar cultural associations of mind with masculinity and body with femininity; that is, he reproduces the mind/body dichotomy in addition to revealing the slippage between its terms. Indeed, James plays with notions of reproduction as a textual phenomenon even as he replicates gendered notions of what constitutes consciousness and femininity. The sense that the Princess "duplicates" her value, as James's boasts in his Preface, gestures toward her capacity to give birth, not only to a child, but also to those episodes in the novel where her consciousness produces something outside of herself; a sort of metaphorical monument to her powers of creation. Certainly, part of Maggie's value is precisely compositional; she becomes a part of the composition and a composer herself. Thus, her "value" is aesthetic as well as pragmatic. Adorning and shaping the text, Maggie adds harmony to the piece *and* establishes or "arranges" (to use James's word) proper relationships among characters.

Consciousness, in *The Golden Bowl*, depends upon actions such as "taking things in," identifying with others, arranging relations, seeing through another's eyes. As such, consciousness, for Maggie, is always about other people's consciousnesses. Maggie fits what might seem to be a conventional prescription of femininity perfectly where compliance, passivity and formlessness reign. Yet she also, repeatedly, transgresses these notions of femininity, especially as she learns the art of concealment. Moreover, James's fiction shows both women *and* men occupying this role: Lambert Strether, the perfectly plastic ambassador who is as transformed by Paris as the wayward Chad Newsome, but who cannot seem to act out his own entreaties to "live all you can"; John Marcher whose obsession with waiting for the spring of the "beast" traps him in a passivity that blinds him to the invitation for life and love offered by May Bartram; Ralph Touchett, Isabel Archer's consumptive cousin, whose ailing health confines him to the position of spectator.[11] All of these men—and there are more—reveal the artificial associations that we often attribute to gender.[12]

In *The Golden Bowl*, Maggie Verver will be forced to stretch beyond the supposed confinements of "femininity" as they are presented in passivity, inactivity, enclosures, and protected domesticity. Consequently, what Maggie sees and learns to see is rarely confined to an interior version of the self; instead, consciousness rears itself in the social field. Thus the discourse of consciousness is social, relational, even, ironically, when it is silent. Examining the language that renders consciousness in this novel often leads us to discussions of silence.[13] While James's narrative is certainly about the power of language, in many ways, it is also about what happens when words fail. Though the preoccupation of most Jamesian critics is with silence as an unspoken form of communication, they are also, simultaneously, discussing how meaning is produced and shared, how characters understand each other, and how, or whether, consciousness is communicable. For the troubling thing about silence in *The Golden Bowl* is not simply that it makes meaning problematic; rather, it is that silent meditation is no longer indicative of a closed, interiorized consciousness. One mind can "overhear" what another mind "thinks." Consequently, characters seem to enter in and out of each other's consciousnesses, sometimes without any apparent restrictions.[14] And the character who seems most attentive to these transactions among minds is James's Princess, Maggie Verver. Maggie, in fact, becomes a repository for other characters' thoughts and feelings. The structure of James's narrative, even, supports this impression. If, in part one, Maggie is the only major character through whose consciousness the action and events are never perceived,[15] in part two, her perception appears to replace that of each character—she perceives all. It is no wonder, then, that Maggie resembles both the figures of the golden bowl and the brimming cup, which is too full to carry. Associating Maggie with these receptacles, James reminds us of the fantastic union of minds represented in the receptacle that occupies William's "world" of pure experience. He also reprises the image of the frail feminine vessel that he created in his Preface to *The Portrait of a Lady*.[16] A series of discourses converge in the object of the receptacle: consider that all these objects that contain (receptacle, vessel, bowl, cup) become metaphors for both consciousness *and* femininity; the female mind *and* body; productivity in thought *and* reproductive capacity. The metaphor of an enclosed space is predictable, but its function is not. Maggie is, certainly, trapped inside the metaphors that define her and that, in turn, define femininity, but she also oversteps the bounds of these containers. In fact, though James maintains in his Preface and chapter titles that the narrative of *The Golden Bowl* is equally split between the Prince and the Princess, Maggie appears to subsume the Prince's perspective and acquire the controlling vision of the novel.[17] Maggie's feminine identity, as such, is formulated by her performance of certain duties: she must accommodate what others are thinking; she must see with their eyes, step into their skin, receive and embody their pain.

Maggie is not unlike her father in the first book; even though they appear to understand each other, both father and daughter present selves that are similarly opaque. Indeed, Adam Verver's "innermost secret" is that he likes to fool himself out of a conscience: "Thus had grown in him a little habit—his innermost secret, not confided even to Maggie, though he felt she understood it, as she understood, to his view, everything—thus had shaped itself the innocent trick of occasionally making believe that he had no conscience, or at least that blankness, in the field of duty, did reign for an hour. . . . " (1.126). Maggie, too, craves this blankness, this "blessed, impersonal whiteness" (1.126). The Maggie of the first book is "the person in the world to whom a wrong thing cannot be communicated. It was as if her imagination had been closed to it, her sense altogether sealed." But, as Fanny Assingham predicts, "her sense will have to open" (1.284). Like a tight bud that must eventually flower, or be "deflowered," Maggie's awakening seems both sexual and epistemological. When Maggie's "sense" opens to receive what she has learned to omit, she also discovers that her consciousness must serve a dual purpose: she must confound others in direct proportion to which she herself finds clarity. It is as important to keep others unconscious (especially her father and Charlotte) as it is to preserve her

own consciousness. Fanny Assingham's reading of Maggie is informative here; she tells us that Maggie wants to "save" her father, to
"keep him from her own knowledge" (1.386). Just as she is in the
process of uncovering something, Maggie must make certain to conceal it from others. Fanny imagines Maggie's dawning revelation and
her necessary camouflage:

> 'She has now as never before to keep him unconscious. . . .
> She has to keep touching it up to make it, each day, each
> month, look natural and normal to him; so that—God for-
> give me the comparison!—she's like an old woman who has
> taken to 'painting' and who has to lay it on thicker to carry
> it off with a greater audacity, with a greater impudence
> even, the older she grows.' (1.396)

James's image of the gaudy old woman that paints her skin to look
more "natural" becomes a hideous example of the lessons in imper-
sonation that Maggie has to master. Fanny continues: "I like the idea
of Maggie audacious and impudent—learning to be so to gloss things
over" (1.396), aligning Maggie's actions with grotesque masquerade.
The "natural" is, in fact, a cover-up, a pose, the most flamboyant of
performances. Fanny Assingham's impression of the painted woman
brings to mind an idea of femininity that challenges propriety and
"naturalness." Yet this metaphor does more than challenge the notion
of some "natural" or "real" Maggie—a Maggie without cosmetic
"*rouge*"—it also asks us to imagine what it would mean to uncover
something beyond all the deceptive maneuvers that constitute communication in this novel. Though James's figure of the painted woman
invites us to see gender as artifice—something one paints on—he
seems reluctant to abandon the notion of an essential self and instead
locates it inside the mind. As a consequence, mind is *the* portion of the
self that must remain protected. Implicit in Maggie's deceptive maneuvers, after all, is a fear that her father might, somehow, be able to read
her mind.[18] The mind, in this sense, becomes like a text, dangerously
available for others to peruse.

When Maggie confronts the pagoda, however, the famous image
that opens book two, she must acknowledge that she has encountered
a text she cannot decipher.[19] The pagoda as text constitutes the sum-
mary of consciousnesses that Maggie has attempted to contain; and
even though it issues forth from her mind, she seems incapable of penetrating it. A comparison to William James's essay is elucidating at
this point: the pagoda, in fact, is not unlike the metaphor of the
Dyak's head that James uses to portray the nucleus through which all

of our experiences are connected. Both the pagoda and the shriveled skull are curious images to signal perception. Both are exotic and foreign in relation to the otherwise familiar figures in each text; both impart a feeling of danger though they remain opaque, hermetic, undecipherable. The Dyak's head, like Maggie's pagoda, illustrates the mystery of relations. Unlike the more domesticated metaphor of the receptacle, the dried skull and the "outlandish pagoda" exaggerate the impossibility of communion between selves. As Maggie faces the change in her situation, she witnesses it as a strange tower, rising in front of her; she experiences it with heightened senses: the color, the texture, even the sound of its tinkling silver bells. Still, whether or not she can "read" this multi-faceted text remains another question entirely—one which James's intriguing image forces Maggie finally to consider. It is as if, at the moment the Princess makes note of a change in her "situation," she loses control; and suddenly this cluster of thoughts and feelings, secrets and sensibilities of the other characters "rears" itself as a mysterious, restricted tower.

> It was not till many days had passed that the Princess began to accept the idea of having done, a little, something she was not always doing, or indeed that of having listened to any inward voice that spoke in a new tone. Yet these instinctive postponements of reflection were the fruit, positively, of recognitions and perceptions already active; of the sense, above all, that she had made, at a particular hour, made by the mere touch of her hand, a difference in the situation so long present to her as practically unattackable. This situation had been occupying, for months and months, the very centre of the garden of her life, but it had reared itself there like some strange, tall tower of ivory, or perhaps rather some wonderful, beautiful, but outlandish pagoda, a structure plated with hard, bright porcelain, coloured and figured and adorned, at the overhanging eaves, with silver bells that tinkled, ever so charmingly, when stirred by chance airs. (2.3)

The Princess's awareness comes retrospectively as she begins "to accept the idea" that she has done something different. The "mere touch of her hand" has allowed her to enact a change in her situation, though as the "situation" is figuratively transformed into the pagoda, what becomes most striking about Maggie's relationship to the figure is her inability to gain access to it.

If Maggie's consciousness is a collection of consciousnesses, we are, along with her, looking at what she has produced—she gives birth, in some sense, to a new form of consciousness of which the pagoda is illustrative. Maggie's fertility, as we have seen, is a fertility of mind *and* body. And here we might begin to ask where it is, precisely, that Henry James locates consciousness; and where indeed does he locate gender? Though these are not the same question, they may indeed have the same answer, or at least invite the same ambiguity. If neither consciousness nor gender are located in the body, if they are instead located in the mind, then sex is irrelevant to the question of how consciousness might be afforded feminine or masculine identification. Twisting the question another way, we see how James's metaphors point to a relationship between consciousness and gender. James's text suggests that gender identity, removed as it is from the biological ground of the body, might be a question of each person's perceptions, a question of how we relate to one another, rather than something fixed, something that we take for granted. Thus, Maggie's "femininity" is dependent upon her actions, just as her consciousness is; furthermore, she "performs" her identity as a result of the various impressions she receives and gives. The pagoda is deeply connected to Maggie's conception of herself; and though James's language indicates that the pagoda "reared itself," as if Maggie had nothing to do with its conception, it soon becomes clear that the pagoda is a result of Maggie's "arrangements." *She* "rears" it, then, like a mother raises and nurtures a child.

Nevertheless, the pagoda towers over her—a massive, intimidating structure. Though Maggie has presumably found a way to "attack" the circumstance that was for so long "practically unattackable," she remains estranged from it. Instead, the pagoda imposes itself upon her, sometimes restricting the area in which she lives. "She had walked round and round it—that was what she felt; she had carried on her existence in the space left her for circulation, a space that sometimes seemed ample and sometimes narrow; looking up, all the while, at the fair structure that spread itself out so amply and rose so high, but never quite making out, as yet, where she might have entered had she wished" (2.3). Reminiscent of the house in *The Portrait of a Lady* from which Gilbert Osmond looks down upon Isabel Archer with mocking expectation,[20] Maggie's pagoda presents no feasible entry. She sees "places that must serve, from within, and especially far aloft, as apertures and outlooks," but no door appears "to give access from her convenient garden level" (2.4). Maggie's garden, like Isabel's, represents her mind. But rather than indicating a private space, the pagoda at its center flaunts its inaccessibility as well as its power to confine.[21]

As Maggie steps "unprecedentally near" the pagoda, she begins to realize the consequences of taking such liberties. "The thing might have been, by the distance at which it kept her, a Mahometan mosque, with which no base heretic could take a liberty; there so hung about it the vision of one's putting off one's shoes to enter, and even, verily, of one's paying with one's life if found there as an interloper" (2.4). The sense that Maggie might be found as an "interloper" in her own garden and that she might, therefore, have to "pay with her life" reveals the danger implicit in entering the recesses of one's own consciousness. Maggie's garden contains something more than she can comprehend; it registers in her own mind, leaves its impression, but deciphering its meaning becomes a process that encompasses the whole of Maggie's consideration and, arguably, the whole of book two. If, in our limited access to the Princess in book one, we imagine her experiencing what it means to "take in" everything that she encounters, now it seems she must face what her mind has made of it all. Furthermore, the "ivory tower" now rises on the "social field" (2.6), indicating that the Princess cannot entirely conceal, within a private self, that which her mind creates and contains. The structure, in fact, exposes its social context.

Indeed, this moment where Maggie circles the pagoda in an effort to understand what she has done, "moving for the first time in her life as in the darkening shadow of a false position" (2.6), marks the first of her endeavors to encompass the relationships between the foursome. To do so, she must move in "darkening shadows," cultivate falsehood, and become a "mistress of shades" (2.142). Maggie attempts to collect what should spill into the minds of others, which explains why she so often gets stuck holding a swelling cup. Another figure James uses to express Maggie's gestures toward containment is a structural one, similar to the pagoda, except this time Maggie has access to the doorway. As Maggie sits and waits for her husband to return from Matcham, her unanswered questions "accumulate" until they appear suspended over her:

> They were there, these accumulations; they were like a roomful of confused objects, never as yet 'sorted', which for some time now she had been passing and re-passing, along the corridor of her life. She passed it when she could without opening the door; then, on occasion, she turned the key to throw in a fresh contribution. So it was that she had been getting things out of the way. They rejoined the rest of the confusion; it was as if they found their place, by some instinct of affinity, in the heap. . . . The sight moreover would doubtless have made her stare, had her attention been more free—the sight of the mass of vain things, congruous, incongruous, that awaited every addition. It

> made her in fact, with a vague gasp, turn away, and what
> had further determined this was the final sharp extinction
> of the inward scene by the outward. The quite different
> door had opened and her husband was there. (2.14–15)

These "accumulations of the unanswered," as James also calls them, are reminiscent of Madame Merle's "cluster of appurtenances" that make up the self.[22] The self is not singular, there are always attachments in this model of subjectivity that reveal its vague outline. Like Isabel, Maggie wants to assert an uncluttered self, to "get things out of the way"; but the vision of this storeroom of ambiguity opposes such naked clarity. Maggie avoids opening the door for as long as she can, though her passages back and forth past this room, along the "corridor of her life," seem as potentially confining as her circuit around the pagoda. An apprehensive Maggie contemplates admission to the pagoda; again, as she faces the imagined room, we sense her trepidation to open another such door. The "sight of the mass of vain things, congruous, incongruous" makes her gasp and turn away, as if she could not stand to look at the disorder of her life. For Maggie, the consummate "arranger" (1.258; 2.5; 2.44–5; 2.110), such chaos could devastate the equilibrium she so skillfully maintains. One wonders, just as James constructs this scene, what would happen if someone other than the Princess could witness this "heap" of uncertainties; and just as one wonders this, the scene inside Maggie's mind gets duplicated or rather, transformed, into the scene of her husband opening a "quite different door." The effect of this "sharp extinction of the inward scene for the outward" is to give us the feeling that someone can walk in and out of another's mental space—a space explicitly configured as domestic—just as easily as one can open a door in one's own home.

As James plays with these metaphorical figures—pagodas, cups, rooms and corridors—it becomes clear that they do more than construct consciousness. James's figurative discourse says something about the relationship between consciousness and gender. The metaphors themselves further establish the connection between images of the female body and images of the mind. Because the body in the Jamesian text is rarely overtly sexualized, we can search instead for patterns of activity in consciousness that contribute to the representation of femininity and masculinity. Mind and body get conflated in these moments; thus, in *The Golden Bowl*, entry into private chambers, signaling sexual intimacy, is synonymous with admission into private thoughts. Almost exclusively, the woman's body and the woman's mind become penetrable sites. Male characters remain protected: Mr. Verver is allowed his opacity; Amerigo remains blessedly obtuse. Male sexuality, furthermore, remains an impenetrable front because it is either sterile (as with Adam Verver) or oppressive (as the Prince demonstrates).

James tells us, as he fills out the image of the "corridor of her life," that Maggie pushes the door open "by a mental act" (2.14); Amerigo, however, opens the "real" door to the room where she is sitting and disrupts Maggie's vision with his physical presence. The sudden interruption acts as annihilation—the Prince's entrance extinguishes Maggie's reverie. Ironically, Maggie has been waiting for him, waiting in "a little crouching posture" like a "timid tigress" (2.10); and despite her timidity, she seems ready to lunge. Maggie watches by the fireside to see how her "design" will work: "She had put her thought to the proof, and the proof had shown its edge; this was what was before her, that she was no longer playing with blunt and idle tools, with weapons that didn't cut. There passed across her vision ten times a day the gleam of a bare blade, and at this it was that she most shut her eyes" (2.9–10). The violence inherent in Maggie's growing awareness is both sexual and psychological.[23] She simultaneously nurtures it in her ready posture, and abhors the sight of it as the bare blade repeatedly flashes its edge in front of her.

Amerigo's presence throughout the novel is ominous—his physical, sexualized power over Maggie, unequivocal. He is often represented looming over her or encircling her with his arms. His embrace suppresses the full expression of consciousness for Maggie. Like many of the silent exchanges in the novel, a touch possesses a coercive intensity that demands each character keep his or her place. Amerigo does not challenge Maggie in this instance, though when he approaches, he is "*visibly* uncertain—this was written in the face he for the first minute showed her" (2.15). Maggie labels it embarrassment, and she wonders why he showed himself thus, only to realize that its significance is precisely in revealing her own significance to him: "the question dangled as if it were the key to everything. With the sense of it on the spot, she had felt, overwhelmingly, that she was significant, that so she must instantly strike him, and that this had a kind of violence beyond what she has intended. It was in fact even at the moment not absent from her view that he might easily have made an abject fool of her" (2.15–16). In James's novel, any question might be the "key to everything"; most of these queries, however, "dangle" before us and remain unanswered. Maggie's quick shift, in this instance, from elation to debasement, from seeing her husband recognize her "significance," to imagining him making an "abject fool" of her, comes with a savage turn, as if such blows were the inevitable result of asking questions that undertake to answer all. The effect of Maggie's action goes beyond her "intention," an excess that betokens a certain kind of violence.

Maggie's question: "'Why, why . . . ?'" is expanded to include her imagination of the cup that she can no longer carry, an image that makes her unspoken words to Amerigo resonate with the poignancy of a plea:

> 'Why, why' have I made this evening such a point of our not all dining together? Well, because I've all day been so wanting you alone that I finally couldn't bear it, and that there didn't seem to be any great reason why I should try to. . . . It's all very well, and I perfectly see how beautiful it is, all round; but there comes a day when something snaps, when the full cup, filled to the very brim, begins to flow over. That's what has happened to my need of you—the cup, all day, has been too full to carry. So here I am with it, spilling it over you—and just for the reason that is the reason of my life. After all, I've scarcely to explain to you that I'm as much in love with you as the first hour; except that there are some hours—which I know when they come because they almost frighten me—that show me I'm even more so. They come of themselves—and, ah, they've been coming! After all, after all—!' Some such words as those were what *didn't* ring out, yet it was as if even the unuttered sound had been quenched here in its own quaver. It was where utterance would have broken down by its very weight if he had let it get so far. (2.18–19)[24]

What remains unspoken, what perhaps cannot be uttered, is Maggie's desire. Maggie's silent confession cannot be expressed fully because there seems to be no place in the narrative for her personal desire (here made explicitly sexual). The sense that Maggie must "bear" it all, must "carry the weight" of everyone, as Fanny predicts (1.381), is taken up in this image of her carrying a cup at the point of overflowing. She seems, in some sense, to hold Desire itself—what *everyone* is "so wanting"—in her brimming cup, and therefore, to be responsible for the way that desire plays itself out amongst the entire cast of characters in the novel. What we find happening in this passage, moreover, is that words cannot sustain the weight of desire. Even the sound of it must be "quenched" before it is spoken. Maggie's voiceless appeal gets cut off. She cannot finish her last sentence; "utterance" threatens to break down. The Prince, consequently, ends his wife's silent testimony by holding her close to him, a foreboding gesture that speaks to the importance of containing the self. Maggie's soundless dialogue with the Prince reveals the precariousness of their positions— "a matter of a hair's breadth for the loss of the balance" (2.17). That she is "frightened" by how she feels, that she experiences something "snapping," "breaking," "quavering," as she thinks these words in the presence of her husband, highlights her own need to share the contents of her cup and the Prince's tacit resistance to taking it from her.

After her passage through the garden of her life, Maggie begins to sense that she must keep her blooming consciousness to herself. Though, at the same time, her husband's reception of her new idea— her "plan"—moves her to realize her own power to "do something":

> This consciousness of its having answered with her husband was the uplifting, the sustaining wave. He had 'met' her—so she put it to herself . . . which she wore in her breast as the token of escape for them both. . . . Even at that moment, in fact, her plan had begun to work; she had been, when he brightly reappeared, in the act of plucking it out of the heart of her earnestness—plucking it, in the garden of thought, as if it had been some full-blown flower that she could present to him on the spot. (2.25–6)

James uses naturalistic language and internalizes it in order to collapse distinctions between the material world surrounding her and Maggie's interior life. This moment where the Princess "plucks out of the heart" of her own "earnestness," picks this "flower" to present to Amerigo, rehearses the scene at the balcony as the Prince and Charlotte prepare to go together to Gloucester. Reminding us of the "continuity" of experiences that William James insists upon in radical empiricism, the rehearsal of the figure of the flower and later, of the cup, connects the sexual experiences of at least three of the novel's characters. The uncanny possibility that Charlotte's and the Prince's and Maggie's experiences might be thus continuous with one another threatens the distinct order that Maggie pursues. Such radical continuity also threatens the idea of individuality as well as notions of privacy that underlie the regulation of sexuality in the novel. James tells us that the secret couple will feel their "cup is full"—a cup they "carried and steadied and began, as they tasted it, to praise" (1.356). The flower that the Prince has "only to gather," the flower that is the fragrant, "exquisite day" he wishes to offer Charlotte, like the flower that Charlotte "detaches from her dress" and tosses to the Prince (1.355–7), also becomes this flower that Maggie desires to give her husband. Maggie learns, however, that her offering has to be on the Prince's terms. She cannot easily carry over the fruits of her contemplation in the pagoda garden, the flowers from her "garden of thought." She is repeatedly answered, in this remarkable scene of Amerigo's return, by her husband's smiling, silent embraces. At first, Maggie's release in the arms of her husband is enough to make her feel she is safe: "She gave up, let her idea go, let everything go; her one consciousness was that he was taking her again into his arms. It was not until afterwards that she discriminated as to this; felt how the act operated with him *instead* of the words he hadn't uttered—operated, in his view, as probably better than any words, as always better, in fact, at any time, than anything" (2.28–9). Giving way to the emotional intensity of this moment, Maggie is able, for an instant, to "let go." But this surrender into "one consciousness," the singular consciousness of desire, does not last long. Maggie's discrimination, an explicit act of revision, comes during her reflection on this scene. Oddly enough, she imagines how the Prince must view it, how his silent act operates "in *his* view." At this moment, Maggie is learning to do what she will gradually have to master—she is making the imaginative leap from her own consciousness to someone else's. She is letting the Prince's "view" occupy her mind. So while the Prince embraces her, she is, in fact, embracing and encircling the Prince until she encompasses his view, she beholds his perspective, she possesses his vision.

Maggie's acceptance of Amerigo's touch, her response to it, is "inevitable, foredoomed"; its effect is to make Maggie vulnerable. The Prince's "tenderness" and her own "sensibility" gives Maggie a taste "of a sort of terror of the weakness they produced in her. It was still, for her, that she had positively something to do, and that she mustn't be weak for this, must much rather be strong" (2.29). Irena Auerbach Smith argues that Maggie's power is "'extraordinary' because it derives not from a show of force, but from a show of vulnerability. She learns to speak—fluently—the language of those she dominates rather than thrust her own narrative on them through force."[25] In an assessment of Maggie's transformation in consciousness that speaks directly to this moment at the opening of book two, Smith explains: "In order to understand her private world, Maggie must turn inward and begin to understand herself, but in order to reshape it, she must, armed with her as yet untested powers, direct her energies to a realm outside of herself and begin to understand others."[26] The split between the private and public sector—the personal, innermost self and the social self—reprises gender rifts which say that the feminine must remain private and secluded while the masculine is active and social. James repeatedly traverses, crosses and re-crosses, these lines so that consciousness in *The Golden Bowl* manifests itself in the slippage *between* the interior and the social. We might imagine that Maggie's walk around the pagoda in her figurative garden coincides with a turn "inward" to understand herself. The outward motion consists of her subsequent gestures toward the Prince, as well as her sense that she still has "positively something to do." It is important to note that these motions must occur simultaneously for the Jamesian center of consciousness: Maggie is forced, at once, to look inward *and* outward, to discover herself in the very process of detachment, and precisely in the moments when she endeavors to inhabit the mind of others.

Maggie's "one rule of art," we learn, is "to keep within bounds and not lose her head" (2.33). This "rule," like the equilibrium she tries to maintain, or the constant arranging of partners and of her life, is motivated by and helps to enforce secrecy. James makes clear that Maggie's struggle to keep her head is countered by the immense, sexual potency of Prince Amerigo. When Maggie, "in a final reflection, a reflection out of the heart of which a light flashed for her like a great flower grown in a night" realizes that Amerigo and Charlotte have been "*treating* her . . . proceeding with her—and for that matter, with her father—by a plan that was the exact counterpart of her own" (2.41), she finds, once again, that she needs to reestablish her place. Reviving the figure of the "flower" in Maggie's imagination, James brings her back to her point of origin, the point where her consciousness began to grow, even in the formidable and strange shadow of the pagoda. As a result of her awareness, the Princess continues to struggle between the pull she feels in her attraction to the Prince, and her need to understand what the other couple—her father and Charlotte—are thinking.

Amerigo's embrace represents an attempt to confine Maggie to the limits of her person, to the singular relation between husband and wife. Though the Prince has the power to close her in, Maggie continues to extend herself farther than the arms clasped around her:

> It was in their silence that the others loomed, as she felt; she had had no measure, she afterwards knew, of this duration, but it drew out and out—really to what would have been called in simpler conditions awkwardness—as if she herself were stretching the cord. Ten minutes later, however, in the homeward carriage . . . she was to stretch it almost to breaking. (2.54)

If the "cord" is the delay and the silence, which Maggie stretches during this scene, "almost to breaking," it is also something like a tether binding each couple together. In the homeward carriage, Maggie's exertions against this feeling of being fastened, make her "stretch the cord" to the point of painful strain. Once again, the Prince puts his arm around Maggie, a "demonstration" that brings "the infinite pressure of her whole person to his own. Held accordingly . . . she felt, even more than she felt anything else, that whatever she might do, she mustn't be irresponsible. Yes, she was in his exerted grasp, and she knew what that was; but she was at the same time in the grasp of her conceived responsibility, and the extraordinary thing was that, of the two intensities, the second was presently to become the sharper" (2.56). Being "irresponsible" would mean succumbing to the Prince's "unfailing magic" (2.56), his intimate invitation for her to submit to his caress. Maggie's "conceived responsibility," however, has a hold on her that proves to be stronger than Amerigo's grasp. Nonetheless, the effort it takes for her to obey this second, "sharper" intensity indicates that both alternatives are equally oppressive. Abandoning herself to sexual desire would mean obliteration—it is impossible for Maggie to give in to Amerigo and continue to know where she is. What would seem to be the opposite gesture, preserving herself by incorporating the lives of others, will become as precarious a task.

The conflict, for Maggie, is explicitly rendered as she strives to articulate an idea to Amerigo while he keeps her "in her compressed state" (2.56), close to his side. Even while Maggie is thus confined, she has the sense of "possessing some advantage that, absolutely then and there . . . she might give up or keep" At the same time, she sees that "what her husband's grasp really meant, as her very bones registered, was that she *should* give it up":

> She should have but to lay her head back on his shoulder with a certain movement to make it definite for him that she didn't resist. To this, as they went, every throb of her consciousness prompted her—every throb, that is, but one, the throb of her deeper need to know where she 'really' was. By the time she had uttered the rest of her idea, therefore, she was still keeping her head and intending to keep it; though she was also staring out of the carriage window with eyes into which the tears of suffered pain had risen, indistinguishable, perhaps, happily, in the dusk. She was making an effort that horribly hurt her, and, as she couldn't cry out, her eyes swam in her silence. (2.57)

Maggie's "resistance" is, in this instance, both her salvation and the cause of her pain; it is born of her need to know "where she 'really'" is, and yet, it comes with an aching effort. The mental and the physical become commensurable as the "head" that Maggie refuses to lay on the Prince's shoulder becomes the "head" that she struggles to "keep," as symbolic proof of self-possession. Consciousness becomes a "throbbing" entity as if it spoke for "needs" both psychological and sexual. It is also what allows Maggie to locate herself, to know where she stands, in the midst of the deceptive arrangements surrounding her. Furthermore, control over one's physical being is clearly a part of controlling one's consciousness and, thereby, controlling one's self. When Maggie sits upright in the carriage, "keeping her head and intending to keep it," rather than resting it against the Prince's shoulder, she is refusing to surrender her awareness.

James uses metaphors that suggest that consciousness, as inwardness, should be hidden and contained—such as Maggie's "keeping her head," a crucial, self-imposed gesture to retain composure over herself and her thoughts. Such metaphors also indicate an obsession over the proper expression of "femininity" where female sexuality is obligated to remain restricted or, better yet, invisible. Representations of consciousness and representations of gender are surrounded by similar anxieties. Restrictions appear to be crucial, yet at the same time, other figures in James's narrative imply that consciousness (like sexual desire) cannot be stashed away or kept within bounds. And in a novel that turns upon various levels of adultery and deception, the threat of uncontrolled sexuality pervades. Significantly, it is a threat that gets displaced onto Maggie who, though she does not commit sexual extravagances, is still imagined to be excessive. Certainly, the overflowing cup she often holds is a perfect indication of this excessiveness; another such example occurs at the moment James envisions the relationships between the foursome as a chamber in a house. "They learned fairly to live in the perfunctory; they remained in it as many hours of the day as might be; it took on finally the likeness of some spacious central chamber in a haunted house, a great overarched and overglazed rotunda, where gaiety might reign, but the doors of which opened into sinister circular passages" (2.288). Though the image begins as an enclosed domestic space, indeed, the most insulated, *central* chamber in a house, James accentuates the profuseness of the dwelling with words like "overarched" and "overglazed." It is as if the house swells into a circus tent with a room that exceeds its own capacity, teeming over into doors and passageways. What's more, the house is "haunted." Its rotunda might be a place where "gaiety reigns," but it opens out to "circular" passages that seem dizzying as well as "sinister." James's intricate figures rehearse the terms of consciousness because they reveal how his characters live. In this example from later in the novel, most of the characters have already been exposed, thus they learn to live mechanically and super-ficially, they live "in the perfunctory," craving the interruption of society and its distracting frivolity. We are invited to imagine, howev-er, that something remains hidden in the chamber even as it stands with its doors gaping open.

Fanny Assingham seems to locate something hidden in Maggie's self that pulls us to the other extreme of these metaphorical figures since it coincides with an interiorized version of consciousness. Fanny calls it Maggie's "character," and it is something that the Princess keeps a secret:

> 'What I've always been conscious of is your having con-cealed about you somewhere no small amount of character; quite as much in fact,' Fanny smiled, 'as one could suppose a person of your size able to carry. The only thing was . . . that thanks to your never calling one's attention to it, I had-n't made out much more about it, and should have been vague, above all, as to *where* you carried it or kept it. Somewhere *under*, I should simply have said—like that lit-tle silver cross you once showed me, blest by the Holy Father, that you always wear, out of sight, next to your skin. That relic I've had a glimpse of. . . . But the precious little innermost, say this time little golden, personal nature of you . . . *that* you've never consentingly shown me. I'm not sure that you've ever consentingly shown it to any-one. . . .' (2.112)

Fanny indulges, somewhat humorously, in this sense that Maggie "carries" her character—that she houses "no small amount" of it, more than a person of her size might seem able to carry. Yet the qual-ities comprising Maggie somehow exceed her person. Identity is a function of one's "nature," but one's "nature" is realized as both sub-ject (since it is "personal") and object (because it is something one wears, an adornment that one can show or conceal.) The Princess appears, furthermore, to deny the full assumption of her character. James's representation of Maggie, through Fanny's eyes, as the bearer of her own character, brings us closer to an understanding of how the Princess arrives at a position also to carry the "character" of the Prince, her father and her stepmother. Her "size" belies her capacity to contain all of this; furthermore, Maggie does not call attention to her own character, she keeps it "out of sight" like the little silver cross she wears around her neck. For Fanny, this "relic" speaks for the "precious little innermost" that is Maggie. *That* piece of Maggie, however, that "golden, personal nature" that Fanny names but has never been shown, seems to be even more concealed than the blessed cross under her dress. With such metaphorical figures, James clings to the sense that one's "insides" are what is real, that they are somehow an untouchable, stable source for the self. Yet, as we have seen in our discussion of the intersections between gender and consciousness in *The Golden Bowl*, such identities are upheld by their configurations alone. This picture of the Princess stresses that her value lies in what is hidden, her "precious" and "golden" insides, as it were. Still, nothing in this novel adequately carries or holds anything, whether that vessel be a person trying to embody his or her character, a cup or bowl filled with desire, a chamber that houses our daily lives, or words themselves, which attempt to incorporate meaning.

James's central metaphor in this novel is, of course, his golden bowl; and the wonderful thing about James's bowl is that it represents the perfect container even as it shows the impossibility of containment.[27] We can align the bowl with an impression of consciousness as inwardness because the bowl seems to store meaning inside itself; yet the metaphor of the golden bowl is, as often, spilling over, creating a sense that the contents of one mind are too many to hold. Such an explication is not far from our understanding of the discourse of gender either. The bowl opens up the question of where to locate identity and whether or not it can be stabilized, held on to, contained. In addition we question whether it is the mind or the body that provides an anchor for self-identification, the essence of identity and a locus for relations as they get communicated and expressed. The bowl unites the characters of this novel in a way that brings us back to William James's image of the receptacle in which, over which and through which minds join. As we saw with our discussion of William's essay, once the contents of our minds find their way into the "receptacle," our thoughts are no longer our own. They become common property, erasing individuality. The matter of what a mind can and cannot accommodate without breaking or cracking or overflowing is implicit in the story of the golden bowl.

Though the story of the bowl pervades the entire novel, James inserts two complementary narrative pieces for the discovery of the article, both of which begin as somewhat daring escapades. When Charlotte and the Prince set out to buy something for Maggie in book one, their risk is all in the secrecy of it; Maggie's trek through London in book two is less audacious, but even she has a "shy hope of not going too straight. To wander a little wild is what would truly amuse her" (2.155). Both trips are motivated by a desire to find a gift for a specific social occasion—first as a wedding present for Maggie, and later, as a token for Mr. Verver's birthday. Charlotte and Amerigo do not purchase the bowl for Maggie. Perhaps more importantly, the former lovers do not purchase the bowl for themselves (though Charlotte admires it) because it would have no meaning; it would be, as Charlotte insists, a "*ricordo* of nothing. It has no reference" (1.108).[28] But the bowl, of course, gets "discovered" twice. It is Maggie, finally, who will purchase the bowl from the antiquario's shop, though she cannot offer it as a gift because it has come to mean *everything*. The bowl, bewilderingly, means everything and nothing. It would seem, nonetheless, that Maggie has somehow detected the proper significance of the bowl; for as the Bloomsbury shopman uncovers it before Charlotte and the Prince, he presents his piece, ceremonially, with an august importance. "'My Golden Bowl,' he observed—and it sounded, on his lips, as if it said everything" (1.112). We might presume that he has the same words for Maggie, though James does not detail the scene of her encounter in the small shop as he does Charlotte's and the Prince's. Maggie must ascertain what this "capacious bowl" (2.159) holds through a series of social interactions, rather than receive its meaning in one pronouncement. Moreover, what is striking about Maggie's revelation is that the bowl does not offer its testimony to her alone; she must study it along with the reactions it evokes from other characters.

Maggie's encounter with the bowl invites an increase in consciousness, a fuller knowledge; but this "gilt cup" (2.159), a receptacle that is itself layered with concealment because its old gold covers a cracked crystal, also demands that she achieve expansion through her interactions with other minds. James explicitly contrasts Maggie's expansion of consciousness to his earlier portrait of Isabel Archer who learns about the scheme surrounding her by sitting alone, thinking. As Paul Armstrong argues, "Maggie's process of awakening does involve solitary reverie, but it depends more on another facet of reflexivity. She comes to a more satisfactory awareness of her situation by conversing with others and interpreting the text of what they say and do not say . . . Maggie's awakening is an intersubjective and hermeneutic experience."[29] And so the Princess invites Fanny to observe the bowl and to decode its meaning along with her; she watches as she offers her reading to this other, self-confessed, "woman of imagination" (2.114) and considers what the reflection reveals. As Fanny and Maggie gaze at the bowl, the question of what they "see" becomes imperative. Once Fanny recognizes the piece, "new to her own vision" upon which the Princess will rest her entire theory of the intrigue that surrounds her, Maggie repeatedly asks her friend to take it in. Yet the meaning that comes out of the bowl, an "inscrutable" piece (2.165), which is likewise a "document" (2.165), is imputed by *both* Maggie and Fanny. It is a meaning that seems, in fact, to be exchanged back and forth through the vehicle of the bowl itself. James's language during this scene is primarily focused on the visual.[30] Looking *at* the bowl is somehow looking into it, as if its covered glass were also a crystal ball. Thus, the bowl that failed twice to be a proper gift, bequeaths its own reward to its newest owner.

When Fanny asks what the bowl has to do with the change in her happiness, Maggie says: "It has everything. You'll see" (2.160). Fanny, in turn, finds herself looking at the precious thing, "found herself in fact eyeing it as if, by her dim solicitation, to draw its secret from it rather than suffer the imposition of Maggie's knowledge" (2.167). Knowledge can be gained by looking; but when such knowledge is shared, it becomes an "imposition"—a word that suggests both the obligation that comes with knowing, and the sense that the knowledge issuing from this bowl forms a grand and imposing quantity. Again, William James's sense of what happens to knowledge when it is shared, when it becomes a social commodity, is informative. Given the images in "A World of Pure Experience" that depict intense moments of communion, it would seem that, on the one hand, sharing knowledge is a step toward the ideal union between minds that he imagines. However, knowledge is also transformed as a result of this transaction—thoughts do not appear to be "owned"—and if we lose ownership of our thoughts, we might, in fact, erase their impact. Thinking, as a process the self experiences, might become superfluous. Characters in *The Golden Bowl*, however, are reluctant to relinquish their hold on knowledge, even when it becomes cumbersome. Maggie thinks at one point that "Knowledge, knowledge was a fascination as well as a fear" (2.140); consequently, she will insist upon complete knowledge though it encumbers her, and though she takes it in with dread. As Fanny indicates, gleaning the secret from the bowl itself promises to be less burdensome than receiving its mystery from another person; exchanging truths, sharing thoughts prove to be painful transactions in this novel. Jennifer Travis details what she calls the "cost of injury" in *The Golden Bowl*, arguing convincingly that at the center of the novel is a surprising commerce "defined not by the traffic in aesthetic objects, not even of well-placed persons, but of psychic duress."[31] As if recognizing the danger in human exchange, Maggie and Fanny appear to channel their mutual, albeit tentative, awarenesses through the bowl, depositing their accumulated answers in its "bold, deep hollow" (2.167).

That the bowl breaks, that it is so positively doomed to break because it has a crack, does little to change its significance as a conduit for the thoughts and emotions that surge throughout this scene. Split into three pieces, the bowl still affirms Maggie's knowledge: "she *knew*, and her broken bowl was proof that she knew" (2.183). Moreover, as Maggie reveals the story of the bowl to her husband, *she* becomes the conduit, she holds the key, she carries the knowledge. In this sense, she replaces the broken bowl, taking the shape of a vessel with more profound depths. Suddenly unafraid of knowledge's complications, Maggie enters the Prince's domain in a way that might once have seemed impossible: "Hadn't she fairly got into his labyrinth with him?—wasn't she indeed in the very act of placing herself there, for him, at its centre and core, whence, on that definite orientation and by an instinct all her own, she might securely guide him out of it?" (2.187). Not only does she enter, but she "guides" him out, stressing, in her silent monologue, that it is he who must "look" now. And if Maggie recognizes the maze out of which the Prince must emerge, then she also, undoubtedly, perceives her own course. In addition, *her* passage creates a place where she and the Prince can meet: "It was wonderful how she felt, by the time she had seen herself through this narrow pass, that she had really achieved something—that she was in fine emerging with the prospect a little less contracted. She had done for him, that is, what her instinct enjoined; had laid a basis not merely momentary on which he could meet her" (2.189). Emphasizing the relational aspect of consciousness, James creates what he calls a "moral exchange" here; and though the Princess emerges with "a superior lucidity" over the Prince (2.189), relishes even, "with her sharpest thrill how he was straitened and tied" (2.192), her ability to win control has a double edge. That which is imagined to be contained within the conscious mind is communicated in this scene through a variety of such "exchanges" between husband and wife; and though Maggie passes "in a time incredibly short, from being nothing for him to being all" (2.228), she finds that gaining such control can be as harrowing as it is liberating.

Maggie's coming to consciousness is a direct result of her interactions with other minds, her increased social relations. Once she enters this arena, however, she struggles with her desire to keep something of herself separate, private, safe. This conflict brings us back, once again, to William James and to questions about gender in *The Golden Bowl*; considering the terms of consciousness that "A World of Pure Experience" sets up, we might ask whether the notion of self, with a pure, protected consciousness, is a delusion. At first glance, it seems that William James has made such a consciousness impossible because

everything in the world of pure experience is continuous, fluid, inter-
changeable. If the idea of the autonomous individual is a delusion,
though, it is a delusion that both William and Henry James desperately try to maintain. Uncovering the ways that language manufactures identity through figures of consciousness, as we have noted,
leads us to consider how language manufactures gender identity in
*The Golden Bowl.* Because their discourses intersect, we can see the
social entanglements that contribute to the representation of both
gender and consciousness; however, Henry James seems especially
reluctant to give over the category of mind, and instead, surrounds it
with calculated mystery. Because it can never precisely be named, the
metaphors sustain the illusion, making consciousness that which is
impossible to surround or delineate, completely. To this end, James
depicts Maggie's consciousness as if it were split into parts that can
be shared as well as certain portions that only she might "visit."
"Maggie inwardly lived in a consciousness that she could but partly
open even to so good a friend [Fanny], and her own visitation of the
fuller expanse of which was for that matter still going on. They had
been duskier still, however, these recesses of her imagination—that,
no doubt, was what might at present be said for them" (2.219).
Living "inwardly," leaving something of one's consciousness closed—
both gestures focus on keeping the self sealed off from others. The
"dusky recesses" of Maggie's imagination seem to be an omen for the
darkness that she will sometimes meet as she attempts to visit the
minds of her father, the Prince and Charlotte. Indeed, Maggie learns
to penetrate her own consciousness at the same time as she uncovers
the layers of others' consciousnesses; thus she is as likely, in this dual
journey, to find beauty as she is to discover depravity.

Maggie alone discerns the value of entering into another's experience. She tells her father: "'One must always . . . have some imagination of the states of others'" (2.258).[32] It is Maggie's peculiar gift,
one that brings her triumph as well as tragedy, to have just such an
imagination. The Princess perceives the minds of other characters as
if in an intimate encounter. Though she achieves some degree of
power as a result of her "empathic improvisations,"[33] she also suffers
from this intimacy. Maggie cannot always manipulate the relationships to her advantage. Once she learns completely to inhabit something outside of herself, she finds herself unintentionally immersed in
the mind of another character. Once again, Maggie staves off her own
desire in order that she might occupy the scene of someone else's consciousness: "There were hours enough, lonely hours, in which she let
dignity go; then there were others when, clinging with her winged
concentration to some deep cell of her heart, she stored away her

hived tenderness as if she had gathered it all from flowers" (2.281). The intensity with which Maggie "stores away" her tenderness—here made sweet like honey—ironically, makes way for an excruciating awareness of Charlotte's misery.

> She saw her, face to face with the Prince, take from him the chill of his stiffest admonition, with the possibilities of deeper difficulty that it represented for each. She heard her ask, irritated and sombre, what tone, in God's name—since her bravery didn't suit him—she *was* then to adopt; and by the way of a fantastic flight of divination she heard Amerigo reply, in a voice of which every fine note, familiar and admirable, came home to her, that one must really manage such prudences a little for one's self. It was positive in the Princess that, for this, she breathed Charlotte's cold air—turned away from him in it with her, turned with her, in growing compassion, this way and that, hovered behind her while she felt her ask herself where then she should rest. (2.282)

The confusion of pronouns at the end of this passage enhances the feeling that Charlotte's consciousness gets transposed onto Maggie's; or rather, that the Princess becomes a translucent site through which we see other characters interact. But instead of becoming invisible, the Princess seems omnipresent; she serves as the locus of relationships in the novel, a capacious cavern in which their voices echo.

Maggie, in this "flight of divination," "turns away" from the Prince *along with* his spurned lover. Then, remarkably, she steps into Charlotte's place: she "breathes" her air as she "hovers behind her"; she "feels" Charlotte ask herself a question; she experiences *her* uncertainty in the face of the Prince's rebuff. If the Princess envisions Charlotte in a gilded cage, it is because she "understood the nature of cages" (2.229). When the imprisoned "creature" escapes, Maggie continues attentively waiting. The narrator interposes, revealing a moment of total communion between the two women: "If, as I say, her attention now, day after day, so circled and hovered, it found itself arrested for certain passages during which she absolutely looked with Charlotte's grave eyes" (2.283). It is difficult to tell, in this moment, whether "looking with" Charlotte's eyes empowers Maggie or imprisons her. Significantly, her attention is "arrested" when she "sees" with this other woman's eyes. Thus she moves from a position of surveillance— "circling and hovering"—to something like confinement behind the gaze of her rival. And yet, it is precisely because

Maggie can permeate Charlotte's thoughts and preempt Charlotte's vision, that she expands her own consciousness. We must ask ourselves, however, whether it matters that these two "creatures," experiencing such mental anguish, are women. What is the admission price for the Jamesian woman who enters the arena of consciousness? Because an expansion of perception borders on cruelty, both taken and given, it seems as if the expense of consciousness, for the Jamesian heroine, cannot be divorced from intense suffering.[34] Thus, at this moment in *The Golden Bowl*, an amplification of consciousness invites, or at least cannot avoid, something as hideous as Charlotte's cry. "[I]ts quaver was doubtless for conscious ears only, but there were verily thirty seconds during which it sounded, for our young woman, like the shriek of a soul in pain" (2.292).[35] The Princess can enter into Charlotte's experience, hear her inaudible scream, see with her eyes, feel her pain, detect her thoughts. Yet in order to appoint Charlotte victim, Maggie must occupy the role herself, compromising her authority at the same time she exercises it.

Maggie finds herself, similarly, entering the Prince's thoughts with a presence so potent that it is almost physical. In an extraordinary mental encounter, the Princess meets the Prince, as it were, when she creeps restlessly about her house because she cannot sleep. The Prince, residing at Portland Place for the night, nevertheless enters Maggie's "rosily coloured" vision. Amerigo goes, ostensibly, to "arrange" some books that he has purchased:

> But when her imagination tracked him to the dusty town, to the house where drawn blinds and pale shrouds, where a caretaker and a kitchenmaid were alone in possession, it wasn't to see him, in his shirt-sleeves, unpacking battered boxes. She saw him, in truth, less easily beguiled—saw him wander, in the closed dusky rooms, from place to place. . . . She made him out as liking better than anything to be alone with his thoughts. Being herself connected with his thoughts, she continued to believe, more than she had ever been, it was thereby as a good deal as if he were alone with *her*. She made him out as resting so from that constant strain of the perfunctory to which he was exposed at Fawns. . . . (2.293–4)

Maggie's "imagination" trails Amerigo to the precise place where he should be. Yet when she pursues her husband thus, tracing the path that he ought to have taken, it is not to "see" him as she expected. But Maggie is capable of more than simply "tracking" him to the "dusty town" and the shrouded house. She sees him wandering, much like she herself wanders, in the middle of the night; "connected to his thoughts," she even enters the "closed dusky rooms" with him. Though Maggie is sensitive to the Prince's desire to "be alone with his thoughts," she does not allow him to remain in solitude. James states twice "she made him out as," as if to say that Maggie's traveling imagination does more than establish fantastic connections: she is the maker of this moment. The Prince may want to "rest" from the "strain of the perfunctory," but he cannot rest from his wife's presence. She is joined to his thoughts; therefore, "being alone with his thoughts" is the same thing as being alone with his wife. Intimacy, in any case, remains portentous and inescapable.

This moment shows Maggie pursuing her prince to the point of attaching herself to his mind, thereby conflating mental and physical space. And if the Princess "sinks to her knees" after this moment of communion with her husband, it is because she sees something she cannot bear: she "sees" Amerigo's idea. "[S]he blinded her eyes from the full flare of seeing that his idea could only be to wait, whatever might come, at her side. It was to her buried face that she thus, for a long time, felt him draw nearest; though after a while, when the strange wail of the gallery began to repeat its inevitable echo, she was conscious of how that brought out his pale hard grimace" (2.295). Foreshadowing the final scene, this imagined embrace, concluding Maggie's imaginative journey to Amerigo's side, hints at the impossibility both of closure and complete communication between the two. Maggie simultaneously "sees" his idea and wants to "blind" her eyes when confronted with it. When the Prince "draws near" her, she becomes conscious, not of sympathy in his expression, but of his "hard, pale grimace." The entire scene, though it is imagined, indeed *because* it is imagined, gives Maggie an intensely vivid, almost brutal indication of what will come in her final union with the Prince. Maggie's imagination provides her with the connective tissue for the variety of relationships that she encounters. She must, for example, experience conversations with the Prince fantastically in order to determine where she stands with him. When her imagination cannot supply the link, James indicates that she herself settles into the crack: "What was clearest always in our young woman's imaginings was the sense of being herself left for any occasion in the breach. She was essentially there to bear the burden, in the last resort, of surrounding omissions and evasions . . . ." (2.302). The image of Maggie as a bridge, a conveyance that covers a wide breach, or holds things together in the same way that her hands fuse the segments of the cracked bowl, also symbolizes her dexterity in keeping things suspended. Though a moment like this seems to intensify the impression of Maggie as victim, her position in the narrative is more ambivalent: James may rely on gendered views of femininity which decree that the female must be rescued, but he as often overturns them to reveal the lapse between characteristically masculine and feminine notions of identity. James's princess does more than bear the "burden" of others' consciousnesses. Indeed, Maggie learns that having the capacity to "hold" the pieces together—the pieces of the bowl, the pieces of her life—also means having the capacity to control and to transform the lives around her.

The scene that closes *The Golden Bowl* brings to bear the issues surrounding relationships and consciousness that both Henry and William James address. In this final episode of the narrative, consciousness manifests itself in an exchange between the Prince and Princess. We are prepared for this ending, in some sense, by the momentous meeting between Fanny and the Princess over the golden bowl. When Maggie invites Fanny Assingham into her private chamber to face the object that has so amplified her consciousness, she bids her to participate in a peculiar intimacy. Together, the two women stand, imputing knowledge, reading the vessel, reading each other, understanding the truth of their situation, through the medium of the bowl. But by the end of the novel, the Prince and Princess have cleared the deck—the bowl is gone, the Ververs have left the country, even the Principino is conveniently removed—so that Maggie is face to face with the consequences of her sacrifice.

> Here it was, then, the moment, the golden fruit that had shone from afar; only, what *were* these things in the fact, for the hand and for the lips, when tested, when tasted—what were they as reward? Closer than she had ever been to the measure of her course and the full face of her act, she had an instant of the terror that, when there has been suspense, always precedes, on the part of the creature to be paid, the certification of the amount. (2.367)

What Maggie will take and what she will give get somewhat confused during the culmination of her union with the Prince. The omnipresent golden bowl, a gift that is intended for a number of people, a gift that never gets delivered, is here rendered as the "golden fruit." But Maggie is left questioning what this fruit really winds up being, or rather, what it is she ends up holding—when "tested," when "tasted," it is an equivocal reward at best.

In the scene with her friend, Fanny Assingham, Maggie repeatedly summons the bowl as her source: she uses her newly acquired piece as a means of communication; she speaks through it and for it, giving voice to its silent witness. At the end, thoroughly alone with her husband, taking in "her reason for what she had done," she has little use for words. "All she now knew accordingly was that she should be ashamed to listen to the uttered word; all, that is, but that she might dispose of it on the spot for ever" (2.368). Perhaps this moment of final communion—like the moment that William James entertains where our thoughts meet until they fill a vast receptacle—brings an end to speech, to discussions, to difference. Perhaps the crossing and re-crossing of gender lines in *The Golden Bowl* allows Maggie and the Prince to change places, to create a space untouched by social patterns. Perhaps as the Prince "takes in" what Maggie so wonderfully gives, their identification with each other is so absolute that their vision becomes one vision. Most critics read this last scene as a final statement on Maggie's consciousness or her vision.[36] Linking this concluding image to William James's idea of the coupling of minds, however, we cannot forget that dwelling in the receptacle means dwelling in the possibility that individual thought might terminate. If, as William writes, our thoughts "terminate in a complete empirical identity" at the moment they become "common property," then the notion of the individual gets fundamentally elided. This moment in *The Golden Bowl* provides an uncanny conclusion to the quest for self-definition that the works of both William and Henry James enact—any definitive idea of selfhood, any clearly defined concept of the individual, is forfeited. A better way to put it might be that the concept of the individual unravels, revealing the jumble of rhetorical arrangements, constructed relations, social configurations that constitute what we call the self. And though the same figurative language that builds identities also systematically deconstructs them—whether that language generates gender or consciousness through its discursive apparatus—we still read these moments as representative of ourselves. At any rate, the frustrating ambivalence of the novel's ending leaves us decidedly uncertain about how to understand the union of husband and wife, symbolized by their embrace. In turning away from the Prince's eyes—eyes with which, he insists, he sees "nothing" except his wife—Maggie may be resisting this inexorable push toward a commonality of minds. Characters in *The Golden Bowl* might approach something like William James's imagination of complete continuity among minds, but they are always only on the edge; they touch, so to speak, the rim of the bowl without settling into it. Henry's novels, like William's philosophy, thus move back and forth between a reliance

upon figurative language to depict their ideas of human consciousness and experience, and the belief that language can never be adequate to the task of explaining all human phenomena. Indeed, both
writers must insist on language's nonequivalence in order to create
consciousness as an elusive entity and in order to create the self as
something that is not completely, not transparently, figured out.[37]

The experience of human intimacy that James depicts at the out-
come of *The Golden Bowl* suggests that consciousness is realized
through relations. James's last completed novel sustains the tension
between preserving or protecting a consciousness that is inward,
sacred, and all for oneself and learning that such a construction cannot exist nor survive on its own because the self is socialized, attends
to customs, enters institutions, relationships, even conversation.
Maggie Verver learns, just as every Jamesian character seems destined
to learn, that one cannot live one's life in the private garden of one's
mind. Consciousness, so internalized and self-enclosed, does not
appear to allow for relationships or for love. Jamesian consciousness
must integrate, must, indeed, accommodate itself to include social
relations. Hence, James's concluding scene hinges upon an exchange:
at the same time the Prince encloses the Princess in his arms, she
encompasses him and provides him with his vision, as if each were
attempting to possess the other. Though this Jamesian heroine repeatedly bridges the gap between other minds and her own, she finds that
her consciousness cannot wholly penetrate another mind to allow for
total communion. Despite Maggie's ability to make herself a conduit
for the thoughts of others, in the end, the only mind she possesses is
her own. A mind constituted by the very same discursive forces that
reveal the contingency between subjectivity and social relations.

## CHAPTER FIVE

# Designing Our Interiors:
## Self-Consciousness and Social Awareness in Edith Wharton's *The House of Mirth*

> "I believe I know the only cure, which is to make one's center of life inside of one's self, not selfishly or excludingly, but with a kind of unassailable serenity—to decorate one's inner house so richly that one is content there, glad to welcome anyone who wants to come and stay, but happy all the same when one is inevitably alone."
>
> Edith Wharton

Much of the energy of Henry James's novels, as we have seen, centers on balancing oppositions, especially rhetorical ones. Conflicting, diametric, antithetical, James's metaphors explicitly generate the intensity of opposition. Because the culture at large shapes his metaphorical figures, James's elaborate designs sometimes elude him. Yet he still attempts to reorder his fictional world as he concludes and thus establish a secure vocabulary for the self, anchoring subjectivity so that we might know, as he so often phrases it, where we are. Though her work also sustains the contest of metaphors that the Jamesian novel illustrates, Wharton dramatizes the conflict over the question of consciousness, suggesting that it is precisely in the linguistic flux that we come to understand subjectivity. Moreover, the social valence of figures for consciousness escalates in Edith Wharton's novels because Wharton focuses, specifically, on the contest between a defining interior life and a socially constructed self. The exclusive sanctuary of the individual mind exposes its permeability the moment Wharton insists that neither social nor personal space have an absolute border.

In *The House of Mirth* (1905), as in most of her fiction, Edith Wharton uses cultural possessions such as houses not only to build the interior life of particular characters, but also to secure and preserve

social class.[1] Wharton erects houses as definitive representations of
the self and its place in society; that is, Wharton produces a concept
of the self through metaphors of drastically interiorized structures
and perfect enclosures. Social markers, therefore, provide Wharton
with a measure for the mind and a vocabulary for consciousness. But
despite evidence that society engenders the subject, Wharton's texts
contain repeated, paradoxical attempts to endorse an authentic self,
which might transcend social configurations. My epigraph, which
comes from one of Wharton's letters, reveals this paradox.[2] For the
moment one's "inner house" welcomes visitors, that seemingly exclusive center of "serenity" becomes, simultaneously, a private and a
public sphere. One must, Wharton writes, be glad to welcome *anyone*
interested in entering this presumably "unassailable" core. Thus
Wharton's metaphor breaks open, even as it asserts its impregnabili-
ty, at the prospect of social intercourse.[3] Her fiction, likewise, reveals
the impossibility of separating the self from its cultural furnishings at
the same time her texts designate that very self as an individual subject.
Wharton's fiction, we might imagine, answers Henry James's creation of
the highly crafted center of consciousness and likewise situates itself
amongst a host of American writers who designate the mind as consecrated space, the individual as an inviolate, compelling center.
Wharton dismantles the view of the mind as a builder of its own private
world as she designs consciousness through metaphors that combine
protected interiors with social domains. Locating the seat of consciousness in Wharton's fictional spaces, therefore, remains difficult. Rather
than meticulously establishing the life within, Wharton's novels
extend the self, challenging any stable notions of inwardness through
constant attention to the current of the social world.

While the question of essential selfhood breaks along the lines of
the personal and the social in Edith Wharton's novels, her work also
accentuates the ways in which this alluring idea of a "real self" splits
along gender lines. Even when women occupy the central position in
her novels, Wharton resists making their minds the center of her
story; instead, her fiction maintains a social center around which
female activity and feminine articles revolve. When the self *is* social
relations, when it materializes as an item from the cultural world such
as art, clothing, jewelry, fabric, we might question whether it could
depreciate or even deteriorate. One wonders to what extent Wharton
was aware of her own precarious relationship to this dynamic,
revealed as it is in her first attempt at writing—a guidebook for the
decoration of houses.[4] In *The House of Mirth*, a woman's clothing,
her social position, her public behavior, the manner in which she carries herself, all appear to anchor society, to formulate social class, and

in turn, to bring individual consciousness into being. Contrary to this model, as we have seen, stands the James novel; Henry James's fiction explicitly resists such identification of the self through social and cultural fixtures. Many of James's women express indifference to the elements of the social world such as houses, clothing and money, even though the Jamesian novel depicts a social scene riddled with, indeed dependent upon, a wealth of material goods. *The Portrait of a Lady*'s Isabel Archer, in a famous instance, provides a negative inventory of the self, insisting that nothing outside of her expresses who she is.[5] Yet, as I have argued, Isabel's neatly framed self-portrait eventually explodes and the language, consequently, shifts in order to execute consciousness as a social drama. *The Golden Bowl*, more explicitly, reveals this movement from a self-enclosed consciousness to a social, interrelational consciousness, still fixing women as the hinge upon which such a motion depends. Wharton's fiction responds to the notion of the individual instituted in a host of American texts of the nineteenth and early twentieth century precisely through metaphors that collapse boundaries between the personal and the social. At the same time, Wharton's novels express the author's own anxiety about the relationship between metaphysical categories linked to the self and social categories such as gender and social class. Wharton's work, consequently, invites us to consider questions about the discourse of consciousness as it becomes implicated in debates over what constitutes personal identity.

Certainly, Wharton experiences characteristic ambiguity over whether or not there exists an adequate language to define, or perhaps *confine*, the self in its interior realm; but even these deliberations presuppose that there is a self, *per se*, to outline. As we saw in the philosophy of William James and the novels of Henry James, exclusively interiorized language inevitably explodes to reveal a tangle of relations; consciousness accordingly materializes through social encounters. Both William and Henry James craft metaphors of enclosure, which they then insist, will not sufficiently accommodate the elusive versions of self and mind that they cultivate. William James, in one instance, attempts to capture the ever-changing quantity of human experience by domesticating it. He constructs a metaphor, which enhances our sense that consciousness is interiorized, closed off from the rest of the world: it is the mind with a house inside.[6] Henry James employs narrow hallways, doors with slippery bolts, cups, chambers, and cages as containers for the self. Indeed, his famous "house of fiction" seems to preside over each of his narratives—foreboding, imposing, encompassing, but because of his attention to its many windows, somehow a structure more open than closed.[7] The Jameses, as

I have elsewhere suggested, capitalize on the metaphor of the self and the mind as house, often pointing inward, as if in an effort to contain meaning rather than allow for its germination. What we find, of course, is that metaphors are always fraught with meaning, they always multiply, and both Henry and William James become particularly anxious about controlling these multiplications. Wharton's work reveals similar anxieties, though she seems to move back and forth more fluidly between possibilities. Consequently, she expands the field upon which we might ask questions about self-consciousness and identity. Indeed, her texts seem to invite fluctuations over meaning as if to suggest that it may be in the vacillation itself that we find our answers.

In the Wharton text houses signify a heightened cultural consciousness in that they announce social status, establish families, exclude marginal individuals; in addition, houses become models for the architecture of the mind. The house embodies those ruling forces of manners, rituals, and social customs, which, Wharton insists, occasion the self. Wharton lays bare the social meaning of houses. At the same time she challenges the privacy of any inner realm, though, she also yearns for the serenity that might come inside it. Perhaps the most striking aspect of Wharton's novels is, in fact, our sense that the self cannot escape being implicated in the outside world. When the mind or the self materializes into a house, it is as if its chambers open automatically and we immediately invite the prospect of social exchange. Indeed, Wharton scarcely entertains the possibility that consciousness might be an inviolate, individualized entity or function—a possibility both of the Jameses continually, if equivocally, hold. And though Wharton's metaphor of the "inner house" reveals that she too domesticates the mind with a rather insouciant spirit, inhabiting the world of the mind, exclusively, remains a ticklish feat for the Wharton character: self-reflection is an indulgence or a nuisance or a torment. Her characters are not allowed a refuge from social affairs—her characters *are* their social affairs—in addition, the self hardly seems a welcome place in which to seek asylum. Wharton provides no idealized moments of self-communion, and though we can sometimes find that hidden, sacred room of one's own in her stories, the space is not rejuvenating or healing, but rather, brings a solitude commensurate with loneliness, pain and even death.

Despite any individual character's efforts to disentangle him or herself from the society represented in Wharton's fiction, outside of the social matrix, there might seem to be no self at all.[8] This, at least, is what Wharton sometimes suggests; but her texts are conflicted over this issue, they resist settling upon any one answer. Identity, therefore, remains in perpetual transition.[9] In the novels of Edith Wharton, the discourse for consciousness becomes a language fluid and supple enough to maneuver in and out of intricate caches that lure us with the possibility of self-containment—houses, brains, bodies, books—as well as flexible enough to accommodate itself to different social situations. *The House of Mirth* presents its heroine, a lily in full bloom, in all the flush of her beauty and self-centeredness—a quality that indicates the ultimate irony of the text, for Lily Bart seems to have no "center." If she does, it is the artful cluster of relationships she has accumulated in the hopes of securing a social position for her "self" as a wife. Tracing her history, from the plush drawing rooms of the wealthy set to the room in her shabby boarding house, Wharton makes clear that, for Lily, consciousness remains that room that she cannot enter, the edge of which she reaches without quite crossing the threshold; though Lily approaches this threshold repeatedly, persistently, perversely.[10] Still, in her early novel, Wharton renders the reality of consciousness and the material of the self, alluring, though bare, possibilities. In *The Age of Innocence* (1920) Wharton will dispute the notion of a stimulating interior life; however, consciousness, in the later novel, fails to insulate the self because the mind is too accessible. Newland Archer, the central character, cannot close his consciousness to others nor assume it as personal property. Like the mind reading that constitutes consciousness in *The Golden Bowl*, Wharton's Pulitzer prize-winning novel shows a communion of minds. But the sense that one's thoughts can be "read" instigates, more profoundly, the loss of any autonomous self. Wharton, throughout her fiction, conceives of individual consciousness as emerging out of society, yet she seems unwilling to forfeit claims of privacy and seclusion for the individual in her recurring figures of the self's interior.

Wharton writes out of a tradition of philosophy and psychology in the midst of speculations over where to locate identity; most often, identity settles within the mind which makes the self a sacred, private entity. Because the mind provides no tangible matter, no specific bearings, its elusiveness conveys its exclusiveness. Consistently in her novels, Wharton refers to what she calls a "real self," an entity that appears to exist without reference or attachment to anything social, though she simultaneously establishes a network of connections between such selves and their environment. Personal consciousness fuses with social awareness until they emerge as one discursive entity. In this sense, Wharton's work anticipates debates between essentialism, which relies upon some natural, irreducible "essence" for human identity and the social construction of identity.[11] While Wharton seems to have no faith in symbols—items from the social world always fail to elucidate the rhetorically persistent "real self"—she cannot, finally, discard the social from her understanding of the self. Though she proudly identifies herself with philosophers and scientific writers, when Wharton crafts her idea of individual consciousness, she resorts to the objects and tokens that surround her, items traditionally defined as "feminine." Despite her distaste for domestic fiction, she produces consciousness out of an explicitly domestic and social sphere.[12]

Wharton sometimes authorizes interiorized versions of identity, sometimes challenges them; consequently, her work makes manifest the tension between individuality and social conditioning, a distinction that we continue to dispute in defining subjectivity. Apart from the philosophy and psychology of William James, debates over the social basis of consciousness among social psychologists such as Charles Horton Cooley and George Herbert Mead help to contextualize Wharton's work.[13] Particularly, Mead's writings elucidate the exchanges that took place among Wharton's contemporaries in their attempts to understand the self and the mind in society. For instance, Mead's essay entitled "The Problem of Society—How We Become Selves" argues that the self is attained only as it assumes the attitude and identity of the social group; the self, that is, must become socialized to become itself:

> [T]he human self arises through its ability to take the attitude of the group to which he belongs—because he can talk to himself in terms of the community to which he belongs and lay upon himself the responsibilities that belong to the community; because he can recognize his own duties as over against others—that is what constitutes the self as such. And there you see what we have emphasized, as peculiar to others, that which is both individual and which is habitual. The structure of society lies in these social habits, and only in so far as we can take these habits into ourselves can we become selves.[14]

Strikingly, Mead imagines society as antecedent to the self. Indeed, the human self arises only when it incorporates social habits or "takes" them "into" itself. The self and society do not emerge as two separate entities: one emerges out of the other; one must contain the other in order for it to come into being. Some separation appears to exist, however, since the self learns the language of the community. "He" talks it to "himself" in order to understand those things that

constitute the self, namely, "responsibilities" and "duties."
Significantly, the self must heroically forfeit its claims to selfhood for
the good of the community. Indeed, the self emerges at the very
moment it abandons its claims on individuality; thus a literal "self"-
sacrifice becomes the hallmark of the individual inside social psychology. Placing the social community first, Mead's work shows that
the self materializes through the process of social initiation. Mead
does allow for some version of consciousness that he calls the self
"talking to itself"; and elsewhere he states that this conversation, the
"inner flow of speech" that occurs within the self is "what constitutes
his mind."[15]

For George Herbert Mead, the self would develop through language, through the process of thinking, as the self "talks to itself";
this dialogue, however, always grounds itself within the duties and
habits of a certain community. Charles Horton Cooley will reinforce
Mead's theories, emphasizing the way that society, in fact, "makes"
the individual:

> Most people not only think of individuals and society as
> more or less separate and antithetical, but they look upon
> the former as antecedent to the latter. That persons make
> society would be generally admitted as a matter of course;
> but that society makes persons would strike many as a star-
> tling notion. . . . We ordinarily regard society, so far as we
> conceive of it at all, in a vaguely material aspect, as an
> aggregate of physical bodies, not as the vital whole which
> it is; and so, of course, we do not see that it may be as orig-
> inal and causative as anything else. Indeed, many look
> upon 'society' and other general terms as somewhat mysti-
> cal, and are inclined to doubt whether there is any reality
> back of them.[16]

For Cooley, as for Mead, social groups and processes have a life of
their own, they are, as Cooley says elsewhere, "living wholes."[17] We
might be inclined to think of society as only "vaguely material" or as
some "mystical entity" with no reality "back of" it, like a magic show
that uses smoke screens, props and strings. But society is, in fact,
"vital," "original," "causative." Thus, according to Cooley, society
becomes an organic, living being that produces other living beings.
We are naive, he further states, who think that the individual is the
only agent, the only cause of events. Contemporary studies in the
emerging field of social psychology such as George Herbert Mead's
and Charles Horton Cooley's impress themselves upon Wharton's

work. Her novels often ask similar questions about what constitutes self and mind in society: Is there a self that exists apart from society? Does social habit transform or corrupt a "purer," "truer" version of the self? Do social circumstances simply shape the human mind or, more radically, construct it? Might figures for consciousness and the process of thought reveal themselves through figures for the social world? In "'Hunting for the Real': Wharton and the Science of Manners," Nancy Bentley argues that Wharton's work embodies the connection between what she calls the "professional study of culture," which, she reminds us, was established during this period within the disciplines of anthropology, sociology and social psychology, and "scientific knowledge" that, for Wharton, "was indispensable for discovering our 'inward relation to reality.'"[18] And inward reality, more than the province of "material forces and human instincts" crucially includes "the irreducible reality of social forms."[19] Thus manners, customs, rituals, social observances—whether they are of the "civilized" or primitive kind—engender the self.

In *The Writing of Fiction* (1925) Wharton's response to the work of Balzac and Stendhal indicates her theory of how identity originates in social relations, making the reproduction of a person within a text, more like an impressionist painting than a definitive sketch: "[T]hese novelists are the first to seem continuously aware that the bounds of the personality are not reproducible by a sharp black line, but that each of us flows imperceptibly into adjacent people and things."[20] The "bounds" of subjectivity are not "reproducible," in fact; they are "imperceptible." The self has no definitive outline; it remains transitory, possibly even invisible, yet continuously "flowing." In *The House of Mirth*, Lily Bart, appropriately, reveals her distinction while exposing the ambiguous boundaries between herself and others. She is stunning spectacle and appropriate background; a rare species and a crude composite. When Lily Bart makes her entrance, she embodies these contrasts. For Lawrence Selden, her first, and certainly, her principal observer, Lily is a refreshing "sight" mostly because of the way she stands apart from the otherwise dull crowd; but she also appears to blend in because she is made up of the same material as these other, prosaic women. Of course, Lily becomes a baffling element in the world of Wharton's New York society because she systematically moves through every one of its class distinctions until she has crossed all boundaries. She remains, though, somehow conspicuous in and unfit for each social class. In the opening scene of the novel, we hear Selden's confused appraisal of Lily—though he considers her a "highly specialized" specimen, she is also, disturbingly, a mere product of her environment. We follow Selden's thoughts as he notices the points of contrast between Lily and the other women flocking the train station:

> He led her through the throng of returning holiday-makers, past sallow-faced girls in preposterous hats and flat-chested women struggling with paper bundles and palm-leaf fans. Was it possible that she belonged to the same race? The dinginess, the crudity of this average section of womanhood made him feel how highly specialized she was.[21]

Simultaneously fascinated and repulsed by these contrasting species of women, Selden wonders whether the Lily on his arm could actually belong to the same "race" as those other women who are pressed flat, burdened by bundles, and preposterously decked. A fastidious critic, Selden pronounces them, in a word, "dingy." And Lily, a woman who flees dinginess, exists somehow as the refinement of all the average and the crude that one must inevitably meet in railway stations. In this scene, we become aware of the ways in which Selden contributes to the fabrication of Lily as the beautiful, unparalleled object of his gaze. Nevertheless, as Wharton insists, Lily manages her image with the skill of a virtuoso. Artist, actress, expert dramatist, Lily, as critics have repeatedly noted, is extremely invested in herself as an object. Her own best stage manager, Lily is the creator, director, and producer of some of the most striking scenes in the novel.[22]

Selden surmises, immediately upon spying Lily, that her "desultory air," her "air of irresolution" might be the "mask of a very definite purpose" (3). Whether or not Lily might embody dual purposes and plans, the sense that there is something hidden or "masked" in her character reinforces our desire to "read into" her. At the same time, Wharton continues to draw our attention to surfaces, insisting upon outward rather than inward dimensions or deep recesses of consciousness. Wharton challenges the belief that the self prevails as some private entity, socialized only at the moment of articulation; that is, she complicates this notion, though she will not entirely abandon it. Despite what we have seen of the social psychologist's argument that the self originates in society, the notion of the individual persists at this moment in America's literary and intellectual history, across genres. George Herbert Mead may develop a radically socialized self, but even he will preserve the "privacy" of the mind:

> What we attach to the term mind particularly is its privacy.
> It belongs to the individual. And what takes place there

> takes place, we say, in the experience of the individual. He
> may make it accessible to others by telling about it. He may
> talk out loud. He may publish. He may indicate even by his
> uncontrolled gestures what his frame of mind is. But there
> is that which goes on inside of a man's mind that never gets
> published, something that takes place there within the
> experience of the individual.[23]

Mead indicates that even if we choose to share the contents of our
minds—by telling, talking about, publishing them—there is "that
which goes on inside" which never gets announced, presumably
because it never can be articulated, perhaps because we cannot vio-
late it with words. We may see the "frame" of the mind but we cannot reach within its casing. "Experience" denotes a privileged realm.
Keeping a sense of the mind as sanctuary, the individual as an
inescapably private category, Mead's words represent the majority of
turn-of-the-century texts preoccupied with questions of consciousness. The Wharton text will attempt to sort out these same issues, presenting that which "takes place within" as that which is inevitably
generated in the social world. Turning the privatized notion of self
inside out, Wharton divulges the "insides" of a character, as it were:
a mere replica of our public world. Consequently, those inviolate, universal categories—mind, consciousness, spirit, soul—carry social and
cultural imprints. In *The House of Mirth*, the Lily Bart who wears a
"mask" and puts on "airs" invites a double reading; and yet, despite
the mystery she promotes, its seems that nothing exclusive, nothing
private, nothing detached from her social bearings, exists behind this
"mask."

Wharton's preoccupation with veils, costumes, disguises, reminds
us that the discursive construction of gender and class are both performative. And Lily "performs" the role of the high society woman
with exquisite panache.[24] Selden's gestures to look beyond the mask,
gestures that the reader invariably mimics, go unrewarded. Wharton
fashions Lily to be merely the sum of closet and curtain, skirts and
setting, as if anticipating the ways in which gender roles rely upon
action and attitude more than some authentic interior. At the same
time, Wharton seems uncomfortable with this equation, a discomfort
we can read from her repeated hints that there might be something
behind the curtain, something that could be considered the "real"
Lily Bart, something beyond gender and the trappings of social class.
Selden attempts to scrape past the layers of lace and veils that Lily
presents, even in his first encounter with the heroine. Though he grat-
ifies himself with her looks, the mere externals of her face, hair, fig-

ure, do not satisfy his study. Instead, Selden tries to imagine exactly what it is that Lily Bart is "made of":

> Selden was conscious of taking a luxurious pleasure in her nearness: in the modeling of her little ear, the crisp upward wave of her hair—was it ever so slightly brightened by art?—and the thick planting of her straight black lashes. Everything about her was at once vigorous and exquisite, at once strong and fine. He had a confused sense that she must have cost a great deal to make, that a great many dull and ugly people must, in some mysterious way, have been sacrificed to produce her. He was aware that the qualities distinguishing her from the herd of her sex were chiefly external: as though a fine glaze of beauty and fastidiousness had been applied to vulgar clay. Yet the analogy left him unsatisfied, for a coarse texture will not take a high finish; and was it not possible that the material was fine, but that circumstances had fashioned it into a futile shape? (5)

The curves and waves and lines of Lily's beauty are not lost on a connoisseur like Selden. Still, there is something beyond what he notices in the shape of her ear, the coloring of her hair. Lily incorporates paradoxes: "vigorous *and* exquisite," "strong *and* fine," she is somehow the ideal combination of Selden's taste for elegant, flawless femininity as well as his attraction to a strength and vigor that might better fit a traditional view of masculinity. Given the union of these forces in the person of Lily, neither portion seems threatening. But what Selden cannot be sure of is her value. Wharton speaks of her heroine being "produced," and endows Selden with the sense that it "cost" a great deal to "make" a person like Lily. She seems, simultaneously, to be a work of art and a factory production. Furthermore, Wharton's mixed metaphors complicate the question of Lily's origins: is she natural or somehow invented? Though the language explicitly makes her a "product," it also suggests something personally unique and "mysterious" about her. We do not know, however, whether it is simply artistic "brightening" or some inward, essential nature.

Selden is dissatisfied with his own analogy because it occurs to him that one cannot imagine a Lily Bart into being without considering "circumstances"—a word that seems synonymous with social class in this novel. Appropriately, Selden ends his meditation with a question, one that he is repeatedly incapable of answering no matter how diverse the variety of "circumstances" in which he witnesses Lily. But the question is important for other "readers" of Lily as well, for in a narrative which follows its heroine down each step of society's ladder, while still insisting upon her specialized quality, we are compelled to ask what it is, exactly, which gives rise to a self—"material" or "circumstances," the clay or the finish, some individualized identity or social class? The shape into which Lily Bart is fashioned seems an inescapable mold, a brittle, empty vessel. Nevertheless, Wharton suggests that the circumstances reveal the quality of the material; examining the hands that shape the clay, we may come to know the clay itself. Lily herself, certainly, has made a careful study of the shaping hands of society. Entering Selden's flat, she reminds him that such study is necessary on the part of a woman. Lily must be aware of her place, not simply whose rooms and houses she might be welcome in, but also how she might situate herself within those rooms.

She allows herself, at once, a rare moment of spontaneity and release in the privacy of Selden's slightly shabby library as well as an occasion to reflect on her circumstances. While Selden watches her measure out the tea, he considers her "so evidently the victim of the civilization which had produced her, that the links of her bracelet seemed like manacles chaining her to her fate" (7). Lily "seems to read his thought," at first, rehearsing the melodramatic tropes of fate and imprisonment. Comparing herself to Selden's cousin, Gerty Farish, who lives in her own flat and who "likes to be good," Lily states that *she* "likes to be happy." Yet if the fundamental difference between these two women, according to Lily, is that Gerty is "free" while Lily "is not," then by implication, freedom comes to those who choose to defy the dominant cultural expectations. Ironically, Lily beholds freedom for women in the guise of the single life, though society will insist that freedom comes with marriage and wealth—the only institutions that provide women with status in their social circle.[25] And of course, Lily continues to be a consummately social creature; she, no doubt, realizes that Gerty's brand of "freedom" would be impossible for her because it entails mandatory separation from the very soil in which she is rooted. Indeed, though she delivers her line somewhat playfully, Lily suggests that the only way *she* can think of changing something like her "self" is by transforming the surroundings in which she poses: "If I could only do over my aunt's drawing-room I know I should be a better woman" (7).

Wharton uses the same language for transformations of self as for transformations of social spaces: doing-over, making-up, renovating. Because surfaces are her specialty, because she must be savvier than any other character in *The House of Mirth*, Lily has mastered the art of decorating and becoming decoration. Lily's life demonstrates how a woman must learn to insert herself into the social scene as if she were a picture. Marriage, then, becomes the inevitable result of finding the proper room in which to be displayed or hung. Consequently, Lily alleges, a woman "must" marry where a man has a choice:

> Ah, there's the difference—a girl must, a man may if he chooses. . . . Your coat's a little shabby—but who cares? It doesn't keep people from asking you to dine. If I were shabby no one would have me: a woman is asked out as much for her clothes as for herself. The clothes are the background, the frame, if you like: they don't make success, but they are a part of it. Who wants a dingy woman? We are expected to be pretty and well-dressed till we drop—and if we can't keep it up alone, we have to go into partnership. (12)

What is the difference, we are pressed to ask, between a woman and her clothes? Lily concedes that there is a distinction—a woman is asked out "as much for her *clothes* as for her*self*," implying that they are separate articles—and yet it is difficult to draw a distinct line between the clothes and the self. Clothes, that is, *make* the female self. A man's clothes do not define him in the same way; a shabby coat does not translate into a seedy man. One wonders what a woman becomes without her clothes—not a ridiculous question when we consider that tableaux vivants, which occupy a pivotal scene in *The House of Mirth*, often employed women "dressed" in nothing more than paint to portray certain famous portraits of nudes.[26] Lily calls clothes the "background, the frame, if you like." And though they don't make for success, they are "a part of it." A crucial part, it seems, for Lily's words indicate that without this "background," the social world stands bereft of its finest scenery. Perhaps a woman and her clothes are, in fact, *the* center of society, the crux at which social class gets established. Certainly, Lily realizes that class distinctions are drawn along the lines of the clothes she wears as much as the houses she visits.

Wharton continually revisits this matter of socialization when it comes to questions of authentic selfhood. Conflating issues of social class, gender and self-knowledge, it is as if Wharton's novel entices the reader into looking for a "natural self" beneath, beyond or underneath the drapes of a woman's clothing at the same time the text produces answers that make that notion untenable. As such, Wharton's articulation of the self seems suspicious of itself: we enter into a reading of a socially constructed self only to be confronted with metaphors that cling to an essential self somewhere "inside" us. Wharton debunks the notion of self-reflection, for example, through

Lily's constant, superficial appraisals before her mirror, but the repeated act invites readers to consider that these self-evaluations could probe deeper. Most often, however, Lily's scrutinizing looks search out the image that *others* see when they observe her. When Lily leaves Selden's apartments, she pauses to glance at her reflection in the mirror; yet this moment does not allow for the kind of reflection that corresponds with self-consciousness. As Lily looks herself over, she may produce a reflection in the glass, but Wharton gives us a string of impressions, which belong to Selden. His "reflection" supplants any self-reflection on Lily's part:

> She paused before the mantelpiece, studying herself in the mirror while she adjusted her veil. The attitude revealed the long slope of her slender sides, which gave a kind of wild-wood grace to her outline, as though she were a captured dryad subdued to the conventions of the drawing-room; and Selden reflected that it was the same streak of sylvan freedom in her nature that lent such savour to her artificiality. (13)

Pointing forward to Lily's crowning moment when she will master the illusory arts to such an extent that she establishes a correlation between art and reality, this instance where Lily studies her image reveals the tenuous border between "nature" and "culture," expressed as the contrast between the "woods" and the "drawing room." Selden compares Lily to a "captured" nymph who still possesses a "sylvan streak of freedom"; interestingly, he finds these metaphors synthesizing as he gazes at what he calls her "outline." As a metaphor for the woman's body, this outline emphasizes the contours of her figure, but more emphatically, the exterior, the frame of the self. Selden tries to penetrate her image with a reading of those "lines," but the paradoxes inherent in his metaphors convey the difficulty Selden has in seeing Lily: the image she advertises gets tangled in the images he manufactures. That Lily is adjusting her "veil" as he stares, heightens Selden's fancy that she is concealing a truer self beneath the folds.

Wharton's vacillation between the notion of a "real self," hidden behind masks or veils, and a socially generated self that corresponds to and is constituted by those presumed disguises, emerges most emphatically in her depiction of Lily Bart alone. If Lily comes to life, as it were, in social company and if social intercourse, as Wharton likewise suggests, generates the self, then what happens to that self when unaccompanied? Wharton wants to create a protective house for the self, as we saw in the epigraph, to ensconce the "center of life" inside it, but the realization of such spaces becomes complicated, especially for the women in her stories. The unaccompanied self, the self in communion with itself, becomes an impossible fantasy, perhaps, even, a dangerous fiction because this society requires that women provide a *social* center for life precisely through their public display. Consequently, Wharton's gestures toward some "real self" within seem troubled, convoluted, contradictory. In *The House of Mirth*, Lily Bart flees any sort of solitary communion with herself as though such activity were a bold deceit. But even while the social arena appears meticulously to breed its Lilies, Wharton alludes to a portion of the self that cannot be expressed in this light, illustrating the double bind in the discourse of consciousness. Despite her acute sense of a socially determined self, Wharton reveals the difficulty most writers of this period had in eschewing the concept that each human being possesses some portion of the self that constitutes his or her essence. Locating this core in the mind, spirit or soul, writers furthered the notion that the essential self remains elusive, incorporeal, metaphysical, but nevertheless, remains. Wharton suggests, in her fluctuations between positions that we cannot rest in either position; that is, the shifts between them, ironically, provide us with our principle. *The House of Mirth,* as Maureen Howard tells us, is a novel of "concealment and revelation, of what is presumed socially and what must be discovered morally and emotionally."[27] Metaphors for consciousness pulsate between these multiple forces.

Lily Bart, at one point, thinks of social intercourse as a way to elude the self, as if one might extinguish consciousness, temporarily, by talking. "She had just time to take her seat before the train started; having arranged herself in her corner with the instinctive feeling for effect which never forsook her, she glanced about in the hope of seeing some other member of the Trenors' party. She wanted to get away from herself, and conversation was the only means of escape that she knew" (18). If the self is constituted by society, such an "escape" would be inconceivable; nonetheless, Wharton continually represents the self as layered, contributing to our sense that something else, something real, exists underneath. As Lily enters into conversation with the wealthy, tedious Percy Gryce, the reader is privy to the undercurrent of thoughts it appears she cannot prevent. Lily begins to analyze her situation, how she stands with respect to her circumstances, though it takes the form mostly of a meditation on the possibilities for her future position as a wealthy wife. Consciousness, for Lily, has a decidedly calculating tinge. She has, as she thinks, a talent for "profiting by the unexpected" (21). By splitting her thoughts along these two lines—one polite talk, and the other, an analysis of her situation—Wharton implies that Lily's calculations hint at a deeper awareness that cannot betray itself on the surface. Rather than leaving traces of a stable interior life, however, this form of duplicitous thought separates the self, implying, at once, that the self retains a public/private border and that certain expressions of consciousness threaten to unhinge it.

We learn that "Miss Bart had the gift of following an undercurrent of thought while she appeared to be sailing on the surface of conversation" (22), which again suggests the division between some awareness inside the self and social awareness. Wharton's attention to surfaces and depth, currents and sailing invites comparisons to the water imagery with which William James famously imagined consciousness. Yet James frequently envisioned a picture of the mind detached from any explicitly "social" source, often amidst natural surroundings like birds and streams.[28] In her novels, Wharton relocates these torrents of thought explicitly within the social world. Drawing rooms offer specific entries and exits, thresholds to cross; as such, Lily Bart's mind becomes comparable to these recesses. Provoking and faltering, however, are her sallies into these spaces. Lily attempts, instead, to dislodge unpleasant thoughts as if consciousness were a dwelling with limited capacity. Once in command of her particular situation, Lily tends to dismiss any difficulties she faces, until they "vanish beyond the edge of thought" (24). Figuring the "edge" of thought, Wharton invites us to think about how the mind might also have such a border, a periphery toward which thoughts recede; envisioning this edge, we perceive Lily continually skirting its fringes, uncertain of whether they offer a buffer or a barrier. If each mind does have such a margin, it most often resembles a permeable membrane through which the activities and articles of the social world pass back and forth. Wharton will push these images of edges and borders to produce an array of metaphors for consciousness, the mind and the self that explicitly call upon the language of interior design and the objects of the social sphere. Appropriately, it becomes difficult, in *The House of Mirth,* to separate houses, money, art, clothing from something we might otherwise feel secure in calling the "self."

Wharton's figures insist that we read the markers of inwardness with a social ruler; that we consider how outward décor might define a richness within. Women, in particular, in *The House of Mirth* demonstrate a flexibility between inwardness and exteriors, though sometimes with a dangerous precariousness. At the center of a society that thrives on speculation, women are speculated about, they are the objects of speculation, eventually becoming spectacles themselves.

Considering that "speculation" means both looking and trading, considering and purchasing, meditating and selling, it is a perfect metaphor for the ways in which consciousness, rather than remaining suspended in the world of the mind, corresponds to social activity, money, commerce and commodities.[29] Such a formula is not unproblematic, however. Though Wharton rehearses familiar references to the self's interior, she also destabilizes such notions of identity, replacing them with the capricious and hazardous world of commerce. A woman like Lily falls between the crevices of this metaphor: she is rendered an object and yet she perceives the buying and selling of herself as merchandise. In fact, she promotes herself, squanders herself, participating in her own objectification. That Lily seems to know what she is doing, that she has a "clear perception" of those moments when she becomes, in Rosedale's mind for instance, a "long coveted object" to the "collector" (315), and that something in her remains detached from the very project that might rescue her from dinginess and poverty, pulls us back from an easy reading of her character.

Never fully illuminated, Lily's interior life, nonetheless, becomes a locus for a certain *resistance* to self-awareness:

> Feeling no desire for the self-communion which awaited her in her room, she lingered on the broad stairway, looking down into the hall below. . . . There were moments when such scenes delighted Lily, when they gratified her sense of beauty and her craving for the external finish of life; there were others when they gave a sharper edge to the meagreness of her own opportunities. (26)

Scenes of beauty "delight" Lily; but she often craves them, consumes them, as an escape from a sense of inner isolation. The colors and sparkles and glimmer of the guests in the hall, this time, cannot gratify Lily's sense of the beauty of life's "external finish"; they merely highlight the sharp edge between her aesthetic imagination and her scanty opportunities. Lily sees her fate as a choice between "being" two different types of women: "It was a hateful fate—but how to escape from it? What choice had she? To be herself, or a Gerty Farish" (27). Of course, Lily cannot "be" a Gerty Farish, but what is interesting about her understanding of her own fate here is the uncomplicated way in which she introduces her choice, as if "being" herself were something completely or unambiguously worked out. In fact, we do not know what it means for Lily to "*be* herself." Nor does Lily, though Wharton implies that she will count the cost of such an endeavor. As Lily enters her guest bedroom at the Trenors, she shows us that apart from the usual distraction of conversation and calculation, one invariably succumbs to the inevitability of self-reflection. Any private space, Wharton here suggests, proves uncomfortable because it produces encroaching visions and memories. First, a "vision" of Gerty's "cramped flat" which she interrupts with a confident, "No; she was not made for mean and shabby surroundings, for the squalid compromises of poverty. Her whole being dilated in an atmosphere of luxury; it was the background she required, the only climate she could breathe in" (27). Here Lily's dependence upon a luxurious atmosphere becomes symbiotic: she "requires" a sumptuous background—it is her sustenance—the climate of opulence is the only one in which she can "breathe." Again, the question of Lily's "being," what she is "made for" or made *of*, highlights the conflict between the socialized self and some pure, essential version of self. Here, Wharton makes the struggle between the two a struggle for survival. Feeling the obligations of living off someone else's luxury makes Lily aware that she is a "mere penshioner on the splendour which had once seemed to belong to her. There were even moments when she was conscious of having to pay her way" (27). Lily senses that there is a price she must pay, that this "splendour" does not, cannot, belong to her without extracting some sacrifice.

When the image of Gerty's place and contrasting fantasies of luxury dissolve to make way for memories of Lily's mother and her family household, we begin to see what form this sacrifice might take. A late-night perusal of her face reveals two lines near Lily's mouth; she considers these wrinkles the very product of unpleasant thoughts: "'It is only because I am tired and have such unpleasant things to think about,' she kept repeating; and it seemed an added injustice that petty cares should leave a trace on the beauty which was her only defence against them" (29). Thoughts, which presumably exist "inside" the self, are here imagined as literally transcribing themselves on Lily's face, altering her outward appearance. Thinking, or any form of self-reflection, therefore, becomes a dangerous occupation for an unmarried woman vigilant about her appearance. After all, Lily's appearance, her beauty, can alter her social situation. More than a defense, Lily's face empowers her to act, offering the possibility for redemption from poverty and worry. Lily remembers "how her mother used to say to her, after they had lost their money, used to say to her with a kind of fierce vindictiveness: 'But you'll get it all back—you'll get it all back with your face'" (30). Just as Lily draws attention to the metonymic way that clothes stand for a woman, her mother reduces any sort of fuller version of self Lily might assume to the derivative of her face. Likewise, Lily's memory of her mother clusters around specific house-

hold images, images that appear to stand for this "vigorous and determined figure" who rules their home: "a door-bell perpetually ringing;
a hall-table showered with square envelopes which were opened in
haste, and oblong envelopes which were allowed to gather dust in the
depths of a bronze jar . . . ransacked wardrobes and dress-closets . . .
gorged trunks" (30). Mrs. Hudson Bart shows how a woman
becomes the sum of these parts: social duties and household arrangements, visitors, invitations, wardrobe, and trunks. Lily's sense of her
mother does not exist apart from these externals.

The only access we have to Mrs. Bart's interior life consists of her
interest in Lily's looks; the one "thought" which, we learn, consoles
Lily's mother is "the contemplation" of Lily's beauty. "She studied it
with a kind of passion, as though it were some weapon she had slowly fashioned for her vengeance. It was the last asset in their fortunes,
the nucleus around which their life was to be rebuilt. She watched it
jealously, as though it were her own property and Lily its mere cus-
todian" (35). That Lily's looks might be an object for her study and
contemplation makes for an ironic portrait of Mrs. Bart; but Wharton
extends her travesty of Mrs. Bart's meditations to make Lily's appearance the nucleus, the core, around which mother and daughter might
make-over their lives. This conflation between insides and outsides
culminates in a confusion over ownership. It is Lily's mother who
seems, really, to "possess" Lily's beauty while Lily merely carries it
for safekeeping. Whether or not we are to read Lily's beauty as a mere
covering a fund of inner strength, outside polish or inner spirit,
remains dubious. Lily does seem capable of turning herself inside out
with a disturbing effortlessness; her responsive nature becomes her
most identifiable trait. Indeed, life has molded Lily; she has yielded to
experiences, receiving each impression as a form of definition: "the
girl showed a pliancy which, to a more penetrating mind than her
aunt's, might have been less reassuring than the open selfishness of
youth. Misfortune had made Lily supple instead of hardening her, and
a pliable substance is less easy to break than a stiff one" (31). Not
only is Lily harder to break, she is also harder to pin down; reacting
to each circumstance with the flexibility of a survivor, Lily Bart
becomes the most bendable of substances, a handful of clay repeatedly reshaped.

Creating these images of malleability, Wharton repeatedly urges us
to ask what a woman is made of: what brings a Lily Bart into being?
If we consider Lily's beauty alone, we find no stability, no uniform
substance; all is fluctuating, plastic, changeable. Yet just when we
begin to concede that Lily Bart becomes nothing more than fluff and
finish, Wharton hints at an interior life in conflict with the outer

form: "Her intentions, in short, had never been more definite; but poor Lily, for all the hard glaze of her exterior, was inwardly as malleable as wax. Her faculty for adapting herself, for entering into other people's feelings, if it served her now and then in small contingencies, hampered her in the decisive moments of life. She was like a waterplant in the flux of the tides. . . ." (55). It should not surprise us that any inner existence replicates the mutations of Lily's exterior beauty. Still, Wharton's reference to Lily's "inwardness" invokes the conflict between a consciousness that is aware of the self and a consciousness that not only must account for "other people's feelings," but also, specifically, takes shape through others' feelings. Wharton conceives of Lily's genius for adaptation in terms both natural and artistic: she is water lily and wax; the fragrant product of nature and the material an artist might use to form a sculpture. "Like a water-plant in the flux of the tides," Lily flows along the current, though she is as often "dragging herself up again and again above its flood" to gain the foothold of success that presents "a slippery surface to her clutch" (40). And with a hard glazed surface that belies metamorphosis, Lily, nonetheless, offers herself up like a wax model to be molded by the artist's hands. Interior life does not stabilize or anchor the self. On the contrary, "inwardly," Lily presents a substance uncannily susceptible to changes. Wharton answers the debate over the essential self with these fluid metaphors, which are impossible to classify. Everything in Lily's being must be fluid, slippery, elastic; no solid core or essence can emerge securely out of the flux. Suspicious of arguments for a "natural" self, Wharton nonetheless adopts the language of her contemporaries. Her solution, however, suggests that she transforms that language, enhancing the flexibility of the discourse, maneuvering her metaphors in order to express the self's potential permutations.

The *tableaux vivant* scene at the center of the novel brings Wharton's inquiry into the social formation of the self together with questions surrounding the issue of a "real" self that might exist beyond social articulation and exhibition. When Lily offers herself as a "living picture" for the occasion of the Welly Brys entrance into society, she embodies the conflict between these selves. More emphatically, she reveals that the self is not realized so much through a process of uncovering or disclosing, as it is through the application of layers of drapes, and through the careful poses and changes in light that accompany them. During the scene of Lily's infamous display of herself as Sir Joshua Reynold's "Mrs. Lloyd," it is difficult to locate any references to inwardness. Certainly, Wharton accentuates Lily's body over her mind, and insists relentlessly upon our viewing her body as the place where these questions about self are figured out. We are meant to focus on her diaphanous clothing, the outline of her fig-ure, the position of her limbs, the grace of her pose. But even Lily's body seems a mere rack upon which social accessories are arranged. Lily's acceptance of her position is disturbing, though Wharton will push her acceptance to the point of "exhilaration." Lily is "in her ele-ment on such occasions" (138), eager to show off her artistic skills on more than the mundane occupations of dress-making and upholstery.

Exhibition reaches the level of performance in the *tableaux vivants*; and perhaps Lily's realization of the "plastic" possibilities of her being might actually reveal a deeper component in Wharton's project for the discourse of consciousness and its correspondent articulation of the self. That is, the "real" Lily Bart (as she is twice named) who emerges in this scene does not occupy a private space, nor does dis-closure occur in conjunction with a visit to the inner corridors of her mind. In this way, Wharton insists upon the ways that social and cul-tural forces author any articulation of consciousness. When we com-pare this central episode in *The House of Mirth* with, for instance, the pivotal moment in Henry James's *The Portrait of a Lady*, we find in Lily no gestures toward inward deliberation. Isabel Archer's land-mark vigil casts a sort of "spell" over her and she sits "motionlessly seeing" the images in her mind; Lily Bart casts a spell over her audi-ence, conscious of her power in being *seen*.[30] James's insistence on this episode as central to Isabel's career suggests that Isabel is most "herself" when alone, thinking; Lily is most herself with an audience, through the vehicle of performance. Furthermore, Wharton repeated-ly insists in the *tableaux* scene that the self can be disclosed only in the guise of another—it is most itself when dressed up as someone else. Lily "had shown her artistic intelligence in selecting a type so like her own that she could embody the person represented without ceasing to be herself" (141–2). Authentic selfhood ascends through art; consequently, the corporeal self merges with something beyond the body, reminding us of William James's sense that art, like experi-ence, turns ordinary material into something spiritual.[31] Lily "steps into" the frame of the Reynolds canvas, replacing the deceased phan-tom of Mrs. Lloyd with the "beams of her living grace" (142). She not only resurrects the dead, but also transforms herself into a work of art—a transformation that, Wharton proposes, allows her to reveal her "real" self.

It is Lily's beauty, as Wharton would have it that enacts this subtle transaction from art to life back to art again:

> Her pale draperies, and the background of foliage against
> which she stood, served only to relieve the long dryad-like
> curves that swept upward from her poised foot to her lift-
> ed arm. The noble buoyancy of her attitude, its suggestion
> of soaring grace, revealed the touch of poetry that Selden
> always felt in her presence, yet lost the sense of when he
> was not with her. Its expression was now so vivid that for
> the first time he seemed to see before him the real Lily Bart,
> divested of the trivialities of her little world, and catching
> for a moment a note of that eternal harmony of which her
> beauty was always a part. (142)

Lily's beauty may be frozen in its pose, but as Selden imagines, it
somehow "soars" beyond what her poised attitude can reveal, beyond
even what her physical presence captures, and outside the margins of
her trivial world, to approach something "eternal." Dress and props,
as features of art, "serve" to make Lily appear more alive. Her stat-
uesque pose and the reference to her as a poem, nonetheless, accentuate the sense that she is preserved as static image. Wharton's
metaphors shift uneasily between a desire to arrest, in art, that which
resonates most vividly and an anxiety about what such an apprehension might entail. When Lily steps into, not out of, the painting, she
indulges—just as Selden will indulge—in the fantasy that she might
escape social inscriptions to submit to the design of art. "Divested"
of her "little world," we might guess that Lily would walk naked into
some natural, Edenic scene. And she almost does. But the world she
walks into must necessarily be manufactured and artificial, not unlike
the "improvised" look of the ballroom whose marble columns "one
had to touch" to learn they were not cardboard and whose chairs one
had to seat one's self in to be sure they were not "painted against the
wall" (139). If, as Wharton's language proposes, a "real self" gets
fabricated through art, then such a self simultaneously underscores
the inventiveness and the artfulness of identity. The expression, the
existence, of Lily's "real" self depends upon selecting the right
"type," stepping into the appropriate persona. There is no question of
something private or concealed; instead, Lily refits herself with a new
background, pose and costume. Wharton writes that Lily has "not an
instant's doubt as to the meaning of the murmur" that greets her
appearance, she senses her "triumph," she feels an "intoxicating sense
of recovered power," she knows she has "produced an impression"
(143), all gestures that push us outward to the impact of Lily's performance, not inward towards an understanding of the thoughts and
feelings that might shape Lily's identity. Rather, Lily achieves her
identity by producing and displaying it as art.[32]

If, as Wharton insists through Lily's transfiguration into "living picture," the self exists as a series of staged performances, then the self must also, necessarily, become fragmented. The discourse of consciousness in *The House of Mirth* generates these fragmentations of the self; Lily's consciousness is embodied in metaphors that bring to life other "beings," other "selves," often in conflict with each other. As if anticipating the impending, momentous encounter with Selden during their conversation about the "republic of the spirit," Lily's equivocal thoughts materialize into two distinct beings. Lily appears calm, though she is "throbbing inwardly with a rush of thoughts. There were in her at the moment two beings, one drawing deep breaths of freedom and exhilaration, the other gasping for air in a little black prison-house of fears. But gradually the captive's gasps grew fainter, or the other paid less heed to them: the horizon expanded, the air grew stronger, and the free spirit quivered for flight" (67). Here Wharton directs us "inward" to Lily's thoughts, though not for calm meditation. Lily is "throbbing inwardly" as much in excitement as in fear. Clearly, these two "beings" her consciousness begets cannot coexist with one another. One is "gasping for air" in a "prison-house of fears" while the other "quiver[s] for flight," relying, it seems, on the widening expanse of sky for its freedom. But it is difficult to tell what it is, precisely, that makes for the danger here. Both the captive spirit and the free spirit lead a precarious existence and we might question whether Lily sees the threat in free flight, fears the prospect of love she begins to contemplate, or recognizes some sort of danger in the "throb" and "rush" of her own interior life.

Certainly the self, in *The House of Mirth*, is rarely in communion with itself, or perhaps a better way to put it is that in this novel Wharton attempts to articulate a series of selves which make up that category we call the individual. One consequence of revealing these ruptures in selfhood is the proliferation of beings—sometimes threatening, sometimes exhilarating—that figure as manifestations of Lily's thoughts. Indeed, though Lily cannot control these dissociations, she seems excruciatingly aware of them. As Gus Trenor thrusts before her the view of herself that other men appear to have, Lily reels from the idea of it as if from a physical blow; but all the while "another self was sharpening her to vigilance, whispering the terrified warning that every word and gesture must be measured" (153). Lily combats an unpleasant, embellished version of herself with yet another version—"another self" sharpened to vigilance, scrupulously measuring its response. Though she eventually escapes the physical, sexual threat that Trenor represents, Lily cannot escape the proliferation of selves that emerge out of her frightened thoughts. One of these selves threatens to "drag" her down (154); when she finally speaks "she heard herself in a voice that was her own yet outside herself" (155); driving from the empty Trenor home, "she seemed a stranger to herself, or rather there were two selves in her, the one she had always known, and a new abhorrent being to which it found itself chained" (156). Looking at these moments in conjunction with Wharton's identification of certain social discourses with the discourse of consciousness, we become aware of her critique of the social conditions that restrain intimacy—intimacy between two people as well as intimacy with one's self. Wharton launches her critique of society by immersing her characters in it, emptying them out, making their "insides" a mere involution of the social, so that introspection and meditation are strained if not impossible.[33]

When Lily Bart looks inside herself, it is as if there exists a splintering so profound it threatens to destroy her. Lily recognizes the destructive, alien, repulsive beings that exist as part of her, though she does not know what to make of them. Mingled together, they appear to her as a monstrous disfigurement: "Can you imagine looking into your glass one morning and seeing a disfigurement—some hideous change that has come to you while you slept? Well, I seem to myself like that—I can't bear to see myself in my own thoughts" (173). Lily's imagined picture of herself, one she confesses to Gerty and one she envisions she might see in the mirror, presents a sight so hideous that she cannot contemplate it. Lily states specifically that she cannot "bear to see" herself in her own thoughts, hinting that her consciousness cannot sustain this deformed version of herself, that it shrinks from ugliness with rigorous discrimination. A moment later, Lily states more explicitly that from such a change "there's no turning back—your old self rejects you, and shuts you out" (174). Lily doubles herself, imagining that an old self stands guard against this newly distorted self; even if it must "shut you out," your former self somehow survives.

Survival might be the force behind the transformation that occurs in Lily's beauty as well. For ironically, as Lily's vision becomes more penetrating, as she comes to face the monster in the mirror that is herself, she presents an even more dazzling, seemingly impervious, exterior to others. The more Lily masters the ability to make herself into a work of art, the more she sustains the text's illusion that her interior life gets crystallized into a synthetic material. Lily's beauty, as Selden laments at one point, has the capacity to become hard and impenetrable: once it had a "transparency through which the fluctuations of the spirit were sometimes tragically visible; now its impenetrable surface suggested a process of crystallization which had fused her whole being into one hard brilliant substance" (199). Lily's protection against herself comes through this "process of crystallization"; yet she retains her skill in "renewing herself" through various "scenes" and "surroundings." Thus her beauty cannot entirely close her off from the social world—for better or for worse—nor can her brilliance blind her from the lucidity that suffering will bring. Indeed, Lily strives to escape her self throughout the entire course of the novel, avoiding communion with herself; she seeks "refuge from the sound of her own thoughts" (244). Though Wharton's text remains conflicted over the notion of the individual and the generative power of social systems, Lily, nevertheless, ends up alone at the close of the text, absorbed with the activity of her mind, until she finally transcends thought and reaches a permanent suspension of consciousness.

In Lily's final conversation with Selden, Wharton emphasizes the conflict between the intimacy of shared thoughts and the gravity of social convention. Lily's "passionate desire to be understood" seems to lead her to a "strange state of extra-lucidity" (322), though Wharton's attention to her emaciated figure, her tears, her pallour, oddly enough, indicates that Lily's heightened consciousness emerges out of the decline of her body. The implication here is that mental and corporeal states cannot correspond: Lily's body, specifically her physical beauty, must degenerate to make way for the increased power of her mind. As Lily's "consciousness put[s] forth its eager feelers" (323), she notes Selden's contrasting aloofness, his constraint. Her actions in this scene are striking because, unlike most moments in *The House of Mirth*, Lily disregards convention, opening up the possibility for communication instead of calculated reactions.[34] Wharton articulates Lily's emotions and desires apart from the cultural codes she has perpetrated: "She had passed beyond the phase of well-bred reciprocity, in which every demonstration must be scrupulously proportioned to the emotion it elicits, and generosity of feeling is the only ostentation condemned" (323). Selden, however, cannot receive her generous words to him; nor will he recognize any part he had in forming Lily. Lily may press beyond decorum to "make him understand that she had saved herself whole from the seeming ruin of her life" (323); but she remains ambivalent about her own role in this process of salvation. She wants to give Selden all the credit, though his rejoinder removes him completely: "I am glad to have you tell me that; but nothing I have said has really made the difference. The difference is in yourself—it will always be there" (324). That Selden locates the difference, the saving power, *in* Lily reminds us of his acute observation that "Lily has it in her to become whatever is believed of her" (165). What precisely is *in* Lily Bart remains questionable, for Selden's words at once suggest that she easily synthesizes into what others believe her to be, but that there exists something inside her that, nevertheless, defines, differentiates and even "saves" her. Intimacy would be possible only if Lily might find a way to share what is "in" her, not give it away entire as she first suggests:

> There is someone I must say goodbye to. Oh not *you*—we are sure to see each other again—but the Lily Bart you knew. I have kept her with me all this time, but now we are going to part, and I have brought her back to you—I am going to leave her here. When I go out presently she will not go with me. I shall like to think that she has stayed with you—and she'll be no trouble, she'll take up no room. (325)

Lily has not settled upon a version of herself, neither the "old self" that she eventually realizes she cannot leave with Selden—"it must still continue to be hers" (326)—nor some new self that she might discover in the midst of her good-byes to him. Indeed, Selden's shifting imagination of her, the self she performs as art, the "real self," the "old self," the disfigured and lonely self she has come to face in the mirror; in short, each self that emerges out of the social climate complicates any single notion of selfhood upon which Lily, or readers of *The House of Mirth*, might rest. As her words to Selden indicate, the self remains detached or portable; she can "keep" it or "leave" it, whichever she chooses. What's more, the self seems barely noticeable, is "no trouble" and "takes up no room." Lily appears to recognize that, though she may hold this self for some time, her claim upon it is by no means final. Furthermore, if this portion of Lily can be passed from person to person, if she can walk out of Selden's apartments without that "self," then the self multiplies up until the final moment of the novel. That is, Lily's motion here repeats, and deceptively completes, her motions throughout the novel, revealing a proliferation of selves rather than a stable location for identity.

Wharton represents these versions of self as a product of the social imagination of Lily that materializes out of her stops along society's ladder. In this instance, there is no pure, untouched principle for the self. Perhaps this is why Lily's final retreat into her own consciousness provides no refuge; in fact, Lily tries "to shut out consciousness by pressing her hands against her eyes" (339) presumably because she knows she will "see" what others have made of her as well as what she has made of herself. For Lily, consciousness turns on a blazing light within her that leaves nothing hidden: "It was as though a great blaze of electric light turned on in her head, and her poor little anguished self shrank and cowered in it, without knowing where to take refuge. She had not imagined that such a multiplication of wakefulness was possible: her whole past was reenacting itself at a hundred different points of consciousness" (339). "Consciousness" multiplies with too much intensity; its "hundred different points" offer a penetration that pierces like a succession of wounds. Wharton figures Lily's self trapped inside her head, "cowering" in the sudden glare of light that awareness of her past "reenacting itself," and an almost forced evaluation of her life, brings. In fact, Lily's crisis culminates as she struggles to find a place to locate the self; when she does at this moment, she seems imprisoned inside it. More characteristically, though, she experiences the feeling of "being something rootless and ephemeral, mere spin-drift of the whirling surface of existence, without anything to which the poor little tentacles of self could cling before the awful flood submerged them" (336). The rare flower that she is, Lily nevertheless gets plucked out of her soil only to be subject to "whirling" forces and the threatening "floods" that appear to stand for life.

These metaphors, despite their melodramatic excess, eventually bring us back round to Wharton's imagination of a personal existence that might actually withstand the flood. This image comes to Lily, significantly, after she has experienced the warmth and security of Nettie Struther's kitchen hearth.[35] Such a moment of intimacy invites Lily into an understanding of "the continuity of life," a continuity that begins inside a home:

> She herself had grown up without one spot of earth being dearer to her than another: there was no centre of earthly pieties, of grave endearing traditions, to which her heart could revert and from which it could draw strength for itself and tenderness for others. In whatever form a slowly accumulated past lives in the blood—whether in the concrete image of the old house stored with visual memories, or in the conception of the house not built with hands, but made up of inherited passions and loyalties—it has the same power of broadening and deepening the individual existence, of attaching it by mysterious links of kinship to the mighty sum of human striving. (336–7)

In this consummate representation of the home, Wharton constructs a "centre" for Lily even as she insists upon its actual absence in her life. For the moment Lily conceives of the image of the house, she possesses that "power" both to establish the self and to expand the self.[36]

And Wharton explicitly makes the vision her heroine's own, she specifies that "such a vision of the solidarity of life had never before *come to Lily*" (337; my emphasis). Indeed, when it comes, Lily feels an attachment to something despite an infamously transient past, an upbringing where no "one spot of earth" is dear to her. Wharton combines natural and architectural imagery in this passage: like the roots of a plant, Lily's individual existence "broadens" and "deepens" once she receives the image of the home within. Moreover, if the "form" of the past comes in the form of a house, one recognizes attachments, "mysterious links of kinship," as if somehow the house were a shared thought, a communal memory, bringing individuals together into a "mighty sum of human striving."[37]

Of course, Wharton's novel does not end with this image of solidarity and kinship; it ends with a suspended word, a word that never gets spoken or revealed. The word "passes between" Lily and Selden over her deathbed, making, as Wharton tells us, "all clear" (347). Such forms of silent communion might be like those "mysterious links" Wharton draws between idealized individuals whose roots spread broad and deep, and who share the imagined interior space of the home. Yet, in a novel where communication amounts to social maneuvers and dodges, careful repartee and wordplay, and where the central character dwells only in the *possibility* of a home, this verbal standstill looms portentously. Indeed, *The House of Mirth* closes upon pure possibility—the possibility of a silent, one might even say sterile, communication between two minds. But we question the prospect of such a union even as we are invited to conceive of it.

*The House of Mirth* asks what it might mean for social realities to constitute mental realities. In repeatedly constructing her female characters out of the configurations of their social and cultural domain, Wharton further complicates the tensions between the personal and the social. The language of the Wharton text, moreover, exposes the ambiguities of human subjectivity as it rehearses a prevalent anxiety over the constitution of individual consciousness and the idea of the self, particularly the female self. As we have seen, Wharton repeatedly dramatizes the conflict between a natural self, or what she refers to as the "real" self, and the notion of socially constructed identities. Wharton's metaphors direct her narrative, creating multiple versions of subjectivity until it becomes difficult to determine which one she endorses. In *The House of Mirth*, especially, metaphors for consciousness generate competing accounts, sometimes fabricating a self identical to its social texture, sometimes preserving a version of self-consciousness that indicates some separate, intrinsically private, room inside the mind. Wharton thus consummates the conflict over the question of consciousness, suggesting that it is precisely in the flux of language that we come to understand subjectivity and to embrace our own identities.

## CHAPTER SIX

# The Price of a Conscious Self in Edith Wharton's *The Age of Innocence*

"I have often thought that the best way to define a man's character would be to seek out the particular mental or moral attitude in which, when it came upon him, he felt himself most deeply and intensely active and alive. At such moments there is a voice inside which speaks and says: '*This* is the real me!' And afterwards, considering the circumstances in which the man is placed, and noting how some of them are fitted to evoke this attitude, whilst others do not call for it, an outside observer may be able to prophesy where the man may fail, where succeed, where be happy and where miserable."

William James

In this letter, written in 1875 to his wife, the newly-married William James reflects on the ways in which one might trace one's own character, one's "deepest" self, as it were, in order to define it.[1] The process by which we gain access to that self appears to be twofold: we hear an inner voice speaking and later consider what produces it and what it means. "*This* is the real me!" the voice inside exclaims fervently. The self thereby discloses itself, announcing its reality, to a rapt audience of one. James's demonstrative pronoun, vague as it is, appears to offer conclusive evidence for a distinctive self, "intensely active and alive." Moreover, the self appears explicitly identified by its consciousness of itself, a consciousness that signals its reality. And yet, James immediately follows this instinctive voice with a remarkably detached, philosophical reflection on "circumstances." The moment James mentions "circumstances," or where the man is "placed," the energy of the letter moves further and further outward, so much so that it requires an "outside observer" to determine the fate of the self. Understanding character no longer requires attention to an inner voice, but rather, to an ability to "fit" together situation and "attitude"—a term that suggests that identity rests not upon deep inner recesses, but upon one's manner. James's letter goes on to discuss the balance between "holding [one's] own" and "trusting outward things to perform their part," revealing the fundamental contest between that inner voice and the conditions under which it might pronounce itself.

The dramatic rendering, in William James's letter, of an inner voice and its accompanying adjustments in attitude reveals a split in the discourse of consciousness that the philosopher had tremendous trouble reconciling. Though the letter dates from the earliest part of his career, before the publication of *The Principles of Psychology* (1890), it reflects a central preoccupation in all of James's work: the division between a consciousness that locates itself inside us and a consciousness that pervades the natural and the social world. It is a tension we have seen repeatedly acted out, across genres, within every text of this study; it is this tension that characterizes the history of consciousness. The inner voice in James's letter, which represents the conscious mind, effectively precipitates the outward action, suggesting his investment in that voice as the essence of one's identity. On the other hand, his initial sense that we might understand ourselves by "seeking" out what *attitudes* produce this inner exclamation indicates James's ambivalence about the origin of identity. It is striking that he speaks of "defining a man's character" given the confusion that critics have often enjoyed over who, among the James brothers, emerges as the philosopher and who the fiction writer. Indeed, the sketch that William provides reads like the germ of a novel, with its character waiting to be "placed" inside the action, his dénouement open either to success or failure, happiness or misery. It sounds, moreover, remarkably like Henry James's conception of *The Portrait of a Lady*, which, he insists, "consisted not at all in any conceit of a 'plot'. . . but altogether in the sense of a single character." A single character, moreover, whom James admits he "locked up" as a "precious object" for fear that she might get into the wrong hands.[2] The fiction of his fellow novelist of manners, Edith Wharton, appears to tell a different story. Her work explicitly brings to bear the force of "circumstance" that both William and Henry James work to keep separate or contained. Though Wharton expresses fascination and even sympathy for her characters; more often than not, she suggests that for her, storytelling consists of the conflict between characters and the forces surrounding them, forces that come from the social and cultural sphere.[3] Probably the most famous account of these influences comes in her consideration of the subject of *The House of Mirth*, her sense that a novelist might reveal the values of a society by exposing what it destroys.[4] Thirty years after the publication of her most popular novel, Wharton reflects on that subject again, stating assuredly: "when there is anything whatever below the surface in the novelist's art, that something can be only the social foundation on which the fable is built." This statement characteristically implies that the Wharton novel, at bottom, is purely social, excavate it all you will. But as Wharton continues the discussion of her art, she qualifies the social to make way for the soul.

> [T]he other, supreme preservative of fiction is whatever of unchanging human nature the novelist has contrived to bring to life beneath the passing fripperies of clothes and custom. The essential soul is always there, under whatever disguise; and the storyteller's most necessary gift is that of making its presence felt, and of discerning just how fair it is modified and distorted by the shifting fashions of the hour.[5]

In naming "unchanging human nature" as the basis for her work, Wharton overturns the "social foundation" she previously cited and rests the weight of fiction on more elusive ground: the pursuit of the soul. The Wharton text, not unlike those of her contemporaries in science and psychology, searches for a language to characterize authentic human experience. Though we see the language of the soul repeatedly emerging in nineteenth-century scientific studies of consciousness, such language was once the province of religious texts. The evolutionary scientists combine discussions of the soul with biological and psychological discourse in order to explore the human mind. And Wharton's novels, in their concern over personal psychology, social determinism, cultural criticism, the spiritual and philosophical dimensions of identity, reveal this peculiar heritage. T. J. Jackson Lears explains that in order to understand American modernists, "one has to acknowledge that for them the category of the authentic had more than aesthetic significance. Some of its roots can only be called religious."[6] It is not surprising, then, that Wharton should imagine her work as a novelist in terms of uncovering this spiritual core. "Essential," "unchanging," and "always there," the soul becomes a substantiated being, the most potent presence inhabiting a story. The soul "preserves" fiction, by which I assume Wharton to mean, saves it, from the "passing fripperies" of a fickle society. Yet it might be hard to find; it might even (purposely?) be "disguised," a hint, on the author's part, that sounds like a tip for her readers. As Wharton concludes her meditation on the fiction writer's hunt for the soul, she states that part of the work of the novelist consists of "discerning" what modifications and distortions that soul has undergone, hinting, suggestively, that it may not be quite so "unchanging" after all. At the close of this passage, Wharton comes round, syntactically and perhaps philosophically, to the "fashions of the hour"; but the soul continues to be a throbbing presence, one that both writer and reader must anticipate.

Though Wharton here attests to the power of the soul, which seems, always, to be located "beneath" or "underneath" changing customs, fickle times, clothes, or the body that wears the clothes, her fiction repeatedly questions such formulas. In fact, Wharton makes it impossible to sustain readings that separate cultural furnishings, fashionable manners, or social knowledge from anything we might expect to find "underneath" them, anything, that is, like a conscious self. The discourse of consciousness in the Wharton text makes the clothes stand for the self, and reveals the soul to be socially inscribed. An interior untouched by social codes, consciousnesses set apart as private, are suspicious categories for Wharton, challenged and unsubstantiated in her texts. Indeed, Wharton's fiction expressly demonstrates the hazards of self-consciousness for characters made up of social stuff; as such, she remains intensely skeptical of its power and its reality. Because Wharton details the "circumstances" of her characters in terms, especially, of the ubiquitous force of social class, the process by which she defines them shows precisely how they are bound. In *The Age of Innocence*, any sense of a personalized consciousness will be incorporated into society. In *The House of Mirth*, as I have argued, characters must learn to examine not their own insides, but the spectacle of women displayed around them. Since her female characters, especially, receive scrupulous training over their appearance as the only way to achieve a stronger position in society, the reader questions those rare moments when Wharton allows her characters a "voice inside" that exclaims the "real me." Indeed, the word "real" seems emptied of meaning in Wharton, leaving the reader with immense uncertainty over the status of the self in her world.

As we have seen in the previous chapters, the reversals of metaphor and method that occur within the studies of consciousness themselves—whether written by evolutionary scientist or modern novelist—all reveal this profound ambivalence about what it is that makes a conscious self. Overwhelmingly, the debate over subjectivity at the turn of the century suggests that if consciousness is to sustain one's identity, it must allow for a clear outline around the self, a citadel of one. At the same time, philosophers, sociologists, scientists, and novelists, dealing as they do in language, cannot resist the remaking of their own designs. We are as often confronted with the certainty of an authentic core for the self as we are told that the self is infused with the contents of the world in which it lives. The tensions within every account of consciousness, manifested as they are in conflicting metaphors and figures, make boundaries between public and private fluid. Still, no author in this study (including Wharton) seems ready to abandon entirely the notion that such boundaries might be maintained. The conscious self comes with a price and it is precisely in the negotiations between a self-contained existence and a profound awareness of the social implications of identity where we find Wharton's notions of consciousness evolving.

From her earliest work of nonfiction, *The Decoration of Houses* (1897), to her Pulitzer Prize-winning novel, *The Age of Innocence* (1920), Wharton's preoccupation with structural representations of interior space reveals a deep anxiety about the security of personal identity and self-consciousness. Though her language in *The Decoration of Houses* might be confined to architecture and to the design of domestic interiors, Wharton's insistence upon closed doors and properly proportioned entrances and passageways in the real world of a home informs her understanding of personal, mental "interiors." It is clear, in her book of interior design, that the treatment of openings, doorways and thresholds carries not only aesthetic importance, but also signifies social control.[7] The author that insists, in *The Decoration of Houses,* that "No room can be satisfactory unless its openings are properly placed and proportioned" and "Under ordinary circumstances doors should always be kept shut,"[8] is the same author who will recreate a world impervious to outsiders but full of permeable minds.

Indeed, through her depiction of old New York society, Wharton presents a drastically open version of interior life, a consciousness that looks like mind reading, though she also suggests that the self covets inward escape. Unlike Lily Bart, Newland Archer, the central character of *The Age of Innocence*, spends a great deal of time inside his own head. And though he does not relinquish consciousness as Lily does, neither does he gain from it as, for instance, his literary cousin Isabel Archer, does. There is no richness about consciousness in Wharton's post-war novel, no profit from it, perhaps because there is no safeguard for it. Wharton unveils the social basis of consciousness to such an extent in this novel, that minds become common texts, dangerously available for perusal. Private thoughts refuse to remain hidden, but rather, expose themselves in a language that goes beyond one mind to forge links through social and communal relations. Though it lacks the perfect symmetry of couples that *The*

*Golden Bowl* presents, *The Age of Innocence* resembles James's later novel in its representation of consciousness as shared thinking. Wharton does not overlook the oppressiveness of such alliances, however. Maggie Verver will be granted her secret meditations as the method by which she resituates herself in the world of James's novel. Likewise, as we have seen in *The Portrait of a Lady*, Isabel Archer learns that consciousness includes the social envelope; but her vigil allows her protected mental space. For Wharton, though, the openness of the social system threatens to negate entirely any notion of an inward life, any clear sense of an individual. Newland Archer wonders at one point how the van der Luydens' "merged identities ever separated themselves enough for anything as controversial as a talking-over."[9] This merger of identity, which in the lofty van der Luydens seems haltingly complete, represents the eventual fusion of minds that a shared inner dialogue decrees. Such complete coalescence reveals the potentially stultifying effects of intimacy. Perhaps the ultimate irony of Wharton's text emerges in the conflict between a vigilant enforcement, on the part of "society," of the boundary between public and private,[10] and the inability of any character that has entered this privileged realm, to retain the sense of a personal life. The discourse of consciousness in the Wharton text thus repudiates any explicit form of self-communion for the self exists only through the realization of its role, the confirmation of its place, in society. Archer's question: "What am I?" leads him to the abrupt realization: "A son-in-law—" (1186). His identity is neither contained nor discrete; it is contingent upon his position in the family. There are moments in the novel when the self does create a private refuge, yet here it encounters either emptiness or a mere inversion (which is sometimes an exaggeration) of the social arena. We find no place in the Wharton landscape that sustains a conscious life. As Ellen Olenska—a foreigner and a perpetual outsider—comprehends penetratingly, with a laugh, there is no where in New York where one can be alone (1261).

Newland Archer longs for refuge, nonetheless, in a world of private language and the security of personal thought. In comparison to Wharton's earlier novel, *The House of Mirth*, where characters demonstrate a certain resistance to self-analysis, *The Age of Innocence* gives us characters that long for the kind of solitude that allows for personal reflection. Ellen Olenska's plaintive analysis of the "public" nature of New York society summarizes this desire. She sees that the social world can be reduced to the activities inside one house: "One can't be alone for a minute in that great seminary of a house, with all the doors wide open . . . . Is there nowhere in an

American house where one may be by one's self?" (1120–1). In contrast, *The House of Mirth* follows Wharton's prescription for interior design: a world of closed doors. One might argue, in fact, that the novel enacts a series of enclosures that culminate inside Lily's tiny and solitary boarding house room. The irony of Wharton's early narrative, however, comes as we realize that even though Lily Bart remains a consummately closed and contained character, she does not recognize the value of her privacy. Not only does the virginal Lily rarely open herself to others, but, as Maureen Howard suggests, she also fears introspection.[11] Wharton makes clear that this consummate socialite would prefer *not* to have access to her own self: when Lily "made a tour of inspection in her own mind, there were certain closed doors she did not open."[12] If *The House of Mirth*, in this sense, shows a "closed" self, then *The Age of Innocence* makes these doors radically open.

Wharton repeatedly demonstrates the fallacy of a private, self-enclosed consciousness throughout *The Age of Innocence*, perhaps the most affecting instance of which occurs at the end of the novel. Archer learns that the terrible secret he has harbored, and that he holds inside by an "iron band" around his heart, is really no secret at all. His wife, as he discovers, had "guessed" (1299). It might be more accurate to say that he *re*discovers this truth since he recognizes—earlier in the novel, at the farewell dinner for the Countess Olenska—that he is at the center of a "conspiracy" (1282). Furthermore, he suddenly sees at that point that May "shares" New York's belief that he and Ellen are lovers (1286). At the dinner party, we see a consciousness that fails to insulate the self because the mind is too accessible; the "tribe" has unlimited access to one's interior life. And yet, strangely, the "iron band," which Archer recognizes years later, seems to suggest the opposite; that is, it seems to offer Archer some form of protection, one might even say containment, for a self. The release of this fastening on his heart, therefore, seems a characteristically ambivalent gesture on Wharton's part: if it means freedom, its removal leaves him suspiciously adrift.[13]

As Archer's meditations often make clear, *The Age of Innocence* produces characters who appear to present mysterious depths compelling a keener examination than the sort of superficial self-appraisals that we see in *The House of Mirth*. Yet the two novels effectively reverse our expectations about the role of self-consciousness in the formation of subjectivity. Characters like Newland Archer, who attempt to conceal their thoughts, scrupulously cultivating their insides, end up with a public consciousness that is entirely "readable." In contrast, Lily Bart's energy radiates only outward, to her audience and to her appearance. Though she eschews self-analysis, wants to "get away from herself," prefers to "shut out consciousness," she remains, to those around her, a perverse enigma (18; 339). She is obliged to advertise herself and yet the travesty of her fate is that no one reads her right. Newland's misdirected self-investigation and Lily's reluctance to study her self have the same result. It is as if Wharton courts the desire for a rich interior, but chastises her characters for requiring it either by suggesting the precariousness of seeking such personal sanctuary or by exposing it as false.

Wharton relentlessly shows that Archer cannot have private thoughts, cannot close his consciousness to others nor protect it from some higher form of social proprietorship.[14] At first, he relishes the communication he has with his fiancée, May Welland, one that requires no unpleasant words, indeed, one that seldom requires words at all. Such habits and forms of exchange, however, establish a fierce intimacy that conducts Archer and May through a network of social associations beyond their control. When Archer precipitates the announcement of his engagement, he has only to look at May for her to decipher his intention:

> [H]is eyes met Miss Welland's and he saw that she had instantly understood his motive. . . . The persons of their world lived in an atmosphere of faint implications and pale delicacies, and the fact that he and she understood each other without a word seemed to the young man to bring them nearer than any explanation would have done. (1027–8)

Wharton more famously refers to this type of language as "hieroglyphic" where "the real thing was never said or done or even thought, but only represented by a set of arbitrary signs" (1050).[15] Though Archer here celebrates this inconspicuous form of communication because it brings him "nearer" to his fiancée, in time, he reverses his judgment of May. That same ability he has to read her thoughts eventually fills him "with a secret dismay."[16] Archer laments the very fact of his wife's accessibility: "never in all the years to come, would she surprise him by an unexpected mood, by a new idea, a weakness, a cruelty or an emotion" (1250). Wharton, of course, shows Archer's blindness on this point. What's more, she continually exposes him as a poor reader of women.[17] Consequently, as critics have often suggested, she invites further investigation into the mysteries behind May's blushes. What is disturbing, however, is that Wharton also allows us to read May's thoughts—unchallenged—

through *Archer's* consciousness, emphasizing the exactitude of the rules with which they communicate. Wharton delivers an entire monologue—a "mute message" as she calls it—in May's voice. But it is Archer who is given the authority to tell the reader what she "means" (1227). Of course, as I have been suggesting, Wharton overturns consciousness in this novel so that its contents are no longer personal property. Archer does not possess the power to narrate the story of the novel;[18] but he does, at least initially, participate in the communal consciousness of the organism that is New York. We are meant to understand that Archer can "hear" May precisely because she has been trained out of any sort of individuality. Her message follows standard code. What Archer does not see is that he too remains open for the same sort of decoding. The paradox of this permeability of consciousness is, of course, that it destroys rather than nurtures intimacy. The possibility, then, for meaningful relationship, for mutual exchange, disappears.

Archer has no difficulty receiving or relaying the voice of the family—which is identical to the voice of New York—as the novel opens. He understands unspoken signals, such as the "particular curve" of his mother's eyebrows that reminds him to keep silent before the butler (1047). He recognizes distinctions, as only one of his set would, like the difference between being "merely a Duke and being the van der Luyden's Duke" (1064). And though he strays from the family in his ideas about the Countess's marriage, when he meets her alone to deliver his opinions, he finds himself speaking, "in a voice that sounded in his ears like Mr. Letterblair's," about the ruling forces of New York society (1103). Indeed, the Countess's response, "that's what my family tell me," implies that there is no other answer Archer could make (1104). We see Archer's repeated attempts to "strike out" for himself—words that he uses to convince May to hasten their marriage—each met with a countermove that suggests the impossibility of original thought (1081–2). His mother assumes, for instance, as the controversy over the Countess's behavior heightens, that he "sees only the Mingott side" (1086). Aligned with a larger body, Archer's participation in the consciousness of the clan appears explicit and definitive. Moreover, it appears to obliterate any chance that he might think something like his own thoughts. Possibilities for communication and self-communion, dependent as they are on notions of private and public space, become dubious categories in the Wharton novel. As I have noted in the previous chapter, even in its drive for closure, *The House of Mirth* refuses to settle upon a singular conception of consciousness or of the self. *The Age of Innocence*, likewise, unsettles us, though Wharton appears, in her images of open doors and accessible minds, to be considering the possibility of transcending personal consciousness.

Though Archer might misread the thoughts and motivations of the characters (in particular, the women) around him, he provides, as often, a fascinating look at the competing theories of consciousness and selfhood that operate in the text. When Newland attempts to understand Ellen Olenska's "mysterious faculty of suggesting tragic and moving possibilities," he idealizes her character, explicitly romanticizes her past, and attempts to classify her.[19] At the same time, he also speculates more broadly on the origins of identity. Since the term "faculty" suggests both the natural abilities of an organism, such as seeing or hearing, as well as skills derived from practice or habit, Archer initially leaves open the "tragic possibilities" of the Countess as either inherent *or* learned. Wharton's attention here to the language of evolution, like the many anthropological allusions in the text, gets somewhat convoluted in Archer's mind.[20] As his reading continues, though, he specifies his interpretation in order to locate, as it were, the essence of the Countess: "Archer had always been inclined to think that chance and circumstance played a small part in shaping people's lots compared with their innate tendency to have things happen to them." Madame Olenska, as he says in the same context, "had hardly ever said a word to him to produce this impression, but it was a part of her" (1107). Here circumstances, behavior and social situation all become irrelevant for a woman whose "innate tendency" occasions the dramatic. Wharton uses words such as "innate" and "inherently" to replace Archer's earlier ambivalence regarding Ellen's "faculties" and, consequently, underscores his gloss over the woman whom he calls "quiet, almost passive" (1107). Perhaps more important than Newland's inability to see Ellen as an agent in her own life is the fact that he represents, even in his sentimentalized portrayal, a crucial division in the understanding of personal identity. Archer believes the self to be defined by inborn qualities, not by circumstances or experiences, nor social environment. Certainly, *he* "produces" this elaborate impression of an essentially dramatic woman. And while Wharton may satirize Archer's limited views of identity as an inherent commodity in favor of a socialized self, she will allow Ellen an unqualified moment of self-reliance, indicating the tantalizing possibility of a sustaining interior life.

Readers of *The Age of Innocence* who want to recover the power of women in the novel often lose track of the passionate attachment that Ellen expresses for Archer.[21] In fact, she acknowledges Newland as *the* source of her newfound knowledge. Given the extensive cultural capital that the Countess has gained from her time abroad, it seems strange that Archer, hemmed in as he is, would have something of value to give to the Countess Olenska. Indeed, Wharton represents

Ellen's knowledge (intellectual, cultural, relational) as vastly exceeding Archer's. But the sort of knowledge that Archer provides is knowledge that she appears never to have encountered—knowledge that, we are to understand, nourishes the self. After their first, mutual confession of feeling, where Ellen pronounces that she "cannot love" Newland unless she "gives [him] up" (1153), she consoles herself with this thought: "I shan't be lonely now. I *was* lonely; I *was* afraid. But the emptiness and the darkness are gone; when I turn back into myself now I'm like a child going at night into a room where there's always light" (1153). The Countess first notes that Archer possesses his knowledge because he has learned to resist the "temptation" of what lies beyond the calm order of New York; thus he has shown her something better than "the things [the world] asks of one"—"better," she exclaims, "than anything I've known" (1152). That Archer's rejection, as she names it, of the "world outside" should motivate the Countess to "turn back into [her]self" seems a peculiar lesson indeed, considering that Archer is rarely allowed that inner refuge himself. Nevertheless, Wharton's suggestion here of an interior life that one might choose in lieu of the surrounding world separates and individuates a self. There appears to be so clear a distinction between inner and outer worlds that turning away from the worldly "tug" (1152) necessarily means "turning into" a self.

Archer listens uncomprehendingly to Ellen's valiant speech outlining her new mode of self-reliance. In fact, Wharton tells us repeatedly that Archer cannot "understand" Ellen, nor can she understand him (1148; 1152; 1153). Archer finds that the Countess's inward retreat "envelops her in a soft inaccessibility" (1153); and though Ellen maintains the boundary between them for reasons of sexual propriety, it is clear that Archer has become unaccustomed to anything like a closed consciousness in others. Though he may inspire the Countess to embrace what she has "never known before" (1152), he does not, himself, register the impact of her words. Turning inward, Ellen suggests a desire to transcend the social world even while the text maintains the impossibility of such a gesture. Moreover, the novel may very well suggest that transcendence for female characters can come about only as a result of transgression.[22] But the Countess has already been "beyond" (1246), and she recognizes that such excesses do not enrich the self. She has paid a high price for stepping outside New York's circle, yet she declines participation in its social game. When Ellen assumes an interior for the self, an inner room "where there's always light," she reinvents Emersonian transcendence by bringing it indoors. She does not enter the woods, nor does she come anywhere near transparency; instead, Wharton seems to accentuate her opacity as a way to retain an individualized consciousness even in the wake of social forces. The Countess embraces a self that carries its own light; though she must explicitly turn inward in order to preserve it.[23]

The problem, however, in reading the Countess's words as an instance of heightened selfhood is that most attempts to hold on to a personal, inward cache in this novel receive ambivalent or blatantly ironic treatment from Wharton. If the novel concedes to a self, it is a self with fluid boundaries, saturated with the contents of the social world. Perhaps the most vivid instance of Wharton's skepticism over an autonomous self in this novel comes in the philosophy of Dr. Carver, founder of the Valley of Love. Wharton plays on the language of nineteenth-century mysticism and mesmerism, both of which William James and Alfred Russel Wallace combined, to the chagrin of their colleagues, with their more "legitimate" studies of consciousness and mental life.[24] Such forays into pseudo-science, represented by Agathon Carver in The Age of Innocence, become comical, and as backward as the Gothic script on his calling card. Through her amusing depiction of a man who has made the "illuminating discovery of the Direct Contact" (1141)—with what, we don't know—Wharton aligns herself with scientists, most of whom dismissed popular séances and spiritual communication. She thus presents Dr. Carver, who lives, as Medora Manson reports, "only in the life of the spirit" (1141), conducts "inner thought" meetings (1180), and calls upon the spirit to "List—oh, list!" where it will (1141), as a farcical representative of the discourse of consciousness. When Medora tells her niece, Ellen, that she has received a "spiritual summons" (1147) to be with Dr. Carver, the Marchioness Manson seems, quite absurdly, to represent the flip side of that communal consciousness set on keeping the social order of old New York. Despite all signs of Dr. Carver and Medora's fatuity, though, Wharton will not dismiss completely their brand of spiritualism. Dr. Carver provides, at any rate, something like William James's answer to questions about consciousness in resorting to ephemeral language. When the doctor calls upon the "spirit" to go where it will, he exposes the openness of a system where our "inner thoughts," if we are in tune with such movements, actually resist closure. And if we take "list" to mean harken or attend then his words quite cunningly suggest that survival in a social system such as New York's, relies upon shrewd attention to what is happening around oneself. Outward observance, not inward attention, is the rule. Consequently, though his rhetoric shows inconsistencies, it appears, finally, to indicate a lack of containment for anything associated with the self. He also stands as an alternative to the "blind conformity to tradition" that the novel decries; indeed, his brand of spirituality requires, as the Countess remarks with interest, "all sorts of new and crazy social schemes" (1206).

Ridiculous as he is, Dr. Carver reveals "inner thought" and social action to be inseparable. And perhaps Wharton means for this to be the lesson, as it were, of the novel. Archer will come to understand this, even in his small way, since he does his part in the State Assembly and becomes a sort of locus for social change in his community (1290–1). However, Archer's resistance, throughout most of the novel, his sense that an inner life counts for more, plagues *The Age of Innocence*, continually teasing us with the anticipation of a deeply fulfilling, interior reality. The persistence of the word "real" in Wharton's fiction—one that appears to resist even the most caustic irony on her part—suggests that we might locate an authentic language precisely through the intersection of society and soul. As easy as it is to caricature Archer's quest for transcendence, Wharton continually comes round to the idea, revealing her reluctance to abandon entirely the notion of interiority as a model for subjectivity. Though modern readers have little sympathy for Archer's melodramatic sense that he has missed "the flower of life" (1291), we hold fast to the belief that Ellen Olenska saves something of herself when she removes to Paris. And while we might note Wharton's reversal of certain assumptions about gender—as Marilyn Chandler suggests, she places Archer as the figure trapped in domestic life, a position usually assigned to a female character—it is difficult to know whether this means we might somehow redeem her hero.[25] I have suggested that Wharton appears to allow Ellen a kind of retreat inside herself, one for which, in her mind, she is indebted to Archer. Indeed, the Countess becomes more and more closed even as she enters deeper into New York society. Newland suffers long spells without gaining access to her thoughts, and certainly he never "understands" her as he does one of his own kind. Nor does the reader necessarily. If Ellen indulges in meditative vigils, we are not privy to them. If she takes pains to analyze the messages sent to her by May, or the rest of the family, the reader never knows. We hear simply that Ellen "understands," as May tells her husband, "everything" (1275), a sweeping rhetorical acknowledgment on Wharton's part that is reminiscent of Henry James. But if Ellen understands "everything," Archer seems to understand "nothing." Accordingly, as the novel progresses, he loses his place within the communal mind of New York. As our center of consciousness, he may well be a miserable failure since he cannot read the Countess's gestures and stands paralyzed in the face of his wife's "secret hopes" (1186). What's more, he persists in the fantasy that he might be free of the social forces that make him who he is, all of which unravel before the reader, exposing Archer to our sympathy or our judgment. May's secrets may be deep, but it is the Countess whose privacy—culminating when she returns the key to her potential lover (1278)—closes her off entirely.[26] Though readers of *The Age of Innocence* might imagine that Ellen's withdrawal to some inner space could be more appealing than the restriction that New York offers, Wharton does not let us indulge in such romance. Elizabeth Ammons regards Ellen as a "New Woman," defined by her independence of thought and her desire for freedom, though, unhappily, rejected by America.[27] But such interpretations rely upon privileging the individual over the community—a complicated gesture in the Wharton text. The individual, in Wharton, is never completely free. Indeed, the Countess, of all people, understands that social relations as well as the community that she inhabits shape her identity. Though Ellen eventually lives alone in Paris, she remains linked to New York not only through the support of her grandmother's trust (1278), but also through the parental role she assumes with the more gently transgressive Fanny Beaufort (Archer's future daughter-in-law), a role that brings her connection to the family full circle. Wharton may be looking with irony at old New York society, but she is also looking with nostalgia.[28] She will not go so far as to suggest that one can live without social forms.

Archer attempts such a life. Because he feels constrained by society, he desires complete removal from it.[29] Yet Wharton makes the idea of his removal inconceivable. Though Archer so often seeks a sequestered place—a place where he might live and breathe a different "air" than what New York manufactures; a "country" where he might indulge in a relationship otherwise considered illegitimate (1245); any other place, "other houses, roofs, chimneys. . . the sense of other lives outside his own" (1250)—Wharton reveals the emptiness of this rhetoric at each instance. There is no such country, and Archer has grown accustomed to New York ways, so much so that were he to enter an atmosphere "less crystalline," he would find it "stifling" (1091); he would literally be unable to breathe. What's more, even an escape "inside himself" does not yield the privacy that he fancies. The most elaborately personalized "place" to which Archer retires does appear, at first, to be protected space. But the novel undermines the security of Archer's privacy even as he believes himself to be indulging in it.

> [H]e had built up within himself a kind of sanctuary in
> which she throned among his secret thoughts and longings.
> Little by little it became the scene of his real life, of his only
> rational activities; thither he brought the books he read, the
> ideas and feelings that nourished him, his judgments and
> his visions. (1224)

Wharton explicitly creates this space "within" Archer, hinting that he
has, in fact, acquired a consciousness that is private. The sanctuary
becomes a sort of glorified inward library full of sentimentalized visions
that arise out of the books he has read.[30] Newland, in one memorable
instance, enhances this feeling of enclosure as he follows the image of
the Countess inside the "enchanted pages" of a volume of verse by
Rossetti appropriately called "The House of Life" (1125).[31] And
though Archer might be content remaining in this sacred place,
Wharton makes clear that he will do so at the expense of his existence.
Closed doors in *The Age of Innocence* do not provide privacy so much
as they signify annihilation, as when Archer feels, with a "deathly
sense," "the doors of the family vault" closing in on him (1283).

Though he positions the Countess securely on a throne inside his
head, Newland loses his own footing in the outside world, as Pamela
Knights convincingly argues, moving about "with a growing sense of
unreality," startled to find that anyone "imagines" he is actually there
(1224).[32] More importantly, if thinking of the Countess appears, in one
electric episode, to produce the inner sanctuary for Newland, elsewhere
when he thinks of her, his mind literally empties out. This split in the
manifestation of his consciousness reveals the trouble Archer has in
holding on to any definitive self: is his interior a sanctuary (replete with
images for worship) or a vacuum? Occupied with his familiar routines,
he can indulge in the security of an identity anchored by habit, where
his daily activity serves as a "link with his former self" (1178). But even
that sense of a "former" self indicates a splintering that Archer has yet
to come to terms with, mostly because he clings to the idea of the mind
as the stronghold for a singular self, a notion that Wharton's text disputes. When reflections of Ellen "[make] of his mind a rather empty
and echoing place," or an interior with reckless, slamming doors
(1179–80), we begin to see the price that Archer will pay for his refuge.
At Newport, surrounded by people alive to the business of socializing,
Archer seems distinctly out of place; to him the activity appears shocking "as if they had been children playing in a grave-yard" (1179). As
Newland experiences the evacuation of his mind, he reads the world
around him as an inversion of the dead space inside him. Social activity, significantly, appears to desecrate that hallowed ground.

In a scene that sheds light on the nature of his sanctuary, Archer attempts to create another private space for himself—not a mental space, this time, but a physical space—in the real world of his home. The moment comes after the farewell dinner for Ellen, an event that forces upon Archer, "in a vast flash," his position in "the centre of countless silently observing eyes and patiently listening ears" (1282). Wharton tells us, quite plainly, "[H]e had come up to the library and shut himself in" (1287). Taking the sentence out of context, however, occludes the clever placement of the action and the fact that Wharton encompasses Newland's reclusive moment, literally, inside an intrusion. The rupture to the fantasy of an enclosed self, a break that comes about after he is reminded of the tribe that rules his life, is rendered quite subtly here. Though it has the character of a stage direction, we hear of Newland's position as if it were an afterthought. That is, Wharton does not set the scene with his attempt to absent himself, but, rather, with May's assertion of her presence. Indeed, we do not even observe Newland alone until May enters, and revokes his privacy. Wharton begins her scene with May's abrupt question, spoken "from the threshold of the library," a question that "rouses him with a start." May's voice precipitates the action. So immediately we see that Archer cannot "shut himself in," that such a motion seems incongruous from the start, given May's appearance. Newland's wife stands at the entryway of his room, unbeknownst to him and eventually enters his library, a space clearly designated as his personal chamber. Wharton's meticulous attention to the purpose of doors in *The Decoration of Houses* is instructive here. In detailing the terms for home design, Wharton repeatedly laments the "absence of privacy in modern houses," offering a critique of domestic life along with her assessment of interiors.

> [E]ach room in a house has its individual uses: some are made to sleep in, others are for dressing, eating, study, or conversation; but whatever the uses of a room, they are seriously interfered with if it be not preserved as a small world by itself.[33]

The door, of course, is what "preserves" the integrity of the room, specifically by making its boundaries distinct. However, Wharton makes clear that Newland cannot keep this room closed off from outside intrusion.[34] We learn in the final chapter of the novel that Archer's library is "the room in which most of the real things of his life had happened" (1289). Wharton accompanies that statement with a list of occurrences such as birth announcements, engagements, christenings, pre-wedding arrangements, career discussions, a child's first step and first words, indicating that the library has lost its "individual," sacred purpose. The room no longer stands as its own little world, a place with one distinct "use," because it must contain *all* of Archer's worlds.

To return to the previous scene of May's interruption, we see, then, the futility of Archer's attempt to "shut himself in" this room or anywhere, even though it is designated as "his." We wonder, even, if this room has a door since May's voice opens the scene and obliterates any illusion of privacy that Archer might maintain.[35] May does, as we see, request permission to enter this space that Archer has declared as his own—a room he can furnish and decorate as he pleases—but Archer cannot keep intimacy with himself even here. The scene, in fact, carries on with the progressive encroachment of his wife who ends up "warmly and fragrantly hovering over him" (303). What "shuts" Archer in, is, of course, the news of May's pregnancy, a fact that makes public their intimacy. In approaching the threshold of his study, May refuses Archer the closed consciousness that he so desperately seeks; that is, her opening question acts as a transgression, a breach in the circle that Archer has tried to draw around himself. It is significant that May asks, ultimately, as she breaks the news that they are to have a child, "'You didn't guess—?'" (1288). May assumes that Archer has read the signs—her fatigue, her languid attitude (1248), a face "paler than usual" (1266), perhaps even her "unnatural vividness" (1266)—and conjectured that she is pregnant. She assumes, in short, and thereby almost succeeds in redeeming, the shared inner dialogue with which they began their courtship. Hence her penetrating look into her husband's eyes, to which Archer uncomfortably submits, before he "turns" his own eyes away: "he felt that his wife was watching him intently" (1288). In this sense, May's oft-mentioned "transparent eyes" may indicate the sacrifice of her own privacy, her vigilant attempt to maintain a joint consciousness with her husband at the expense of a closed interior.[36]

Despite May's attempts to keep communion with her husband, Archer loses his ability, or rather, relinquishes his capacity to participate in the consciousness of New York. Yet the novel asserts that his position inside this social repository must be maintained. He must, it seems, empty himself out in order to remain a viable participant in the community. Like William James's receptacle "in which, through which, and over which minds join,"[37] and the imaginary conversations that govern *The Golden Bowl*, the consciousness that Wharton's novel establishes requires attention to social forces as the only way to retain a self. It is a disquieting lesson for the twentieth-century American novel, given our culture's commitment to debased versions of Emersonian individualism.[38] Society may reclaim Archer's thoughts as public, not personal, property; but the process is a vexed one in the Wharton novel. The contortions acted out on the psyche—and sometimes the body—of her main character as he tries to make his inner world "real" reflect the friction within Wharton's imagination of the novel: is it founded on society or the soul? We diminish Wharton's project as a writer when we abandon the more elusive part of this theory; as Carol Singley suggestively argues, Wharton is a writer not only of society but also of spirit.[39] And yet, Wharton herself continually challenges the possibility that the spirit or inwardness might be viable categories for identity. More specifically, she questions whether such categories are "real."

Wharton both deploys and disables the discourse of realism as it applies to interior life. Certainly, Newland Archer's confusion over the "real" reflects his growing detachment from the society that sustains him. Moving back and forth, for instance, between the scene with the Countess by the shore and the view of May "sitting under the shameless Olympians and glowing with secret hopes" (1186), Archer enacts a dizzying series of reversals about "reality" that continue until the final chapter of the novel. The resonance of the word "real" in this text, reminiscent of the meditation on the "real" self I have examined in *The House of Mirth*, underscores the preoccupation Wharton has with questions of identity and existence. As difficult as it is to pin down Archer's perception of what is "real," given his desperate vacillations between the dream world and reality, it is precisely those vacillations that make evident the complications of Wharton's project for the conscious self. If the discourse of consciousness, in some respects, replaces religious discourse in its search for authentic self-expression, interior dimensions of human character, and the experience of the soul, there is something imperative about keeping this language elusive. The problem, of course, is that Wharton and her contemporaries distrust the capacity of language to represent experience; authors of consciousness want to cultivate language's creative capacity without entirely losing control over it. With this in mind, perhaps we might consider Wharton's continual refuge in the word "real"—"real people," "real things," "real self," "real life," "the last shadow of reality"—as more than irony. Perhaps Wharton's relentless repetition of the term shows a desire to maintain some control over language, to rein in the capacity for words to mean too many things. Wharton recognizes, certainly, the various inversions of meaning that language undergoes, inversions that become heightened in the face of the division between personal and social life. Claire Preston suggests that this linguistic demarcation in Wharton's fiction "represents an impoverishment of vocabulary, in which the opposite of a thing is formulated merely as its own cancellation."[40] In these moments, words continually—almost automatically—turn inside out. The notion of reality, then, becomes fluid intimating that an exchange between the two worlds may be the crux of identity. Staring at Ellen, waiting for her to turn to him, Archer is suddenly confronted with the sense that this vision is only a "dream"; " reality" awaits him with May and a family ruled by clocks and dinners. But once Newland enters the Welland house, the "density" of the atmosphere, the overt luxury of its "heavy carpets," the "stack of cards and invitations"—all signs of the influx of the social world— make *that* life the "unreal" one. And the brief scene on the shore, significantly, becomes "as close to him as the blood in his veins" (1187–8). He transposes these scenes, in other words, resisting the pull of the social world, so that the episode he reconstructs, the image he holds of the Countess, literally enters into him, and becomes an interiorized reality.

Archer's desire to make the life inside his consciousness the only "reality," his attempts to keep the social world as remote as a backdrop, come through most powerfully in his impulsive visit to the remote cottage at Skuytercliff, where the van der Luydens have taken Ellen on "retreat." When Archer decides to meet the Countess, he is deceived into thinking that he will find a deeper intimacy with her, perhaps even with himself, here. Their encounter begins, after all, with a flirtatious sense of mind reading where Ellen confesses she "knew" he'd come (1120). Though Wharton rewrites that confident communication a moment later when they each declare they cannot speak the other's language (1120). Wharton seems to assign Ellen a more penetrating vision since she sees that no house in America affords a spot for seclusion: one is perpetually "on stage" in its society (1121), a metaphor that suggests one might be one's "real" self if only some private space could be found. Newland does not deny or defend what Ellen calls the "public" nature of New York; instead, he takes recourse in the fantasy that the van der Luyden's Patroon house, unlocked only for the day, will provide a thoroughly private moment for them. And Ellen too, after all, "ran away" to this place, indicating that she conceives of it as an escape ("I feel myself safe here" [1116])[41] despite her keen awareness of the openness of American society. Newland indulges in extremes, however. He believes they have found a "secret room" (1122) that might protect and conceal them, and insofar as the room stands for the self, he hopes it will contain the feelings he struggles to articulate. The house, as he sees it, waits expressly for him and Ellen, "as if magically created to receive them" (1121). And here, Wharton's language collapses into vagueness: "if the thing was to happen, it was to happen in this way, with the whole width of the room between them, and his eyes still fixed on the outer snow" (1122). The "thing" most likely is the Countess's motion toward an embrace that Newland imagines, that he "almost" hears; and, arguably, the vagueness is all his. But the fact that Wharton keeps this thing unnamed preserves the sense that the deepest imaginings, the most real moments, defeat our powers of description. The immediacy of Archer's feeling where "soul and body [throb] with the miracle to come" (1122) utterly bursts, of course, at the sight of Julius Beaufort. Newland's dramatic gesture in "throwing open the door of the house" (1122), therefore, appears ridiculous. The society that they suppose they have left looms in the snow-covered shelter of the Patroon house. Even the most exclusive, the most secluded houses, Wharton suggests, cannot secure intimacy.

Though Skuytercliff appears to offer the possibility of "escape" from the social world to a safer spot, a place where, as the Countess remarks, they might have a "quiet talk" (1121), Beaufort's entrance, with the din of New York at his heels, closes the gap between public and private space to the point of obliteration. It is no surprise, then, that Beaufort's interruption should carry them into a conversation about the telephone, a technology that requires directness of communication and, as Wharton shows in the final chapter, makes evasion nearly impossible.[42] Certainly, in a novel that turns upon calculated ellipses, punctuated silences, "implication and analogy" (1282), conversation becomes a valuable commodity. Archer esteems good conversation such as the kind he finds with Ned Winsett; it allows him, the narrator tells us, to "take the measure of his own life" (1114). And he seems quite moved by the talk he has with the French tutor, Monsieur Riviere, especially by the idea of "intellectual liberty" that he details when they first meet. "'[I]t's worth everything, isn't it, to keep one's intellectual liberty, not to enslave one's powers of appreciation, one's critical independence?'" (1174). Riviere tells Archer that he left journalism in order to "preserve" his "moral freedom," a concept that is directly linked to his ability, as it were, to "speak" his mind. Elaborating on the notion of moral freedom, "what we call in French one's *quant a soi*," the Frenchman tells Archer, "when one hears good talk one can join in it without compromising any opinions but one's own; or one can listen, and answer it inwardly. Ah good conversation—there's nothing like it, is there?" (1174). The sense that one can "preserve" one's freedom by choosing when and what to speak; that one might "answer inwardly" without compromising one-self, works against the transparency of mind that the social world of New York dictates. In that respect, it is remarkably "foreign." We see, in the way that Archer is immediately drawn to the notions of the Frenchman, the allure of a mind that can open or close itself; that can speak for itself. Like the French phrase, *quant a soi*, which indicates guardedness or a desire not to be read, Riviere's speech oddly shows self-protection as the ultimate form of personal freedom. And we might assume, since this inspiring speech comes from the voice of a writer who affirms the importance of "critical independence," that Wharton would endorse such a mode of life. What is troubling about it, however, is how quickly we learn that Monsieur Riviere is far from independent. The limitations placed upon him by his social position seriously interfere with the authority he derives from his free mind. Indeed, he confesses, in this same conversation, that the idea of end-ing his days living in a garret is "chilling to the imagination." Social class, which relegates the Frenchman to the garret, invariably infringes upon—that is, literally diminishes—the space in which he can circulate. What's more, it hints at a lifeless existence for him or at least a deadening of that which he most reveres: the imagination. When Riviere shows up later in the novel, as Count Olenski's mes-senger, we see the effects of his limited power. He comes, literally, to speak *for* the Count. The moment he speaks for *himself* (in a conver-sation that reveals to Archer how far removed *he* is from the family negotiations), Riviere sacrifices his position (1218). Furthermore, as Medora Manson assures Archer, the home that the Countess aban-doned, in addition to its material opulence, has "brilliant conversa-tion" (1143), making the value of such talk immediately suspect.

Wharton constructs an open consciousness in this book, but com-munication falters nonetheless, partly because it is difficult to know what kind of "talk" to trust in *The Age of Innocence*. There is little room for meditation, for something like a self talking to itself, in the strained world that Wharton presents. It is telling that when such inner conversations do occur, they often consist in "conjectures" about the thoughts or actions of another, a gesture that inevitably brings minds closer together. When Archer wonders, at one point, what has been keeping his wife, he finds such guesswork allows him to enter yet another mind, her father's: "He had fallen into the way of dwelling on such conjectures as a means of tying his thoughts fast to reality. Sometimes he felt as if he had found the clue to his father-in-law's absorption in trifles; perhaps even Mr. Welland, long ago, had had escapes and visions" (1248). Archer's consciousness here aligns itself with Mr. Welland's, through their mutual "absorption."

More specifically, Newland's speculations about the contents of another man's mind afford a distinct link between his thoughts and another's, a sort of mental cross-checking that keeps this society orderly. The mind, thus defined by its relations, is never independent or autonomous. Thoughts of May lead Newland to thoughts of his father-in-law in an unstinting logic that reveals the impossibility of escaping some collective social accord. Newland, as we have seen, strains to remove himself from this system of shared thinking; he perhaps senses that such an order not only obliterates privacy, but also threatens to erase all difference, as if his inner life were automatically to duplicate his father-in-law's. After all, Archer recognizes with exasperation how May begins "to humour him like a younger Mr. Welland" (1227). May's gestures to "relegate" him to "the category of unreasonable husbands" (1187) certainly correspond as rigidly to Newland's insistence on making his wife represent a "type rather than a person" (1164). Identity, constructed in these instances through strict classification, becomes distinctly homogeneous, repetitious even, as if to suggest that there are only so many "types" society knows. Hence the exigency of Newland's wish to operate outside the "silent organization" that holds his world together (1285), a wish significantly figured as an attempt to move beyond "inarticulateness."

Finding agency apart from the clan proves difficult for the characters inside the "powerful engine" that is New York (1074). Archer realizes during his encounter with Ellen in Boston, that to remove himself from the communal consciousness he must withstand an interruption, a gap between thought and articulation, that literally disables his voice. "[H]e really had no idea what he was saying: he felt as if he were shouting at her across endless distances" (1198). Though Wharton configures Newland's detachment in the melodramatic tropes of flustered and frustrated courtship, she also suggests that consciousness, as one's relation to oneself, gets profoundly severed here. The voice, as one vehicle for self-expression, falters when divorced from communal utterance. Archer resists the only form of consciousness endorsed by his society; that is, he attempts to extricate himself from it, retreating to his "sanctuary," hiding in May's brougham, flitting off to Boston, tucking himself away in his library, meeting the Countess secretly in the museum. He even dreams, as he tells May, of going "ever so far off—away from everything"—to Japan (1287–8). What he finds, as a result of all his maneuvers, is a self divided against itself. Wharton explicitly configures this division as an estrangement of voice: he seems to be speaking "a strange language" (1198); "he could not trust himself to speak" (1218); "the sound of his voice echoed uncannily" (1273); "he could not find his voice" (1274). Moreover, Newland hears other voices without recognizing their meaning or being able to identify them; the talk, at the final dinner party for Ellen, sweeps past him "like some senseless river running and running because it did not know enough to stop" (1285). Similarly, he does not recognize Countess Olenska's voice when he contrives to meet her in Boston, despite his habit of lingering over images of her. "The words hardly reached him: he was aware only of her voice, and of the startling fact that not an echo of it had remained in his memory" (1199).

Though the novel advances toward a virtual depletion of the inner life—we continually witness its absorption, its consumption, by the public world—the great leap in the final chapter over twenty-six years appears to open up a space for private reflection. It is difficult to know how to read this motion, however, considering the exhaustive gestures of the rest of the narrative, which work against any notion of authentic self-expression, any "inner voice" or "real me." Still, at the close of this novel, we find Archer in his library, in the midst of solitary contemplation. Wharton highlights this seclusion through contrast: Archer has just returned from a crowd—"the throng of fashion" (1289)—that has been circulating through the galleries of the Museum, and that seems to represent the society from which he has long wished to extricate himself. Yet the associations that visit him in his library do not exactly ground him, or stabilize his identity; they seem rather strangely to dislodge him. Newland remains metaphorically suspended while he reviews his past: "There are moments when a man's imagination, so easily subdued to what it lives in, suddenly rises above its daily level, and surveys the long windings of destiny. Archer hung there and wondered. . . ." (1294; ellipsis original). This is not the first time we've witnessed Archer in this odd state. At the bon voyage dinner for the Countess, he appears to be "float[ing] somewhere between chandelier and ceiling"; Wharton calls this condition "imponderability" (1282), thus disabling Newland's consciousness and making him decidedly unable to think. The gesture toward suspension is not unlike the indefinite closure that Wharton achieves in *The House of Mirth*. An ellipsis, similarly, keeps Lily "hanging." Even *before* she finds a certain mental hiatus with the sleeping drug, Lily imagines herself in limbo, detached from all that is real: "But this was the verge of delirium . . . she had never hung so near the dizzy brink of the unreal" (339). The difference is that Lily stands at the edge of an abyss while Archer's position—in the final chapter at least—allows him to rise above what he has been used to seeing. Precarious as this dangling state might be, the repeated use of the ellipsis interestingly indicates that it is also nonverbal. Wharton thereby echoes a prevailing sentiment regarding the inadequacy of language among writers seeking to define a conscious self. Words cannot authentically translate the experience of Archer's "wondering" or Lily's "delirium" because there is no language equivalent to the varied manifestations of consciousness.

The picture of Archer's imagination "rising" and hanging above its daily level literalizes the idea of the "free mind" that Monsieur Riviere pronounces in the text. As we have seen, it is a displacement that brings with it an exacting cost. When the mind lifts itself beyond "what it lives in," it may acquire proportionate moral elevation; but it seems clear that one cannot remain long in such a pendulous state. In his Preface to *The American*, Henry James addresses this idea of "experience liberated, so to speak; experience disengaged, disembroiled, disencumbered, exempt from the conditions that we usually know to attach to it." James explicitly states that such a model allows one to operate in a medium that relieves experience of its "relations"; but the balloon of experience, as James describes it, belongs to the realm of romance, a mode that he realizes crept into his narrative unawares.[43] The Wharton novel strains against realism but will not abandon it for romance.[44] Wharton cannot fully endorse a self apart from "relations," yet her multiple ellipses (there are seven) in the final chapter suggest her fascination with the gaps that such a self might fill.

Archer alights from his suspended condition, as it were, in Paris. And perhaps the foreignness of this place along with the fact that he is accompanied by a son untrained in the old ways, "unconscious of what was going on in his father's mind" (1299), allows him to move beyond the claustrophobic compass of New York. But his decision not to enter the Countess's home; his belief that uncertainty is equivalent to passion ("Only, I wonder—the thing one's so certain of in advance: can it ever make one's heart beat as wildly?" [1296]), like his sense that "thinking over a pleasure to come" gives a "subtler satisfaction than its realization" (1018) shows a perverse desire to remain in the suspended state, to make that anticipatory condition the whole reality. "'It's more real to me here than if I went up,' he suddenly heard himself say; and the fear lest that last shadow of reality should lose its edge kept him rooted to his seat" (1302). As opposed to the closing moments of *The House of Mirth* (rendered not through *Lily's* voice, but via a narrative voice), this moment delivers Archer's vision in Archer's spoken words. Such a maneuver on Wharton's part has prompted many readers to divert any ambivalence regarding the potential for authentic inner reality onto Archer. As such, Archer is either a victim of society's constraints or a victim of his own constrained vision.[45] But the ambivalence is also Wharton's. For a novel intensely devoted to transparency of consciousness, this final moment, showing characters entirely closed off from one another's thoughts appears to enact a strange reversal.

While reading Wharton's fiction through the facts of her biography is a tricky business, we might learn something by paying attention to the figurative language she employs across genres. It seems important, at this juncture, to remember that she fills *A Backward Glance* with references to "inner voices," "real" selves, the "acquisition" of her "real personality," the discovery of "authentic human nature," the "inmost self," and her "inner world," all terms which it seems clear she intends without irony. [46] Indeed, these references make for some of the most deeply felt emotion in the text, a response that Wharton appears quite self-consciously to invite. At the same time, she records entirely unsentimental examples of her keen critical eye, like her earnest inquiry to Henry James about the characters inside his *Golden Bowl*. Disturbed by what she sees as a lack of "atmosphere" in James's late novels, the sense that they are "more and more severed from that thick nourishing human air in which we all live and move," she approaches James with this "preoccupation." "I one day said to him: 'What was your idea in suspending the four principle characters in 'The Golden Bowl' in the void? What sort of life did they lead when they were not watching each other. . . ? Why have you stripped them of all the *human fringes* we necessarily trail after us through life?'"[47] Wharton's language in both instances reveals, with characteristic sharpness, a theory of consciousness remarkably balanced on its edge. The "human fringe," which we trial behind us, itself an echo of William James's language for consciousness, seems to spill from us despite our efforts to contain ourselves. And it is for Wharton material indispensable to fiction. At the same time, as we see penetratingly, even poignantly in *A Backward Glance*, she will not abandon the possibility that language can render authentically some core of the self that she alternately names the soul, the inner life or one's *real* self. Though she could imagine the "suspended" existence, Wharton will not attempt to sustain it in the way she sees James's fiction uncomfortably poised. But it is really the same anxiety over language, over the central question of translating one's conscious life into words, that brings Wharton and James to linguistic "suspension." Both authors, writing as they do at the intersection of society and selfhood, struggle to find a language adequate to inward reality; it is a problem vital to the modern novel as well as the new psychology at the turn of the century.

Perhaps, too, as I have suggested with respect to the evolutionary writers to whom William James's philosophy of consciousness owes so much, the impulse to record the conscious life necessarily carries with it a profound fear of the loss of creative power. This concern might explain the phenomenon so familiar in the modern novel of leaving the ending, as Henry James would have it, *en l'air* as well as the almost obsessive impulse toward revision that we have seen among scientific texts intent on defining consciousness. Both gestures indicate the impossibility of settling upon any one answer, any singular term, any positive fate for consciousness or for the characters whose lived experience we follow. The language for consciousness, as we have repeatedly seen, vacillates in these texts between the certainty of inner life as the essence of identity and the sense that we come to know ourselves through our relationships and through the inevitable imprint of the social world. All of these texts are preoccupied with the desire to locate an authentic expression for the life of the mind; and in some sense, all of them fail to do so—an awareness that the authors sometimes painfully relate. The history of consciousness, soaked through as it is by the cultural environment, reveals itself through a complex series of metaphors that move in and out of, but never rest upon, one linguistic system. Unwilling to relinquish the language of the soul, novels, scientific studies, texts of psychology and social psychology combine spiritual and social influence as they bring consciousness into being. The belief in the "real me," the sense that interior life is (and must remain) a mystery that we are awakened to again and again, rubs up against the sense that who we are is bound by social ties, collective responsibilities, and our history within a community. The narrative of consciousness does not resolve this split, but rather, intensifies it, maybe even elevates it so that it becomes *the* question and thereby the legacy of the culture of the modern mind.

# Notes

## Preface

[1] May Sinclair, "The Novels of Dorothy Richardson" *The Little Review*, vol. 5, (April 1918): 3–11.


## Chapter 1

[1] Along with interior designer Ogden Codman, Jr., Edith Wharton wrote the first American handbook of interior decoration, explicitly intending to repair the gap between interiors and exteriors that seemed to proliferate in the gaudy excesses of the houses of the Gilded Age. See Edith Wharton and Ogden Codman, Jr., *The Decoration of Houses* (1897; reprint, New York: Charles Scribner's Sons, 1901), xix. Also see Shari Benstock, *No Gifts From Chance: A Biography of Edith Wharton* (New York: Charles Scribner's Sons, 1994), 83–88 for a useful discussion of the history and production of Wharton's first book.

[2] Wharton and Codman, Jr., p. xx.

[3] Julian Jaynes makes this point in the introduction to his study of human consciousness as he surveys some of the solutions to the question of consciousness that have been proposed over the centuries. Jaynes's book makes the radical claim that human consciousness did not begin far back in animal evolution; rather, he contends that consciousness is a learned process, still developing, which was brought into being out of an earlier hallucinatory mentality. Jaynes's introduction is especially adept at showing how trends in science—from nineteenth-century studies in geology, chemistry and biology to twentieth-century discoveries in physics and neuroscience—transformed notions of consciousness. See Julian Jaynes, *The Origin of Consciousness in the Breakdown of the Bicameral Mind* (1976; reprint, Boston: Houghton Mifflin Company, 1990).

[4]  Charles Darwin, *The Foundations of the Origin of Species* (Cambridge: Cambridge University Press, 1909), 113. This book, edited by Darwin's son, Francis Darwin, is actually a collection of two essays which anticipated *The Origin of Species by Means of Natural Selection or the Preservation of Favoured Races in the Struggle for Life* (1859). Francis Darwin reminds readers, in the introduction, that *Origin* was an abstract for a much bigger book and that the essay of 1844 (from which I take my excerpt) was an expansion of the sketch of the first essay (1842): "It is not therefore surprising that in the *Origin* there is occasionally evident a chafing against the author's self-imposed limitation. Whereas in the 1842 essay there is an air of freedom, as if the author were letting himself go, rather than applying the curb" (xxv). Darwin's son does *not* mention that the *Origin* was also written hurriedly in order that Darwin might not be outstaged by Alfred Russel Wallace who, concurrently, discovered a theory "On the Tendency of Varieties to depart indefinitely from the Original Type" (1858). See Bert James Loewenberg, ed., *Charles Darwin: Evolution and Natural Selection* (Boston: Beacon Hill Press, 1959), 138.

[5]  Gillian Beer, *Darwin's Plots: Evolutionary Narrative in Darwin, George Eliot and Nineteenth-Century Fiction* (London: Routledge & Kegan Paul, 1983), 88. Beer further states that the "profound importance of Darwin's idea [of natural selection] was in revealing a new dynamic for change and in disclosing a fresh space occupied neither by concepts of design nor use. The abiding problem for Darwin was how to express it in a language which was imbued with intentionality" (88). Beer takes a literary approach to Darwin's *Origin*, illuminating the connections between Darwin's creative strategies and textual devices to those of nineteenth-century fiction writers. Her seminal work on Darwin consistently stresses that the multivalent "quagmire" of metaphorical language was necessary for the articulation of Darwin's theory; according to Beer, Darwin relies on uncontrolled "surplus meaning," he needs the metaphor's tendency to multiply. For a sharp criticism of Gillian Beer's approach to Darwin, see Ted Benton's "Science, ideology and culture: Malthus and the *Origin of Species*" in David Amigoni and Jeff Wallace, ed., *Charles Darwin's The Origin of Species: New Interdisciplinary Essays* (Manchester: Manchester University Press, 1995).

[6]  Jeff Wallace provides an excellent discussion of the problems of the notion of "origin" in Darwin's *Origin of Species*; he cites recent studies of Darwin's text that argue that if there is one thing that *Origin* is *not* about, it is the origin of species. Wallace also reminds us that we should not be completely misled by the second part of the book's title, "by means of Natural Selection," for while the metaphor and the theory of natural selection as a mechanism for species-generation was clearly the "central and the most revolutionary proposal of the text," Darwin's use of the word "origin" exposes many of the text's ambiguities. While Darwin felt compelled to challenge the principles of independent species-creationism, Wallace argues that the issue of an ultimate beginning for species inevitably impinged upon his project in the *Origin*. Wallace's introduction is particu-

larly apt at demonstrating the ways in which the *Origin* "reveals tensions in its assumed relationship between language and scientific knowledge which often hinge on the role of metaphor" (24). See "Introduction: Difficulty and Defamiliarisation —Language and Process in *The Origin of Species*" in Jeff Wallace, ed., *Charles Darwin's The Origin of Species: New Interdisciplinary Essays* (Manchester: Manchester University Press, 1995), 3–8.

7    Most studies of Darwin even remotely interested in his language take up this metaphor. Some studies of the significance of language in Darwin's scientific texts include Gillian Beer, "Darwin and the Growth of Language Theory," in *Nature Transfigured: Science and literature, 1700–1900,* ed., John Christie and Sally Shuttleworth (Manchester: Manchester University Press, 1989), "The Face of Nature": Anthropomorphic Elements in the Language of *The Origin of Species*" in *Languages of Nature: Critical Essays on Science and Literature,* ed., Ludmilla Jordanova (New Brunswick: Rutgers University Press, 1986) and her *Darwin's Plots*; Stanley Edgar Hyman, *The Tangled Bank: Darwin, Marx, Frazer and Freud as Imaginative Writers* (New York: Atheneum, 1962); also, Robert M. Young, *Darwin's Metaphor: Nature's Place in Victorian Culture* (Cambridge: Cambridge University Press, 1985).

8    Charles Darwin, *The Origin of Species by Means of Natural Selection or the Preservation of Favoured Races in the Struggle for Life* (1859; reprint, New York: Collier Books, 1962), 136–7.

9    Darwin, *Origin*, 243.

10   Darwin, *Foundations*, 114–15.

11   Darwin, *Foundations*, 127–8.

12   Darwin, *Origin*, 484.

13   Charles Darwin, *The Descent of Man, and Selection in Relation to Sex* (New York: A.L. Burt, Publisher, 1874), 1. See also Gillian Beer, "'The Face of Nature': Anthropomorphic Elements in the Language of *The Origin of Species.*" Beer argues that Darwin was very aware of the problems "man" posed for him in *Origin* and that he made what seems like a conscious decision to remain silent on the question: "there seem to have been as good social as there were religious reasons for Darwin to attempt to conceal man in the interstices of his text—or to permit him almost to escape beyond its parameters" (222). Beer is particularly good at pointing out how Darwin's metaphors have consequences beyond the control of the text that engenders them: "The quagmire of the metaphoric troubles Darwin, yet he needs it. He needs its tendency to suggest more than you meant to say, to make the latent actual, to waken sleeping dogs, and equally its powers of persuasion through lassitude, through our inattention. Analogy, suspect though it has always been to scientists, was one of the great tools of nineteenth-century evolutionary theory. Moreover, analogy was not simply a tool of theory,

but was itself part of theory" (238). I would qualify Beer's statement to argue that metaphor, in fact, explicitly constructs those theories.

[14] Darwin, *The Descent of Man*, 74.

[15] Darwin, *The Descent of Man*, footnote, 79.

[16] Darwin, *The Descent of Man*, 112; 113; 126–7.

[17] Charles Darwin, *The Expression of the Emotions in Man and Animals* (1872) reprinted in Bert James Loewenberg, ed., *Charles Darwin: Evolution and Natural Selection* (Boston: Beacon Hill Press, 1959), 405.

[18] Darwin, *The Descent of Man*, 123.

[19] Loren Eisely, *Darwin's Century: Evolution and the Men Who Discovered It* (New York: Doubleday Anchor Books, 1958) offers a useful introductory study of the Darwin-Wallace relationship.

[20] Alfred Russel Wallace, *Darwinism: An Exposition of the Theory of Natural Selection with Some of its Applications* (London: Macmillan and Company, 1891), 461.

[21] In the preface to a later work entitled *On Miracles and Modern Spiritualism* (London: James Burns, 1875), Wallace explains that he is "well aware" that his ventures into metaphysics made other scientists nervous or disdainful. Wallace acknowledges that his scientific friends "are somewhat puzzled to account for what they consider to be my delusion, and believe that it has seriously affected whatever power I may have once possessed of dealing with the philosophy of Natural History" (vi), but goes on to explain his progression from confirmed materialist to the "science" of Spiritualism. As a materialist, Wallace says "I could not find a place in my mind" for the conception of spiritual existence; nor could he locate any other agencies in the universe apart from matter and force. The shift in Wallace's thinking occurs dramatically, though the drama of the incident itself seems barely detectable: "My curiosity was at first excited by some slight but inexplicable phenomena occurring in a friend's family, and my desire for knowledge and love of truth forced me to continue the inquiry. The facts became more and more assured, more and more varied, more and more removed from anything that modern science taught or modern philosophy speculated on. The facts beat me. They compelled me to accept them, *as facts*, long before I could accept the spiritual explanation for them" (vii). Strikingly, Wallace represents the mind as "making room" for the spiritual as if the intellectual and the spiritual were combative entities trying to fit into one spot; the "facts" must fight their way in until "by slow degrees a place [is] made." Though this obscure incident from his past obviously transforms his thought, Wallace gives no specific indication of the event or the emotions surrounding it; the spiritualist's "cardinal maxim" is that everyone must "find out the truth for him or her self (223), thus Wallace will do no more than invite readers to consider his oblique evidence and discover meaning for themselves. Unlike the scientist whose job

it is to present proven research which makes their findings incontrovertible, the spiritualist leaves open the possibilities for meaning.

22 Wallace, *Darwinism*, 474.

23 Wallace, *Darwinism*, 466; 474.

24 Wallace, *Darwinism*, 474–5; 476.

25 Julian Jaynes discusses the shift from a "tough-minded" materialism to "emergent evolution" which asserted that consciousness issued forth as "something genuinely new" at a critical stage of evolution; emergent evolutionists believed consciousness came from living things, but they claimed that it emerged at some point in evolution in a way underivable from its constituent parts. Jaynes cites G.H. Lewes as an early proponent of this theory; he also evokes William James's discussion of the conscious automaton theory in chapter five of *The Principles of Psychology*, vol. 1 (1890; reprint, Cambridge: Harvard University Press, 1981), 132–147. However, Jaynes specifies that the phrase, "conscious automata," comes from an essay by T.H. Huxley, *Collected Essays* (New York: Appleton, 1896), vol. 1, 244. See Jaynes, 11–12.

26 G.H. Lewes, *Problems of Life and Mind* (Boston: Houghton, Osgood and Company, 1880), 5.

27 Lewes, *Problems of Life and Mind*, 81–3; 86.

28 Lewes, *Problems of Life and Mind*, 87.

29 Lewes, *Problems of Life and Mind*, 145; 149.

30 Lewes, *Problems of Life and Mind*, 181.

31 Lewes, *Problems of Life and Mind*, 201. The remainder of this passage illustrates what Lewes considers to be the *individual* character of "personality." Lewes narrates the experience of "four men" who observe a sunset: "Of four men gazing on a sunset, all will have similar visual impressions, but each will react on these according to his personal disposition—one will interpret them according to the abiding religious attitude of his mind; a second, according to the aesthetic attitude; a third will interpret the signs as favourable to the condition of his crops, or tomorrow's expedition; a fourth will be as indifferent as a cow to the splendours of the sky: the light of the setting sun enables him to find his way across the fields, but he is only subconscious even of this." His explication of this scene sounds remarkably like the sketch of the "four men," in William James's *Principles of Psychology*, who visit Europe. "Let four men make a tour in Europe. One will bring home only picturesque impressions—costumes and colors, parks and views and works of architecture, pictures and statues. To another all this will be non-existent; and distances and prices, populations and drainage-arrangements, door- and window-fastenings, and other useful statistics will take their place. A third will give a rich account of the theatres,

restaurants, and public balls, and naught beside; whilst the fourth will per-haps have been so wrapped in his own subjective broodings as to tell little more than a few names of places through which he passed. Each has select-ed, out of the same mass of presented objects, those which suited his pri-vate interest and has made his experience thereby." See William James, *The Principles of Psychology*, vol. 1, 275–6. While Lewes suggests that one's perception of a scene results from the attitude of mind already present—religious, aesthetic, pragmatic,—James's four men seem to take in these impressions whole as if they could displace or remake subjectivity as a result of their notions of experience. For a fuller discussion of this passage with respect to William James's account of experience, see chapter two.

[32] George Henry Lewes, *The Physical Basis of Mind* (London: Kegan Paul, Trench, Trubner & Co. Ltd., 1893), 353–4; 360.

[33] Lewes, *The Physical Basis of Mind* , 365; 366.

[34] In the preface to the first edition of the text, Spencer tells us that portions of *The Principles of Psychology* were originally published in the *Westminster Review* of October 1853, though he expands and revises his text repeatedly. See *The Works of Herbert Spencer*, third edition, 2 vols. (1899; reprint, Osnabruck: Otto Zeller, 1966), vol. 1, 151. One wonders whether the compulsion to revise a text, so prevalent among the evolution-ary psychologists, discloses a concern over keeping the concepts inside it unresolved.

[35] *The Works of Herbert Spencer* , vol. 1, 15; 42; 44.

[36] *The Works of Herbert Spencer* , vol. 1, 184.

[37] See Peter Dear, "Narrative, Anecdotes, and Experiments: Turning Experience into Science in the Seventeenth Century" in *The Literary Structure of Scientific Argument*, ed., Peter Dear (Philadelphia: University of Pennsylvania Press, 1991), 135; 163.

[38] Sally Shuttleworth makes this point and provides both of these quotations (from the 1855 version of Spencer's, *The Principles of Psychology* ) in her essay on George Eliot's, *Silas Marner*. Shuttleworth argues that the novel sheds light on nineteenth-century science, philosophy and social thought; she specifically examines the prose of Lewes and Spencer for an under-standing of Eliot's articulation of the complex interrelationships between scientific and social theories of this period. While Spencer provided an organic theory of history, Shuttleworth maintains that Lewes allowed Eliot to explore the internal psychological conflict and breakdown of individual identity. See Sally Shuttleworth "Fairy Tale or Science?: Physiological Psychology in *Silas Marner*" in *Languages of Nature: Critical Essays on Science and Literature*, ed., L.J. Jordanova (New Brunswick: Rutgers University Press, 1986), 265–6.

[39] *The Works of Herbert Spencer* , vol. 1, 187–192.

[40] *The Works of Herbert Spencer* , vol. 1, 159.

[41] *The Works of Herbert Spencer* , vol. 1, 159.

[42] *The Works of Herbert Spencer* , vol. 1, 161.

[43] *The Works of Herbert Spencer* , vol. 1, 132–3.

[44] At one point in *Principles*, Spencer directly confronts the "alarm" he assumes would ensue were we actually to understand mind or consciousness completely: "While reading the last two sections, some will perhaps have thought that they stand in direct contradiction to the section preceding them. After alleging that the substance of Mind cannot be known, an attempt is forthwith made to show that Mind is, certainly in some cases and probably in all, resolvable into nervous shocks; and that these nervous shocks answer to the waves of molecular motion that traverse nerves and nerve-centers. Thus not only is the substance of Mind supposed to be knowable as having this universal character, but it is closely assimilated to, if not identified with, nervous change. The alarm is groundless however. The foregoing reasoning brings us no nearer to a solution of the final question." This passage amounts to a scholarly sigh of relief; we see, in a moment like this, Spencer's investment in keeping the mind and its "substance" an unsolvable riddle. See *The Works of Herbert Spencer* , vol. 1, 156–7.

[45] *The Works of Herbert Spencer* , vol. 1, 140.

[46] In his excellent book on American pragmatism and its originators (Oliver Wendell Holmes, Jr., William James, Charles Sanders Peirce, and John Dewey), Louis Menand specifically discusses Darwin's influence on William James. See Louis Menand, *The Metaphysical Club: A Story of Ideas in America* (New York: Farrar, Straus and Giroux, 2001), 140–146; 357.

[47] See James's chapter on Attention; William James, *The Principles of Psychology*, vol. 1, 380–1.

## CHAPTER 2

[1] James's work responds to the theories of nineteenth-century scientists such as Darwin, Spencer and G.H. Lewes who wrestled with questions about the natural origin of the mind, reflecting their paradoxical tendencies to place consciousness inside elaborate physiological systems while still maintaining its elusive properties. See, also, chapter one.

[2] An exemplary instance of this debate is John Dewey's "The Vanishing Subject in the Psychology of William James," *Journal of Philosophy, Psychology and Scientific Method* 37 (1940): 589–99, reprinted in *Problems of Men* (New York: Philosophical Library, 1946) which argues

that there are "two incompatible strains" in Jamesian psychology: episte-mological dualism, which argues for a definitive, psychical self, and natu-ralism which "purges" psychology of the traditional notion of "subject," describing mental phenomena in terms of the organism exclusively. Milic Capek rejects Dewey's claim, arguing that what James denies is "a timeless, ghostly, and diaphanous entity, common to all individuals and consequent-ly impersonal." Capek argues that James's work, despite its discrepancies, supports the notion of a "potential self"—based on what James calls "vir-tual experience"—and opposes naturalism. See Milic Capek, "The Reappearance of the Self in the Last Philosophy of William James," *The Philosophical Review* 62 (1953): 526–544.

3   William Joseph Gavin, *William James and the Reinstatement of the Vague* (Philadelphia: Temple University Press, 1992) discusses language with respect to Jamesian "metaphysics," arguing that James's language exists as a "provocation" to the reader, gesturing to what lies beyond it, and that James remains suspicious of words even when he is "bewitched" by them.

4   William James, *The Principles of Psychology*, volume 1, (1890; reprint, Cambridge, University Press, 1981), 233. All subsequent references will be to this edition of the text.

5   For example, in the chapter entitled "The Consciousness of Self," James speaks of the "Spiritual Self" and its faculties: "This is an abstract way of dealing with consciousness . . . we may insist on a concrete view, and then the spiritual self in us will be either the entire stream of our personal con-sciousness, or the present 'segment' or 'section' of that stream, according as we take a broader or a narrower view—both the stream and the section being concrete existencies in time, and each being a unity after its own peculiar kind" *(PP,* 1.284).

6   On the place of natural imagery and the aesthetic in James, see Russell B. Goodman, *American Philosophy and the Romantic Tradition* (Cambridge: Cambridge University Press, 1990). Goodman considers Emerson, James and Dewey in conjunction with literary Romanticism; he borrows ideas from Wordsworth such as naturalization of the spiritual, the "feeling intel-lect" and the marriage of self and world in order to study the Romantic aspect of James's thought. See also Donna Farantello, "'The Picture of the Mind Revives Again': Perception in William James's Psychology and "Tintern Abbey,'" *The Wordsworth Circle* 22 (1991): 131–5. In comparing James with Wordsworth, Farantello emphasizes each writer's focus on con-structing a picture of the mind. She takes us through Wordsworth's poem, reading it alongside James's *Principles of Psychology.*

7   Olaf Hansen calls our attention to James's investment in the aesthetic: "In a veritable tour de force and as a kind of climax, William James in *Principles* explains that there is 'a mental structure which expresses itself in aesthetic and moral principles. Many of the so-called metaphysical princi-ples are at bottom only expressions of aesthetic feeling.'" See Olaf Hansen,

*Aesthetic Individualism and Practical Talent: American Allegory in Emerson, Thoreau, Adams, and James* (Princeton: Princeton University Press, 1990), 181.

8 Peter Marcus Ford, *William James's Philosophy* (Amherst: University of Massachusetts Press, 1982), 15.

9 William James, *Psychology: Briefer Course* (New York: Henry Holt and Co., 1892), 466–67.

10 Gerald Myers expresses the tenacity with which James held to the words "consciousness" and "stream" despite his rejection of consciousness as an introspectable entity. He goes on to say that James "burdened" his reader with the task of determining the proper conceptualization of both consciousness and experience. James was "always confident that continuity as well as other characteristics are essential aspects of what we introspect and experience. We can overlook or neglect the continuity, but if we introspect carefully, we will find it, however perplexed we are about verbalizing it and the ways we recognize it." See Gerald Myers, *William James: His Life and Thought* (New Haven: Yale University Press, 1986), 80.

11 Michael S. Kearns, *Metaphors of Mind in Fiction and Psychology* (Lexington: The University Press of Kentucky, 1978), 37; 227. Kearns speaks of mind-as-living-being as the concept, which replaces mind-as-entity. In his Afterward on William James, he attempts to sketch out how mind-as-living-being functions as a generative metaphor, manifested in what he calls the "surface metaphor" of the stream of consciousness.

12 Jamesian consciousness is a selecting agency: consciousness "is always interested more in one part of its object than in another, and welcomes and rejects, or chooses, all the while it thinks" *(PP,* 1.273).

13 Daniel Bjork, *William James: The Center of His Vision* (New York: Columbia University Press, 1988), 160.

14 Discussing William James's relationship to British empiricism, John E. Smith uses this passage in *Principles* to explain James's insistence on analyzing actual *experiencing* as a process: "the experience of thunder is not exhausted as an instantaneous datum of sound . . . but is part of a temporal episode which James sought to represent by the use of hyphens. . . ." Smith notes that James was "above all a thinker in participles"; he glosses this example of the thunder and reads it as an experience that "has the character of an event and belongs to the ongoing biography of the one who has it; to abstract from the total episode the bare sense quality of sound and call that the delivery of 'experience' is, in James's view, to confuse the concrete experiencing with an abstraction and one which has been dictated by the demand that experience be preeminently sensory in character. James's conception of 'radical empiricism' follows in the same vein since it involves both a criticism and the expansion of the classical view. . . ." See John E. Smith, *America's Philosophical Vision* (Chicago: University of Chicago Press, 1992), 26.

[15] Ironically, in his later essay, "Does 'Consciousness' Exist?," James will attempt to erase the significance of consciousness as a "word" and focus his attention precisely on its "function." See William James, *Essays in Radical Empiricism* (New York: Longmans, Green and Co., 1922), 4.

[16] Richard Poirier suggests a connection between Emerson and William James in their emphasis on transitions and on action; he claims that Emersonians (including James) want to prevent words from ever coming to rest. James himself calls our attention to transitions, though he states in *Principles* that in the stream of our thought, language tends to give more stress to the substantives. Poirier weaves in and out of Emersonian and Jamesian texts, pointing to the similarities in their language, showing James's indebtedness to Emersonian figures. Implicit in Poirier's project is the sense that Emerson's work and his subsequent influence is somehow unsettling: "denial of the Emerosnian influence reveals . . . an instinctive recognition that Emerson and his influence, if its nuances and skepticisms were deeply enough explored, would prove disturbing, even disruptive of the critical-interpretive enterprise as people practice it." See Richard Poirier, *The Renewal of Literature: Emersonian Reflections* (New York: Random House, 1987), 25–6.

[17] Gerald Myers discusses introspection in his study of William James: "The natural sciences depend upon sense-perception, whereas psychology, it was commonly assumed in James's time, relies upon introspection as its distinct method of inquiry. . . . Like sense-perception, introspection is fallible and can at times be troublesome and difficult, yet *'the difficulty is simply that of all observation of whatever kind'* (PP, 1.191)." Myers, 64–5.

[18] As John E. Smith notes at the beginning of *America's Philosophical Vision*, James insisted on "distinguishing within experience a central focus of attention from what he called the 'fringe.' Adopting a 'field' theory, an approach which he described at the time as the most important advance to take place in psychology for decades, he claimed that there is always more in experience than is being attended to by what we may call the 'spotlight' consciousness. Attention, as selective and hence abstractive, must in the nature of the case ignore the fringe but from that it does not follow that it does not exist. How seriously he took this conception can be seen in the *Varieties* where the 'trans-marginal' consciousness plays a key role in the analysis of phenomena of religion." See Smith, 25.

[19] A remarkably similar illustration occurs in a text by James's contemporary, George Henry Lewes. Lewes discusses "four men" who observe a sunset: "Of four men gazing on a sunset, all will have similar visual impressions, but each will react on these according to his personal disposition" (201). See G.H. Lewes, *Problems of Life and Mind* (Boston: Houghton, Osgood and Company, 1880). For a fuller discussion of Lewes, see chapter one.

[20] Richard Poirier, ed. *Ralph Waldo Emerson*, (Oxford: Oxford University Press, 1990), 36. See also Poirier, *A World Elsewhere: The Place of Style in*

*American Literature* (New York: Oxford University Press, 1966), which suggests that American writers have been "addicted" to metaphors of building.

[21] In the introduction to his study of Modernist writing, Frank Lentricchia considers what he calls the "Philosophy of Modernism at Harvard circa 1900." He rehearses these metaphors of James's (the innermost centre within the circle, the sanctuary within the citadel, the self of all other selves) to give witness to James's overt commitment to "the inalienable private property of selfhood." Lentricchia claims that James thus inscribes a contradiction at the very heart of capitalism: because property under capitalism can be property only if it is alienable. Arguing that James's later writing is explicitly anti-imperialist, Lentricchia states that James eventually found that nothing was inalienable, not even this secret self we think we possess, but that James "employed the literal language of private property against itself by making the discourse literal so as to preserve a human space for freedom." See Frank Lentricchia, *Modernist Quartet* (New York: Cambridge University Press, 1994), 31.

[22] Hughes states: "In the shifting, transitional world in which they dwelt, the problem of consciousness early established itself as crucial. Another way of defining their intellectual epoch would be to suggest that it was the period in which the subjective attitude of the observer of society first thrust itself forward in peremptory fashion. . . . By slow stages of reorientation—and often against their original intention—they were led to discover the importance of subjective 'values' in human behavior." Though Hughes's study is confined mostly to European writers, James fits this paradigm beautifully. See H. Stuart Hughes, *Consciousness and Society: The Reorientation of European Social Thought 1890–1930* (New York: Vintage Books, 1958), 15–16.

[23] Studies in a variety of disciplines from philosophy to cognitive science to linguistics to psychology to intellectual history comment on the development of the professional study of psychology. David Cole begins his collection of essays on the field of cognitive inquiry with a comment about the representation of philosophical issues in cognitive science; as an interdisciplinary field, cognitive science continues to reiterate some of the questions that arose when the disciplines were beginning to split. See David Cole, *Philosophy, Mind and Cognitive Inquiry* (Dordrecht: Kluwer Academic Publishers, 1990), 5.

[24] John E. Smith asserts: "It is generally agreed that the most important single influence on the course of Western Philosophical thinking since the early eighteenth century was the appeal to experience as a touchstone for judging all claims to knowledge and the possession of power." See Smith, 4.

[25] William James, *Essays in Radical Empiricism* (New York: Longmans, Green and Co., 1922), 3. This essay was first published in *Journal of Philosophy, Psychology and Scientific Methods*, vol. 1. No. 18, September, 1904. All subsequent references will be to this edition of the text.

[26] In *William James's Radical Reconstruction of Philosophy* (Albany: State University of New York Press, 1990), Charlene Haddock Seigfried notices the bipolar organization of Jamesian metaphors, suggesting that the opposing pairs illustrate extremes: "Although James is an indefatigable defender of pluralism, his thoughts are often organized dialectically into dualisms" (227). Seigfried emphasizes the importance of analogy for James, though she reads metaphors as reflective of James's creativity without speculating about their function in the text.

[27] Paul de Man discusses the particular problem that metaphor poses for philosophy in its resistance to proper boundaries: "Metaphors, tropes, and figural language in general have been a perennial problem and, at times, a recognized source of embarrassment for philosophical discourse and, by extension, for all discursive uses of language including historiography and literary analysis. It appears that philosophy either has to give up its own constitutive claim to rigor in order to come to terms with the figurality of its language or that it has to free itself from figuration altogether. And if the latter is considered impossible, philosophy could at least learn to control figuration by keeping it, so to speak, in its place, by delimiting the boundaries of its influence and thus restricting the epistemological damage that it may cause." See Paul de Man, "The Epistemology of Metaphor" in Sheldon Sacks, ed. *On Metaphor* (Chicago: University of Chicago Press, 1979), 11. de Man's sense that philosophy must "give up" its claim to "rigor" if it insists on metaphors enhances the notion that metaphor is flighty, embarrassing, perhaps even irreverent. Metaphor provides a disturbing reminder that language cannot be controlled; words lead to misapprehension, even "epistemological damage," as easily as they lead us to meaning.

[28] In the chapter entitled "Superfluous Emerson," Poirier highlights the connection between the Jamesian desire for vagueness and Emersonian "superfluity." He reminds us that James "had already said in *Principles of Psychology*, 'It is, in short, the re-instatement of the vague to its proper place in our mental life which I am so anxious to press on the attention.' There are etymological connections among the words 'vague,' 'vagrancy'—a particular favorite of James's, 'extravagance,' and 'extravagant,' connecting them to superfluity. . . ." See Richard Poirier, *Poetry and Pragmatism* (Cambridge: Harvard University Press, 1992), 44.

[29] Gerald Myers explains: "Pure experience, the aboriginal stream of consciousness that occurs unbroken by conceptualization, is a catchall for space, time, conjunctive relations, change, activity—everything required for it to bloom into the structured world we learn to perceive"; and again, "Radical empiricism is the idea that the world's essentials are all found in the flux of intuited or perceived experience; this concept transmuted the stream of consciousness of James's psychology into the pure experience of his metaphysics." Myers, 314; 324.

## CHAPTER 3

1  The epigraph comes from James's letter to Grace Norton (1883), quoted in Henry James, *Selected Letters*, ed. Leon Edel (Cambridge: Harvard University Press, 1974), 190–2.

2  Richard Hocks provides the first comprehensive examination of the connection between William and Henry James in his book, *Henry James and Pragmatistic Thought: A Study in the Relationship between the Philosophy of William James and the Literary Art of Henry James* (Chapel Hill: University of North Carolina Press, 1974). Hocks argues from the outset that Henry James "embodies" William James's thought—"where William is the pragmatist, Henry is, so to speak, the pragmatism" (4); Hocks is even more explicit in stating that he is not arguing "influence," but rather claiming that one writer (Henry) "personifies" the other's (William's) thought (18). His book anticipates such work as Paul Armstrong, *The Phenomenology of Henry James* (Chapel Hill: University of North Carolina Press, 1983) and Merle Williams, *Henry James and the Philosophical Novel* (Cambridge: Cambridge University Press, 1993). Armstrong sets up a relationship between Henry James's fascination with consciousness and what is commonly called his "moral vision" (vii). He speaks of the "impression" as a way of knowing; comparing it to consciousness, he contends that the word gives us the sense that consciousness is not something Henry James creates, but rather, something "pressed upon him," there to be absorbed by the artist (37). See also John Carlos Rowe, *The Theoretical Dimensions of Henry James* (Ithaca: Cornell University Press, 1976). Rowe emphasizes James's acknowledgement of the textuality of consciousness; such figures as the "house of fiction" show that there is no consciousness outside a book: "the imagined activity by which such rhetorical figuration brings about the image is less a faculty of consciousness than a property of language" (216). For a range of studies that link the James brothers, see Eliseo Vivas, "Henry and William (Two Notes)," *Kenyon Review* 5 (1943): 580–587; F.O. Matthiessen, *The James Family* (New York: Alfred A. Knopf, 1947); H.B. Parkes, "The James Brothers," *Sewanee Review* 56 (1948): 323–28; Joseph Firebaugh, "The Pragmatism of Henry James," *Virginia Quarterly Review* 27 (1951): 419–35, and "The Ververs," *Essays in Criticism* 4 (1954): 400–410; William McMurray, "Pragmatic Realism in *The Bostonians*," in *Henry James: Modern Judgments*, ed., Tony Tanner (London: Macmillan & Co., 1968) 160–65; Ellwood Johnson, "William James and the Art of Fiction," *Aesthetics and Art Criticism* 30 (1972); as well as Hocks, *Henry James and Pragmatist Thought*.

3  In a frequently quoted passage from a letter to his brother, Henry writes: "Then I was lost in the wonder of the extent to which all my life I have (like M. Jourdain) unconsciously pragmatised. You are immensely and universally *right*." Henry James, *The Letters of Henry James*, ed., Percy Lubbock, 2 vols. (New York: Charles Scribner's Sons, 1920), 2.83.

[4]   Leon Edel insists upon a lifelong psychic antagonism between the brothers in his comprehensive study of Henry's life. See Leon Edel, *The Life of Henry James* (Harmondsworth: Penguin Press, 1977).

[5]   Parkes offers a representative appraisal of these roles, parenthetically, as if it were a given: "Although William and Henry were temperamentally so opposed to each other, and although they deal with their neurotic difficulties by such different methods (William's robust self-assertiveness being, by normal standards, much healthier than Henry's retreat into the role of a spectator and the rigid protective shell of mannerisms which he gradually built up around himself), yet the two brothers were alike in that the fundamental premise of all their intellectual activity was an acceptance of the moral freedom of the individual human being." See Parkes, 325.

[6]   Matthiessen, 321.

[7]   Ignas K. Skrupskelis and Elizabeth M. Berkeley, ed., *William and Henry James, Selected Letters* (Charlottesville: University Press of Virginia, 1997), 239.

[8]   Hocks argues that the relationship between the James brothers is one of "polarity"—where contraries exist by virtue of each other—rather than paradox—the union of two opposites. He states that Henry's later manner "is just the mode of presentation which most thoroughly embodies William's own views" though William repeatedly says he is opposed to his brother's method. Hocks, 19.

[9]   Matthiessen, 339.

[10]  Matthiessen, 340.

[11]  Matthiessen, 341–2; also *The Letters of William James*, ed. by his son Henry James (Boston: Atlantic Monthly Press, 1920), 2:277–78 and Skrupskelis and Berkeley, ed., *William and Henry James, Selected Letters*, 484.

[12]  William James, *The Principles of Psychology* (1890; reprint, Cambridge: Harvard University Press, 1981), 1.234.

[13]  Matthiessen 341–2; also *The Letters of William James*, ed. by his son Henry James (Boston: Atlantic Monthly Press, 1920), 2:277–78 and Skrupskelis and Berkeley, ed., *William and Henry James, Selected Letters*, 485.

[14]  An example in the philosophy which has a similar feel to it comes from James's *Principles* where he describes images in the mind: "Every definite image in the mind is steeped and dyed in the free water that flows round it. With it goes the sense of its relations, near and remote, the dying echo of whence it came to us, the dawning sense of whither it is to lead. The significance, the value of the image is all in this halo or penumbra that surrounds and escorts it. . . ." (*PP*, 1.246). As I demonstrate in chapter two,

James often uses metaphysical or ethereal references to describe something like the "fringe" of consciousness.

[15] Henry James, *The Portrait of a Lady*, volumes 3 and 4 (New York: Charles Scribner's Sons, 1908), ix–x. All subsequent references will be to this edition of the text.

[16] James makes a similar claim about systematic growth in his Preface to *The Spoils of Poynton*. He imagines his novel growing "symmetrically" under the shade of an ash tree (which is also, incidentally, "trained" to grow as it does): "The horizon was in fact a band of sea . . . while above one's head rustled a dense summer shade, that of a trained and arching ash, rising from the middle of the terrace, brushing the parapet with a heavy fringe and covering the place like a vast umbrella. Beneath this umbrella and really under exquisite protection *The Spoils of Poynton* managed more or less symmetrically to grow." See Henry James, *The Spoils of Poynton*, volume 10, (New York: Charles Scribner's Sons, 1908), xi.

[17] Tony Tanner is one of the first critics to argue that James brings together two opposing worlds in this name. Tanner states that Isabel is "happiest . . . at Gardencourt, and the very name points to the fact that this is the locale in the book which most exudes a mood of mellow reciprocity between the civilized and the natural." See Tanner, 153.

[18] See Sandra K. Fischer, "Isabel Archer and the Enclosed Chamber: A Phenomenological Reading," *Henry James Review* 7 (1986): 48–58.

[19] Henry's description of the process of growth in terms of these discrete units is reminiscent of William James's use of the metaphor of a kaleidoscope to describe the ever-changing pace of consciousness. Both authors use an image that denotes not so much a process as it does a series of frozen, separate pieces that make up a pattern. The pattern may be constantly moving but it is also always made up of the same units. See William James, *Principles of Psychology*, 1.228–9.

[20] Donatello Izzo discusses what he calls the "freedom/constraint theme" in *Portrait* with respect to theme and technique in the novel. He states that the "closure is reinforced by the title: *Portrait* alludes to an enclosed form, which the frame ostensibly isolates from the surrounding reality and which, in the novel, constitutes a completely formal principle of unity. . . ." (42–3). Izzo also finds that the novel "weaves a dense web of references to itself and to its internal composition. And these self-reflexive references—the novel's dialogue with itself and its thematizing itself, thereby inaugurating the inclusion of a discourse *on* the text *within* the text itself—make *The Portrait of a Lady* a decisively modern text" (46). See Donatello Izzo, "*The Portrait of a Lady* and Modern Narrative" in *New Essays on The Portrait of a Lady*, ed., Joel Porte (Cambridge: Cambridge University Press, 1990), 33–47.

[21] See William James, "Does 'Consciousness' Exist?" from *Essays in Radical Empiricism* (New York: Longmans, Green and Co., 1920), 14. See also chapter two.

[22] William James, *Principles*, 1.275.

[23] William James, *Principles*, 1.275–6. For a fuller explication of this passage and its place in James's philosophy, see chapter two.

[24] Hawthorne begins *The House of the Seven Gables*, for example, with a description of "the venerable mansion" which, he says, "has always affected [him] like a human countenance"; because it bears "traces" of storm and sun; also because it is "expressive . . . of the long lapse of mortal life, and accompanying vicissitudes that have passed within." Hawthorne imagines that recounting these "would form a narrative of no small interest and instruction, and possessing, moreover, a certain remarkable unity, which might almost seem the result of artistic arrangement" (11). Thus the house is a metaphor for the human being as well as the "arrangement" of narrative. See Nathaniel Hawthorne, *The House of the Seven Gables* (New York: Penguin Books, 1990). In *The Grasping Imagination: The American Writings of Henry James* (Toronto: University of Toronto Press, 1970), Peter Buitenhuis notes the influence of Hawthorne on James's house imagery. With respect to Emerson, Elizabeth Jean Sabiston argues that James is indebted to Emerson's "organic theory of art in which the latter describes a poem (or any literary work, for that matter) as having 'an architecture of its own,' derived from the innermost heart of the work, the thought of its creator" (126). She briefly discusses the distinctions between James's use of architectural metaphors and landscape metaphors. See Elizabeth Jean Sabiston, *The Prison of Womanhood* (London: The Macmillan Press. Ltd, 1987), 114–138. See also Richard Poirier, *A World Elsewhere: The Place of Style in American Literature* (New York: Oxford University Press, 1966). Poirier claims that American literature is preoccupied with theories about "proper housing for expanded states of consciousness" (vii).

[25] Richard Poirier, ed. *Ralph Waldo Emerson* (Oxford: Oxford University Press, 1990), 200.

[26] Poirier, ed., 215.

[27] James writes, the "price" of the novel as literary form is "its power not only, while preserving that form with closeness, to range through all the differences of the individual relation to its general subject-matter . . . but positively to appear more true to its character as it strains, or tends to burst, with a latent extravagance, its mould" (x).

[28] Even the neat frame of the Preface pinches tightly on the account James longs to provide. His final words are sounded with exasperation: "There is really too much to say" (xxi).

29 Ellen Frank, *Literary Architecture* (Berkeley: University of California Press, 1979), 3–4. In her introduction, Frank discusses the analogue of literature to architecture: "it represents an embodied consciousness or form of consciousness, as it represents an awareness (idea) of consciousness. The four writers I have chosen [Pater, Hopkins, Proust, and James] select architecture in order to give to language and thought spatial extension. . . . By means of the analogue, they may give, or seem to give, substance to that which is no-thing, to that which does not occupy what we call substantial space. . . ." (12). More than connecting architecture and literature in literary history, Frank wants to suggest a connection between architecture and literature in terms of perceptual experience: "to writers more and more fearful of disappearance not only of the temporal past but of familiar concepts of identity (and such are those writing toward the close of the nineteenth century and on into the first decades of the twentieth), architecture provides a means of preserving or memorializing the past, and identity, even as it provides for the transformation of that past and of being into literary art" (13).

30 Frank, 172.

31 See Diana Collecott, "Framing *The Portrait of a Lady*: Henry James and Isabel Archer," from Amritjit Singh and K. Ayyappa Paniker, ed., *The Magic Circle of Henry James* (New York: Envoy Press, 1989). Recent debates about the representation of women in the cinema and about the role of the female spectator influence Collecott's thinking about James's ways of writing and the ways in which he can be read.

32 The metaphor of Isabel as "house" is present within the novel as well. At one point in the *Portrait*, Ralph compares Isabel first to a work of art, then claims she is "finer . . . than a great Titian, than a Gothic cathedral." He thinks to himself: "The key of a beautiful edifice is thrust into my hand, and I'm told to walk in and admire." The narrator finishes the image, however, indicating that Ralph's imagination of Isabel is not quite complex enough, for if she is a house, she is not so readily accessible by key: ". . . it was not exactly true that Ralph Touchett had had a key put into his hand. His cousin was a very brilliant girl, who would take, as he said, a good deal of knowing; but she needed the knowing. . . . He surveyed the edifice from the outside and admired it greatly; he looked in at the windows and received an impression of proportions equally fair. But he felt that he saw it only by glimpses and that he had not yet stood under the roof. The door was fastened, and though he had the keys in his pocket he had a conviction that none of them would fit" (1.86).

33 A.D. Moody argues that we feel an "uneasiness" all along because James has been covertly protecting his heroine; "she remains for him an ideal being, cherished in defiance of her fate" (21). James's "flaw," he states, occurs when his critical sense bows before the force of his admiration. Moody finds signs of the lapse of James's critical faculty in the last three

chapters where James is "unwilling to expose [Isabel] in a really frank light
. . . there is in it an effect of obfuscation, as if a veil were being drawn over
her" (32–2). See A.D. Moody, "James's Portrait of an Ideal," from Amritjit
Singh and K. Ayyappa Paniker, ed., *The Magic Circle of Henry James* (New
York: Envoy Press, 1989).

³⁴ This sense that Isabel possesses the freedom to *make* herself or make her
world is often connected to the influence of Emerson's writings on Henry
James. Elizabeth Jean Sabiston discusses Isabel's Emersonian roots, stating
at one point that for Isabel, "the initiation into life and the shaping of character have been dangerously postponed. . . . The result is Isabel's illusion
that she can 'build therefore [her] own world'; that her choices are completely free and that she is adventuring on life." See Elizabeth Jean
Sabiston, *The Prison of Womanhood*, 119. Also, Philip Rahv's chapter,
'The Heiress of All the Ages,' in *Image and Idea: Fourteen Essays on
Literary Themes* (New York: New Directions, 1949); Richard Chase, *The
American Novel and its Tradition* (New York: Doubleday, 1957) who
argues for a connection between Isabel's romanticism and the transcendental tradition; Richard Poirier, *The Comic Sense of Henry James* (London:
Oxford University Press, 1960); Annette T. Rubinstein, "Henry James,
American Novelist; or, Isabel Archer, Emerson's Granddaughter" in
*Weapons of Criticism: Marxism in America and the Literary Tradition*,
edited by Norman Rudich (Palo Alto, Calif: Ramparts Press, 1976) who
claims that James is an abstract or metaphysical novelist and that *Portrait*
"takes as its theme an examination of the indigenous American philosophy
of transcendentalism . . . specifically, it poses the question of perfect freedom, a question earlier posed in one way by Emerson and Thoreau. . . ."
(319); and Leon Edel, "The Myth of America in *The Portrait of a Lady*,"
*Henry James Review* 7 (1986): 8–17. This essay also develops the
Emersonian quality of Isabel, though Edel argues that James is undermining the Emersonian doctrine 'Trust thyself.'

³⁵ Tony Tanner, "The Fearful Self: Henry James's *The Portrait of a Lady*,"
from *Modern Judgments* (London: Macmillan & Co., 1968) offers the
exemplary argument on Isabel's fear of herself.

³⁶ Commenting specifically on this passage, Sharon Baris states that this
notion of the "vagabond mind" is "the portrait of an Emersonian transcendental thinker; Isabel's mind leaps over the particulars of place and
time, so that she feels an 'elation of liberty' although sitting still. She adds
that as the novel progresses, Isabel becomes more and more unable to read;
in each case, her attention wanders because, in an Emersonian way, Isabel
adds 'observation upon observation' in the act of creatively reading her
own independent self or text" (147). See Sharon Baris, "James's
Pyrotechnic Display: The Book in Isabel's Portrait," *Henry James Review*
12 (1991): 146–153.

³⁷ The worst and most obvious instance of Isabel's "misreading" occurs in her
interpretation of Osmond's character. Isabel's "imagination supplied the

human element" in a rather "dry account" of Gilbert Osmond (1.383). Consequently, as James puts it: "She had not read him right" (2.192). Various critics take up the idea of the imagination and how it relates to Isabel's role as a reader. D. Buchanan claims that Isabel's imagination is "flawed—gothic, ridiculous, manipulable, and hyperactive." See D. Buchanan, "'The Candlestick and the Snuffers': Some Thoughts on *The Portrait of a Lady*," *Henry James Review* 16 (1995): 124; A.D. Moody concurs: hers is "an abuse of the imagination," a "grave moral blindness." See A.D. Moody, "James's Portrait of an Ideal," from Amritjit Singh and K. Ayyappa Paniker, ed., *The Magic Circle of Henry James* (New York: Envoy Press, 1989). Sandra K. Fischer calls this Isabel's particular form of "misreading" and claims that when we, as readers, pose possible answers to questions about Isabel's decisions (specifically, her much-debated choice to return to Osmond), we "partake of Isabel's own style of misreading reality." See Sandra K. Fischer, "Isabel Archer and the Enclosed Chamber: A Phenomenological Reading," *Henry James Review* 7 (1986): 55. Dorothy Berkson, "Why Does She Marry Osmond?: The Education of Isabel Archer," *American Transcendental Quarterly* 60 (1986): 53–71, is more sympathetic to Isabel; she traces Isabel's journey as a typical novel of initiation—bildungsroman—which is, instead, an "initiation crisis" because female characters cannot escape corruptions on a raft (like Huck Finn), a whaling ship (like Ishmael), or by entering the wilderness (like Natty Bumppo). Berkson emphasizes Isabel's innocence, though she reluctantly charges Isabel with "misreading" as well.

38   With the delight of discovery, James announces his decision to "place the center of the subject *in* the young woman's own consciousness" (Preface, xv; my emphasis).

39   This passage relates to William James's metaphorical language in *Principles of Psychology*. Madame Merle's image of the self as flowing and overflowing is like his image of the "stream" (*PP*, 1.233). Isabel's sense that the self gets protected and remains separate and guarded is more explicitly connected to William's sense that there is a sanctuary, a "self of selves," a citadel of consciousness (*PP*, 1.284–5).

40   Laurence Holland cites this conversation between Isabel and Ralph in *The Expense of Vision*, namely because it suggests "the antithesis between *seeing* and the full partaking of experience which is important to the novel." See Laurence B. Holland, *The Expense of Vision* (Princeton: Princeton University Press, 1964), 48.

41   Millicent Bell, *Meaning in Henry James* (Cambridge: Harvard University Press, 1991), 94.

42   Naomi Lebowitz argues that the dynamic of relationships becomes the central point of James's novels, but that it is the "burden" of the novel to see relationship as morality: "The plea that James addresses to both novelist and reader to undergo 'intimate exploration,' to face the difficulties and

discomforts of honest and deep exploration, becomes for all writers who place at the center of the novel's form and meaning the concept that morality is shaped by individual personal relationship, a plea to educate for intimacy." See Naomi Lebowitz, *The Imagination of Loving* (Detroit: Wayne State University Press, 1965), 54.

43  Ellen Frank briefly discusses the etymology of the word "dwelling" in her study, *Literary Architecture*. She points out that the word "dwelling" if traced to its Indo-European root, "comes from a word that means 'to rise in a cloud,' the 'dust,' 'vapor,' or 'smoke' which makes seeable, that is, gives substantial form to, the soul or spirit, our breath-being. . . . Constructing a building is *bringing into being*; constructing a dwelling is bringing of being *into seeable form*." Frank, 12. Such a reading of the word suggests how intimately Isabel's "dwellings" are connected to what James represents as her "being."

44  Remarking on this final scene, Debra MacComb says that when Isabel breaks from Goodwood's seductive embrace to regain the Gardencourt threshold on which she began, "she makes the essential transition from 'looking' to 'knowing,' from the literal darkness of her surroundings to what must be termed enlightenment" (138). She argues that Isabel's "very straight path" back to Rome and to Osmond is neither a fear of sexuality nor a capitulation to tradition; rather, she claims Isabel's flight exemplifies James's critique of "America's celebrated tendency to elevate individual liberty over obligation or tradition and its faith that radical breaks—for which the American War for Independence is paradigmatic—are sufficient to secure such liberty" (129). See Debra MacComb, "Divorce of a Nation; or, Can Isabel Archer Resist History?," *The Henry James Review* 17 (1996): 129–148.

45  In her classic study of Jamesian consciousness, Dorothea Krook concludes that Isabel flees Goodwood toward the path she knows because, like James, she possesses "fear of, and revulsion from sexual passion in its more violent and importunate forms." Dorothea Krook, *The Ordeal of Consciousness in Henry James* (Cambridge: Cambridge University Press, 1963), 368. More recently, Sandra Fischer has summed up arguments by saying that critics debate whether Isabel goes back to Rome with a new sense of power (and a desire to give this to Pansy), reconciled to what lies beyond the door; or if she flees, walks into the house for safety, and therefore regresses into the private world. She says it is more realistic to see Isabel doing the latter; "her way of life with Osmond is like coming home because it is the private life of the enclosed, isolated chamber." Fischer, 48. As I argue, however, personal and social domains get conflated in the novel; consciousness must make way for the social interactions that Isabel cannot fasten the door against. Robert White argues that it is important to see James's novel in its context—not post-Freudian, not the 1908 New York edition, but the original 1881 edition. He alerts us to the nineteenth century discourse on sexuality, referring to Michel Foucault's *History of*

*Sexuality.* Rather than fearing passion, Isabel's reaction to Goodwood "springs from a recognition of the power of the passion that has all but engulfed them" (69). Though, he states, "Isabel's definition of freedom, her assumption of the 'very straight path' back to Rome is not apt to evoke a great deal of sympathy from her readers a century later . . . it is finally amiss to think that Isabel runs back to Rome because she is frightened of her awakened sexuality" (69–70). Interestingly, in a footnote, he states that James's resolution savors a bit of the Gospel of St. Mark: "Is not the 'very straight path' an allusion to Christ's terrible insistence: 'strait is the gate and narrow is the way which leadeth unto life, and few there be that find it'? Matt 7:14." See Robert White, "Love, Marriage and Divorce: The Matter of Sexuality in *Portrait of a Lady*," *The Henry James Review* 7 (1986): 59–71. Speaking more generally about ending in narrative, Torgovnick claims that James uses "confrontational endings" and plays with the notion of the "epilogue as an after-history," thus neatly disposing of his characters' after-fates. She goes on to say that James refuses to over-simplify Isabel's complex act in returning to Osmond; rather, he "demands that readers retrospectively appreciate Isabel's development. . . . He refuses both to make the ending saccharine and to make interpretation an easy, automatic process for his reader." See Marianna Torgovnick, *Closure in the Novel* (New Jersey: Princeton University Press, 1981), 134.

[46] In an insightful critique of recent film versions of *The Scarlet Letter* and *The Portrait of a Lady*, Boudreau links James and Hawthorne, explicitly pitting them against Emersonian individualism, "one of our more abiding cultural legacies" (43). She argues that, through the depiction of Hester Prynne and Isabel Archer, both Hawthorne and James imply that a "valuable existence calls for a compromise between self and society" (44). According to Boudreau, a character like Isabel initially "stumbles because she fails to understand that identity is historically and socially constituted" (50). Kristin Boudreau, "*Is* the World Then So Narrow? Feminist Cinematic Adaptations of Hawthorne and James," *The Henry James Review* 21 (2000): 43–53. Similarly, Robert Weisbuch asserts that James understands the self as a "result of accumulated experience, a Hawthornian rather than an Emersonian self" (226). See Robert Weisbuch, "James and the American Sacred, " *The Henry James Review* 22 (2001): 217–228.

## CHAPTER 4

[1] In his excellent study, *Manhood at Harvard: William James and Others* (New York: W.W. Norton & Co., 1996), Kim Townsend speaks about the way in which James's use of language highlighted *man's* individuality: "What James illuminated was not just a technique (stream of consciousness) but rather what that technique served to approximate or re-create: namely the condition in which we live and use language. What James gives us is a world in which men are cut off from one another in their essential

individuality" (176). Jamesian individuality, Townsend implies, seems to be a crucial component not of humanity, but of *manhood*. Townsend goes on, not surprisingly, to quote James's *Principles of Psychology*: 'The breach from one mind to another is perhaps the greatest breach in nature. . . . Absolute insulation, irreducible pluralism is the law.' Furthermore, he reminds us that though James "insisted upon the sanctity of the individual," he did so "while engaging with the social and political world" (235). Townsend opens his study with a statement of purpose: he writes "about an ideal of manhood that came into being in the decades following the Civil War and about a select group of men who were influential in its creation—or, as in a few significant cases—who called it into question" (11). In some sense, James himself (according to Townsend) is one of these men who questioned the construction of ideal manhood; though Townsend also gives us these challenges with the same subtlety and canniness that characterizes James's writing. Thus, the portrait of William James that emerges in *Manhood* is eloquent, highly sympathetic, and mostly attuned to the price of constructing notions of masculinity for those like James who sought (and suffered) desperately to uphold them.

2   In *Principles of Psychology*, James tells us: "It seems as if the elementary psychic fact were not *thought* or *this thought* or *that thought*, but *my thought*, every thought being *owned*. Neither contemporaneity, nor proximity in space, nor similarity of quality and content are able to fuse thoughts together which are sundered by this barrier of belonging to different personal minds. The breaches between such thoughts are the most absolute breaches in nature." See William James, *The Principles of Psychology* (1890; reprint, Cambridge, Harvard University Press, 1981), vol. 1, 221.

3   For a fuller discussion of the performative quality of gender, see Judith Butler, *Gender Trouble* (New York: Routledge, 1990).

4   See William James, *Essays in Radical Empiricism* (New York: Longmans, Green and Co., 1922). All subsequent references will be to this edition of the text.

5   In *Manhood at Harvard: William James and Others*, Townsend stresses James's intense commitment to personal experience and how much of his philosophy rested on just such "feelings." He quotes James from his Gifford Lectures: "'Who knows whether the faithfulness of individuals here below to their own poor over-beliefs may not actually help God in turn to be more effectively faithful to his own greater tasks? God himself, in short, may draw vital strength and increase of very being from our fidelity. For my own part, I do not know what the sweat and blood and tragedy of this life mean, if they mean anything short of this. If this life be not a real fight, in which something is eternally gained for the universe by success, it is no better than a game of private theatricals from which one may withdraw at will. But it *feels* like a real fight' (Writings I, 463)." Quoted in Townsend, 36.

6   As I argue in chapter two, James produces metaphors that create a sense of
    mystery when it comes to consciousness, as if he were unable to capture its
    essence with language; thus he states: "At present, then, the only conclu-
    sion I come to is the following: That (in some persons at least) the part of
    the innermost Self which is most vividly felt turns out to consist for the
    most part of a collection of cephalic movements of 'adjustments' which, for
    want of attention and reflection, usually fail to be perceived and classed as
    what they are; that over and above these there is an obscurer feeling of
    something more; but whether it be of fainter physiological processes or of
    nothing objective at all, but rather of subjectivity as such, of thought
    become 'its own object,' must at present remain an open question. . . ."
    *Principles of Psychology*, vol. 1, 291–2. James's qualifiers: "in some per-
    sons at least," "for the most part," and of course his vague reference to the
    obscurer "something more" that exists over and above the physiological
    processes, allow him to engender the elusive, ungraspable fringe of con-
    sciousness.

7   Martha Banta makes a similar point about Isabel Archer in her study of the
    images of women—both visual and verbal—that came into being in the
    United States between the Philadelphia Centennial Exposition in 1876 and
    the close of World War I. Considering the power of imaging and imagining
    in *The Portrait of a Lady*, Banta states: "Isabel does what the writers of
    novels have traditionally done: she renders a "portrait" of Gilbert Osmond.
    Significantly, she does this by imagining Osmond's mind. Even more signif-
    icantly, Isabel images his mind by defining it as the process that has turned
    her into a looked-at object—a portrait for his collection. Once she is able
    to look at him looking at her, she snatches back her mind from his grasp
    for her own uses and becomes herself." See Martha Banta, *Imaging
    American Women: Idea and Ideals in Cultural History* (New York:
    Columbia University Press, 1987), 333.

8   Henry James, *The Golden Bowl*, volumes 23 and 24, (New York: Charles
    Scribner's Sons, 1909), vii. All subsequent references will be to this edition
    of the text.

9   Assumptions about femininity or masculinity with respect to consciousness
    emerge tellingly in the language of literary critics as well. In her attempts to
    carve out a space for something she calls "feminine consciousness," Sydney
    Janet Kaplan insists upon an essential split between authorial depictions of
    feminine and masculine consciousness or, as she sometimes names it, sensi-
    bility. She assumes, it seems, that "feminine consciousness" issues not only
    from a female character, but also from a female novelist (Dorothy
    Richardson, May Sinclair, Virginia Woolf, and Doris Lessing are part of the
    host of all-female authors she studies.) Kaplan also implies that "feminine
    consciousness" is a reaction to the "male consciousness" that male authors
    were consistently creating. Attempting to get around the premise that all
    women have the same (feminine) consciousness, Kaplan explains that her
    study traces the effects of a "literary device" in a novel: "[W]hen I use the

term 'feminine consciousness' here, I hope the reader understands that I am using it in a rather special and limited way. I use it not simply as some general attitude of women toward their own femininity, and not as something synonymous with a particular sensibility among female writers. I am concerned with it as a literary device: a method of characterization of females in fiction." See Sydney Janet Kaplan, *Feminine Consciousness in the Modern British Novel* (Urbana: University of Chicago Press, 1975), 3. Kaplan's book is an example of early feminist criticism, but interestingly, this problem is apparent in later works as well. Diana Fuss discusses the double bind of the feminist critic in her book *Essentially Speaking: Feminism, Nature and Difference* (New York: Routledge, 1989). Feminists want to speak as and for women, but while it might seem crucial for political reasons, creating a category "woman," actually erases differences among women and among feminisms. Consequently, writers fall prey to a kind of essentialism that mirrors the patriarchal systems they seek to subvert.

10  Cynthia Russett, *Sexual Science: The Victorian Construction of Womanhood* (Cambridge: Harvard University Press, 1989), discusses the quandary over sexual identity that nineteenth-century evolutionary science enhanced: "the sexual science that arose in the late nineteenth century . . . attempted to be far more precise and empirical than anything that had gone before. In addition, it was able to draw on new developments in the life sciences as well as on the new social sciences of anthropology, psychology and sociology. And, finally, it spoke with the imperious tone of a discipline newly claiming, and in large measure being granted, decisive authority in matters social as well as strictly scientific" (3–4). She makes the point that Nature, after Darwinian evolution, had decreed a secondary role for women: "The great principle of division of labor was brought to bear: men produced, women reproduced. This was called complementarity" (12). In this sense, we understand more thoroughly Maggie's excessiveness, her extravagance; she is both producing and reproducing in James's text.

11  These characters people James's novels and short stories—*The Ambassadors*, "The Beast in the Jungle," and *The Portrait of a Lady*, respectively. Priscilla Walton argues that "in James's writing, the Feminine is frequently located in female characters, but it is not restricted to them and is also often found in the plurality of writing and production." Specifically, she speaks of *The Ambassadors* as a text that can be read as a critique of the realist/referential doctrine of knowability because it "offers suggestions for an alternative interpretation, in which Strether embraces Feminine multiplicity." See Priscilla Walton, "'A mistress of shades': Maggie as Reviser in *The Golden Bowl*," *Henry James Review* 13 (1992): 32; 103.

12  Linda S. Kauffman's study of James's *The Turn of the Screw* reveals what she calls the "artifice" of gender. Specifically, Kauffman argues that critics don't pay enough attention to the governess' desire and that she is hardly

the stereotypical spinster that critics of the tale have made her out to be. Kauffman elaborates on her entire project with respect to *Turn*: "In previous examples of this genre, I have described how stereotypical representations of gender have been subverted and transgressed repeatedly; James's tale similarly reveals the artifice of the literary construction of gender, for rather than being the helpless victim of unrequited love, the governess demonstrates an aggressive will to power." See Linda S. Kauffman, *Discourses of Desire: Gender, Genre and Epistolary Fictions* (Ithaca: Cornell University, 1986), 226.

13  In his study entitled *Silence in Henry James*, John Auchard contends that the silences in *The Golden Bowl* are an attempt to control a "pervasive and growing terror" (about which both he and James remain ambiguous) and that silence itself, as "positive, psychological method rather than as spiritual evacuation, faces profound social breakdown and actively works for reorganization." See John Auchard, *Silence in Henry James* (University Park: Penn State University Press, 1986), 3. Virginia Fowler states that words do not disclose truth in this narrative so much as they evade it: "language becomes a way of concealing knowledge rather than revealing it, and silence comes to be more communicative of truth than speech is." Any traditional use of words (in dialogue, for example) is represented as untrustworthy; silence becomes an alternative mode of communication, a vehicle for truth that somehow lifts the veil from language. See Virginia Fowler, "The Later Fiction" in Daniel Mark Fogel, ed., *A Companion to Henry James Studies* (Connecticut: Greenwood Press, 1993), 204. According to Sharon Cameron, speech is emptied of meaning in *The Golden Bowl*, but what the novel consistently demonstrates is that the "unsaid is not commensurate with the unheard." In other words, crucial exchanges between characters are carried on in moments that look like mind reading; meaning is conveyed haltingly, and characters are forced to intuit others' thoughts if they are to understand each other at all. Sharon Cameron, *Thinking in Henry James* (Chicago: University of Chicago Press, 1989), 97.

14  In this sense, I would modify Sharon Cameron's claim that "to look into another's mind is to be blocked by its impenetrability" (108). This is not *always* the case. Just as often in *The Golden Bowl*, a character finds he or she is sharing mind-space with another character despite a desire to remain a separate, autonomous self with access to one's own mind alone. One character's thoughts or voice might thus resonate in another character's consciousness beyond his or her control.

15  McWhirter makes this point in his chapter on *The Golden Bowl*, "For the Sake of This End." For him, this sense that Maggie's consciousness is entirely absent in the first part of the novel is yet another indication, a "device," which "serves to emphasize her incapacity for life, as well as the degree to which her identity is subsumed in her father's. Our sudden, total immersion in Maggie's consciousness at the beginning of the second book thus reflects something of the shock she herself undergoes when the Prince

returns from Matcham." See David McWhirter, *Desire and Love in Henry James* (Cambridge: Cambridge University Press, 1989), 192.

[16] James expresses his "wonder" at "the Isabel Archers, and even much smaller fry, [who] insist on mattering." He quotes George Eliot who, he says, "admirably noted it— 'In these frail vessels is borne onward through the ages the treasure of human affection.'" Henry James, *The Portrait of a Lady*, volumes 3 and 4 (New York: Charles Scribner's Sons, 1908), xiii.

[17] For example, Marcia Ian in "Consecrated Diplomacy and The Concretion of Self," *Henry James Review* 7 (1985): 27–31 states that the two sections of the narrative are generally assumed to represent two points of view, but "as a whole they represent the mind of Maggie Verver, divided from itself, precisely in the center where Maggie first experiences herself as separate from her father and others. . . . Part I becomes subsumed by Part II just as the Prince becomes subsumed by Maggie when she takes possession of her own mind" (31). Critics read Maggie's role in the narrative in a variety of ways, but frequently represent her as the character with the most influential, sometimes the governing, position and perspective. Mark Seltzer sees Maggie as a socially conditioned agent of power; Maggie's power is "a power of love, a vigilance of 'care'" (65). Seltzer continues, "Far from being opposed, love and power in *The Golden Bowl*, are two ways of saying the same thing" (66). See Mark Seltzer, *Henry James and the Art of Power* (Ithaca: Cornell University Press, 1984). Cheryl Torsney, in "Specula(ariza)tion in *The Golden Bowl*," *Henry James Review* 12 (1991): 141–5 claims that Maggie, finally, refuses to engage in the speculative economy, "electing to control her own fate" (141); David McWhirter, in his *Desire and Love in Henry James* (Cambridge: Cambridge University Press, 1989), argues that Maggie's "new and empowering consciousness of 'possessing the constructive, the creative hand'" allows her to "author a text which she willfully imposes on everything and everyone around her" (194); Irena Auerbach Smith, in "The Golden Goal: Toward a Dialogic Imagination in James's Last Completed Novel," *Henry James Review* 16 (1995): 172–90 modifies McWhirter's view, stating that "as she moves steadily toward her goal (to be an autonomous being in her world as both author of herself and of others)," Maggie "does and does not" author and impose her text on everyone and everything; Virginia Fowler, in her essay entitled "The Later Fiction" in Daniel Mark Fogel's *A Companion to Henry James Studies* (Connecticut: Greenwood Press, 1993) claims Maggie as "the only one of the American girls who possesses and accepts sexual passion, and in fact this passion is what propels her into selfhood" (200). Maggie triumphs, in this sense, as she "relinquishes innocence and claim(s) the rights and responsibilities of power" (205). In her essay, "What Can a Woman Do for the Late Henry James?," *Raritan* XIV (1994): 1–17 Mary Ann Caws considers the force Maggie has on the narrative itself. Caws asserts that we as readers are "permitted to see that Maggie is working the plot, developing her language as she does her imagination" (4).

[18] Dale Bauer argues that female characters in James's fiction create and reproduce, in their deceptions, "an alienated protest that can only serve to foreground, as James's narrative strategy, their need for dialogue in lieu of patriarchal monologue or, worse, silence." Bauer claims that "all of the women in James's novels construct illusions and test them: Charlotte lies to the Prince about the price of the golden bowl; Fanny lies about her suspicions of the Prince's and Charlotte's affair; finally, Maggie lies about her jealousy and her knowledge and lives in 'horror of finding out if [her father] would really have consented to be sacrificed' (2.107). These lies indicate the tenuous position of American women in European society, in sexual relations generally. In other words, Maggie comes to understand the necessity of lying, as well as the power of interpretation to compensate for her own betrayal of her father. . . . For Maggie, interpretation results in a confrontation with her father's authoritative discourse, in the possible failure of the utterance. . . ." See Dale Bauer, *Feminist Dialogics: A Theory of Failed Community* (Albany State University Press, 1988), 66.

[19] Priscilla Walton makes this point in her essay; she opens her piece with a discussion of a series of (male) critics and their views on Maggie's process of revision; she states: "My reading differs from those male critics for I do not perceive Maggie's revisions as destructive or confining. On the contrary, I would argue that these revisions constitute her means of opening the closed text of book I. Indeed, her methodology is in accord with the tenets of post-structuralist feminism since her revisions disrupt the masculine referentiality of book I by privileging the pluralizing nature of the feminine other in book II." Walton, 144. See also Eileen Watts, "*The Golden Bowl*: A Theory of Metaphor," *Modern Language Studies* 13 (1983): 169–176. Watts states that "the pagoda is an expression of the inscrutability of language," but that it is primarily Maggie's "ability to make connections" (between the Prince and the golden bowl, for instance) which "creates her reality" (169). Watts concludes that "language, here represented by metaphor, is concurrent with the consciousness of the character and of the reader, therefore, not only does language become consciousness, but intellection and reality become indistinguishable" (175).

[20] Laurence Holland compares Maggie's pagoda to Osmond's "formidable house" in his classic study of James: "But if the pagoda suggests the complex social, psychological, and sexual situation which Maggie confronts, it presents also an exotic version of Gilbert Osmond's formidable house in *The Portrait of a Lady* with its 'jealous apertures' which defied entrance, its 'small high window' from which Osmond scrutinized the world and looked upon Isabel Archer to court, to use, and to 'mock at her.'" See Laurence B. Holland, *The Expense of Vision: Essays on the Craft of Henry James* (Princeton: Princeton University Press, 1964), 337.

[21] Marcia Ian argues that in the pagoda scene, Maggie "conceives of her own mind as an image of enclosure"; this image, "shifts," however, when relationships reveal themselves to be false. Indeed, Maggie "experiences the

sudden sanctification of her own inner life as it invites her to approach its exotically private precincts. . . . Maggie, in other words, experiences simultaneously her psychological separateness from her father, her ontological individuality, and her own moral responsibility. Selfhood, self-consciousness and conscience, therefore, are virtually synonymous terms for the moment. . . ." (31). See Marcia Ian, "Consecrated Diplomacy and the Concretion of Self," *Henry James Review* 7 (1985): 27–31.

[22] Henry James, *The Portrait of a Lady*, 1.287.

[23] Hugh Stevens argues that "sexuality in this novel is *that which cannot be figured*, that which is always alluded to but rarely directly portrayed" (55). Calling this James's "most passionate novel," Stevens states: "In *The Golden Bowl*, violent fantasy can accompany the most delicate manners, and 'sexuality' consists not so much in bodily contact as in the endless working out of scenarios, and of variations of scenarios. James has created sexuality as discourse—a formidable eroticism of the text" (56). See Hugh Stevens, "Sexuality and the Aesthetic in *The Golden Bowl*," *Henry James Review* 14 (1993): 55–71.

[24] Making note of this scene as an instance of psychic communication, Sharon Cameron explains that Maggie's "unspoken words are so well perceived—I am pressed to say 'heard'—that Amerigo breaks them off because he can no longer endure them. . . . Maggie registers her own words not . . . from the vantage of wishing to speak them . . . but more complexly from the vantage of (virtually) hearing them understood. In passages like these, crucial exchanges are carried on in spite of the spoken, or in the midst of the spoken, or explicitly as a counter to it." See Cameron, 97.

[25] Irena Auerbach Smith, "The Golden Goal: Toward a Dialogic Imagination in James's Last Completed Novel," *Henry James Review* 16 (1995): 173.

[26] Smith, 173.

[27] Jennifer Gribble is attentive to these paradoxical tendencies apparent in the primary metaphor of *The Golden Bowl*. Discussing the role of "value" in James's novel, she reminds us of the enigma of this Jamesian image, contending that the bowl is "a repository of ambiguous, often contradictory values for the characters in the novel as a whole: deception and revelation, costliness and cheapness, beauty and tawdriness, wholeness and fragmentation; it contains and curbs fullness; it is an emblem of generosity and of manipulativeness. It hovers between metaphoric and dramatic functions, now image, now tangible object. The atmosphere it generates changes from the toughest of financial, emotional and sexual transactions to rhapsodic lyricism and blatant theatricality" (51). See Jennifer Gribble, "Value in *The Golden Bowl*," *The Critical Review* 27 (1985): 50–65.

[28] Sharon Cameron's insightful discussion of *The Golden Bowl* in the third chapter of her book turns on James's use of the word "reference." See Cameron, 83–121.

[29] Paul Armstrong, *The Phenomenology of Henry James* (Chapel Hill: University of North Carolina Press, 1983), 160. Armstrong invokes phenomenology in order to interpret James because, he argues, it provides a conceptual framework that can illuminate the connections between two dimensions of Jamesian fiction—his fascination with consciousness and what is commonly called his 'moral vision.' Armstrong states: "Guided by phenomenology's theories about the workings of consciousness and the structure of existence, I have identified and analyzed five major aspects of experience that, together, map James's understanding of the human being—the impression as a way of knowing, the imagination, freedom, personal relations, and the politics of the social world" (vii). Placing James within the context of such intellectual figures as his brother William, the British empiricists, Swedenborg, and Nietzsche, Armstrong claims that his study is a comparative one, between philosophy and literature, and that it belongs to the tradition of cultural criticism.

[30] Stephen Arata examines Jamesian perception as a form of hermeneutics rather than of epistemology. Interested in the way that James ties "proper seeing" to the development of various kinds of interpretive practices, Arata claims that what has been neglected in discussions of *The Golden Bowl* is "the role played by the fine-arts museum in shaping perception. The very ubiquity of the museum in James's fiction as a whole . . . has perhaps made it difficult to discern the particular configuration assumed by this institution in *The Golden Bowl*" (200). Arata informs us that James's writing career overlaps with the rise of the fine arts museum in America, but it is not the emergence of the art museum alone which accounts for the modes of perception characteristic of this novel. Rather, Arata explores the connections between perception, museums, and various types of power. Museums are implicated in imperial power and domination, and the kind of perception that the museum fosters saturates the entire novel. Arata calls this the "skiascopic sensibility," named for an instrument developed at the turn of the century which fit over the eyes to act as blinders; thus the viewer found his field of vision restricted to a single item at a time (206). He states: "While it is tempting to argue that such a sensibility cuts along gender lines—fine-arts museums were often imagined as feminine spaces passively awaiting the male museum patron—in *The Golden Bowl* skiascopia in fact defines the relations among all the main characters" (208). See Stephen D. Arata, "Object Lessons: Reading the Museum in *The Golden Bowl*" in *Famous Last Words: Changes in Gender and Narrative Closure*, ed., Alison Booth, (Virginia: University of Virginia Press, 1993). See also Susan M. Griffin, *The Historical Eye: The Texture of the Visual in Late James* (Chapel Hill: University of North Carolina Press, 1983) for a study of perception and epistemology in James and Jean-Christophe Agnew's "The Consuming Vision of Henry James," in *The Culture of Consumption: Critical Essays in American History, 1880–1980*, ed., Richard Wightman Fox and T. J. Jackson Lears (New York: Pantheon, 1983).

31  In "The Cost of Feeling: Emotional Injury in Henry James's *The Golden Bowl*," *Modern Fiction Studies* 44.4 (1998): 837–864, Jennifer Travis discusses pain as a manifestation not of an individualized consciousness, but rather a measure of the exchanges that occur between characters in this novel. She asserts that "feelings here are not a model for the deep structure of human consciousness . . . but rather a question of commerce, and their novelization not a domain of a discernible 'inside,' but a complex field in which literary fiction helps to negotiate how depth and pain are inflicted, owned and compensated" (854).

32  Philip Sicker calls attention to this moment as a revelation of the way in which "Maggie's love for Amerigo triumphs over Charlotte's because it inspires what she modestly calls 'some imagination of the states of others'—not simply *another*, but the Prince, Charlotte, and Adam all at once." See Philip Sicker, *Love and the Quest for Identity in the Fiction of Henry James* (Princeton: Princeton University Press, 1980), 164.

33  The phrase is Mark Seltzer's. He argues that Maggie achieves control by putting herself in the place of others, as *both* victim and victimizer: "Critics have debated whether Maggie triumphs through the creative force of a "sympathetic imagination" that affirms the "imaginative autonomy" of others (Yeazell) or whether she wins by using her intelligence to control others, by denying "vital interchange with others" (Rowe). But I have already suggested that James insists on the interchangeability of these characterizations. Control and sympathy are not opposed here; in fact, Maggie controls precisely through a power of sympathy. . . . Maggie's empathic improvisations—her ability to put herself at once into the place of victim and victimizer—are the measure of her power. I can't put myself into Maggie's skin, Charlotte confesses, but it is just this ability to put oneself into another's skin that Maggie demonstrates" (71). See Mark Seltzer, *Henry James and the Art of Power* (Ithaca: Cornell University Press, 1984).

34  I think, here, of Lambert Strether in *The Ambassadors* who remains enclosed within his own protected consciousness even when he recognizes, even when he can no longer avoid, the fullness of knowledge about the relationships around him. Though we might concede that consciousness is also a drama of social relations for Strether, and that his expansion of consciousness depends upon a growing awareness of the interrelationships and intrigues of the Parisian set, Maggie's mind seems to have a different, a trickier social function than his. Strether cannot accommodate the social into his personal consciousness; or rather, he is never forced to do so. He seems able to keep it aestheticized, to walk in and out of the picture, as it were, and thus avoid mixing the world stuff with the stuff of consciousness. Maggie has no choice but to integrate the two.

35  Irena Auerbach Smith tells us that even though Maggie and Adam seem unquestionably to have triumphed over Charlotte and Amerigo in the end, "Charlotte's consciousness nevertheless continues to live in Maggie"

(Smith, 185), which leads me to infer that Smith finds this habitation somewhat more menacing than, or at least as equally imposing as, Maggie's "triumph" over her stepmother.

[36] As the title of his book indicates, *Love, in James's fiction, is tied to the Quest for Identity*; thus Philip Sicker reads this final scene as a commentary on what happens when two people love with such intensity as to obliterate each others' identities: "James's Prince and Princess have learned to love each other with a frightening intensity . . . their passion must inevitably consume their identities." Though at first, he imagines Maggie transcends the "self-obliterating fusion of single love to establish multiple circuits of relationships," Sicker still reads the final scene as a kind of "blackout" that amounts to a mutual loss of self for the couple. See Sicker, 167; 164. Sharon Cameron suggests that in order to understand the final scene, we have to step outside of the bounds of psychological realism and consider how the exchange between the couple works beyond its reference to the plot: "Finally, the context of psychological realism seems inadequate to explain why the victory of the novel, as experienced by the reader of it, is less associated with retrieving Amerigo (who has never, to most readers, seemed worth it) than it is associated with the fact that, as if outside the story—outside any story—consciousness, for a moment, is made unequivocal. That is, *Maggie's* consciousness which is made definitive seems less the point of the novel's final paragraph than does the stark imperialism of consciousness's domination. Such domination, absolute, can't quite be owned, can't even quite be identified with. This is the fact I take Maggie to appreciate when she, like Amerigo, perceives herself victimized by it. Thus one way to explain what happens in the novel is not to say that Maggie rearranges the quartet and gets Amerigo back, but rather that consciousness (as it happens, hers) is made adequate in the sense of made ultimate; in the sense of empowered; in the sense of made to have the last, the only, word." Cameron, 12–13. Mary Ann Caws more explicitly locates Maggie's victory in her vision, specifically, her ability to transfer her vision to her prince: "That final burial of her sight I read not just as not wanting to see the Prince's eyes, or as refusing to see anymore, or in order to see that nothing around herself, as he does, but as symbolically transferring her sight to his own. For him to see, she has to sacrifice her seeing. . . ." Caws names this gesture of Maggie's "an act of unprecedented generosity" and concludes with this statement about Jamesian heroines: "The heroine for James is, I believe, the one who makes the space for the other, for the exchange of visions." Caws, 4; 14.

[37] My formulation of this predicament of language's nonequivalence, a predicament that both of the Jameses face, borrows from Wai Chee Dimock, "Gender, the Market, and the Non-Trivial in James," *Henry James Review* 15 (1994): 24–30. Dimock addresses *The Bostonians* and the peculiar "cognitive gymnastics" that both the female/mentor character, Olive, and James's text itself enact; she states that James's novels "write about sex and gender without bowing to the pressure of explanation."

Further, Dimock makes a statement about the representation of gender or sexual identity in James's text that sounds remarkably similar to what James himself might want to propose about consciousness. Dimock writes: "[The Jamesian text] switches back and forth between an adequating rationality on the one hand, self-confident that every human phenomenon has an explanatory equivalence, and a kind of charmed stupor on the other hand, stunned by the utter disparity, the utter lack of equivalence between a person and all those things supposed to explain that person, between a nameable identity and the thing it is supposed to name" (28). I would argue that it is this "nonequivalence" that the Jameses promote. Dimock mostly marvels at what she calls "the precarious space of nonequivalence" created in Henry James's handling of sexuality, but she does not consider that this space might be cannily constructed—I would say by both of the Jameses, and for consciousness as well as gender identity—through their very insistence upon the impossibility of linguistic equivalence.

## CHAPTER 5

1  Many critics have discussed the significance of houses in Wharton's fiction. For instance, Marilyn R. Chandler, *Dwelling in the Text: Houses in American Fiction* (Berkeley: University of California Press, 1991) discusses what she calls Wharton's fascination with the "semiotics of houses and the peculiar mores and ironic inconsistencies of American domestic and social life" (149); speaking of Wharton's investment in "the politics of space," (149) Chandler stresses that living space is always "significant space," revealing an intricate network of symbolic systems that "reinforce the behavioral mores and severe social stratification" (157) of Wharton's work. Judith Fetterly, *Felicitous Space: The Imaginative Structures of Edith Wharton and Willa Cather* (Chapel Hill: The University of North Carolina Press, 1986) is concerned with the relationship of space to the female imagination; she discusses Wharton's first book, *The Decoration of Houses*, as an elaborate mapping of ideal domestic spaces, "where public and private are carefully distinguished and movement carefully controlled" (83). I argue, however, that while Wharton may attempt to map out social or domestic spaces, such a gesture ultimately reveals the impossibility of confining or separating categories like public and private. The metaphors used to articulate a "private" self are necessarily culled from the social world.

2  Wharton's letter to Mary Berenson is quoted in R.W.B. Lewis, *Edith Wharton: A Biography* (New York: Harper and Row, 1975), 413.

3  More famous, perhaps, than this figure in my epigraph is the image from Wharton's short story, "The Fullness of Life," which depicts a woman's "nature" as if it were a house, each room, portioned out for certain purposes and persons: "I have sometimes thought that a woman's nature is like a great house full of rooms: there is the hall, through which everyone pass-

es going in and out; the drawing room, where one receives formal visits; the sitting room, where the members of the family come and go as they list; but beyond that, far beyond, are other rooms, the handles of whose doors are never turned; no one knows the way to them, no one knows whither they lead; and in the innermost room, the holy of holies, the soul sits alone and waits for a footstep that never comes." Apart from the plaintive portrait of the soul, forever awaiting a "footstep that never comes," what is striking is that the soul awaits anyone at all. Every other portion of this "house" is clearly delineated as social space, and yet Wharton seems deeply ambivalent about the privacy of this "innermost room." Edith Wharton, "The Fullness of Life" (1893), in *The Collected Short Stories of Edith Wharton*, ed., R.W.B. Lewis, 2 vols. (New York: Charles Scribner's Sons, 1968), 1: 14.

4    Wharton's first book takes seriously the aesthetics of domestic life; a catalogue of rules for decorating, *The Decoration of Houses*, was the first American handbook of interior design. See Edith Wharton and Ogden Codman, Jr., *The Decoration of Houses* (1897; reprint, New York: Charles Scribner's Sons, 1901).

5    I refer, of course, to the famous argument between Isabel Archer and Madame Merle, over what constitutes the self. See Henry James, *The Portrait of a Lady*, volumes 3 and 4 (New York: Charles Scribner's Sons, 1908), 1.287–8.

6    See William James, *Essays in Radical Empiricism* (New York: Longmans, Green and Co., 1922), 11; 14. See also chapter two.

7    Henry James recounts his well-known construction of the house of fiction in the Preface to *The Portrait of a Lady*. See Henry James, *The Portrait of a Lady*, x.

8    Pamela Knights makes this point in her study of *The Age of Innocence*: "Readers soon discover that any observation about an individual character—about his or her consciousness, emotions, body, history or language—also entangles us in the collective experience of the group, expressed in the welter of trifles, the matrix of social knowledge, within and out of which Wharton's subjects are composed. . . . Where and how far that entangle extends is one of the novel's questions. Its hero, Archer, raises the inquiry, but . . . we realize his limits. Though acknowledging social formation, he still assumes that somewhere a 'real' self survives. The suggestion of the unfolding narrative is, more radically, that without the shape, the social mold, there may be no self at all." See Pamela Knights, "Forms of Disembodiment: The Social Subject in *The Age of Innocence*" in Millicent Bell, ed., *The Cambridge Companion to Edith Wharton* (New York: Cambridge University Press, 1995), 20–21.

9    Maureen Howard discusses the significance of transition in *The House of Mirth* as an issue which touches the question of self-identity (in this instance, the author's) as well as a writer's choice among fictional genres: "The quest for Lily's character and for her own identity as more than a

passing literary fancy drew Wharton away from the solutions of melodrama and the satisfying end games of social comedy. Perhaps that is why Henry James found *The House of Mirth* to be 'two novels and too confused.' But if we are to understand that the novel is purposely rent in two, the confusion, if there is any, can be seen as the insoluable dilemma of Lily Bart. She is in transit, literally—between trains, house parties, friends and false friends, high life, low life. Wharton was also on the move, and in writing *The House of Mirth*, she found that there was no prefab house of fiction, social satire or deterministic naturalism, that would accommodate Lily, a modern heroine." See Maureen Howard, "The Bachelor and the Baby: *The House of Mirth*" in Millicent Bell, ed., *The Cambridge Companion to Edith Wharton* (New York: Cambridge University Press, 1995), 141–2.

[10] Others read these same falterings in Lily's career as her failure to find a home. Jeanne Boydston locates Wharton's novels within the tradition of the Domestic novel, pointing out that, like the domestic novelists, Wharton has much to say about homes, though in her novels, "home appears the embodiment of all that is wrong in society" (31). She goes on to consider the apprehensions that Wharton and the domestic novelists shared, apprehensions about industrial society, capitalism, specifically, its "power to permeate social relations and to establish itself as the wellspring of individual identity" (33). Boydston stresses that Wharton locates Lily Bart's tragedy in the failure of the home. "Mirroring the social relations of the society in which they exist, the households of *The House of Mirth* are but stages for an ongoing spectacle of wealth, mere 'improvisations' of relationships, created and dissolved according to their success in providing the props and trappings of fashion. . . ." (34). See Jeanne Boydston, "Grave Endearing Traditions: Edith Wharton and the Domestic Novel" in Alice Kessler-Harris and William McBrien, ed., *Faith of a (Woman) Writer* (New York: Greenwood Press, 1988).

[11] Diana Fuss discusses the ways in which essentialism and social constructions come together especially through the relation between the natural and the social; she emphasizes that the essentialist/constructionist tension often results in a collapsing of the bar between these two terms. Fuss argues, specifically, that essentialism is *essential* to constructionism; she highlights feminist theory as a particularly vexed site for this debate since feminism seems to take for granted a shared identity, some "essential" point of commonality among its members. With the type of stunning turn that characterizes her argument, Fuss takes her conviction about the politics of feminism to its furthest conclusion to suggest that "it is politics that feminism cannot do without, politics that is essential to feminism's many self-definitions" (37). See Diana Fuss, *Essentially Speaking: Feminism, Nature and Difference* (New York: Routledge, 1989).

[12] Though Wharton identified herself almost exclusively with male writers, her writing has much in common with her female contemporaries.

Charlotte Perkins Gilman's "The Yellow Wallpaper" and Kate Chopin's *The Awakening* as well as some of the local colorists like Sarah Orne Jewett and Mary Wilkins Freeman create female characters whose identity—for better or for worse—is linked to, indeed, made identical to, their surroundings. Thus the yellow wallpaper woman merges with the wallpaper and the nursery where she stays; Edna Pontellier's consciousness moves in and out of the rhythms of the sea, unconfined by the various houses she tries to inhabit; the narrator of *The Country of the Pointed Firs* is so sympathetic to her new neighbors, so receptive to her new environment as to blend into it; and a character like Louisa Ellis in "The New England Nun" accepts placidly the tiny domestic hermitage where her "little feminine appurtenances," as Freeman writes, become "a very part of her personality" (62). See Candace Ward, ed., *Great Short Stories by American Women* (New York: Dover Publications, 1996).

13  Wharton, certainly, read widely in the emerging field of social psychology, but readers of her fiction have also found it tempting to consider how her own experience with professional psychologists influenced her work. The most interesting connection remains contestable, that is, the belief that Wharton underwent the "rest cure" for cases of nervous exhaustion, invented by the well-known neurologist, S. Weir Mitchell. R.W.B. Lewis, in his biography, concedes that Wharton did not stay in Mitchell's Orthopedic Hospital, but rather, was an outpatient in a hotel. Lewis bases his account, however, on a supposition: "It must be supposed that Dr. Mitchell looked in on Mrs. Wharton once or twice—he would have taken a special interest in the younger literary colleague and fellow Newporter—but Edith's chief physician during her three months at the Stenton Hotel was a Dr. McClellan." See R.W.B. Lewis, *Edith Wharton: A Biography* (New York: Harper & Row Publishers, 1975). Shari Benstock, in her biography *No Gifts From Chance: A Biography of Edith Wharton* (New York: Charles Scribners Sons, 1994), is deeply invested in discrediting this "popular belief." Though she provides the proof for her claims, she attacks Mitchell's "cure," first: "demanding, severe, and in some sense brutal, the Weir Mitchell 'cure' was not something one entered into casually. It required confinement, isolation, round-the-clock observation, rest, and regular feeding under supervision . . . patient dependency and 'infantilization' were central features of the cure." More specifically, Benstock's research reveals evidence that casts serious doubt on the belief that Wharton underwent any formal rest cure of the kind administered by Mitchell. She notes that Wharton read and wrote both letters and fiction during this time, though patients were forbidden any kind of intellectual or creative work under Mitchell's treatment. Mitchell's patient records, which Benstock cites, contain no references to Wharton, nor do her own papers state that she took the rest cure during these years (1898–99). Benstock's strongest claim comes in Wharton's own words: "In 1918, when her editor, W.C. Brownell had a severe nervous breakdown, she commiserated with his suffering while denying any personal experience of neurasthenia: 'I am not neurasthenic, or

anything approaching it.'" Despite this emphatic statement, oddly enough, the rumor that Wharton had suffered a "nervous breakdown" due to overwork was an explanation she herself let stand. See Benstock, 93–96.

[14] George Herbert Mead, *Movements of Thought in the Nineteenth Century* (Chicago: University of Chicago Press, 1936), 375. Mead's work would have been available to Wharton through a variety of journals in philosophy, psychology and sociology. He published extensively (from 1895 to his death in 1931) on theories of social process and self-identity. This text was published posthumously by Mead's students at Chicago.

[15] See Mead, 381; 385.

[16] Charles Horton Cooley, *Human Nature and the Social Order* (1902; reprint, New York: Schocken Books, 1964), 42.

[17] Cooley, 48.

[18] The phrase, "inward relation to reality," is actually William James's. In a letter to Sara Norton, Edith Wharton discusses a lecture by Wilhelm Ostwald entitled *Individuality and Immortality* with respect to the other "voices" of contemporary psychology among which, of course, is William James's: "Ah, how it lifts one up to hear such a voice as that [Ostwald's] in the midst of all the psychological-pietistical juggling of which your friend W. James is the source & chief distributor! It has a fine Stoic note—the note of Seneca & Epictetus. . . . Thank you for sending me such a book.—It refreshed me all the more because I chanced to get out of the library here last night Paulsen's 'Introduction to Psychology,' with a 'foreward' by Iedit James—& at the first page I was in the thick of the familiar jargon: 'Religion & atheism stand opposite each other not as theories, but as expressions of the will, & differing practical attitudes toward life'—& 'humanity will never be satisfied with scientific knowledge to explain its inward relation to reality.' What other kind of knowledge is it capable of receiving? Oh, dear—oh, how slowly the wheels turn, & how often the chariot slips back!—" See *The Letters of Edith Wharton*, ed., R.W.B. Lewis and Nancy Lewis (New York: Charles Scribner's Sons, 1988), 101–2. Wharton concentrates her attack of William James's theories on his use of "psychological-pietistical" jargon; she prefers the apparent stoicism of Ostwald. But what is especially interesting is Wharton's rhetorical question regarding the province of scientific knowledge. She asks it, that is, as if to suggest that scientific evidence presents the only way to understand the intersection between "inwardness" and "reality," and furthermore, as if such terms were themselves transparent.

[19] Bentley writes that "customs and manners, long the province of letters—conduct books, the novel, the travel essay—came under the scrutiny of science. And during the same period, the traditional novel of manners acquired a scientific inflection" (51). Wharton's method, Bentley asserts, amounts to superimposing exotic and civilized manners so that she "not only recognizes the ethnographic as a reflection of modern taste, she makes

taste ethnographic—the New York tribal god of Taste . . . far from subordinating the current interest in primitivism to a traditional form, Wharton invokes the exotic to refashion from within the established understanding of social form itself. Though affixed to a narrow axis of elite manners, Wharton's fiction delineates the broadest questions of culture addressed in early anthropology: what culture is, how it works, its power and its limits. In self-consciously exploring these questions, Wharton participated in the emergence of a whole 'science of manners.'" (48). See Nancy Bentley, "'Hunting for the Real': Wharton and the Science of Manners" in Millicent Bell, ed., *The Cambridge Companion to Edith Wharton* (New York: Cambridge University Press, 1995), 47–67.

[20] Edith Wharton, *The Writing of Fiction* (New York: Charles Scribner's Sons, 1925), 7.

[21] Edith Wharton, *The House of Mirth* in *Edith Wharton: Novels*, ed., R.W.B. Lewis, (1905; reprint, New York: Library of America, 1985), 5. All subsequent references will be to this edition of the text.

[22] In "Reading *Mrs. Lloyd*," Judith Fryer argues that it is Lily, not Selden, who occupies the role of artist in *The House of Mirth*: "that Selden is a connoisseur and not an artist—Lily is the artist—is important . . . for Lily, creating her own design, her self as Mrs. Lloyd, is her great moment." See Alfred Bendixen and Annette Zilversmit, ed., *Edith Wharton: New Critical Essays* (New York: Garland Publishing Company, Inc., 1992), 52. In "Lily Bart and Masquerade Inscribed in the Female Mode," Cynthia Griffin Wolff expands her reading of "Lily Bart and the Beautiful Death" where she argued that in creating Lily, Wharton depicted a woman whose own construction of self had been fatally compromised by society's demand that she become no more than an aesthetic object, a collectible piece of art, to consider the ways that Wharton's experience with theater influences the novel. Wolff demonstrates that theater taught Wharton to focus on appearance and action; thus, she argues that "the core of Miss Bart's dilemma might best be characterized as the plight of a heroine in search of an appropriate scenario." See Katherine Joslin and Alan Price, ed. *Wretched Exotic* (New York: Peter Lang Publishing, 1993), 259; 269. Gloria Erlich states that "Lily's supreme investment in herself as object reduces her capacity for subjective wholeness"; calling attention to the ways in which spectating and spectatorship complicate issues of power in this novel, Erlich argues that "in making a spectacle of herself—in making herself into an object of speculation—for all to interpret, Lily can awe and impress, but she cannot fully control audience response." See Gloria C. Erlich, *The Sexual Education of Edith Wharton* (Berkeley: University of California Press, 1992), 71.

[23] Mead, 384.

[24] Amy Kaplan, *The Social Construction of American Realism* (Chicago: The University of Chicago Press, 1988), discusses the role of the upper-class

woman as spectacle; she states that as Lily steps into this role, she gets defined against the backdrop of the lower classes. Kaplan analyzes the scene when Lily attends her cousin's wedding ceremony because it is a moment when she occupies, for a change, the place of the spectator. She imagines, however, what it would be like to trade her place with the 'mystically veiled figure occupying the center of attention.' Kaplan writes: "Lily's contradictory self-image encapsulates that of her class, which to maintain its power as the center of attention must also remain mystically veiled. The combination of conspicuousness and elusiveness empowers the elite as the center of desire by simultaneously attracting the notice of the audience beneath them and keeping that audience at bay" (91).

25 Maureen Howard argues that marriage, in Lily Bart's unstable society, is "at best, a flimsy institution in which to house one's ambitions. *House* may be read as a perverse marriage novel, for if we track Lily's business, the business of getting married, she is, at 29, a failure. And what is most evident, she has no inner desire to be wed. The pressures are all external . . . it is not fate, afterall, but a fastidious irresolution: she defaults at the marriage game, finding it insufficient." While I agree with Howard's assessment of the degeneration of marriage in the novel, I would like to complicate the sense that Lily's "inner desire" reveals whether or not she wants to be wed. Wharton's ambivalence toward Lily's interior life characterizes most of the novel, thus it is difficult, if not impossible, to state what Lily's "inner desires" might be. See Howard, 143.

26 Judith Fryer explains that tableaux vivants drew mixed public reactions in the latter half of the nineteenth century, mostly because of their risque quality: "on the one hand, respectable audiences [were] given 'permission' to stare at women in a state of semi-nudity (often the only covering would be paint sprayed on the body) under the guise of viewing 'great art' . . . on the other hand, certain segments of the population . . . were outraged by the indecent displays." See Fryer, "Reading *Mrs. Lloyd*, 30.

27 Howard, 137.

28 As we saw in chapter two, William James sees consciousness as a stream: "Consciousness, then, does not appear to itself chopped up in bits. . . . It is nothing jointed; it flows. A 'river' or a 'stream' are the metaphors by which it is most naturally described. *In talking of it hereafter, let us call it the stream of thought, of consciousness, or of subjective life.*" James also imagines that the movements of consciousness look like a bird in flight: "As we take, in fact, a general view of the wonderful stream of our consciousness, what strikes us first is this different pace of its parts. Like a bird's life, it seems to be made of an alternation of flights and perchings." Of course, James's imagination of consciousness goes through multiple conversions. His notion of the self, as such, cannot be contained. In fact, his discussion of the "empirical self, or me," reveals the ways in which the self acquires its identity by what we accumulate around us:

> The Empirical Self of each of us is all that he is tempted to call by the name of *me*. But it is clear that between what a man calls *me* and what he simply calls *mine* the line is difficult to draw. We feel and act about certain things that are ours very much as we feel and act about ourselves. . . . *In its widest possible sense . . . a man's Self is the sum total of all that he CAN call his*, not only his body and his psychic powers, but his clothes and his house, his wife and his children, his ancestors and friends, his reputation and works, his land and horses, and yacht and bank account.

One wonders to what extent Wharton's preoccupation with the notion of a "real" self, emptied though it is of meaning, stemmed from an express desire to separate what is "mine" from what is "me." The consuming culture that breeds Lily makes such distinctions at the self's peril. See William James, *The Principles of Psychology*, volume 1, (1890; reprint, Cambridge, Harvard University Press, 1981), 233; 236; 279.

[29] Wai Chee Dimock, "Debasing Exchanges: Edith Wharton's *The House of Mirth*," *PMLA* 10 (October 1985): 783–792 argues that "the power of the marketplace" resides "not in its presence, which is only marginal in *The House of Mirth*, but in its ability to reproduce itself, in its ability to assimilate everything else into its domain. As a controlling logic, a mode of human conduct and human association, the marketplace is everywhere and nowhere, ubiquitous and invisible. Under its shadow even the most private affairs take on the essence of business transactions, for the realm of human relations is fully contained within an all-encompassing business ethic" (783).

[30] In his preface to the novel, Henry James expresses the importance of showing "what an 'exciting' inward life may do for the person leading it." Isabel Archer "sits up, by her dying fire, far into the night, under the spell of recognitions on which she finds the last sharpness suddenly wait." See Henry James, *Portrait*, xx.

[31] William James uses an illustration with paint and painting in order to show "experience" as a cohesive entity that cannot be separated into "parts": "*Experience, I believe, has no such inner duplicity; and the separation of it into consciousness and content comes, not by way of subtraction, but by way of addition* . . . paint will also serve here as an illustration. In a pot in a paint-shop, along with other paints, it serves in its entirety as so much saleable matter. Spread it on a canvas, with other paints around it, it represents, on the contrary, a feature in a picture and performs a spiritual function." See William James, *Essays in Radical Empiricism*, 9.

[32] Critics, upon reading this scene, frequently call attention to the figure of Lily as artist. Shari Benstock asserts that in the tableaux vivant scene Lily "so successfully masters illusory arts that she becomes, at one and the same time, both her subject and herself. The narrative voice . . . assures us that such reinventions of reality are not easy to effect . . . distinctions blur in this boundary world, and one cannot merely draw aside the veil of artifice

to reveal the reality it hides: artifice and actuality intermesh." See Shari
Benstock, "'The word which made all clear': The Silent Close of *The House
of Mirth* ," Alison Booth, ed. *Famous Last Words: Changes in Gender and
Narrative Closure* (Charlottesville: University of Virginia Press, 1993), 236.
Maureen Howard writes that Lily "constructs herself; she wants to be
viewed, framed as a society woman in staged nature. She underestimates
the risk." See Howard, 148. Judith Fryer states: "That Lily has consider-
able skill as an actress, that she can create her own persona, comes as no
surprise, for Wharton has been careful to establish from the first pages of
the novel that her heroine's constant and all-consuming project has been
and is to turn herself into a work of art." See Fryer, "Reading *Mrs. Lloyd*,"
50.

[33] Judith Fryer, for example, explains that Wharton redefines Emerson's version of the transcendent self, and instead insists upon the self's social and
cultural circumstances: "Emerson imagined the possibility of transcending
the world of physical experience in order to reach an ideal state of perception; Wharton demonstrated the fallacy of such transcendence, the way in
which one—if female—is tied to one's cultural context." Fryer, "Reading
*Mrs. Lloyd*," 44.

[34] Shari Benstock comments on this scene, arguing that Wharton took a "double gamble" in *The House of Mirth*, holding up the mirror to her own
social set. "Although her values were those of an earlier, less affluent, and
less worldly community, she understood the double standard of 'modern'
society's mores, the tensions between personal desires and public codes of
behavior." Benstock asserts that Wharton rewrote the denouement of the
novel of manners to reflect these tensions: "the classic ending of comedy (in
which marriage renews society and extends its power) and tragedy (where
death is a cleansing and renewing social force) draw together in a single
closing image in *The House of Mirth* that combines both meanings: death-
in-marriage and marriage-in-death." See Benstock, 245–6. Wai Chee
Dimock emphasizes Lily's moral stance in this scene, noting that the scru-
ples she feels toward the end of the book come from herself and not from
anyone else; she argues that her sudden decision to burn Bertha Dorset's letters "probably has something to do with another mistake she makes during
the same visit, the mistake of indulging in 'the passion of her soul.' Hardly
anyone else in the book has been guilty of this mistake, and it becomes all
the more startling against the background of Selden's tepid civilities." In
destroying Bertha's letters, Dimock asserts, Lily "is offering Selden a great
deal more than he has offered her or ever will offer her. But Lily no longer
weighs and 'proportion[s]' her feelings; she is no longer deterred by
thoughts of 'profits' and 'returns.'" See Dimock, 789. Ruth Bernard
Yeazell, "The Conspicuous Wasting of Lily Bart," *ELH* 59 (1992): 713–34,
also makes note of this scene in order to discuss Wharton's use of fiction to
give us "real life": "like any novelist who professes to give us 'real life,'
Wharton also takes advantage of the possibilities of fiction: insisting that
in Lily Bart's world only appearances count, she nonetheless offers us an

interior view, the privileged access to another's consciousness that only fiction can provide. Unlike all those who watch Lily Bart, we know, for example, that she chooses to burn Bertha's letters rather than to use them; and for us, at least, such knowledge does make a difference. That difference should not be exaggerated: what the novel actually gives us through its heroine is not an alternative vision, just the faltering pulse of resistance, which the novelist and reader register to the bitter end" (734).

35 Critics deliberate over the significance of this scene, especially because as Lily enters this home, she experiences a relationship that seems to carry over to the moment of her death. Carol Wershoven, *The Female Intruder in the Novels of Edith Wharton* (Rutherford: Fairleigh Dickinson University Press, 1982), for instance, suggests that this moment with Nettie is the symbol of Lily's "potential rebirth" (53); Elizabeth Ammons, *Edith Wharton's Argument with America* (Athens: University of Georgia Press, 1980), states that this connection, this blending of the leisure and working class, is a symbol of the emergence of the "New Woman" (43); Cynthia Griffin Wolff, *A Feast of Words: The Triumph of Edith Wharton* (New York: Oxford University Press, 1977) addresses the encounter between Lily and Nettie in a footnote, emphasizing the link between Lily and Nettie's child: "Lily's powerful identification with the baby gives silent testimony to the infantilizing force of the mutilating image of women that society fosters" (130); Elaine Showalter, "The Death of the Lady (Novelist): Wharton's *House of Mirth*" in Alfred Bendixen and Annette Zilversmit, ed., *Edith Wharton: New Critical Essays* (New York: Garland Publishing Company, Inc., 1992), calls this "the strongest moment of female kinship in the novel." Though some feminist critics read the extension of this scene—where Lily imagines holding the baby in a deathbed hallucination—as "sentimental and regressive," Showalter argues that the hallucination "speaks for Lily's awakening sense of loving solidarity and community, for the vision she has had of Nettie's life as representing 'the central truth of existence'" (20); Kathy Fedorko, *Gender and the Gothic in the fiction of Edith Wharton* (Tuscaloosa: The University of Alabama Press, 1995), wants to contest critics who read Nettie's role "as wholly positive, as heroic, female kinship." Nettie's warmth, she argues, is "deceptive" because she "invalidates" Lily's words; Fedorko suggests, furthermore, that Nettie's baby makes Lily "intensely, debilitatingly aware of her own vulnerability and need for love and nurture as well as her fear of becoming the sexual, child-bearing mother" (45). Though Wharton intensifies the significance of this scene in a way that invites strong readings of rebirth, female solidarity, and awakening, I would suggest that she remains ambivalent about the power of the home—whether it be Nettie's hearth or the home that Lily figuratively takes in—precisely because it represents the self. The home in the mind and the series of houses Lily inhabits offer only elusive foundations for identity.

36 Annette Larson Benert, "The Geography of Gender in *The House of Mirth*," *Studies in the Novel* 22:1 (1990): 26–39, argues that the novel

addresses the "use of physical space as a means of self expression, or, more accurately, class expression and social control" (30). Benert discusses Wharton's image of the house in Lily's mind with respect to Henry James: "in this we may see an important difference from Henry James; for Wharton a house is not primarily an image of the self or even its 'envelope' but an embodiment of time and place, the intersection of the traditions and ties, the diachronic and the synchronic, that inform human life" (36). Though I also argue that Wharton's figure of the house carries with it social implications, customs and traditions, signifying Wharton's heightened cultural consciousness, this moment when Lily conceives of a home in her mind becomes significant because, as Wharton states, such an image "broadens and deepens individual existence" as well. Thus, "class expression" and "self expression" in Benert's own words, combine in this figure.

[37] Wai Chee Dimock offers a reading of this moment in Wharton's novel which accentuates the idealism of the representation of a home, especially in contrast to the encroaching world of the marketplace: "Wharton's image of the sanctified ancestral home . . . is a quintessentially aristocratic ideal. As a metaphor and as fact, the ancestral house stands aloof, in all its feudal strength, from the contemporary world of commodities. . . . It is Wharton's fantasy of a transcendent order, for an organic life based on 'blood' and 'roots' is indeed antithetical to the mechanical exchange of capitalism. . . . The ideal is declared impossible even as it is invoked. The ancestral home is no alternative to the commodified house of mirth, irrevocably present and here to stay." See Dimock, 790. While I agree with Dimock's formulation of the omnipresence of the "commodified house of mirth," I argue that Wharton's texts embody a tension between the commodified house with its ties to the social world and the idealized house in the mind; hence Wharton's invocation and simultaneous renunciation of the inner home; hence her almost obsessive configurations of houses both inside and outside the mind.

## CHAPTER 6

[1] *The Letters of William James*, edited by his son, Henry James (Boston: Atlantic Monthly Press, 1920), 1.199–200. As the letter continues, James defines the feeling accompanying what he calls the "characteristic attitude," that is, the encounter with the "real me." "I feel a sort of deep enthusiastic bliss. . . which translates itself physically by a kind of stinging pain inside my breastbone (don't smile at this—it is to me an essential element of the whole thing!), and which, although it is a mere mood or emotion to which I give no form in words, authenticates itself to me as the deepest principle of all active and theoretic determination which I possess" (1.200) By locating the "feeling," ultimately, inside his breastbone, as a physical sensation, James materializes what is otherwise immaterial and intangible; he will struggle with this same mind/body split throughout *Principles of Psychology* and later essays examining the conscious mind.

[2] Henry James, *The Portrait of a Lady*, volumes 3 and 4 (New York: Charles Scribner's Sons, 1908), vii; xii.

[3] Though Wharton critics have generally been attuned to the forces of gender and social class in her fiction, Elizabeth Ammons asserts that we must add race to the list. Ammons argues that both the erasure and the presence of race in Wharton's writing (especially the representation of whiteness as racial) needs to be addressed and that we cannot continue to approach her work as if race were not an operative category in it. See Elizabeth Ammons, "Edith Wharton and the Issue of Race" in Millicent Bell, ed., *The Cambridge Companion to Edith Wharton* (New York: Cambridge University Press, 1995), 68–86.

[4] About the origins of *The House of Mirth*, Wharton writes: "In what aspect could a society of irresponsible pleasure-seekers be said to have, on the 'old woe of the world', any deeper bearing than the people composing such a society could guess? The answer was that a frivolous society can acquire dramatic significance only through what its frivolity destroys. . . . The answer, in short, was my heroine, Lily Bart." See Edith Wharton, *A Backward Glance* (New York: D. Appleton Century Company, 1934), 207. For more on *The House of Mirth*, see chapter five.

[5] *Edith Wharton: The Uncollected Critical Writings*, ed., Frederick Wegener (Princeton: Princeton University Press, 1996) 265; 267. Wharton's introduction accompanied the Oxford University Press, "World Classics" edition of *The House of Mirth*, published in 1935.

[6] See "Looking for the White Spot" in T. J. Jackson Lears, *The Power of Culture: Critical Essay in American History* (Chicago: University of Chicago Press, 1993), 15. Lears focuses his discussion of the modernist discourse of authenticity on a study of Sherwood Anderson. He argues that "the white spot," a Transcendentalist notion of a pure space that exists between the individual and God, becomes, for Anderson, a symbol of intense communion with another person. Thus, it might be "the way that modern people experience authentic spiritual life—now that the question of 'immortal life' had become too embarrassing to discuss" (31). Though Lears begins the essay with an acknowledgement that the ideal of authentic self-expression has been cast aside now that we recognize it as a "cultural construction," his analysis of Anderson shows that we need not automatically discard the discourse of authenticity.

[7] In her discussion of the architecture of The Mount, one of Edith Wharton's homes, Sarah Luria claims that doors reveal "an inwardly projected domestic order [that] seems determined to probe the inner life as it is to defend its sanctity" (309). She argues that Wharton's domesticity is inseparable from her work and that the design of her house made possible the space she needed to create her life's work. Though Luria claims that Wharton's architectural creed allows her to maintain private space in her own home, the novels so deeply complicate the tensions between public and private space

that it seems likely the issue remained a vexed one in Wharton's own life. See "The Architecture of Manners: Henry James, Edith Wharton, and The Mount," *American Quarterly* 49 (1997): 298–327.

8   Edith Wharton and Ogden Codman, Jr., *The Decoration of Houses* (1897; reprint, New York: Charles Scribner's Sons, 1901), 23; 49.

9   *The Age of Innocence* in *Edith Wharton: Novels*, ed., R.W.B. Lewis, (1920; reprint, New York: Library of America, 1985), 1057. All subsequent references will be to this edition of the text.

10  A wonderfully telling example of this scruple comes as Archer contemplates the Mingott clan's act in bringing the Countess "out": "he was glad that his future wife should not be restrained by false prudery from being kind (*in private*) to her unhappy cousin; but to receive Countess Olenska in the family circle was a different thing from producing her *in public*, at the Opera of all places" (1024; my emphasis).

11  See Maureen Howard, "The Bachelor and the Baby: *The House of Mirth*" in Millicent Bell, ed., *The Cambridge Companion to Edith Wharton* (New York: Cambridge University Press, 1995), 137–156.

12  *The House of Mirth* in *Edith Wharton: Novels*, ed., R.W.B. Lewis, (1905; reprint, New York: Library of America, 1985), 85. I am grateful to Jennifer Klein Hudak for making clear to me Lily's intensely closed nature here.

13  My understanding of the dissemination of Archer's consciousness owes much to Pamela Knights's essay, "Forms of Disembodiment: The Social Subject in *The Age of Innocence*" in Millicent Bell, ed., *The Cambridge Companion to Edith Wharton* (New York: Cambridge University Press, 1995), 20–45. Knights makes note of Wharton's interest "in what happens to the self when separated, by will or circumstances, from the world that has formed it" and states that the author's examination of Archer in *The Age of Innocence* "parallel[s], in its own terms, contemporary debates about the social basis of consciousness" (21).

14  James Robinson was the first to make explicit the sense that Archer cannot divorce himself from society and maintain a self. Robinson argues that Archer is a creature of the old ways, and "cannot break away from them without destroying himself psychologically in the process" (4). See James A. Robinson, "Psychological Determinism in *The Age of Innocence*," *Markham Review* 5 (Fall 1975): 1–5. Pamela Knights complicates this argument in helpful ways through her attention to disembodiment.

15  Emerson, too, uses the notion of the hieroglyphic in conjunction with communication, but specifically, communication with oneself. In *Nature*, he claims that there are no questions we cannot answer, "whatever curiosity the order of things has awakened in our minds, the order of things can satisfy. Every man's condition is a solution in hieroglyphic to those inquiries he would put." Thus, he suggests that we might look for answers inside ourselves, though, troublingly, what we find is a "hieroglyphic," something

mysterious and difficult to decipher. See Richard Poirier, ed., *Ralph Waldo Emerson* (Oxford: Oxford University Press, 1990), 3.

[16] Archer's dismay at the loss of this more delicate form of "nearness," which he shares with May in place of any sexual intimacy before their marriage, might explain his "curious indifference to [the Countess's] bodily presence," even as he is on the verge of a love affair with her. Wharton sets Archer's indifference toward the sensual Ellen inside a moment where he sits "with her face abandoned to his gaze. . . . The face exposed her as much as if it had been the whole person, with the soul behind it" (1208). Though Wharton may be suggesting a demureness on the part of Archer that rivals May's and that goes as deep as his love of tradition, it seems important to consider his wish here for an intimacy beyond the body. If we dismiss the possibilities for such intimacy as mere prudishness or sentimentality, we ignore the complications of Wharton's idea of the self—conflicted as it is— her sense that fiction must bring to life both the "social picture" *and* the soul.

[17] For a rich discussion of Archer's blindness and misreadings, see Emily J. Orlando, "Rereading Wharton's 'Poor Archer': A Mr. Might-have-been' in *The Age of Innocence*," *American Literary Realism* 30 (Winter 1998): 56–76.

[18] As Pamela Knights puts it, he is Wharton's "specimen rather than her spokesman." Knights, 21.

[19] See Martha Banta's study, *Imaging American Women: Ideas and Ideals in Cultural History* (New York: Columbia University Press, 1987) for a comprehensive discussion of the typology of American women.

[20] Most discussions of Wharton's social Darwinism center on *The House of Mirth*, though the rest of her fiction, certainly, shows the influence of Darwin's theories as well as his language. For a fine discussion of these influences, see Claire Preston, *Edith Wharton's Social Register* (New York: St. Martin's Press, 2000), 49–60. Also, see Nancy Bentley, "'Hunting for the Real': Wharton and the Science of Manners" in Millicent Bell, ed., *The Cambridge Companion to Edith Wharton* (New York: Cambridge University Press, 1995), 47–67 for further discussion of Wharton's use of anthropology, primitivism and what Bentley calls "culture consciousness" in the novel.

[21] Clare Virginia Eby cautions readers to modify what she calls the "dominant" interpretations of the novel that overstate both Wharton's sympathy for her central character and "the power of New York women." See Clare Virginia Eby, "Silencing Women in Edith Wharton's *Age of Innocence*," *Colby Quarterly* 28 (June 1992): 93–104.

[22] Julie Olin-Ammentorp and Ann Ryan make this point in their study of *The Custom of the Country*. See "Undine Spragg and the Transcendental I," *Edith Wharton Review* 17 (Spring 2001): 1–8.

23 The fact that Ellen Olenska ends up, at the close of the novel, in a room where "a light shone through the windows" (1302), a room that remains closed to Archer (and to the reader), shows Wharton's ambivalence, to the end, over the privacy of the Countess's inner realm.

24 See Alfred Russel Wallace, *On Miracles and Modern Spiritualism* (London: James Burns, 1875) and William James, *Varieties of Religious Experience: A Study in Human Nature* (New York: Random House, 1929). Chapters one and two also provide a fuller discussion of Wallace and James.

25 Marilyn Chandler seems quite ready to do so. She reads Archer's enslavement to society as a variation on the theme of entrapment that feminist critics have recognized in women's stories of domestic life. But she explicitly replaces the female character a feminist reading would be set on redeeming with Wharton's male center: "It would be hard to accuse Wharton . . . of partiality to one sex over the other, as some have tried to do. Her complaint is always with structures and systems, institutions and customs—products of human desire and human politics, entrapping all in them, even those who most assiduously work for their preservation." See Marilyn Chandler, *Dwelling in the Text: Houses in American Fiction* (Berkeley: University of California Press, 1991), 178.

26 Kathy Miller Hadley suggests that Wharton purposely draws the reader's attention to the "untold stories" of May and Ellen. She claims that Archer's "obsessive curiosity" about Ellen's life invites the reader to speculate about it, an activity that, she asserts, undermines the structure of the novel and its focus on Newland Archer. See "Ironic Structure and Untold Stories in *The Age of Innocence*," *Studies in the Novel* 23:2 (1991): 262–272. Gwendolyn Morgan makes a similar gesture in calling May the "unsung heroine" of the novel; she joins other critics in redeeming May as a character that transcends the behavioral formulas of old New York. See Gwendolyn Morgan, "The Unsung Heroine—A Study of May Welland in *The Age of Innocence*" in Pat Browne, ed., *Heroines of Popular Culture* (Bowling Green: Bowling Green State University Popular Press, 1987), 35; Evelyn E. Fracasso, "The Transparent Eyes of May Welland in Wharton's *The Age of Innocence*," *Modern Language Studies* 21:3 (1991): 43–8; Linette Davis, "Vulgarity and Red Blood in *The Age of Innocence*," *The Journal of the Midwest Modern Language Association* 20 (1987): 1–8; and Elsa Nettels, *Language and Gender in American Fiction: Howells, James, Wharton and Cather* (Charlottesville: University Press of Virginia, 1997) for similarly redemptive readings of May.

27 Elizabeth Ammons, *Edith Wharton's Argument with America* (Athens: The University of Georgia Press, 1980) 146. Ammons's argument depends upon her conviction that Wharton was committed to a feminist critique of the role of women in America throughout her entire career. Kathy Fedorko, likewise, reads Ellen as "the aware feminine self," "a woman comfortable with autonomy, with her body, with self-knowledge" (69). Fedorko claims

that Wharton "press[es] the limits of rationality, to utter the unutterable about sexuality, rage, death, fear, and especially, the nature of men and women" in her work (ix). The fact that Fedorko's argument rests upon Wharton's use of gothic elements in her fiction, especially her ghost stories, shows how complicated this maneuver might be in a novel (mostly) devoted to realism. Susan Goodman, *Edith Wharton's Friends and Rivals* (Hanover: University Press of New England, 1990), shows a different spin on the question of female autonomy, taking issue with studies that claim Wharton's work places women in isolation. Goodman argues that Wharton's "heroines" define themselves through their connections with other women; but she still assumes a "female community" set apart from the larger social body.

28 John Updike claims that Wharton learned from Proust "the "dignity of nostalgia." Updike finds that Wharton owes much to Proust, whom she admired, but never met: "Proust's simultaneously telescopic and microscopic view, his recognition that grandeur and absurdity coexist; his sense of society's apparent rigidity and actual fragility—these inform Wharton's enchanted caricature of her own tribe" (18). See John Updike, "Archer's Way," *The New York Review of Books* 42, no. 19 (1995 November 30): 16, 18.

29 Kenneth D. Pimple states that when Archer falls in love with Ellen and contemplates abandoning May, "he does not for an instant think of challenging society, but only of fleeing it" (147). In his essay, Pimple also makes the point that Wharton's books give us an "exceedingly rare glimpse of the traditions, mores and beliefs of a privileged segment of nineteenth-century America whose doors were firmly closed to any outside observer" (138). Calling to mind the advice Wharton herself gives in *The Decoration of Houses*, Pimple's observation reveals further subtleties regarding Wharton's ambivalence about the privacy of/in the world she presents in her fiction. See "Edith Wharton's 'Inscrutable Totem Terrors': Ethnography and *The Age of Innocence*," *Southern Folklore* 51 (1994): 137–152.

30 Hildegard Hoeller's reading of Wharton is informative here. Though she does not discuss *The Age of Innocence*, her study suggests that Wharton's fiction is best understood as a dialogue between two genres: sentimental fiction and realism. She stresses the fact that Wharton plays with sentimental love plots at the same time that she destabilizes them with the economies of realism. If, as I have suggested, the word "real" appears to be emptied of meaning in Wharton, then the detailed rendering of Archer's "real life" in the sanctuary is merely ironic. However, I am more interested, along with Hoeller, in the ways that Wharton maintains the tension between two discourses—whether they be sentimentality and realism or the language of the "real self" versus the socialized self—until the end. See Hildegard Hoeller, *Edith Wharton's Dialogue with Realism and Sentimental Fiction* (Gainesville: University Press of Florida, 2000).

[31] For a provocative reading of this scene see Orlando, 58–9.

[32] See Knights for a fuller discussion of Archer's "disembodiment" or loss of being.

[33] Edith Wharton, *The Decoration of Houses*, 22. Wharton refers, in various places, to the "newness" of the couple's house, which seems to align it with the modernism that she criticizes. At one point she even indicates that their home exemplifies an express resistance to the uniformity of architecture in New York. The Archers live in "a newly built house in East Thirty-ninth Street. The neighborhood was thought remote, and the house was built in a ghastly greenish-yellow stone that the younger architects were beginning to employ as a protest against the brownstone of which the uniform hue coated New York like a cold chocolate sauce; but the plumbing was perfect" (1072). This wry look at his own future dwelling comes as a result of Archer's response to Ellen's interiors; so it is difficult to tell whether he admires or laments the newness. The fact that he twice dwells on the strange color (1072; 1178) and here calls it "ghastly" indicates his distaste for this departure from form. But Archer does like the latest trends, even as he clings to traditions. The engagement ring he chooses for May has "the new setting . . . but it looks a little bare to old-fashioned eyes" and he dreams of decorating his library with "plain new bookcases without glass doors" (1072), a plan that he follows through with despite family disapproval.

[34] Claire Preston suggests that these intrusions—mere interruptions in the beginning of the story—have become "institutionalised in a room of their own." Preston, 42.

[35] The room does, in fact, have a door. If we follow Archer's string of memories in Chapter 34, we hear that his son Dallas, as a young boy, "first staggered across the floor shouting 'Dad,' while May and the nurse laughed behind the door" (1289).

[36] I cannot help but wonder if Wharton's recurrent description of May's "transparent eyes" might be referring playfully to Emerson's famous "transparent eyeball." If this is the case, May's self-effacing nature ("I am nothing. I see all") might, in a perverse reworking of Emerson's code, indicate the only form of consciousness available in the world of *The Age of Innocence*.

[37] William James, *Essays in Radical Empiricism* (New York: Longmans, Green and Co., 1922), 85. See chapter four for a discussion of this essay, "A World of Pure Experience," with respect to Henry James's *The Golden Bowl*.

[38] Kristin Boudreau asserts the abiding power of Emerson's rhetoric in her study of recent film versions of Hawthorne and James. See Kristin Boudreau, "*Is the World Then So Narrow?* Feminist Cinematic Adaptations of Hawthorne and James," *The Henry James Review* 21

(2000): 43–53. Robert Weisbuch repeats this sentiment in "James and the American Sacred," *The Henry James Review* 22 (2001): 217–228. He claims that James asserts a Hawthornian self, as opposed to an Emersonian one, a self that participates in the world and is defined by it. However, it seems as if Emerson's language has more staying power since Weisbuch (inadvertently?) echoes the philosopher's rhetoric ("Build, therefore, your own world") when he states that "Isabel chooses to *make her world*" (226; my emphasis).

[39] Singley's book is a comprehensive study of "the dimensions of Wharton's religious, spiritual and philosophical search in the context of American intellectual thought and religious history" (xi). See Carol Singley, *Edith Wharton: Matters of Mind and Spirit* (New York: Cambridge University Press, 1995).

[40] Preston makes this point with respect to Wharton's binary of "nice" and "not-nice" or the "not-x" phrase in general: "The semantic opposite of 'x', expressed as the category 'not-x', is a descriptive evasion which relieves the mind of imaginative, verbal, or social exercise. This evasion is a kind of restrictive antithesis which in semantic terms leads nowhere" (2). Preston's discussion of *The Age of Innoence* turns on this binary opposition. See Preston, 1–8.

[41] Irving Howe astutely notes that even Ellen Olenska, despite her obvious experience and sophistication, "affirms the value of social innocence" in the novel. Here and elsewhere, the Countess indicates a desire to come under the shelter of New York. Howe cites the instance where the Countess tells Archer: "I want to do what you all do—I want to feel cared for and safe" (1074). She also, later in the novel, tells him: "I promised Granny to stay with her because it seemed to me here I should be safer" (1263). See Irving Howe, "Perception, Communication and Growth as Correlative Themes in Edith Wharton's *The Age of Innocence*," *Agora: A Journal in the Humanities and Social Sciences* 2, no. 2 (1973): 71.

[42] In Newland's telephone conversation with his son, Wharton reveals this directness: "Dallas seemed to be speaking in the room: the voice was as near by and natural as if he had been lounging in his favorite armchair by the fire." At the same time Wharton makes the voice a force that presses upon another ('Think it over? No sir: not a minute. You've got to say yes now'), she also implies something about its detachment by calling attention to Dallas' voice as if it stood apart from him: "The voice began again" (1293). The sense that Dallas' voice is almost too direct, too forceful might indicate a certain longing on Wharton's part for more subtle forms of communication.

[43] Henry James, *The American*, volume 2 (New York: Charles Scribner's Sons, 1907), xvii–xviii.

[44] Pamela Knights maintains that the novel resists stability, that "when Archer seems to be pushing toward a different kind of self (one, impossibly,

beyond the social). . . the mimetic code of realism . . . seems to feel beneath it other pressures, as the novel of manners shifts into the fantastic" (35). Also relevant here is Hildegard Hoeller's engaging discussion "Economy and Excess: Realism and Sentimental Fiction Reconsidered" (her book's introduction). She asserts, quite aptly for *The Age of Innocence*, that the realist narrative, as opposed to the sentimental, "is more likely to be struggling against its own form, which tends to remind us of the very fact that it is artificial, artistic, constructed." See Hoeller, 25–37.

[45] Cynthia Griffin Wolff argues that Archer triumphs over society in his acceptance of reality, a reading that rests upon the belief that he has been its victim. Emily Orlando and Claire Preston offer arguments for the contrary. For these readers, Archer's only victimization is self-imposed. See Wolff, *A Feast of Words*, 323–5; Orlando, 72–73 and Preston, 24.

[46] See *A Backward Glance*, 89, 104, 112, 127, 173, 197 respectively.

[47] Wharton continues by saying that James was surprised at her question, "and I saw at once that the surprise was painful, and wished I had not spoken. I had assumed that his system was a deliberate one, carefully thought out, and had been genuinely anxious to hear his reasons. But after a pause of reflection he answered in a disturbed voice: 'My dear—I didn't know I had!'" *A Backward Glance*, 190–1.

# Bibliography

Abramson, Harold, ed. *Problems of Consciousness*. New York: Corlies, Macy & Company, Inc., 1952.

Agnew, Jean-Christophe. "The Consuming Vision of Henry James." In *The Culture of Consumption: Critical Essays in American History, 1880–1980*, edited by Richard Wightman Fox and T. J. Jackson Lears. New York: Pantheon, 1983.

Anderson, Quentin. *The American Henry James*. New Brunswick: Rutgers University Press, 1957.

Allen, Elizabeth. *A Woman's Place in the Novels of Henry James*. New York: St. Martin's Press, 1984.

Alter, Robert. "The Novel and the Sense of the Past." *Salmagundi* 68 (1985–6): 91–106.

Ammons, Elizabeth. *Edith Wharton's Argument with America*. Athens: University of Georgia Press, 1980.

———. "Edith Wharton and the Issue of Race." In *The Cambridge Companion to Edith Wharton*, edited by Millicent Bell. Cambridge: Cambridge University Press, 1995.

Arata, Stephen D. "Object Lessons: Reading the Museum in *The Golden Bowl*." In *Famous Last Words: Changes in Gender and Narrative Closure*, edited by Alison Booth. Virginia: University of Virginia Press, 1993.

Armstrong, Paul. *The Phenomenology of Henry James*. Chapel Hill: University of North Carolina Press, 1983.

———. *The Challenge of Bewilderment: Understanding and Representation in James, Conrad, and Ford*. Ithaca: Cornell University Press, 1987.

Auchard, John. *Silence in Henry James*. University Park: Penn State University Press, 1986.

Baars, Bernard J. *In the Theater of Consciousness: The Workspace of the Mind*. New York: Oxford University Press, 1997.

Banta, Martha. *Imaging American Women: Idea and Ideals in Cultural History*. New York: Columbia University Press, 1987.

Baris, Sharon. "James's Pyrotechnic Display: The Book in Isabel's Portrait." *The Henry James Review* 12 (1991): 146–153.

Barrish, Phillip. *American Literary Realism, Critical Theory, and Intellectual Prestige, 1880–1995*. Cambridge: Cambridge University Press, 2001.

Barzun, Jacques. *A Stroll with William James*. New York: Harper and Row, 1983.

Bauer, Dale. *Feminist Dialogics: A Theory of Failed Community*. Albany State University of New York Press, 1988.

———. *Edith Wharton's Brave New Politics*. Madison: University of Wisconsin Press, 1994.

Beer, Gillian. *Darwin's Plots Evolutionary Narrative in Darwin, George Eliot and Nineteenth-Century Fiction*. London: Routledge & Kegan Paul, 1983.

———. "The Face of Nature": Anthropomorphic Elements in the Language of *The Origin of Species*." In *Languages of Nature: Critical Essays on Science and Literature*, edited by L.J. Jordanova. New Brunswick: Rutgers University Press, 1986.

———. "Darwin and the Growth of Language Theory." In *Nature Transfigured: Science and Literature, 1700–1900*, edited by John Christie and Sally Shuttleworth. Manchester: Manchester University Press, 1989.

Bell, Daniel. *Cultural Contradictions of Capitalism*. New York: Basic Books, 1976.

Bell, Millicent. "Henry James, Meaning and Unmeaning." *Raritan* 4 (1984): 29–46.

———. *Meaning in Henry James*. Cambridge: Harvard University Press, 1991.

———. ed. *The Cambridge Companion to Edith Wharton*. Cambridge: Cambridge University Press, 1995.

Benert, Annette Larson. "The Geography of Gender in *The House of Mirth*." *Studies in the Novel* 22:1 (1990): 26–39.

Benstock, Shari. "'The word which made all clear': The Silent Close of *The House of Mirth*." In *Famous Last Words: Changes in Gender and Narrative Closure*, edited by Alison Booth. Charlottesville: University of Virginia Press, 1993.

———. *No Gifts From Chance: A Biography of Edith Wharton*. New York: Charles Scribner's Sons, 1994.

Bentley, Nancy. "'Hunting for the Real': Wharton and the Science of Manners." In *The Cambridge Companion to Edith Wharton*, edited by Millicent Bell. Cambridge: Cambridge University Press, 1995.

Benton, Ted. "Science, ideology and culture: Malthus and the *Origin of Species*." In *Charles Darwin's The Origin of Species: New Interdisciplinary Essays,* edited by David Amigoni and Jeff Wallace. Manchester: Manchester University Press, 1995.

Berkson, Dorothy. "Why Does She Marry Osmond?: The Education of Isabel Archer." *American Transcendental Quarterly* 60 (1986): 53–71.

Biddle, Arthur William. "The Emerging Consciousness: A Study of the Development of the Centre of Consciousness in the Early Novels of Henry James." Ph.D. diss., Michigan State University, 1970.

Bjork, Daniel. *William James: The Center of His Vision*. New York: Columbia University Press, 1988.

Blackall, Jean Frantx. "Charity at the Window: Narrative Techniques in Edith Wharton's *Summer*." In *Edith Wharton: New Critical Essays*, edited by Alfred Bendixen and Annette Zilversmit. New York: Garland Publishing Company, Inc., 1992.

Blackmur, R. P. *The Art of the Novel: Critical Prefaces by Henry James*. New York: Charles Scribner's Sons, 1934.

Booth, Wayne. *The Rhetoric of Fiction*. Chicago: University of Chicago Press, 1961.

Boudreau, Kristin. "Henry James's Inward Aches." *The Henry James Review* 20 (1999): 69–80.

———. "*Is* the World Then So Narrow? Feminist Cinematic Adaptations of Hawthorne and James." *The Henry James Review* 21 (2000): 43–53.

Bowler, Peter J. *Darwinism*. New York: Twayne Publishers, 1993.

Boydston, Jeanne. "Grave Endearing Traditions: Edith Wharton and the Domestic Novel." In *Faith of a (Woman) Writer*, edited by Alice Kessler-Harris and William McBrien. New York: Greenwood Press, 1988.

Bradbury, Malcolm. *The Expatriate Tradition in American Literature*. Durham: British Association for American Studies, 1982.

Bradbury, Nicola. *Henry James: The Later Novels*. Oxford: Clarendon Press, 1979.

———. *An Annotated Critical Bibliography of Henry James*. New York: St. Martin's Press, 1987.

Buchanan, D. "'The Candlestick and the Snuffers': Some Thoughts on *The Portrait of a Lady.*" *The Henry James Review* 16 (1995): 121–30.

Bucke, Richard Maurice. *Cosmic Consciousness, A Study in the Evolution of the Human Mind.* New York: E.P. Dutton and Co., Inc., 1947.

Budick, E. Miller. *Fiction and Historical Consciousness.* New Haven: Yale University Press, 1989.

Buitenhuis, Peter. *The Grasping Imagination: The American Writings of Henry James.* Toronto: University of Toronto Press, 1970.

Butler, Judith. *Gender Trouble: Feminism and the Subversion of Identity.* New York: Routledge, 1990.

Butler, Thomas. *Memory: History, Culture and the Mind.* Oxford: Basil Blackwell, 1989.

Cameron, Sharon. *Thinking in Henry James.* Chicago: University of Chicago Press, 1989.

Campbell, Percy. *Consciousness, Brain Child.* East Cleveland: The Caxton Co., 1933.

Capek, Milic. "The Reappearance of the Self in the Last Philosophy of William James." *The Philosophical Review* 62 (1953): 526–544.

Carpenter, W.B. *Principles of Mental Physiology.* New York: Appleton, 1874.

Carroll, David. *The Subject in Question: The Languages of Theory and the Strategies of Fiction.* Chicago: University of Chicago Press, 1982.

Caws, Peter, ed. *Two Centuries of Philosophy in America.* New Jersey: Rowman and Littlefield, 1980.

Caws, Mary Ann. "What Can a Woman Do for the Late Henry James?" *Raritan* XIV (1994): 1–17.

Chandler, Marilyn R. *Dwelling in the Text: Houses in American Fiction.* Berkeley: University of California Press, 1991.

Chase, Richard. *The American Novel and its Tradition.* New York: Doubleday, 1957.

Clubbe, John. "Interiors and the Interior Life in Edith Wharton's *The House of Mirth.*" *Studies in the Novel* 28 (Winter 1996): 543–564.

Cohn, Dorrit. *Transparent Minds: Narrative Modes for Presenting Consciousness in Fiction.* Princeton: Princeton University Press, 1978.

Cole, David, ed. *Philosophy, Mind and Cognitive Inquiry.* Boston: Kluwer Academic Publishers, 1990.

Colgrove, F.W. *Memory: An Inductive Study.* New York: Henry Holt and Company, 1901.

Collecott, Diana. "Framing *The Portrait of a Lady*: Henry James and Isabel Archer." In *The Magic Circle of Henry James*, edited by Amritjit Singh and K. Ayyappa Paniker. New York: Envoy Press, 1989.

Colquitt, Clare, Susan Goodman, and Candace Waid, ed. *A Forward Glance: New Essays on Edith Wharton*. Newark: University of Delaware Press, 1999.

Connolly, Francis X. "Literary Consciousness and Literary Conscience." *Thought* 25 (1950): 663–680.

Cooley, Charles Horton. *Human Nature and the Social Order*. 1902. Reprint, New York: Schocken Books, 1964.

Crews, Frederick. *The Tragedy of Manners: Moral Drama in the Later Novels of Henry James*. New Haven: Yale University Press, 1957.

Crowley, Frank Edward. "Identity Themes and Double Consciousness in Henry James, James Joyce and John Fowles: The Myth in the Metaphor." Ph.D. diss., State University of New York, Buffalo, 1980.

Cuddy, Lois. "Triangles of Defeat and Liberation: The Quest for Power in Edith Wharton's Fiction." *Perspectives on Contemporary Literature* 8 (1982): 18–25.

Darwin, Charles. *The Foundations of the origin of species; 2 essays written in 1842 and 1844*. Cambridge: Cambridge University Press, 1909.

———. *The Origin of Species by Means of Natural Selection or the Preservation of Favoured Races in the Struggle for Life*. 1859. Reprint, New York: Collier Books, 1962.

———. *The Expression of the Emotions in Man and Animals*. London: J. Murray, 1872.

———. *The Descent of Man, and Selection in Relation to Sex*. New York: A.L. Burt, Publisher, 1874.

———. *Evolution and Natural Selection*. Boston: Beacon Press, 1959.

Daugherty, Sarah. "James, Renan, and the Religion of Consciousness." *Comparative Literature* 16 (1979): 318–31.

Davis, Linette. "Vulgarity and Red Blood in *The Age of Innocence*." *The Journal of Midwest Modern Language Association* 20 (1987): 1–8.

Davison, Richard, Gary Schwartz and David Shapiro, ed. *Consciousness and Self-Regulation*. New York: Plenum Press, 1983.

Dear, Peter. "Narrative, Anecdotes, and Experiments: Turning Experience into Science in the Seventeenth Century." In *The Literary Structure of Scientific Argument*, edited by Peter Dear. Philadelphia: University of Pennsylvania Press, 1991.

de Man, Paul. "The Epistemology of Metaphor." In *On Metaphor*, edited by Sheldon Sacks. Chicago: University of Chicago Press, 1979.

———. *Blindness and Insight: Essays in the Rhetoric of Contemporary Criticism*. 2nd rev. ed. London: Methuen, 1983.

Dennett, Daniel. *Consciousness Explained*. Boston: Little, Brown and Co., 1991.

Dewey, John. "The Vanishing Subject in the Psychology of William James." *Journal of Philosophy, Psychology and Scientific Method* 37 (1940): 589–99, reprinted in *Problems of Men* (New York: Philosophical Library, 1946).

Dimock, Wai Chee. "Debasing Exchanges: Edith Wharton's *The House of Mirth*." *PMLA* 10 (October 1985): 783–792.

———. "Gender, the Market, and the Non-Trivial in James." *The Henry James Review* 15 (1994): 24–30.

Djwa, Sandra. "Ut Pictura Poesis: The Making of a Lady." *The Henry James Review* 7 (1986): 72–85.

Dove, John R. "Tragic Consciousness in Isabel Archer." *Studies in American Literature* 8 (1960): 78–94.

Dupee, F.W. *The Question of Henry James*. New York: Henry Holt and Company, 1945.

———. *Henry James*. New York: William Sloane, 1951.

Dyman, Jenni. *Lurking Feminism: The Ghost Stories of Edith Wharton*. New York: Peter Lang Publishing, 1996.

Dyson, John Peter. "The Soft Breath of Consciousness: A Critical Analysis of Some of the Later Tales of Henry James." Ph.D. diss., Princeton University, 1971.

Eby, Clare Virginia. "Silencing Women in Edith Wharton's *The Age of Innocence*." *Colby Quarterly* 28 (1992): 93–104.

Edel, Leon. *Henry James: The Master, 1909–1916*. New York: J.B. Lippincort Co., 1972.

———. *The Life of Henry James*. Harmondsworth: Penguin Press, 1977.

———. *Henry James: A Life*. New York: Harper and Row Publishers, 1985.

———. "The Myth of America in *The Portrait of a Lady*." *The Henry James Review* 7 (1986): 8–17.

———. *Henry James: Selected Letters*. Cambridge: Harvard University Press, 1987.

Edel, Leon, and Lyall H. Powers, ed. *The Complete Notebooks of Henry James*. New York: Oxford University Press, 1987.

Edelman, Gerald. *Bright Air, Brilliant Fire: On the Matter of the Mind*. New York: Basic Books, 1992.

Eisely, Loren. *Darwin's Century: Evolution and the Men Who Discovered It*. New York: Doubleday Anchor Books, 1958.

Ellmann, Mary. *Thinking About Women*. New York: Harcourt, Brace & World, Inc., 1968.

Engelberg, Edward. *The Unknown Distance: From Consciousness to Conscience*. Cambridge: Harvard University Press, 1972.

Eriksen, Richard. *Consciousness, Life and the Fourth Dimension*. New York: Hazell, Watson & Viney, Ltd., 1923.

Erlich, Gloria C. *The Sexual Education of Edith Wharton*. Berkeley: University of California Press, 1992.

Esch, Deborah, ed. *New Essays on The House of Mirth*. Cambridge: Cambridge University Press, 2001.

Faery, Rebecca Blevins. "Wharton's Reef: The Inscription of Female Sexuality." In *Edith Wharton: New Critical Essays*, edited by Alfred Bendixen, and Annette Zilversmit. New York: Garland Publishing Company, Inc., 1992.

Farantello, Donna. "'The Picture of the Mind Revives Again': Perception in William James's Psychology and 'Tintern Abbey.'" *The Wordsworth Circle* 22 (1991): 131–5.

Fedorko, Kathy. *Gender and the Gothic in the Fiction of Edith Wharton*. Tuscaloosa: The University of Alabama Press, 1995.

Feidelson, Charles. "The Moment of *The Portrait of a Lady*." *Ventures* 8 (1968): 47–55.

Feinstein, Howard. *Becoming William James*. Ithaca: Cornell University Press, 1984.

Fetterly, Judith. *Felicitous Space: The Imaginative Structures of Edith Wharton and Willa Cather*. Chapel Hill: The University of North Carolina Press, 1986.

Firebaugh, Joseph. "The Pragmatism of Henry James." *Virginia Quarterly Review* 27 (1951): 419–35.

———. "The Ververs." *Essays in Criticism* 4 (1954): 400–410.

Fischer, Sandra K. "Isabel Archer and the Enclosed Chamber: A Phenomenological Reading." *The Henry James Review* 7 (1986): 48–58.

Fogel, Daniel. *Henry James and the Structure of the Romantic Imagination.* Baton Rouge: Louisiana State University Press, 1981.

———. ed. *A Companion to Henry James Studies.* Westport: Greenwood Press, 1993.

Ford, Peter Marcus. *William James's Philosophy.* Amherst: University of Massachusetts Press, 1982.

Forster, E.M. *Aspects of the Novel.* New York: Harcourt, Brace and Co., 1927.

Fowler, Virginia. *Henry James's American Girl.* Madison: The University of Wisconsin Press, 1984.

———. "The Later Fiction." In *A Companion to Henry James Studies*, edited by Daniel Mark Fogel. Connecticut: Greenwood Press, 1993.

Fracasso, Evelyn. "The Transparent Eyes of May Welland in Wharton's *The Age of Innocence.*" *Modern Language Studies* 21: 4 (1991): 43–8.

———. *Edith Wharton's Prisoners of Consciousness.* Westport: Greenwood Press, 1994.

Frank, Ellen. *Literary Architecture.* Berkeley: University of California Press, 1979.

Freedman, Jonathan. *Professions of Taste: Henry James, British Aestheticism and Commodity Culture.* Stanford: Stanford University Press, 1990.

Freidman, Alan. *The Turn of the Novel.* New York: Oxford University Press, 1966.

Friedling, Sheila. "Problems of Perception in the Modern Novel: The Representation of Consciousness in Works of Henry James, Gertrude Stein, and William James." Ph.D. diss., University of Wisconsin, Madison, 1973.

Friedman, Melvin. *Stream of Consciousness: A Study in Literary Method.* New Haven: Yale University Press, 1955.

Fryer, Judith. *The Faces of Eve: Women in the Nineteenth Century Novel.* New York: Oxford University Press, 1976.

———. "Purity and Power in *The Age of Innocence.*" *American Literary Realism* 17 (1984): 153–168.

———. "Women and Space: the Flowering of Desire." *Prospects* 9 (1984): 187–230.

———. "Reading *Mrs. Lloyd.*" In *Edith Wharton: New Critical Essays*, edited by Alfred Bendixen and Annette Zilversmit. New York: Garland Publishing Company, Inc. 1992.

Fullerton, W. Morton. "'The Art of Henry James.' A review of The Novels and Tales of Henry James. New York ed. 24 vols. London: Macmillan, 1907–1909." *The Quarterly Review* 212 (1910): 394–5.

Funston, Judith. *Henry James: A Reference Guide*. Boston: G.K. Hall & Co., 1991.

Fuss, Diana. *Essentially Speaking: Feminism, Nature and Difference*. New York: Routledge, 1989.

Gale, Robert. *The Caught Image: Figurative Language in the Fiction of Henry James*. Chapel Hill: University of North Carolina Press, 1964.

Gard, Roger. *Henry James The Critical Heritage*. London: Routledge and Kegan Paul, 1968.

Gass, William. "The High Brutality of Good Intentions." *Accent* 18 (1958): 62–71.

Gavin, William Joseph. *William James and the Reinstatement of the Vague*. Philadelphia: Temple University Press, 1992.

Gibbons, Tom. *Rooms in the Darwin Hotel: Studies in English Literary Criticism and Ideas: 1880–1920*. Nedlands: University of Australia Press, 1973.

Gibson, William. "Metaphor in the Plot of *The Ambassadors*." *New England Quarterly* 24 (1951): 291–305.

Gilbert, Sandra M., and Susan Gubar. *No Man's Land: The Place of the Woman Writer in the Twentieth Century*. New Haven: Yale University Press, 1989.

Goetz, William. *Henry James and the Darkest Abyss of Romance*. Baton Rouge: Louisiana State University Press, 1986.

Goldberg, M.A. "'Things' and Values in Henry James's Universe." *Western Humanities Review* 11 (1957): 377–385.

Goodman, Russell. *American Philosophy and the Romantic Tradition*. Cambridge: Cambridge University Press, 1990.

Goodman, Susan. *Edith Wharton's Women: Friends and Rivals*. Hanover: University Press of New England, 1990.

———. *Edith Wharton's Inner Circle*. Austin: University of Texas Press, 1994.

Gordon, Beverly. "Woman's Domestic Body: The Conceptual Conflation of Women and Interiors in the Industrial Age." *Winterthur Portfolio* 31:4 (1996): 281–301.

Gragg, Perry Earl. "The Revelation of Consciousness: The Psychology of William James and Five Novels of Henry James." Ph.D. diss., University of Texas at Austin, 1961.

Graham, Kenneth. *Henry James: the Drama of Fulfillment*. Oxford: Clarendon Press, 1975.

Gregor, Ian and Brian Nicholas. *The Moral and the Story*. London: Faber and Faber, 1962.

Grenier, Richard. "Society and Edith Wharton." *Commentary* 96 (1993): 48–52.

Gribble, Jennifer. "Value in *The Golden Bowl*." *The Critical Review* 27 (1985): 50–65.

Griffin, Susan M. *The Historical Eye: The Texture of the Visual in Late James*. Boston: Northeastern University Press, 1991.

Hadley, Kathy Miller. "Ironic Structure and Untold Stories in *The Age of Innocence*." *Studies in the Novel* 23:2 (1991): 262–272.

Hansen, Olaf. *Aesthetic Individualism and Practical Intellect*. New Jersey: Princeton University Press, 1990.

Hardwick, Elizabeth. *The Selected Letters of William James*. New York: Doubleday Books, 1960.

Hartsock, Mildred. "The Exposed Mind: A View of *The Awkward Age*." *Critical Quarterly* 9 (1967): 49–59.

Hawthorne, Nathaniel. *The House of the Seven Gables*. New York: Penguin Books, 1990.

Hocks, Richard. *Henry James and Pragmatistic Thought: A Study in the Relationship between the Philosophy of William James and the Literary Art of Henry James*. Chapel Hill: University of North Carolina Press, 1974.

Hoeller, Hildegard. *Edith Wharton's Dialogue with Realism and Sentimental Fiction*. Gainesville: University Press of Florida, 2000.

Holbrook, David. *Edith Wharton and the Unsatisfactory Man*. London: Vision Press, 1991.

Holland, Laurence. *The Expense of Vision*. Baltimore: The Johns Hopkins University Press, 1982.

Holt, Edwin. *The Concept of Consciousness*. London: George Allen Company, Ltd., 1914.

Horne, Philip, ed. *Henry James: A Life in Letters*. London: The Penguin Press, 1999.

Howard, Maureen. "The Bachelor and the Baby: *The House of Mirth*." In *The Cambridge Companion to Edith Wharton*, edited by Millicent Bell. Cambridge: Cambridge University Press, 1995.

Howe, Irving, ed. *Edith Wharton: A Collection of Critical Essays*. New Jersey: Prentice-Hall, 1962.

———. "Perception, Communication and Growth as Correlative Themes in Edith Wharton's *The Age of Innocence*." *Agora: A Journal in the Humanities and Social Sciences* 2 (1973): 68–82.

Hughes, H. Stuart. *Consciousness and Society: the Reorientation of European Social Thought*. New York: Vintage Books, 1958.

Humphrey, Nicholas. *Consciousness Regained*. Oxford: Oxford University Press, 1983.

———. *A History of the Mind: Emotion and the Birth of Consciousness*. New York: Simon and Schuster, 1992.

Humphrey, Robert. *Stream of Consciousness in the Modern Novel*. Berkeley: California University Press, 1954.

Hyman, Stanley Edgar. *The Tangled Bank: Darwin, Marx, Frazer and Freud as Imaginative Writers*. New York: Atheneum, 1962.

Ian, Marcia. "Consecrated Diplomacy and The Concretion of Self." *The Henry James Review* 7 (1985): 27–31.

Izzo, Donatello. "*The Portrait of a Lady* and Modern Narrative." *New Essays on The Portrait of a Lady*, edited by Joel Porte. Cambridge: Cambridge University Press, 1990.

James, Henry. *The American. The Novels and Tales of Henry James*. Volume 2. New York: Charles Scribner's Sons, 1907.

———. *The Portrait of a Lady. The Novels and Tales of Henry James*. Volumes 3 and 4. New York: Charles Scribner's Sons, 1908.

———. *The Spoils of Poynton. The Novels and Tales of Henry James*. Volume 10. New York: Charles Scribner's Sons, 1908.

———. *The Ambassadors. The Novels and Tales of Henry James*. Volumes 21 and 22. New York: Charles Scribner's Sons, 1909.

———. *The Golden Bowl. The Novels and Tales of Henry James*. Volumes 23 and 24. New York: Charles Scribner's Sons, 1909.

———. *Great Short Works of Henry James*. New York: Harper & Row, 1966.

James, William. *The Principles of Psychology*. 1890. Volumes 1, 2 and 3. Reprint, Cambridge: Harvard University Press, 1981.

———. *Psychology: Briefer Course*. New York: Henry Holt and Co., 1892.

———. *Essays in Radical Empiricism*. New York: Longmans, Green and Co., 1922.

———. *The Varieties of Religious Experience: A Study in Human Nature.*
New York: Random House, 1929.

———. *The Letters of William James,* edited by his son, Henry James.
Boston: Atlantic Monthly Press, 1920.

Jameson, Frederic. *The Political Unconscious: Narrative as a Socially
Symbolic Act.* Ithaca: Cornell University Press, 1981.

Jaynes, Julian. *The Origin of Consciousness in the Breakdown of the
Bicameral Mind.* 1976. Reprint, Boston: Houghton Mifflin
Company, 1990.

Johnson, Courtney Jr. *Henry James and the Evolution of Consciousness.* East
Lansing: Michigan State University Press, 1987.

Johnson, Ellwood. "William James and the Art of Fiction." *The Journal of
Aesthetics and Art Criticism* 30 (1972): 285–96.

Johnson, Michael and Tracy Henley, ed. *Reflections on the Principles of
Psychology: William James After a Century.* New Jersey: Lawrence
Erlbaum Associates, Publishers, 1990.

Joslin, Katherine. *Edith Wharton.* New York: St. Martin's Press, 1991.

Kahler, Erich. *The Inward Turn of Narrative.* Princeton: Princeton University
Press, 1973.

Kaplan, Amy. *The Social Construction of American Realism.* Chicago: The
University of Chicago Press, 1988.

Kaplan, Sydney Janet. *Feminine Consciousness in the Modern British Novel.*
Urbana: University of Chicago Press, 1975.

Karpinski, Joanne, ed. *Critical Essays on Charlotte Perkins Gilman.* New
York: G.K. Hall & Co., 1992.

Kauffman, Linda S. *Discourses of Desire: Gender, Genre and Epistolary
Fictions.* Ithaca: Cornell University Press, 1986.

Kearns, Michael S. *Metaphors of Mind in Fiction and Psychology.* Lexington:
The University Press of Kentucky, 1987.

Kemp, Anthony. *The Estrangement of the Past: A Study in the Origins of
Modern Consciousness.* New York: Oxford University Press, 1991.

Kelly, Cornelia Pulsifer. *The Early Development of Henry James.* Urbana:
University of Illinois Press, 1965.

Kermode, Frank. *The Sense of an Ending: Studies in the Theory of Fiction.*
New York: Oxford University Press, 1968.

Kiell, Norman, ed. *Blood Brothers: Siblings as Writers.* New York:
International Universities Press, Inc., 1983.

Killoran, Helen. *Edith Wharton: Art and Allusion*. Tuscaloosa: University of Alabama Press, 1996.

Knights, L.C. "Henry James and the Trapped Spectator." *Southern Review* 4 (1938): 600–15.

Knights, Pamela. "Forms of Disembodiment: The Social Subject in *The Age of Innocence.*" In *The Cambridge Companion to Edith Wharton*, edited by Millicent Bell. Cambridge: Cambridge University Press, 1995.

Krook, Dorothea. *The Ordeal of Consciousness in Henry James*. Cambridge: Cambridge University Press, 1962.

Kundu, Gautam. "The Houses that Edith Wharton Built: The Significance of the van der Luyden's Italian Villa and The Patroon's Rock Cottage in *The Age of Innocence.*" *Indian Journal of American Studies* 13 (1983): 127–131.

Labrie, Ernest R. "Henry James's Idea of Consciousness." *American Literature* 39 (1968): 517–529.

———. "The Morality of Consciousness in Henry James." *Colby Library Quarterly* 9 (1971): 409–424.

———. "The Power of Consciousness in Henry James." *Arizona Quarterly* 29 (1973): 101–114.

Lauer, Kristin and Margaret Murray. *Edith Wharton: An Annotated Secondary Bibliography*. New York: Garland Publishing, 1990.

Layton, Lynne and Barbara Shapiro. *Narcissism and The Text: Studies in the Literature and Psychology of Self*. New York: New York University Press, 1986.

Lears, T.J. Jackson. "Sherwood Anderson: Looking for the White Spot." In *The Power of Culture: Critical Essays in American History*, edited by Richard Wightman Fox and T.J. Jackson Lears. Chicago: University of Chicago Press, 1993.

Lebowitz, Naomi. *The Imagination of Loving: Henry James's Legacy to the Novel*. Detroit: Wayne State University, 1965.

Lee, Brian. *The Novels of Henry James: A Study in Culture and Consciousness*. New York: St. Martin's Press, 1978.

Lentricchia, Frank. *Modernist Quartet*. Cambridge: Cambridge University Press, 1994.

Lewes, G.H. *Problems of Life and Mind*. Boston: Houghton, Osgood and Company, 1879–80.

———. *The Physical Basis of Mind*. London: Kegan Paul, Trench, Trubner & Co. Ltd., 1893.

Lewis, R.W.B. *Trials of the Word: Essays in American Literature and Humanistic Tradition.* New Haven: Yale University Press, 1965.

———. ed. *The Collected Short Stories of Edith Wharton.* 2 vols. New York: Charles Scribner's Sons, 1968.

———. *Edith Wharton: A Biography.* New York: Harper & Row Publishers, 1975.

———. ed. *Edith Wharton: Novels,* New York: Library of America, 1985.

———. ed. *The Selected Short Stories of Edith Wharton.* New York: Charles Scribner's and Sons, 1991.

———. *The Jameses: A Family Narrative.* New York: Farrar, Straus and Giroux, 1991.

Lewis, R.W.B. and Nancy Lewis, ed. *The Letters of Edith Wharton.* New York: Charles Scribner's Sons, 1988.

Lindberg, Gary H. *Edith Wharton and the Novel of Manners.* Charlottesville: University of Virginia Press, 1975.

Little, Matthew. "Henry James's 'The Art of Fiction': Word, Self, Experience." *Philological Quarterly* 64 (1985): 225–38.

Loewenberg, Bert James, ed. *Charles Darwin: Evolution and Natural Selection.* Boston: Beacon Hill Press, 1959.

Lubbock, Percy. *The Craft of Fiction.* London: Jonathan Cape, 1954.

———. ed. *The Letters of Henry James.* 2 vols. New York: Charles Scribner's Sons, 1920.

Luria, Sarah. "The Architecture of Manners: Henry James, Edith Wharton and The Mount." *American Quarterly* 49 (1997): 298–327.

Lycan, William. *Consciousness.* Cambridge: The MIT Press, 1987.

Machann, Virginia Sue Brown. "American Perspectives on Women's Initiations: The Mythic and Realistic Coming to Consciousness." Ph.D. diss., University of Texas, 1979.

MacComb, Debra. "Divorce of a Nation; or, Can Isabel Archer Resist History?" *The Henry James Review* 17 (1996): 129–148.

Maini, Darshan Singh. *Henry James: the Indirect Vision.* Ann Arbor: University of Michigan Press, 1988.

Marcell, David W. "High Ideals and Catchpenny Realities in James's *The Portrait of a Lady.*" In *Essays in Modern American Literature,* edited by Richard E. Langford. Deland: Stetson University Press, 1963. First published in *SSH* 1 (1963): 23–34.

Marshall, Adré. *The Turn of the Mind: Constituting Consciousness in Henry James*. Madison: Farleigh Dickinson Press, 1998.

Marshall, Henry Rutgers. *Consciousness*. London: Macmillan and Co., Limited, 1909.

Martin, Robert K. "Ages of Innocence: Edith Wharton, Henry James and Nathaniel Hawthorne." *The Henry James Review* 21 (2000): 56–62.

Matthiessen, F.O. *The James Family*. New York: Alfred A. Knopf, 1947.

———. *Henry James: The Major Phase*. New York: Oxford University Press, 1963.

May, Keith. *Out of the Maelstrom: Psychology and the Novel in the Twentieth Century*. London: P. Elek, 1977.

McDermott, John, ed. *The Writings of William James*. New York: Random House Press, 1967.

McDougall, William. *Body and Mind*. London: Methuen, 1915.

McMurray, William. "Pragmatic Realism in *The Bostonians*." In *Henry James: Modern Judgments*, edited by Tony Tanner. London: Macmillan & Co., 1968.

McWhirter, David. *Desire and Love in Henry James*. Cambridge: Cambridge University Press, 1989.

Mead, George Herbert. *Mind, Self and Society: From the Standpoint of a Social Behaviorist*. Chicago: University of Chicago Press, 1934.

———. *Movements of Thought in the Nineteenth Century*. Chicago: University of Chicago Press, 1936.

Meissner, Collin. *Henry James and the Language of Experience*. Cambridge: Cambridge University Press, 1999.

Menand, Louis. *The Metaphysical Club: A Story of Ideas in America*. New York: Farrar, Straus and Giroux, 2001.

Merish, Lori. "Engendering Nationalism: Narrative Form and Commodity Spectacle in U.S. Naturalist Fiction." *Novel* 29 (Spring 1996): 319–345.

Michaels, Walter Benn. *The Gold Standard and The Logic of Naturalism*. Berkeley: University of California Press, 1987.

Miller, D. Quentin. "'A Barrier of Words': The Tension Between Narrative Voice and Vision in the Writings of Edith Wharton." *American Literary Realism* 27 (1994): 11–22.

Mitchell, Lee Clark. *Determined Fictions: American Literary Naturalism*. New York: Columbia University Press, 1989.

———. "Beyond the Frame of *The Portrait of a Lady*." *Raritan* 17:3 (1998): 90–109.

———. "A Marriage of Opposites: Oxymorons, Ethics, and James's *The American*." *The Henry James Review* 19 (1998): 1–16.

Moi, Toril. *Sexual/Textual Politics: Feminist Literary Theory*. London: Routledge, 1985.

Montgomery, Maureen E. *Displaying Women: Spectacles of Leisure in Edith Wharton's New York*. New York: Routledge, 1998.

Moody, A.D. "James's Portrait of an Ideal." In *The Magic Circle of Henry James*, edited by Amritjit Singh and K. Ayyappa Paniker. New York: Envoy Press, 1989.

Morgan, Gwendolyn. "The Unsung Heroine—A Study of May Welland in *The Age of Innocence*." In *Heroines in Popular Culture*, edited by Pat Browne. Bowling Green: Bowling Green State University Popular Press, 1987.

Morton, Peter. *The Vital Science: Biology and the Literary Imagination: 1860–1900*. London: George Allen & Unwin Publishers, Ltd., 1984.

Myers, Gerald. *William James: His Life and Thought*. New Haven: Yale University Press, 1986.

*New Literary History* 15 No. 1 (Special Issue on "Literature and/as Moral Philosophy") (1983): 1–216.

Needleman, Jacob. *Consciousness and Tradition*. New York: The Crossroad Publishing Company, 1982.

Nettels, Elsa. *Language and Gender in American Fiction: Howells, James, Wharton and Cather*. Charlottesville: University Press of Virginia, 1997.

Nussbaum, Martha. *Love's Knowledge: Essays on Philosophy and Literature*. New York: Oxford University Press, 1990.

Nuttal, A.D. *A Common Sky: Philosophy and the Literary Imagination*. Berkeley: University of California Press, 1974.

Olin-Ammentorp, Julie and Ann Ryan. "Undine Spragg and the Transcendental I." *Edith Wharton Review* 17 (2001): 1–12.

Olney, James. "Psychology, Memory and Autobiography: William and Henry James." *The Henry James Review* 6 (1984): 46–51.

Olsen, Stein Haugom. *The Structure of Literary Understanding*. Cambridge: Cambridge University Press, 1978.

Orlando, Emily J. "Rereading Wharton's 'Poor Archer': A Mr. Might-have-been' in *The Age of Innocence.*" *American Literary Realism* 30 (Winter 1998): 56–76.

Ornstein, Robert, ed. *The Nature of Human Consciousness.* San Francisco: W.H. Freeman and Company, 1973.

Orr, Elaine. "Contractual Law, Relational Whisper: A Reading of Edith Wharton's *The House of Mirth.*" *Modern Language Quarterly* 52 (1991): 53–70.

Orvell, Miles. *The Real Thing: Imitation and Authenticity in American Culture: 1880–1940.* Chapel Hill: The University of North Carolina Press, 1989.

Parkes, H.B. "The James Brothers." *Sewanee Review* 56 (1948): 323–28.

Pimple, Kenneth D. "Edith Wharton's 'Inscrutable Totem Terrors': Ethnography and *The Age of Innocence.*" *Southern Folklore* 51 (1994): 137–152.

Poirier, Richard. *The Comic Sense of Henry James.* London: Oxford University Press, 1960.

———. *A World Elsewhere: The Place of Style in American Literature.* New York: Oxford University Press, 1966.

———. *The Renewal of Literature: Emersonian Reflections.* New York: Random House, 1987.

———. ed. *Ralph Waldo Emerson.* Oxford: Oxford University Press, 1990.

———. *Poetry and Pragmatism.* Cambridge: Harvard University Press, 1992.

Pope, Kenneth, and Jerome Singer. *The Stream of Consciousness: Scientific Investigations into the Flow of Human Experience.* New York: Plenum, 1978.

Porte, Joel, ed. *New Essays on The Portrait of a Lady.* Cambridge: Cambridge University Press, 1990.

Posnock, Ross. *The Trial of Curiosity: Henry James, William James and the Challenge of Modernity.* New York: Oxford University Press, 1991.

Powers, Lyall. "Visions and Revisions: The Past Rewritten." *The Henry James Review* 7 (1986): 105–116.

Preston, Claire. *Edith Wharton's Social Register.* New York: St. Martin's Press, 2000.

Price, Alan. *The End of the Age of Innocence: Edith Wharton and the First World War.* New York: St. Martin's Press, 1996.

Price, Martin. *Forms of Life: Character and Moral Imagination in the Novel.* New Haven: Yale University Press, 1983.

Rahv, Philip. *Image and Idea: Fourteen Essays on Literary Themes*. New York: New Directions, 1949.

Restuccia, Frances L. "The Name of Lily: Edith Wharton's Feminism(s)." *Contemporary Literature* 28:2 (1987): 223–238.

Revonsuo, Antti, and Matti Kamppinen, ed. *Consciousness in Philosophy and Cognitive Neuroscience*. New Jersey: Lawrence Erlbaum Associates, Publishers, 1994.

Richards, Robert. *Darwin and the Emergence of Evolutionary Theories of Mind and Behavior*. Chicago: University of Chicago Press, 1987.

Ricks, Beatrice. *Henry James A Bibliography of Secondary Works*. Metuchen: The Scarecrow Press, 1975.

Ricoeur, Paul. *The Rule of Metaphor: Multi-Disciplinary Studies of the Creation of Meaning in Language*. Translated by Robert Czerny *et al*. Toronto: University of Toronto Press, 1977.

Righter, William. "Golden Rules and Golden Bowls." *Philosophy and Literature* 13 (1989): 262–81.

Rimmon, Shlomith. *The Concept of Ambiguity, the Example of James*. Chicago: The University of Chicago Press, 1977.

Ringuette, Dana. "The Self-Forming Subject: Henry James's Pragmatist Revision." *Mosaic* 23 (1990): 115–129.

Rivkin, Julie. *False Positions: The Representational Logic of Henry James's Fiction*. Stanford: Stanford University Press, 1996.

Roediger, Henry and Fergus Craik, ed. *Varieties of Memory and Consciousness*. Hillsdale: Lawrence Erlbaum Associates, Publishers, 1989.

Rogers, Jaqueline McLeod. *Aspects of the Female Novel*. Wakefield: Longwood Academic, 1991.

Rosenfield, Claire. "The Shadow Within: The Conscious and the Unconscious Use of the Double." *Daedalus* 92 (1963): 326–344.

Rowe, John Carlos. *Henry Adams and Henry James: The Emergence of a Modern Consciousness*. Ithaca: Cornell University Press, 1976.

———. *The Theoretical Dimension of Henry James*. Madison: The University of Wisconsin Press, 1984.

Rubinstein, Annette T. "Henry James, American Novelist; or, Isabel Archer, Emerson's Granddaughter." In *Weapons of Criticism: Marxism in America and the Literary Tradition*, edited by Norman Rudich. Palo Alto, Calif: Ramparts Press, 1976.

Ruddick, Lisa. "Fluid Symbols in American Modernism: William James, Gertrude Stein, George Santayana, and Wallace Stevens." In *Allegory, Myth and Symbol*, edited by Morton W. Bloomfield. Cambridge: Harvard University Press, 1981.

Russett, Cynthia Eagle. *Sexual Science: The Victorian Construction of Womanhood*. Cambridge: Harvard University Press, 1989.

Ryan, Judith. "The Vanishing Subject: Empirical Psychology and the Modern Novel." *PMLA* 95 (1980): 857–69.

Sabiston, Elizabeth Jean. *The Prison of Womanhood*. Basingstoke: The Macmillan Press. Ltd, 1987.

Samuels, Charles. *The Ambiguity of Henry James*. Urbana: University of Illinois Press, 1971.

Schirmeister, Pamela. *The Consolations of Space: The Place of Romance in Hawthorne, Melville and James*. Stanford: Stanford University Press, 1990.

Seager, William. *Metaphysics of Consciousness*. London: Routledge, 1991.

Sears, Sallie. *The Negative Imagination: Form and Perspective in the Novels of Henry James*. Ithaca: Cornell University Press, 1968.

Segal, Ora. *The Lucid Reflector: The Observer in Henry James's Fiction*. New Haven: Yale University Press, 1969.

Seigfried, Charlene Haddock. *William James's Radical Reconstruction of Philosophy*. Albany: State University of New York Press, 1990.

Seltzer, Mark. *Henry James and the Art of Power*. Ithaca: Cornell University Press, 1984.

Sensibar, Judith L. "Edith Wharton Reads the Bachelor Type: Her Critique of Modernism's Representative Man." *American Literature* 60 (1988): 575–90.

Shibles, Warren, ed. *Essays on Metaphor*. Wisconsin: The Language Press, 1972.

Showalter, Elaine. "The Death of the Lady (Novelist): Wharton's *House of Mirth*." In *Edith Wharton: New Critical Essays*, edited by Elaine Showalter. New York: Garland Publishing Company, Inc., 1992.

Shuttleworth, Sally. "Fairy Tale or Science?: Physiological Psychology in *Silas Marner*." In *Languages of Nature: Critical Essays on Science and Literature*, edited by L. J. Jordanova. New Brunswick: Rutgers University Press, 1986.

Sicker, Philip. *Love and the Quest for Identity in the Fiction of Henry James*. Princeton: Princeton University Press, 1980.

Sidlauskas, Susan. "Psyche and Sympathy: Staging Interiority in the Early Modern Home." In *Not at Home: The Suppression of Domesticity in Modern Art and Architecture*, edited by Christopher Reed. London: Thames and Hudson Ltd., 1996.

Sinclair, May. "The Novels of Dorothy Richardson." *The Little Review* vol. 5 (April 1918): 3–11.

Singley, Carol. *Edith Wharton: Matters of Mind and Spirit*. Cambridge: Cambridge University Press, 1995.

Skrupskelis, Ignas and Elizabeth Berkeley, ed. *The Correspondence of William James*. vol. 1. Charlottesville: University Press of Virginia, 1992.

———. ed. *William and Henry James, Selected Letters*. Charlottesville: University Press of Virginia, 1997.

Smith, Irena Auerbach. "The Golden Goal: Toward a Dialogic Imagination in James's Last Completed Novel." *The Henry James Review* 16 (1995): 172–90.

Smith, John. *America's Philosophical Vision*. Chicago: The University of Chicago Press, 1992.

Smith, Stephanie. "The Delicate Organisms and Theoretic Tricks of Henry James." *American Literature* 62 (1990): 583–605.

Spencer, Herbert. *The Works of Herbert Spencer*. Third edition, 2 vols. 1899. Reprint, Osnabruck: Otto Zeller, 1966.

Spender, Stephen. *The Destructive Element: A Study of Modern Writers and Beliefs*. Boston: Houghton Mifflin Press, 1936.

Stein, Allen. *After the Vows Were Spoken: Marriage in American Literary Realism*. Columbus: Ohio State University Press, 1984.

Steinberg, Erwin R. *The Stream of Consciousness Technique in the Modern Novel*. Port Washington, NY: Kennikat Press, 1979.

Stevens, Hugh. "Sexuality and the Aesthetic in *The Golden Bowl*." *Henry James Review* 14 (1993): 55–71.

———. *Henry James and Sexuality*. Cambridge: Cambridge University Press, 1998.

Stevenson, Randall. *Modernist Fiction: An Introduction*. Lexington: University Press of Kentucky, 1992.

Tanner, Tony. *The Reign of Wonder: Naivety and Reality in American Literature*. Cambridge: Cambridge University Press, 1965.

———. "The Watcher from the Balcony: Henry James's *The Ambassadors*." *Critical Quarterly* (1966): 41–56.

————. ed. *Henry James: Modern Judgments*. London: Macmillan, 1968.

Taylor, Anne Robinson. *Male Novelists and their Female Voices: Literary Masquerades*. Troy: The Whitson Publishing Company, 1981.

Taylor, Gordon. *The Passages of Thought: Psychological Representation in the American Novel, 1870–1900*. New York: Oxford University Press, 1969.

Tillotson, Kathleen. *Novels of the 1840s*. Oxford: Clarendon Press, 1956.

Tintner, Adeline. "'In the Dusky, Crowded, Heterogeneous Back-shop of the Mind' The Iconography of *The Portrait of a Lady*." *The Henry James Review* 7 (1986): 140–157.

————. "Jamesian Structures in *The Age of Innocence* and Related Stories." *Twentieth Century Literature* 26 (1980): 332–47.

Torgovnick, Marianna. *Closure in the Novel*. New Jersey: Princeton University Press, 1981.

Torsney, Cheryl. "Specula(riza)tion in *The Golden Bowl*." *The Henry James Review* 12 (1991): 141–6.

Townsend, Kim. *Manhood at Harvard: William James and Others*. New York: W.W. Norton & Co., 1996.

Updike, John. "Archer's Way." *The New York Review of Books*. 42, no. 19 (1995 November 30): 16, 18.

Van Ghent, Dorothy. "On The *Portrait of a Lady*." In *The English Novel: Form and Function*. New York: Rinehart, 1953.

Vivas, Eliseo. "Henry and William James: Two Notes." *Kenyon Review* 5 (1943): 580–594.

————. *Creation and Discovery: Essays in Criticism and Aesthetics*. New York: Noonday Press, 1955.

Waid, Candace. *Edith Wharton's Letters from the Underworld: Fictions of Women and Writing*. Chapel Hill: University of North Carolina Press, 1991.

Wallace, Alfred. *On Miracles and Modern Spiritualism*. London: James Burns, 1875.

————. *Darwinism, an Exposition of the Theory of Natural Selection With Some of its Applications*. London: Macmillan, 1889.

Wallace, Jeff. "Introduction: Difficulty and Defamiliarisation—Language and Process in *The Origin of Species*." In *Charles Darwin's The Origin of Species: New Interdisciplinary Essays*, edited by Jeff Wallace. Manchester: Manchester University Press, 1995.

Walton, Priscilla. "'A Mistress of Shades': Maggie as Reviser in *The Golden Bowl*." *The Henry James Review* 13 (1992): 143–53.

Ward, Candace, ed. *Great Short Stories by American Women*. New York: Dover Publications, Inc., 1996.

Warnock, Mary. *Memory*. London: Faber and Faber Limited, 1987.

Watt, Ian. *Rise of the Novel*. Berkeley: University of California Press, 1957.

———. "The First Paragraph of *The Ambassadors*: An Explication." *Essays in Criticism* 10 (1960): 250–74.

Watts, Eileen. "*The Golden Bowl*: A Theory of Metaphor." *Modern Language Studies* 13 (1983): 169–176.

Webb, Eugene. *Philosophers of Consciousness*. Seattle: University of Washington Press, 1988.

Wegener, Frederick, ed. *Edith Wharton: The Uncollected Critical Writings*. Princeton: Princeton University Press, 1996.

Weinstein, Philip. *Henry James and the Requirements of the Imagination*. Cambridge: Harvard University Press, 1971.

Weisbuch, Robert. "James and the American Sacred." *The Henry James Review* 22 (2001): 217–228.

Wershoven, Carol. *The Female Intruder in the Novels of Edith Wharton*. Rutherford: Farleigh Dickinson University Press, 1982.

———. "*The Awakening* and *The House of Mirth*: Studies in Arrested Development." *American Literary Realism* 19 (1987): 27–41.

West, Rebecca. *Henry James*. London: Nisbet and Co., 1916.

Wharton, Edith. *A Backward Glance*. New York: D. Appleton Century Company, 1934.

———. *The Writing of Fiction*. New York: Charles Scribner's Sons, 1925.

Wharton, Edith and Ogden Codman, Jr. *The Decoration of Houses*. 1897. Reprint, New York: Charles Scribner's Sons, 1901.

White, Allon. *The Uses of Obscurity: Fiction of Early Modernism*. London: Routledge & Kegan Paul, 1981.

White, Robert. "Love, Marriage and Divorce: The Matter of Sexuality in *Portrait of a Lady*." *The Henry James Review* 7 (1986): 59–71.

Williams, Merle. *Henry James and the Philosophical Novel*. New York: Cambridge University Press, 1993.

Wiseman, Adele. "What Price the Heroine?" *International Journal of Women's Studies* 4 (1981): 459–471.

Wolff, Cynthia. *A Feast of Words: The Triumph of Edith Wharton*. New York: Oxford University Press, 1977.

———. ed. *Edith Wharton, Novellas and Other Stories*. New York: Library of America Press, 1990.

———. "Lily Bart and Masquerade Inscribed in the Female Mode." In *Wretched Exotic*, edited by Katherine Joslin and Alan Price. New York: Peter Lang Publishing, 1993.

Wolman, Benjamin B., ed. *Historical Roots of Contemporary Psychology*. New York: Harper & Row, 1968.

Woolf, Judith. *Henry James: The Major Novels*. Cambridge: Cambridge University Press, 1991.

Yeazell, Ruth Bernard. *Language and Knowledge in the Late Novels of Henry James*. Chicago: The University of Chicago Press, 1976.

———. "The Conspicuous Wasting of Lily Bart." *ELH* 59 (1992): 713–34.

Young, Robert M. *Darwin's Metaphor: Nature's Place in Victorian Culture*. Cambridge: Cambridge University Press, 1985.

# Index

## A

Agnew, Jean-Christophe, 215n.30
Amigoni, David, 188n.5
Ammons, Elizabeth, 174, 227n.35, 229n.3, 232n.27
Anderson, Sherwood, 229n.6
anthropology, 93, 138, 170, 210n.10, 222–223n.19, 231n.20
Arata, Stephen, 215n.30
architecture, 203n.29. *See also*, James, Henry, architectural imagery in; Wharton, on architecture
Armstrong, Paul, 121, 199n.2, 215n.29
Auchard, John, 211n.13

## B

Balzac, Honoré de, 138
Banta, Martha, 209n.7, 231n.19
Baris, Sharon, 204n.36
Bauer, Dale, 213n.18
Beer, Gillian, 3, 188n.5, 189n.7, 189–190n.13
Bell, Millicent, 79–80, 205n.41, 219–220n.9, 222–223n.19, 229n.3, 230n.11, 231n.20
Bendixen, Alfred, 223n.22, 227n.35
Benert, Annette Larson, 227–228n.36

Benstock, Shari, 187n.1, 221–222n.13, 225–226n.32
Bentley, Nancy, 138, 222–223n.19, 231n.20
Benton, Ted, 188n.5
Berenson, Mary, 218n.2
Berkeley, Elizabeth M., 200nn.7, 11, 13
Berkson, Dorothy, 204–205n.37
Bjork, Daniel, 31, 195n.13
Booth, Alison, 215n.30, 225–226n.32
Boudreau, Kristin, 86, 207n.46, 234–235n.38
Boydston, Jeanne, 220n.10
Browne, Pat, 232n.26
Buchanan, D., 204–205n.37
Buitenhuis, Peter, 202n.24
Butler, Judith, 90, 208n.3

## C

Cameron, Sharon, 211nn.13, 14, 214nn.24, 28, 217n.36
Capek, Milic, 193–194n.2
Caws, Mary Ann, 212n.17, 217n.36
Chandler, Marilyn R., 173, 218n.1, 232n.25
Chase, Richard, 204n.34
Chopin, Kate, 220–221n.12
Christie, John, 189n.7

Codman, Ogden, Jr., 187n.1
Cole, David, 197n.23
Collecott, Diana, 203n.31
Cooley, Charles Horton, 136,
        137–138
    *Human Nature and the Social
        Order*, 222n.16

**D**

Darwin, Charles, xi–xii, 23
    on consciousness, 2–3, 6, 8–9
    continuity hypothesis of, 4, 7–8, 20
    on evolutionary theory, 3
    materialist theory of, 5
    on the Moral Sense, 8
    on natural selection, 5, 8–9
    on the origin of man, 6
    Wallace and, 9–11, 188n.4
    WORKS:
        *The Descent of Man, and
            Selection in Relation to Sex*,
            6–8, 189n.13
        *The Expression of the Emotions
            in Man and Animals*,
            190n.17
        *The Foundations of the Origin of
            Species*, 188n.4
        *On the Origin of Species by
            Means of Natural Selection
            or the Preservation of
            Favoured Races in the
            Struggle for Life (Origin)*,
            2–6, 10, 188nn.4, 6, 189n.8
Darwinism, 9–11. *See also* social
    Darwinism
Davis, Linette, 232n.26
Dear, Peter, 20, 192n.37
de Man, Paul, 198n.27
Dewey, John, 193–194n.2, 194n.6
Dimock, Wai Chee, 217–218n.37,
        225n.29, 226n.34, 228n.37
domestic fiction, 136, 220–221n.12

**E**

Eby, Clare Virginia, 231n.21
Edel, Leon, 199n.1, 200n.4, 204n.34
Eisely, Loren, 190n.19
Eliot, George, 192n.38, 212n.16
Emerson, Ralph Waldo, 194n.6,
        196–197n.20, 234–235n.38
    architectural imagery and, 72–73
    on hieroglyphic, 230–231n.15
    on individual, 178, 207n.46
    *See also* James, Henry, Emerson
        and; James, William,
        Emerson and; Wharton,
        Emerson and
Erlich, Gloria, 223n.22
evolutionary scientists, 23–24, 163,
        164, 186. *See also* evolution-
        ary theory
evolutionary theory, 2, 3, 9, 11, 89,
        94, 170, 210n.10

**F**

Farantello, Donna, 194n.6
Fedorko, Kathy, 227n.35,
        232–233n.27
Fetterly, Judith, 218n.1
Firebaugh, Joseph, 199n.2
Fischer, Sandra K., 70, 201n.18,
        204–205n.37, 206n.45
Fogel, Daniel Mark, 211n.13,
        212n.17
Ford, Peter Marcus, 29, 195n.8
Foucault, Michel, 206–207n.45
Fowler, Virginia, 211n.13, 212n.17
Fox, Richard Wightman, 215n.30
Fracasso, Evelyn E., 232n.26
Frank, Ellen, 74, 203n.29, 206n.43
Freeman, Mary Wilkins, 220–221n.12
Fryer, Judith, 223n.22, 224n.26,
        226n.33
Fuss, Diana, 209–210n.9, 220n.11

## G

Gavin, William Joseph, 194n.3
Gilman, Charlotte Perkins,
 220–221n.12
Goodman, Russell B., 194n.6
Goodman, Susan, 232–233n.27
Gribble, Jennifer, 214n.27
Griffin, Susan M., 215n.30

## H

Hadley, Kathy Miller, 232n.26
Hamilton, Sir William, 33
Hanson, Olaf, 194–195n.7
Hawthorne, Nathaniel, 72, 202n.24,
 207n.46, 234–235n.38
Hocks, Richard, 199n.2, 200n.8
Hoeller, Hildegard, 233n.30,
 235–236n.44
Holland, Laurence B., 205n.40,
 213n.20
Hopkins, Gerard Manley, 203n.29
Howard, Maureen, 145, 167,
 219–220n.9, 224n.25,
 225–226n.32, 230n.11
Howe, Irving, 235n.41
Hughes, Stuart, 45, 197n.22
Hume, David, 33
Huxley, T.H., 191n.25
Hyman, Stanley Edgar, 189n.7

## I

Ian, Marcia, 212n.17, 213–214n.21
interior design, 219n.4. *See also*
 Wharton, on interior design
Izzo, Donatello, 201n.20

## J

James family, 63
James, Henry, xi, xii, xiii, xiv
 architectural imagery in, 68, 72, 74,
 82, 83, 108–111, 118, 133
 attention to social experience, 62,
 69, 75, 78–82, 84, 85–86,
 88, 105, 110, 115–116,
 121–124, 129–130, 133
 Emerson and, 72–73, 202n.24,
 204nn.34, 36, 207n.46
 evolutionary theory and, 2, 89
 Hawthorne and, 72, 202n.24,
 207n.46
 on individual, 114, 124, 129
 James, William and, 87–89, 103,
 106, 107, 114, 120, 122,
 123, 128, 129–130, 201n.19
 on knowledge, 75–76, 79, 84, 122,
 123
 Norton, Grace, letter to, 61–62,
 199n
 on pain, 61, 106, 117–118,
 122–126, 216n.31
 on power, 114–116, 123–124,
 216n.33
 on pragmatism, 62–63, 199nn.2, 3
 on relationships, 80–81, 89, 104,
 124, 128, 130, 205–206n.42
 role of women in the work of,
 104–107, 111, 126, 128, 133
 sexuality in the work of, 106, 109,
 111–118, 206–207n.45,
 210–211n.10, 214n.23
 on silence, 105, 112–115, 116–117,
 129, 211n.13
 on soul, 76–77
 on vision, 79, 106, 115, 121–122,
 125–127, 129, 130, 205n.40,
 215n.30, 217n.36
 WORKS:
 *The Ambassadors*, 210n.11,
 216n.34
 *The American*, 184, 235n.43
 *The American Scene*, 65
 "The Beast in the Jungle,"
 210n.11
 *The Golden Bowl*, xiv, 64–65, 88,
 89, 103, 104, 105, 106, 111,
 116, 120, 123, 124, 129,
 133, 135, 165–166, 177, 185

*The Portrait of a Lady*, xiii–xiv,
62, 68, 69, 70, 71, 73, 75,
77, 79, 80, 82, 87–88, 106,
109, 133, 151, 162, 166,
201n.15, 202nn. 27, 28,
203n.32, 205n.38, 210n.11,
212n.16, 219nn.5, 7,
225n.30
*The Spoils of Poynton*, 201n.16
*The Tragic Muse*, 63
*The Wings of the Dove*, 65
James, William, xi, xii, 2, 14, 136,
151, 161–162, 177, 228n.1
absolute experience, 50
anthropology and, 93
attention to social experience, 88,
89, 96, 99, 101–103,
133–134, 162
conscious automata theory, 191n.25
consciousness as relational, 31, 51
consciousness as selective, 24, 31,
40, 41, 42, 195n.12
on continuity, 91, 94, 100–102,
114, 129, 195n.10
Darwin and, 193n.1
Dewey and, 193–194n.2
on dualism, 27, 50, 51–54,
193–194nn.2
Emerson and, 42, 91, 194n.6,
196–197n.16, 198n.28
on emotion, 39
empirical self, 224–225n.28
evolutionary theory and, 2, 89, 94,
186
on feeling, 45, 94–95, 208n.5
on identity, 162
on individual, 89, 91, 99, 101, 120,
124, 129, 207–208n.1
on introspection, 36–37, 56–57,
196n.17
James, Henry and, 62–72, 85,
87–89, 103, 106, 107, 114,
120, 122, 123, 128,
129–130, 201n.19

on knowledge, 97, 98, 122
on language, 28, 31–36, 49, 66, 92,
95, 101–102, 185
Lewes and, 191–192n.31, 193n.1,
196n.19
on memory, 37–38
metaphysics of, 29, 55–56, 198n.29
mysticism of, 27, 172
natural imagery, 29, 34, 146,
194n.6
on psychology as discipline, 45–46,
93, 100
pure experience, 28, 52, 55, 95, 97,
100–101, 106, 124, 198n.29
radical empiricism of, 27–28,
49–50, 53, 57, 58, 90,
93–95, 99, 114, 198n.29
Romanticism and, 29, 194n.6
on soul, 45, 47
Spencer and, 193n.1
spiritualism of, 43–45, 47–48,
50–51, 54–57, 172
stream of consciousness metaphor,
xi, 17, 28, 30, 33–35, 39,
43, 54, 56, 78, 194n.5,
195n.10
Wordsworth and, 29, 194n.6
WORKS:
"Does 'Consciousness' Exist?,"
27, 46, 53, 55, 58, 71,
196n.15
*Essays in Radical Empiricism*, 46,
55, 88, 196n.15, 197n.25,
225n.31
*The Principles of Psychology*, xi,
xii, 24, 27, 30, 32–3, 40,
43–46, 48, 50, 54–58, 65,
66, 72, 98, 101, 162,
200–201n.19, 205n.39,
208n.2, 209n.6
*Psychology: Briefer Course*, 30,
195n.9

*The Varieties of Religious Experience*, 196n.18, 232n.24
"A World of Pure Experience," xiv, xv, 88, 90, 100, 122, 123
Jaynes, Julian, 187n.3, 191n.25
Jewett, Sarah Orne, 220–221n.12
Johnson, Ellwood, 199n.2
Jordanova, Ludmilla, 189n.7, 192n.38
Joslin, Katherine, 223n.22
Jourdain, M. 199n.3

K

Kant, Immanuel, 47
Kaplan, Amy, 223–224n.24
Kaplan, Sydney Janet, 209–210n.9
Kauffman, Linda S., 210–211n.12
Kearns, Michael S., 195n.11
Kessler-Harris, Alice, 220n.10
Knights, Pamela, 175, 219n.8, 230n.13, 231n.18, 234n.32, 235–236n.44
Krook, Dorothea, 206n.45

L

Lears, T.J. Jackson, 163, 215n.29, 229n.6
Lebowitz, Naomi, 205–206n.42
Lentricchia, Frank, 197n.21
Lessing, Doris, 209–210n.9
Lewes, George Henry (G.H.), xi–xii, 2, 12–13, 23
  on consciousness, 13–18
  on continuity, 19
  James, William and, 14, 17, 191–192n.31, 196n.19
  on language, 12–13, 14–16, 18, 19
  on the Sensorium, 13
  on soul, 16–18
  Spencer and, 19
  WORKS:
    *The Physical Basis of Mind*, 15

*Problems of Life and Mind*, 14, 191n.31
Lewis, Nancy, 222n.18
Lewis, R.W.B., 218n.2, 218–219n.3, 221–222nn.13, 18, 223n.21, 230n.9
Locke, John, 32
Loewenberg, Bert James, 188n.4, 190n.17
Lubbock, Percy, 199n.3
Luria, Sarah, 229–230n.7

M

MacComb, Debra, 206n.44
Matthiessen, F. O., 199n.2, 200nn.11, 13
McBrien, William, 220n.10
McMurray, William, 199n.2
McWhirter, David, 211–212nn.15, 17
Mead, George Herbert:
  on individual, 139–140
  on language, 136–137
  WORKS:
    *Movements of Thought in the Nineteenth Century*, 222n.14
    "The Problem of Society—How We Become Selves," 136
Menand, Louis, 193n.46
mesmerism. *See* mysticism; spiritualism
Mitchell, Dr. S. Weir, 221–222n.13
modern mind, 28, 186
modern novel, xi, 163, 164, 185–186
Moody, A.D., 203–204n.33, 204–205n.37
Morgan, Gwendolyn, 232n.26
Myers, Gerald E., 195n.10, 196n.17, 198n.29
mysticism, 27, 172. *See also* spiritualism

N

Nettels, Elsa, 232n.26
neurasthenia. *See* rest cure

New Woman, 174, 227n.35
Nietzsche, Friedrich, 215n.29
Norton, Grace, 61
Norton, Sara, 222n.18

O

Olin-Ammentorp, Julie, 231n.22
Orlando, Emily J., 231n.17, 234n.31,
      236.45
Ostwald, Wilhelm, 222n.18

P

Paniker, K. Ayyappa, 203n.31,
      203–204n.33, 204–205n.37
Parkes, H.B., 199n.2, 200n.5
Pater, Walter, 203n.29
Pimple, Kenneth D., 233n.29
Poirier, Richard, 196–197n.20,
      198n.28, 202n.25, 204n.34
Porte, Joel, 201n.20
Preston, Claire, 179, 231n.20,
      234n.34, 235n.40, 236n.45
Price, Alan, 223n.22
Proust, Marcel, 39, 203n.29, 233n.28
psychology, discipline of, 24, 163,
      185, 186, 197n.23, 210n.10,
      221n.13, 222n.18. *See also*
      James, William, psychology,
      discipline of

R

Rahv, Philip, 204n.34
realism, 235–236n.44. *See also*
      Wharton, on realism, lan-
      guage of
rest cure, 221–222n.13
Reynolds, Sir Joshua, 150–151
Richardson, Dorothy, xi, 209–210n.9
Robinson, James, 230n.14
Romanticism. *See* James, William,
      Romanticism and
Rossetti, Dante Gabriel, 175
Rowe, John Carlos, 199n.2, 216n.33
Rubinstein, Annette, 204n.34

Rudich, Norman, 204n.34
Russett, Cynthia, 210n.10
Ryan, Ann, 231n.22

S

Sabiston, Elizabeth Jean, 202n.24,
      204n.34
Sacks, Sheldon, 198n.27
Seigfried, Charlene Haddock, 198n.26
Seltzer, Mark, 212n.17, 216n.33
sentimental fiction, 233n.30
Showalter, Elaine, 227n.35
Shuttleworth, Sally, 189n.7, 192n.38
Sicker, Philip, 216n.32, 217n.36
Sinclair, May, xi, 187n.1, 209–210n.9
Singh, Amritjit, 203–204nn.31, 33,
      204–205n.37
Singley, Carol, 178, 235n.39
Skrupskelis, Ignas P., 200nn.7, 11, 13
Smith, Irena Auerbach, 115, 212n.17,
      214n.25, 216–217n.35
Smith, John E., 195n.14, 196n.18,
      197n.24
social Darwinism, 231n.20. *See also*
      Darwinism
social psychology, 136–139. *See also*
      psychology, discipline of
social science, 93
sociology, 138, 210n.10
Spencer, Herbert, xi–xii, 2, 22
      on consciousness, 19, 20, 21–23
      on continuity, 19–20
      on evolution, 18
      on language, 19, 21
      Lewes and, 19
      on Mind, 19–21, 23, 194n.44
      *The Principles of Psychology*, 20,
            23, 192n.34, 193n.44
spiritualism, xii–xiii, 9–12. *See also*
      James, William, spiritualism
      of; Wallace, Alfred Russel,
      spiritualism of; Wharton,
      spiritualism and

stream of consciousness. *See* James, William, stream of consciousness metaphor
Stendhal, 138
Stevens, Hugh, 214n.23
Swendenborg, Emanuel, 215n.29

**T**

tableaux vivants. *See* Wharton, on tableaux vivants
Tanner, Tony, 199n.2, 201n.17, 204n.35
Torgovnick, Marianna, 206–207n.45
Torsney, Cheryl, 212n.17
Townsend, Kim, 207–208n.1, 208n.5
Transcendentalism, 229n.6. *See also* Emerson; Wharton, on transcendence
Travis, Jennifer, 122, 216n.31

**U**

Updike, John, 233n.28

**V**

Vivas, Eliseo, 199n.2

**W**

Wallace, Alfred Russel, xi, xiii, 2, 23
  on consciousness, 11–12
  on continuity, 9–10, 12
  Darwin and, 9, 10, 188n.4
  on evolution, 9, 11
  on natural selection, 9–10
  spiritualism of, 9–11, 12, 172, 190–191n.21
  WORKS:
    *Darwinism: An Exposition of the Theory of Natural Selection and Some of its Applications*, 9, 11
    *On Miracles and Modern Spiritualism*, 190–191n.21, 232n.24
Wallace, Jeff, 188n.5, 188–189n.6

Walton, Priscilla, 210n.11, 213n.19
Ward, Candace, 220–221n.12
Watts, Eileen, 213n.19
Wegener, Frederick, 229n.5
Weisbuch, Robert, 207n.46, 234–235n.38
Wershoven, Carol, 227n.35
Wharton, Edith, xiv, xv, 2, 24
  anthropology and, 138, 170, 222–223n.19, 231n.20
  on architecture, 1, 134, 165, 229–230n.7, 234n.33
  attention to social experience, 131–136, 140, 143–148, 150, 155–156, 158, 162–166, 168, 170–175, 177–186
  Berenson, Mary, letter to, 132–133, 218n
  on communication, 158, 168–169, 177, 179–183
  Cooley and, 136–137
  on domestic fiction, 136
  Emerson and, 171, 178, 226n.33, 234n.36
  evolutionary theory and, 2, 170
  on individual, 132, 135, 136, 153, 155, 166, 169, 174, 178
  on interior design, 1, 2, 132, 146, 165, 167, 176, 187n.1
  on intimacy, 154, 156, 166, 168–169, 177, 179–180, 231n.16
  James, Henry and, 131–133, 151, 166, 173, 177, 185
  James, William and, 133, 136, 146, 151, 172, 177, 185
  on marriage, 142–143, 224n.25
  Mead and, 136–137
  on New York society, 138, 165–166, 169, 173, 174
  Norton, Sara, letter to, 222n.18
  on privacy, 135, 151, 164–169, 174–177, 179–180, 182–183, 230n.10, 232n.23

realism, language of, xv, 132,
    135–136, 140, 144–145,
    150–152, 156, 158, 164,
    168, 173, 176, 178–179,
    180, 181, 183–185
on silence, 169, 182
on social class, 132, 133, 138,
    140–142, 143, 181
on soul, 140, 145, 163–164, 173,
    178, 185
spiritualism and, 172
on tableaux vivants, 143, 150–153,
    224n.26, 225–226n.32
on transcendence, 171, 173,
    226n.33
Wallace and, 172
on woman's body, 144, 150, 151,
    155, 164
on woman's clothing, 132, 140,
    143–144, 148, 150–151, 164
WORKS:
    *The Age of Innocence*, xiv, xv,
        135, 164–167, 169, 170,
        172–175, 181, 232n.23,
        234n.33, 235n.42
    *A Backward Glance*, 185,
        229n.4, 236nn.46, 47
    *The Decoration of Houses*, 1,
        165, 176, 187n.1, 218n.1,
        219n.4, 234n.33
    "The Fullness of Life,"
        218–219n.3
    *The House of Mirth*, xiv, xv, 131,
        132, 135, 138, 140,
        142–146, 151, 155, 158,
        162, 164, 166–167, 169,
        178, 183, 184
    *The Writing of Fiction*, 138
White, Robert, 206–207n.45
Williams, Merle, 199n.2
Wolff, Cynthia Griffin, 223n.22,
        227n.35, 236n.45
Woolf, Virginia, 209–210n.9
Wordsworth, William, 29, 194n.6

Y

Yeazell, Ruth Bernard, 216n.33,
        226–227n.34
Young, Robert M., 189n.7

Z

Zilversmit, Annette, 223n.22, 227n.35